Kotlin Programming

THE BIG NERD RANCH GUIDE

Josh Skeen & David Greenhalgh

Big Nerd
Ranch

Kotlin Programming: The Big Nerd Ranch Guide

by Josh Skeen and David Greenhalgh

Big Nerd Ranch, LLC
200 Arizona Ave NE
Atlanta, GA 30307
(770) 817-6373
http://www.bignerdranch.com/
book-comments@bignerdranch.com

The 10-gallon hat with propeller logo is a trademark of Big Nerd Ranch, LLC.

Exclusive worldwide distribution of the English edition of this book by

Pearson Technology Group
800 East 96th Street
Indianapolis, IN 46240 USA
http://www.informit.com

ISBN-10 0135161630
ISBN-13 978-0135161630

First edition, first printing, July 2018

Dedication

For Baker, the best little bug.

— J.S.

To Rebecca, a driven, patient, beautiful woman, and the reason that this book came to be. To Mom and Dad, for valuing education above all else.

— D.G.

Acknowledgments

We received a lot of help in writing this book. Without that help, this book would not be what it is, and it may never even have happened. Thanks are due.

First, we need to say thank you to our colleagues at Big Nerd Ranch. Thank you to Stacy Henry and Aaron Hillegass for providing us with the time and space to write this book. It has been immensely gratifying to learn and teach Kotlin. We hope that this book lives up to the trust and the support that we have received.

Particular thanks are also due to our colleagues at Big Nerd Ranch. Your careful teaching revealed many bugs in the text, and your thoughtful recommendations led to many improvements in our approach. It is truly wonderful to have colleagues such as you. Thank you Kristin Marsicano, Bolot Kerimbaev, Brian Gardner, Chris Stewart, Paul Turner, Chris Hare, Mark Allison, Andrew Lunsford, Rafael Moreno Cesar, Eric Maxwell, Andrew Bailey, Jeremy Sherman, Christian Keur, Mikey Ward, Steve Sparks, Mark Dalrymple, CBQ, and everyone else at the Ranch who helped us with this work.

Our colleagues in operations, marketing, and sales are also instrumental. Classes would literally never be scheduled without their work. Thank you Heather Sharpe, Mat Jackson, Rodrigo "Ram Rod" Perez-Velasco, Nicholas Stolte, Justin Williams, Dan Barker, Israel Machovec, Emily Herman, Patrick Freeman, Ian Eze, and Nikki Porter. We cannot do what we do without what you do.

Special thanks and an extra bit of karma are also owed to our amazing students who were adventurous enough to join us for the early access version of the course and were kind enough to help us identify errata. Without your feedback and insights into how to improve the course, this text would not be where it is today. Those students include: Santosh Katta, Abdul Hannan, Chandra Mohan, Benjamin DiGregorio, Peng Wan, Kapil Bhalla, Girish Hanchinal, Hashan Godakanda, Mithun Mahadevan, Brittany Berlanga, Natalie Ryan, Balarka Velidi, Pranay Airan, Jacob Rogers, Jean-Luc Delpech, Dennis Lin, Kristina Thai, Reid Baker, Setareh Lotfi, Harish Ravichandran, Matthew Knapp, Nathan Klee, Brian Lee, Heidi Muth, Martin Davidsson, Misha Burshteyn, Kyle Summers, Cameron Hill, Vidhi Shah, Fabrice Di Meglio, Jared Burrows, Riley Brewer, Michael Krause, Tyler Holland, Gajendra Singh, Pedro Sanchez, Joe Cyboski, Zach Waldowski, Noe Arzate, Allan Caine, Zack Simon, Josh Meyers, Rick Meyers, Stephanie Guevara, Abdulrahman Alshmrani, Robert Edwards, Maribel Montejano, and Mohammad Yusuf.

We want to extend a special thank you to our colleagues and members of the Android community who helped us test the book's accuracy, clarity, and ease of use. Without your external perspective, putting this book together would have been even more daunting. Thank you Jon Reeve, Bill Phillips, Matthew Compton, Vishnu Rajeevan, Scott Stanlick, Alex Lumans, Shauvik Choudhary, and Jason Atwood.

We also need to acknowledge the many talented folks who worked on the book with us. Elizabeth Holaday, our editor, helped refine the book, crystallize its strengths, and diminish its weaknesses. Anna Bentley, our copyeditor, found and corrected errors and ultimately made us look smarter than we are. Ellie Volckhausen designed the cover. And Chris Loper designed and produced the print book and the EPUB and Kindle versions.

Finally, thank you to all our students. Being your teacher offers us the opportunity to be a student in many ways, and for that we are immensely grateful. Teaching is part of the greatest thing that we do, and it has been a pleasure working with you. We hope that the quality of this book matches your enthusiasm and determination.

Table of Contents

Introducing Kotlin

In 2011, JetBrains announced the development of the Kotlin programming language, an alternative to writing code in languages like Java or Scala to run on the Java Virtual Machine. Six years later, Google announced that Kotlin would be an officially supported development path for the Android operating system.

Kotlin's scope quickly grew from a language with a bright future into the language powering applications on the world's foremost mobile operating system. Today, large companies like Google, Uber, Netflix, Capital One, Amazon, and more have embraced Kotlin for its many advantages, including its concise syntax, modern features, and seamless interoperability with legacy Java code.

Why Kotlin?

To understand the appeal of Kotlin, you first need to understand the role of Java in the modern software development landscape. The two languages are closely tied, because Kotlin code is most often written for the Java Virtual Machine.

Java is a robust and time-tested language and has been one of the most commonly written languages in production codebases for years. However, since Java was released in 1995, much has been learned about what makes for a good programming language. Java is missing the many advancements that developers working with more modern languages enjoy.

Kotlin benefits from the learning gained as some design decisions made in Java (and other languages, like Scala) have aged poorly. It has evolved beyond what was possible with older languages and has corrected what was painful about them. You will learn more in the coming chapters about how Kotlin improves on Java and offers a more reliable development experience.

And Kotlin is not just a better language to write code to run on the Java Virtual Machine. It is a multiplatform language that aims to be general purpose: Kotlin can be used to write native macOS and Windows applications, JavaScript applications, and, of course, Android applications. Platform independence means that Kotlin has a wide variety of uses.

Who Is This Book For?

We have written this book for developers of all kinds: experienced Android developers who want modern features beyond what Java offers, server-side developers interested in learning about Kotlin's features, and newer developers looking to venture into a high-performance compiled language.

Android support might be why you are reading this book, but the book is not limited to Kotlin programming for Android. In fact, except in one advanced chapter, Chapter 21, all the Kotlin code in this book is agnostic to the Android framework. That said, if you are interested in using Kotlin for Android application development, this book shows off some common patterns that make writing Android apps a breeze in Kotlin.

Although Kotlin has been influenced by a number of other languages, you do not need to know the ins and outs of any other language to learn Kotlin. From time to time, we will discuss the Java code equivalent for Kotlin code you have written. If you have Java experience, this will help you understand the relationship between the two languages. If you do not know Java, seeing how another language tackles the same problems can help you grasp the principles that have shaped Kotlin's development.

How to Use This Book

This book is not a reference guide. Our goal is to guide you through the most important parts of the Kotlin programming language. You will be working through example projects, building knowledge as you progress. To get the most out of this book, we recommend that you type out the examples in the book as you read along. Working through the projects will help build muscle memory and will give you something to carry on from one chapter to the next.

Also, each chapter builds on the topics presented in the last, so we recommend that you do not jump around. Even if you feel that you are familiar with a topic in other languages, we suggest that you read straight through – Kotlin handles many problems in unique ways. You will begin with introductory topics like variables and lists, work your way through object-oriented and functional programming techniques, and understand along the way what makes Kotlin such a powerful language. By the end of the book, you will have built your knowledge of Kotlin from that of a beginner to a more advanced developer.

Having said that, do take your time: Branch out, use the Kotlin reference at `kotlinlang.org/docs/reference` to follow up on anything that piqued your curiosity, and experiment.

For the More Curious

Most of the chapters in this book have a section or two titled "For the More Curious." Many of these sections illuminate the underlying mechanisms of the Kotlin language. The examples in the chapters do not depend on the information in these sections, but they provide additional information that you may find interesting or helpful.

Challenges

Most chapters end with one or more challenges. These are additional problems to solve that are designed to further your understanding of Kotlin. We encourage you to give them a try to enhance your Kotlin mastery.

Typographical conventions

As you build the projects in this book, we will guide you by introducing a topic and then showing how to apply your new-found knowledge. For clarity, we stick to the following typographical conventions.

Variables, values, and types are shown with fixed-width font. Class, function, and interface names are given bold font.

All code listings are shown in fixed-width font. If you are to type some code in a code listing, that code is denoted in bold. If you are to delete some code in a code listing, that code is struck through. In the following example, you are being instructed to delete the line defining variable y and to add a variable called z:

```
var x = "Python"
var y = "Java"
var z = "Kotlin"
```

Kotlin is a relatively young language, so many coding conventions are still being figured out. Over time, you will likely develop your own style, but we tend to adhere to JetBrains' and Google's Kotlin style guides:

- JetBrains' coding conventions: `kotlinlang.org/docs/reference/coding-conventions.html`

- Google's style guide, including conventions for Android code and interoperability: `android.github.io/kotlin-guides/style.html`

Looking Forward

Take your time with the examples in this book. Once you get the hang of Kotlin's syntax, we think that you will find the development process to be clear, pragmatic, and fluid. Until then, keep at it; learning a new language can be quite rewarding.

1

Your First Kotlin Application

In this chapter you will write your first Kotlin program, using IntelliJ IDEA. While completing this programming rite of passage, you will familiarize yourself with your development environment, create a new Kotlin project, write and run Kotlin code, and inspect the resulting output. The project you create in this chapter will serve as a sandbox to easily try out new concepts you will encounter throughout this book.

Installing IntelliJ IDEA

IntelliJ IDEA is an integrated development environment (IDE) for Kotlin created by JetBrains (which also created the Kotlin language). To get started, download the IntelliJ IDEA Community Edition from the JetBrains website at jetbrains.com/idea/download (Figure 1.1).

Figure 1.1 Downloading IntelliJ IDEA Community Edition

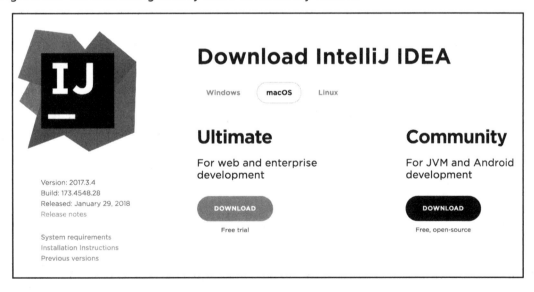

Once it has downloaded, follow the installation instructions for your platform as described on the JetBrains installation and setup page at `jetbrains.com/help/idea/install-and-set-up-product.html`.

IntelliJ IDEA, called IntelliJ for short, helps you write well-formed Kotlin code. It also streamlines the development process with built-in tools for running, debugging, inspecting, and refactoring your code. You can read more about why we recommend IntelliJ for writing Kotlin code in the section called *For the More Curious: Why Use IntelliJ?* near the end of this chapter.

Your First Kotlin Project

Congratulations, you now have the Kotlin programming language and a powerful development environment to write it with. Now there is only one thing left to do: Learn to speak Kotlin fluently. First order of business – create a Kotlin project.

Open IntelliJ. You will be presented with the Welcome to IntelliJ IDEA dialog (Figure 1.2).

Figure 1.2 Welcome dialog

(If this is not the first time you have opened IntelliJ since installing it, you may be brought directly to the last project you had open. To get back to the welcome dialog, close the project using File → Close Project.)

Click Create New Project. IntelliJ will display the New Project dialog, as shown in Figure 1.3.

Figure 1.3 New Project dialog

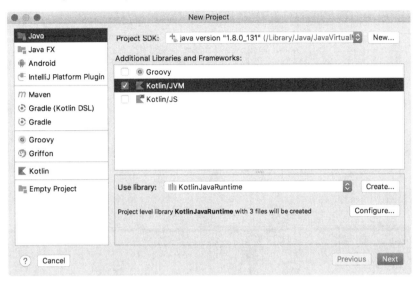

In the New Project dialog, select Kotlin on the left and Kotlin/JVM on the right, as shown in Figure 1.4.

Figure 1.4 Creating a Kotlin/JVM project

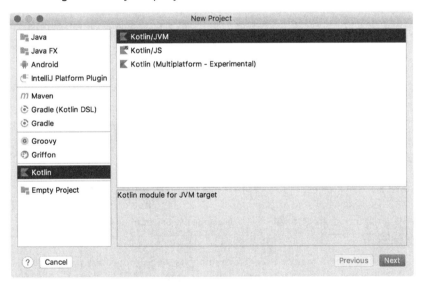

You can use IntelliJ to write code in languages other than Kotlin, including Java, Python, Scala, and Groovy. Selecting Kotlin/JVM tells IntelliJ you intend to use Kotlin. More specifically, Kotlin/JVM tells IntelliJ you intend to write Kotlin code that *targets*, or runs on, the Java Virtual Machine. One of the benefits of Kotlin is that it features a toolchain that allows you to write Kotlin code that can run on different operating systems and platforms.

(From here on, we will refer to the Java Virtual Machine as just "JVM," as it is commonly called in the Java developer community. You can learn more about targeting the JVM in the section called *For the More Curious: Targeting the JVM* near the end of this chapter.)

Click Next in the New Project dialog. IntelliJ will display a dialog where you can choose settings for your new project (Figure 1.5). For the Project name, enter "Sandbox." The Project location field will auto-populate. You can leave the location as is or select a new location by pressing the ... button to the right of the field. Select a Java 1.8 version from the Project SDK dropdown to link your project to Java Development Kit (JDK) version 8.

Figure 1.5 Naming the project

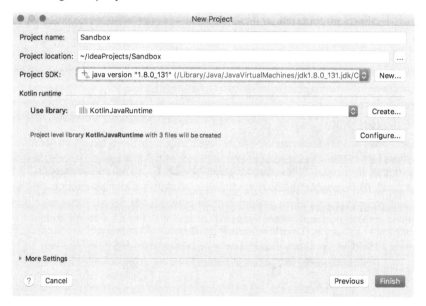

Why do you need the JDK to write a Kotlin program? The JDK gives IntelliJ access to the JVM and to Java tools that are necessary for converting your Kotlin code to bytecode (more on that in a moment). Technically, any version 6 or greater will work. But our experience, as of this writing, is that JDK 8 works most seamlessly.

If you do not see some version of Java 1.8 listed in the Project SDK dropdown, this means you have not yet installed JDK 8. Do so now before proceeding: Download JDK 8 for your specific platform from oracle.com/technetwork/java/javase/downloads/jdk8-downloads-2133151.html. Install the JDK, then restart IntelliJ. Work back through the steps outlined to this point to create a new project.

When your settings dialog looks like Figure 1.5, click Finish.

IntelliJ will generate a project named Sandbox and display the new project in a default two-pane view (Figure 1.6). On disk, IntelliJ creates a folder and a set of subfolders and project files in the location specified in the Project location field.

Figure 1.6 Default two-pane view

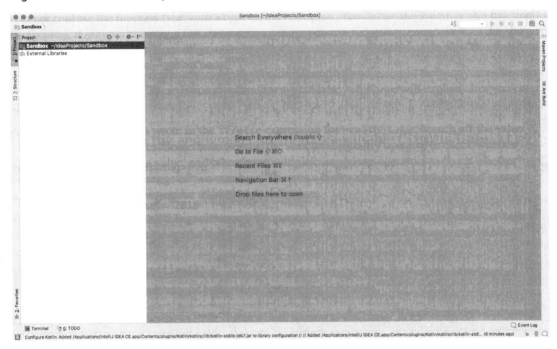

The pane on the left shows the *project tool window*. The pane on the right is currently empty. This is where you will view and edit the contents of your Kotlin files in the *editor*. Turn your attention to the project tool window on the left. Click the disclosure arrow to the left of the project name, Sandbox. It will expand to display the files contained in the project, as shown in Figure 1.7.

Figure 1.7 Project view

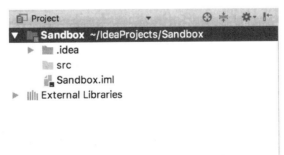

A *project* includes all of the source code for your program, along with information about dependencies and configurations. A project can be broken down into one or more *modules*, which are like subprojects. By default, a new project has one module, which is all you need for your simple first project.

The Sandbox.iml file contains configuration information specific to your single module. The .idea folder contains settings files for the entire project as well as those specific to your interaction with the project in the IDE (for example, which files you have open in the editor). Leave these auto-generated files as they are.

The External Libraries entry contains information about libraries the project depends on. If you expand this entry you will see that IntelliJ automatically added Java 1.8 and KotlinJavaRuntime as dependencies for your project.

(You can learn more about IntelliJ project structure on the JetBrains documentation website at jetbrains.org/intellij/sdk/docs/basics/project_structure.html.)

The src folder is where you will place all the Kotlin files you create for your Sandbox project. And with that, it is time to create and edit your first Kotlin file.

Creating your first Kotlin file

Right-click on the src folder in the project tool window. Select New and then Kotlin File/Class from the menu that appears (Figure 1.8).

Figure 1.8 Creating a new Kotlin file

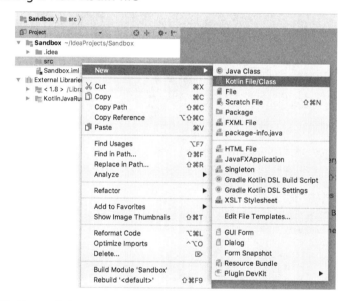

In the New Kotlin File/Class dialog, type "Hello" in the Name field and leave the Kind field set to File (Figure 1.9).

Figure 1.9 Naming the file

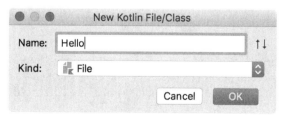

Click OK. IntelliJ will create a new file in your project, src/Hello.kt, and display the contents of the file in the editor on the righthand side of the IntelliJ window (Figure 1.10). The .kt extension indicates that the file contains Kotlin, just like the .java extension is used for Java files and .py for Python files.

Figure 1.10 Empty Hello.kt file displays in editor

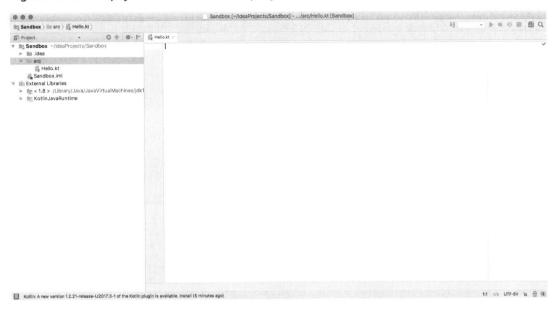

At last, you are ready to write Kotlin code. Give your fingers a little stretch and go for it. Type the following code into the Hello.kt editor. (Remember that throughout this book, code you are to enter is shown in bold.)

Listing 1.1 "Hello, world!" in Kotlin (Hello.kt)

```
fun main(args: Array<String>) {
    println("Hello, world!")
}
```

The code you just wrote might look unfamiliar. Do not fear – by the end of this book, reading and writing Kotlin will feel like second nature. For now, it is enough to understand the code at a high level.

The code in Listing 1.1 defines a new *function*. A function is a group of instructions that can be run later. You will learn in great detail how to define and work with functions in Chapter 4.

This particular function – the **main** function – has a special meaning in Kotlin. The **main** function indicates the starting place for your program. This is called the *application entry point*, and one such entry point must be defined for Sandbox (or any program) to be runnable. Every project you write in this book will start with a **main** function.

Your **main** function contains one instruction (also known as a *statement*): println("Hello, world!"). **println()** is also a function that is built into the *Kotlin standard library*. When the program runs and println("Hello, world!") is executed, IntelliJ will print the contents of the parentheses (without the quotation marks, so in this case Hello, world!) to the screen.

Running your Kotlin file

Shortly after you finish typing the code in Listing 1.1, IntelliJ will display a green ▶, known as the "run button," to the left of the first line (Figure 1.11). (If the icon does not appear, or if you see a red line underneath the filename in the tab or under any of the code you entered, this means you have an error in your code. Double-check that you typed the code exactly as shown in Listing 1.1. On the other hand, if you see a red and blue Kotlin K, this flag is the same as the run button.)

Figure 1.11 Run button

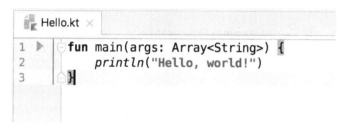

It is time for your program to come to life and greet the world. Click the run button. Select Run 'HelloKt' from the menu that appears (Figure 1.12). This tells IntelliJ you want to see your program in action.

Figure 1.12 Running `Hello.kt`

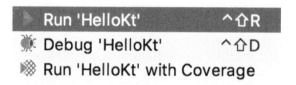

When you run your program, IntelliJ executes the code inside of the curly braces ({}), one line at a time, and then terminates execution. It also displays two new tool windows at the bottom of the IntelliJ window (Figure 1.13).

Figure 1.13 Run and event log tool windows

On the left is the *run tool window*, also known as the *console* (which is what we will call it from now on). It displays information about what happened as IntelliJ executed your program, as well as any output your program prints. You should see `Hello, world!` printed in your console. You should also see `Process finished with exit code 0`, indicating successful completion. This line appears at the end of all console output when there is no error; we will not show it in console results from now on.

(macOS users, you may see red error text stating that there is an issue with JavaLauncherHelper, as shown in Figure 1.13. Do not worry about this. It is an unfortunate side effect of how the Java Runtime Environment is installed on macOS. To remove it would require a lot of effort, but the issue does no harm – so you may ignore it and carry on.)

On the right is the *event log tool window*, which displays information about work IntelliJ did to get your program ready to run. We will not mention the event log again, because you get much more interesting output in the console. (For the same reason, do not be concerned if the event log never opened to begin with.) You can close it with the hide button at its top right, which looks like this: ⌃.

Compilation and execution of Kotlin/JVM code

A lot goes on in the short time between when you select the run button's Run 'HelloKt' option and when you see Hello, World! print to the console.

First, IntelliJ *compiles* the Kotlin code using the kotlinc-jvm compiler. This means IntelliJ translates the Kotlin code you wrote into *bytecode*, the language the JVM "speaks." If kotlinc-jvm has any problems translating your Kotlin code, it will display an error message (or messages) giving you a hint about how to fix the issues. Otherwise, if the compilation process goes smoothly, IntelliJ moves on to the execution phase.

In the execution phase, the bytecode that was generated by kotlinc-jvm is executed on the JVM. The console displays any output from your program, such as printing the text you specified in your call to the **println()** function, as the JVM executes the instructions.

When there are no more bytecode instructions to execute, the JVM terminates. IntelliJ shows the termination status in the console, letting you know whether execution finished successfully or with an error code.

You will not need a comprehensive understanding of the Kotlin compilation process to work through this book. We will, however, discuss bytecode in more detail in Chapter 2.

The Kotlin REPL

Sometimes you might want to test out a small bit of Kotlin code to see what happens when you run it, similar to how you might use a piece of scratch paper to jot down steps for a small calculation. This is especially helpful as you are learning the Kotlin language. Luckily for you, IntelliJ provides a tool for quickly testing code without having to create a file. This tool is called the *Kotlin REPL*. We will explain the name in a moment – for now, open it up and see what it can do.

In IntelliJ, open the Kotlin REPL tool window by selecting Tools → Kotlin → Kotlin REPL (Figure 1.14).

Figure 1.14 Opening the Kotlin REPL tool window

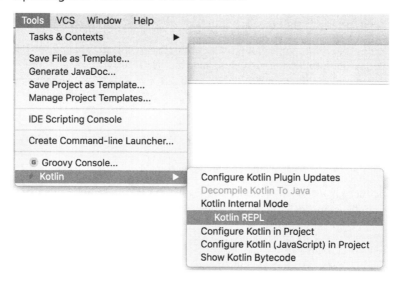

IntelliJ will display the REPL at the bottom of the window (Figure 1.15).

Figure 1.15 The Kotlin REPL tool window

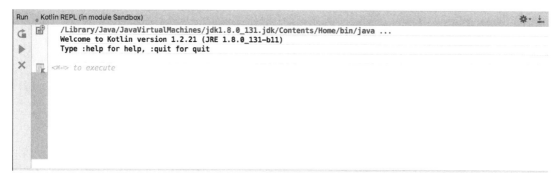

You can type code into the REPL, just like in the editor. The difference is that you can have it evaluated quickly, without compiling an entire project.

Enter the following code in the REPL:

Listing 1.2 "Hello, Kotlin!" (REPL)

```
println("Hello, Kotlin!")
```

Once you have entered the text, press Command-Return (Ctrl-Return) to evaluate the code in the REPL. After a moment, you will see the resulting output underneath, which should read Hello, Kotlin! (Figure 1.16).

Figure 1.16 Evaluating the code

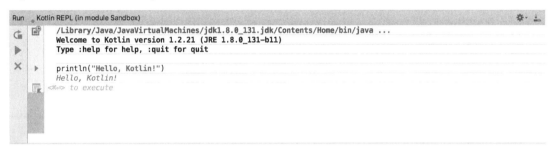

REPL is short for "read, evaluate, print, loop." You type in a piece of code at the prompt and submit it by clicking the green run button on the REPL's left side or by pressing Command-Return (Ctrl-Return). The REPL then *reads* the code, *evaluates* (runs) the code, and *prints* out the resulting value or side effect. Once the REPL finishes executing, it returns control back to you and the process *loop* starts all over.

Your Kotlin journey has begun! You accomplished a great deal in this chapter, laying the foundation for your growing knowledge of Kotlin programming. In the next chapter, you will begin to dig into the language's details by learning about how you can use variables, constants, and types to represent data.

For the More Curious: Why Use IntelliJ?

Kotlin can be written using any plain text editor. However, we recommend using IntelliJ, especially as you are learning. Just as text editing software that offers spell check and grammar check makes writing a well-formed prose essay easier, IntelliJ makes writing well-formed Kotlin easier. IntelliJ helps you:

- write syntactically and semantically correct code with features like syntax highlighting, context-sensitive suggestions, and automatic code completion

- run and debug your code with features like debug breakpoints and real-time code stepping when your application is running

- restructure existing code with refactoring shortcuts (like rename and extract constant) and code formatting to clean up indentation and spacing

Also, since Kotlin was created by JetBrains, the integration between IntelliJ and Kotlin is carefully designed – often leading to a delightful editing experience. As an added bonus, IntelliJ is the basis of Android Studio, so shortcuts and tools you learn here will translate to using Android Studio, if that is your thing.

For the More Curious: Targeting the JVM

The JVM is a piece of software that knows how to execute a set of instructions, called bytecode. "Targeting the JVM" means compiling, or translating, your Kotlin source code into Java bytecode, with the intention of running that bytecode on the JVM (Figure 1.17).

Figure 1.17 Compilation and execution flow

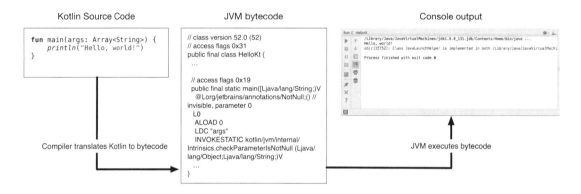

Each platform, such as Windows or macOS, has its own instruction set. The JVM acts as a bridge between the bytecode and the different hardware and software environments the JVM runs on, reading a piece of bytecode and calling the corresponding platform-specific instruction(s) that map to that bytecode. Therefore, there are different versions of the JVM for different platforms. This is what allows Kotlin developers to write platform-independent code that can be written one time and then compiled into bytecode and executed on different devices regardless of their operating systems.

Since Kotlin can be converted to bytecode that the JVM can execute, it is considered a JVM language. Java is perhaps the most well-known JVM language, because it was the first. However, other JVM languages, such as Scala and Kotlin, have emerged to address some shortcomings of Java from the developer perspective.

Kotlin is not limited to the JVM, however. At the time of this writing, Kotlin can also be compiled into JavaScript or even into native binaries that run directly on a given platform – such as Windows, Linux, and macOS – negating the need for a virtual machine layer.

Challenge: REPL Arithmetic

Many of the chapters in this book end with one or more challenges. The challenges are for you to work through on your own to deepen your understanding of Kotlin and get a little extra experience.

Use the REPL to explore how arithmetic operators in Kotlin work: +, −, *, /, and %. For example, type (9+12)*2 into the REPL. Does the output match what you expected?

If you wish to dive deeper, look over the mathematical functions available in the Kotlin standard library at kotlinlang.org/api/latest/jvm/stdlib/kotlin.math/index.html and try them out in the REPL. For example, try min(94, -99), which will tell you the minimum of the two numbers provided in parentheses.

2

Variables, Constants, and Types

This chapter will introduce you to variables, constants, and Kotlin's basic data types – fundamental elements of any program. You use *variables* and *constants* to store values and pass data around in your application. *Types* describe the particular kind of data that is held by a constant or variable.

There are important differences between each of the data types and between variables and constants that shape how they are used.

Types

Variables and constants have a data type that you specify. The type describes the data that is held by a variable or constant and tells the compiler how *type checking* will be handled, a feature in Kotlin that prevents the assignment of the wrong kind of data to a variable or constant.

To see this idea in action, you are going to add a file to the Sandbox project you created in Chapter 1. Open IntelliJ. The Sandbox project will likely open automatically, because IntelliJ reopens your most recent project. If it does not, you can open Sandbox from the list of recent files on the lefthand side of the welcome dialog or by selecting File → Open Recent → Sandbox.

Begin by adding a new file to the project by right-clicking src in the project tool window. (You may need to click the Sandbox disclosure arrow to see src.) Select New → Kotlin File/Class, and name the file TypeIntro. The new file will open in the editor.

The **main** function, as you saw in Chapter 1, defines the entry point for your program. IntelliJ offers a shortcut for writing this function: Type the word "main" in TypeIntro.kt and press the Tab key. IntelliJ will automatically add the basic elements of the function for you, as shown in Listing 2.1.

Listing 2.1 Adding a **main** function (TypeIntro.kt)

```kotlin
fun main(args: Array<String>) {

}
```

Declaring a Variable

Imagine you are writing an adventure game that allows a player to explore an interactive world. You may want a variable for keeping track of the player's score.

In TypeIntro.kt, create your first variable, called experiencePoints, and assign it a value:

Listing 2.2 Declaring an experiencePoints variable (TypeIntro.kt)

```
fun main(args: Array<String>) {
    var experiencePoints: Int = 5
    println(experiencePoints)
}
```

Here, you have assigned an instance of the type Int to a variable called experiencePoints. Let's walk through each part of what happened.

You defined a variable using the keyword var, which indicates that you want to declare a new variable, followed by the new variable's name.

Next, you specified the type definition for the variable, : Int, which indicates that experiencePoints will hold an integer (whole number) value.

Last, you used the *assignment operator* (=) to assign what is on the righthand side (an instance of the Int type, specifically 5) to what is on the lefthand side (experiencePoints).

Figure 2.1 shows the experiencePoints variable's definition in diagram form.

Figure 2.1 Anatomy of a variable definition

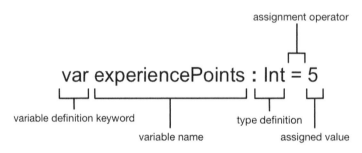

After defining the variable, you print its value to the console using the **println** function.

Run the program by clicking the run button next to the **main** function and selecting Run 'TypeIntroKt'. The result printed to the console is 5, the value you assigned to experiencePoints.

Now, try assigning experiencePoints the value "thirty-two" instead. (The strike-through indicates code you are to delete.)

Listing 2.3 Assigning "thirty-two" to experiencePoints (TypeIntro.kt)

```
fun main(args: Array<String>) {
    var experiencePoints: Int = 5
    var experiencePoints: Int = "thirty-two"
    println(experiencePoints)
}
```

Run **main** again by clicking the run button. This time, the Kotlin compiler displays an error:

```
Error:(2, 33) Kotlin: Type mismatch: inferred type is String but Int was expected
```

When you typed this code, you may have noticed the red underline beneath "thirty-two". This is IntelliJ's signal that the program has an error. Hover over "thirty-two" to read the details of the detected problem (Figure 2.2).

Figure 2.2 Type mismatch disclosure

```
fun main(args: Array<String>) {
    var experiencePoints: Int = "thirty-two"
    println(experiencePoi
                         [TYPE_MISMATCH] Type mismatch.
}                        Required:  Int
                         Found:     String
```

Kotlin uses a *static type system* – meaning the compiler labels the source code you define with types so that it can ensure the code you wrote is valid. IntelliJ also checks code as you type it and notices when an instance of a particular type is incorrectly assigned to a variable of a different type. This feature is called *static type checking*, and it tells you about programming mistakes before you even compile the program.

To fix the error, change the value assigned to experiencePoints to an Int that matches its declared type by changing "thirty-two" back to 5:

Listing 2.4 Fixing the type error (TypeIntro.kt)

```
fun main(args: Array<String>) {
    var experiencePoints: Int = "thirty-two"
    var experiencePoints: Int = 5
    println(experiencePoints)
}
```

A variable can be reassigned in the course of your program. If the player gains more experience, for example, you can assign a new value to the experiencePoints variable. Add 5 to the experiencePoints variable, as shown:

Listing 2.5 Adding 5 to experiencePoints (TypeIntro.kt)

```
fun main(args: Array<String>) {
    var experiencePoints: Int = 5
    experiencePoints += 5
    println(experiencePoints)
}
```

After assigning the experiencePoints variable a value of 5, you use the *addition and assignment operator* (+=) to add 5 to the original value. Run the program again. You will see the number 10 printed to the console.

Kotlin's Built-In Types

You have seen variables that are of the String type and variables of the Int type. Kotlin also has types to handle values like true/false, lists of elements, and key-value pairs for defining mappings of elements. Table 2.1 shows many of the commonly used built-in types available in Kotlin:

Table 2.1 Commonly used built-in types

Type	Description	Examples
String	Textual data	"Estragon" "happy meal"
Char	Single character	'X' Unicode character U+0041
Boolean	True/false values	true false
Int	Whole numbers	"Estragon".length 5
Double	Decimal numbers	3.14 2.718
List	Collections of elements	3, 1, 2, 4, 3 "root beer", "club soda", "coke"
Set	Collections of unique elements	"Larry", "Moe", "Curly" "Mercury", "Venus", "Earth", "Mars", "Jupiter", "Saturn", "Uranus", "Neptune"
Map	Collections of key-value pairs	"small" to 5.99, "medium" to 7.99, "large" to 10.99

If you have not seen all of these types, do not be concerned – you will learn about all of them throughout the course of this book. In particular, you will learn more about strings in Chapter 7 and numbers in Chapter 8, and you will learn about lists, sets, and maps, together called *collection types*, in Chapter 10 and Chapter 11.

Read-Only Variables

So far, you have seen variables whose values can be reassigned. But often, you will want to use variables whose values should not change in your program. For example, in the text adventure game, the player's name will not change after it has been initially assigned.

Kotlin provides a different syntax for declaring *read-only* variables – variables that cannot be modified once they are assigned.

You declare a variable that can be modified using the var keyword. To declare a read-only variable, you use the val keyword.

Colloquially, variables whose values can change are referred to as vars and read-only variables are referred to as vals. We will follow this convention from now on, since "variable" and "read-only variable" are less distinct. vars and vals are both considered "variables," so we will continue to use that term to refer to them as a group.

Add a val definition for the player's name and print it after the experience points:

Listing 2.6 Adding a playerName val (TypeIntro.kt)

```
fun main(args: Array<String>) {
    val playerName: String = "Estragon"
    var experiencePoints: Int = 5
    experiencePoints += 5
    println(experiencePoints)
    println(playerName)
}
```

Run the program by clicking the run button next to the **main** function and selecting Run 'TypeIntroKt'. You will see the values of experiencePoints and playerName printed in the console:

```
10
Estragon
```

Next, try reassigning playerName to a different String value, using the = assignment operator, and run the program again.

Listing 2.7 Trying to change playerName's value (TypeIntro.kt)

```
fun main(args: Array<String>) {
    val playerName: String = "Estragon"
    playerName = "Madrigal"
    var experiencePoints: Int = 5
    experiencePoints += 5
    println(experiencePoints)
    println(playerName)
}
```

You will see the following compilation error:

```
Error:(3, 5) Kotlin: Val cannot be reassigned
```

The compiler complains because you tried to modify a val. Once a val has been assigned, it can never be reassigned.

Delete the second assignment to fix the reassignment error:

Listing 2.8 Fixing the `val` reassignment error (`TypeIntro.kt`)

```
fun main(args: Array<String>) {
    val playerName: String = "Estragon"
    playerName = "Madrigal"
    var experiencePoints: Int = 5
    experiencePoints += 5
    println(experiencePoints)
    println(playerName)
}
```

`val`s are useful for guarding against accidentally changing variables that should be read-only. For this reason, we recommend that you use a `val` any time you do not need a `var`.

IntelliJ can detect when a `var` can be made a `val` instead by analyzing your code statically. If a `var` is never changed, IntelliJ will suggest that you convert it to a `val`. We suggest you follow IntelliJ's suggestion – unless you are about to write the code that reassigns the `var`. To see what IntelliJ's suggestion looks like, change `playerName` to a `var`:

Listing 2.9 Changing `playerName` to be reassignable (`TypeIntro.kt`)

```
fun main(args: Array<String>) {
    val playerName: String = "Estragon"
    var playerName: String = "Estragon"
    var experiencePoints: Int = 5
    experiencePoints += 5
    println(experiencePoints)
    println(playerName)
}
```

Because the value of `playerName` is never reassigned, it does not need to be (and should not be) a `var`. Notice that IntelliJ has added a mustard-colored highlight to the line with the `var` keyword. If you mouse over the `var` keyword, IntelliJ explains the suggested improvement (Figure 2.3).

Figure 2.3 Variable never modified

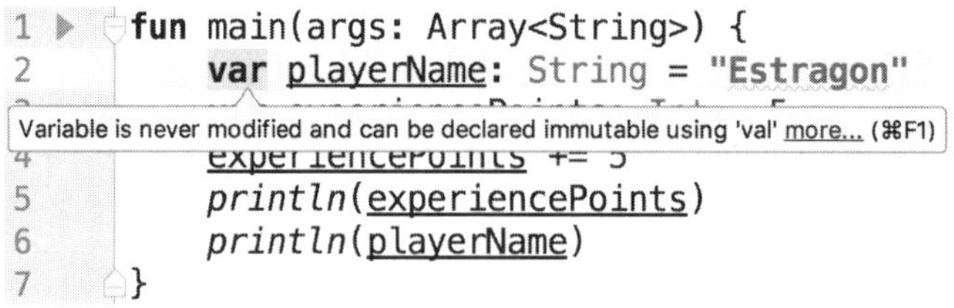

As expected, IntelliJ suggests converting `playerName` to a `val`. To apply the suggestion, click on the `var` keyword next to `playerName` and press Option-Return (Alt-Enter). In the pop-up, select Make variable immutable (Figure 2.4).

Figure 2.4 Making a variable immutable

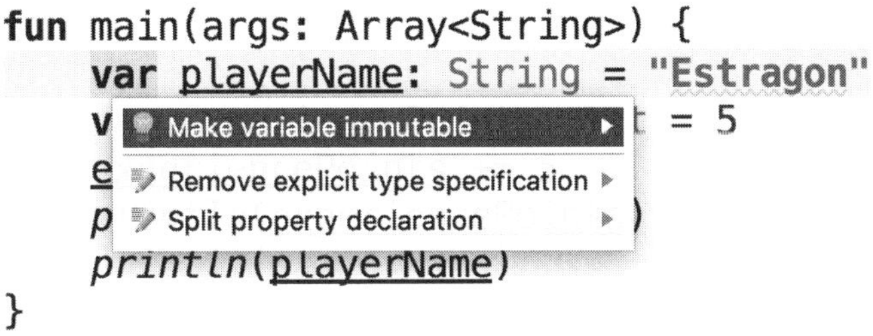

```
fun main(args: Array<String>) {
    var playerName: String = "Estragon"
    v  💡 Make variable immutable          ▶ t = 5
    e  ⤳ Remove explicit type specification ▶
    p  ⤳ Split property declaration          ▶ )
    println(playerName)
}
```

IntelliJ automatically converts the var to a val (Figure 2.5).

Figure 2.5 Immutable playerName

```
fun main(args: Array<String>) {
    val playerName: String = "Estragon"
    var experiencePoints: Int = 5
    experiencePoints += 5
    println(experiencePoints)
    println(playerName)
}
```

As we said earlier, we recommend that you use a val any time you can, so that Kotlin can warn you about accidental reassignments. We also recommend that you pay attention to IntelliJ's suggestions for code improvement. You may not always use them, but they are always worth taking a look at.

Type Inference

Notice that the type definitions you specified for the playerName and experiencePoints variables are grayed out in IntelliJ. Grayed-out text indicates an element that is not required. Mouse over the String type definition, and IntelliJ will provide an explanation about why the element is not required (Figure 2.6).

Figure 2.6 Redundant type information

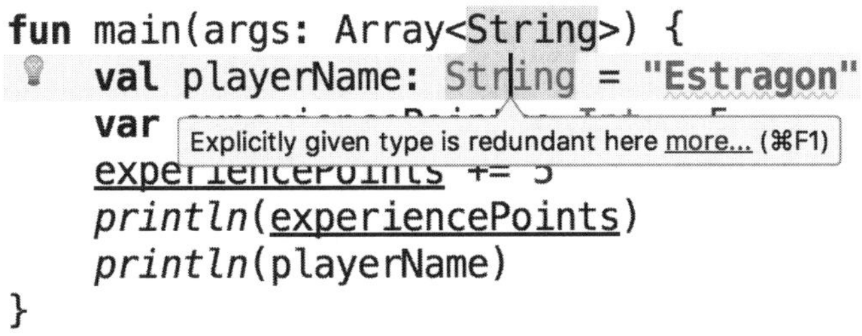

```
fun main(args: Array<String>) {
💡  val playerName: String = "Estragon"
    var
    exper [ Explicitly given type is redundant here more... (⌘F1) ]
    println(experiencePoints)
    println(playerName)
}
```

As you can see, Kotlin indicates that your type declaration is "redundant." What does this mean?

Kotlin includes a feature called *type inference* that allows you to omit the type definition for variables that are assigned a value when they are declared. Because you assign data of the String type to playerName and of the Int type to experiencePoints when you declare them, the Kotlin compiler infers the appropriate type information for both variables.

Just as IntelliJ can help you change a var to a val, it can also help you remove unneeded type specifications. Click on the String type definition (: String) next to playerName and press Option-Return (Alt-Enter). Then click Remove explicit type specification in the pop-up (Figure 2.7).

Figure 2.7 Removing explicit type specification

```
fun main(args: Array<String>) {
    val playerName: String = "Estragon"
    var experiencePoint   Remove explicit type specification ▶
    experiencePoints +=   Split property declaration          ▶
    println(experiencePoints)
    println(playerName)
}
```

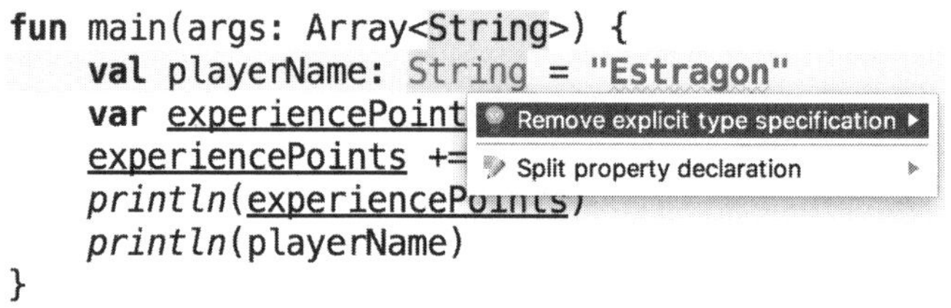

: String will disappear. Repeat the process for the experiencePoints var to remove : Int.

Whether you take advantage of type inference or specify the type when you declare the variable, the compiler will keep track of the type. In this book, we use type inference where it is unambiguous to do so. Type inference helps keep code clean, concise, and easier to modify as your program changes.

Note that IntelliJ will display the type of any variable on request, including those that use type inference. If you ever have a question about the type of a variable, click on its name and press Control-Shift-P. IntelliJ will display its type (Figure 2.8).

Figure 2.8 Displaying type info

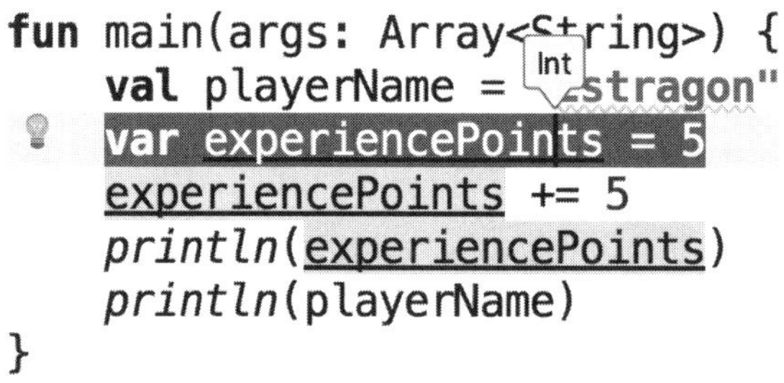

```
fun main(args: Array<String>) {
    val playerName =  Int stragon"
    var experiencePoints = 5
    experiencePoints += 5
    println(experiencePoints)
    println(playerName)
}
```

Compile-Time Constants

Earlier we told you that vars can have their values changed and vals cannot. That ... was a white lie. In fact, there are special cases where a val can return different values, which we will discuss in Chapter 12. If you have a piece of data that you want to be absolutely, positively immutable – to never change – consider a *compile-time constant*.

A compile-time constant must be defined outside of any function, including **main**, because its value must be assigned at *compile time* (that is, when the program compiles) – hence the name. **main** and your other functions are called during *runtime* (when the program is executed), and the variables within them are assigned their values then. A compile-time constant exists before any of these assignments take place.

Compile-time constants also must be of one of the following basic types, because use of more complex types for a constant could jeopardize the compile-time guarantee. You will learn more about how types are constructed in Chapter 13. Here are the supported basic types for a compile-time constant:

- String
- Int
- Double
- Float
- Long
- Short
- Byte
- Char
- Boolean

Add a compile-time constant to TypeIntro.kt, above the declaration of the **main** function, using the const modifier:

Listing 2.10 Declaring a compile-time constant (TypeIntro.kt)

```
const val MAX_EXPERIENCE: Int = 5000

fun main(args: Array<String>) {
    ...
}
```

Prepending a val with the const modifier tells the compiler that it can be sure that this val will never change. In this case, MAX_EXPERIENCE is guaranteed to have the integer value 5000, no matter what. This gives the compiler the flexibility to perform optimization behind the scenes.

Wondering about the format of the const val's name, MAX_EXPERIENCE? While this format is not required by the compiler, our preferred style is to distinguish const vals by fully capitalizing them and replacing spaces with underscores. As you may have noticed, we use camel casing and an initial lowercase for both vars and vals. Style norms like these help keep your code readable and clear.

Inspecting Kotlin Bytecode

You learned in Chapter 1 that Kotlin is an alternative to Java for writing programs that run on the JVM, where Java bytecode is executed. It is often useful to inspect the Java bytecode that the Kotlin compiler generates to run on the JVM. You will look at the bytecode in several places in this book as a way to analyze how a particular language feature works on the JVM.

Knowing how to inspect the Java equivalent of the Kotlin code you write is a great technique for understanding how Kotlin works, especially if you have Java experience. If you do not have Java experience specifically, the Java code will likely share familiar traits with a language that you have worked with – so think of it as a pseudocode to aid your understanding. And, if you are brand new to programming – congratulations! In choosing Kotlin, you have chosen a language that, as you will see in these sections, allows you to express the same logic that Java does, typically in much less code.

For example, you may have wondered how using type inference when defining variables in Kotlin affects the resulting bytecode that is generated to run on the JVM. To learn how, you can use the Kotlin bytecode tool window.

In `TypeIntro.kt`, press the Shift key twice to open the Search Everywhere dialog. Begin entering "show kotlin bytecode" in the search box, and select Show Kotlin Bytecode from the list of available actions when it appears (Figure 2.9).

Figure 2.9 Showing Kotlin bytecode

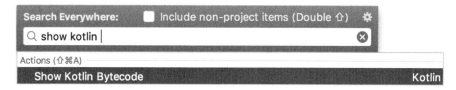

The Kotlin bytecode tool window will open (Figure 2.10). (You can also open the tool window with Tools → Kotlin → Show Kotlin Bytecode.)

Figure 2.10 Kotlin bytecode tool window

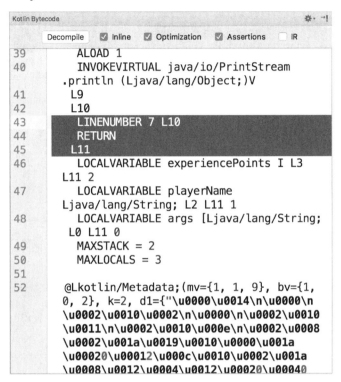

If bytecode is not your native tongue, fear not! You can translate the bytecode back to Java to see it represented in terms you may be more familiar with. In the bytecode tool window, click the Decompile button at the top left.

A new tab will open showing `TypeIntro.decompiled.java` (Figure 2.11), a Java version of the bytecode the Kotlin compiler generated for the JVM.

Figure 2.11 Decompiled bytecode

```
 TypeIntro.kt ×     TypeIntro.decompiled.java ×
   9          d1 = {"\u0000\u0014\n\u0000\n\u0002\u0010\u0002\n\u0000
             \n\u0002\u0010\u0011\n\u0002\u0010\u000e\n\u0002\b\u0002
             \u001a\u0019\u0010\u0000\u001a\u00020\u00012\f\u0010
             \u0002\u001a\b\u0012\u0004\u0012\u00020\u00040\u0003
             ¢\u0006\u0002\u0010\u0005"\u0006\u0006"},
  10          d2 = {"main", "", "args", "", "", "([Ljava/lang/String;)
             V", "production sources for module Sandbox"}
  11      )
  12  ▶  public final class TypeIntroKt {
  13  ▶     public static final void main(@NotNull String[] args) {
  14            Intrinsics.checkParameterIsNotNull(args,
             paramName: "args");
  15            String playerName = "Estragon";
  16            int experiencePoints = 5;
  17            int experiencePoints = experiencePoints + 5;
  18            System.out.println(experiencePoints);
  19            System.out.println(playerName);
  20         }
  21      }
```

(The red underlines in this case are due to a quirk in the interaction between Kotlin and Java, rather than a problem.)

Focus on the variable declarations for `experiencePoints` and `playerName`:

```
String playerName = "Estragon";
int experiencePoints = 5;
```

Although you omitted type declarations from the definitions of both variables in the Kotlin source, the bytecode that was generated includes explicit type definitions. This is how the variables would be declared in Java, and the bytecode gives a behind-the-scenes look at Kotlin's type inference support.

You will dig deeper into the decompiled Java bytecode in later chapters. For now, close `TypeIntro.decompiled.java` (using the X in its tab) and the bytecode tool window (using the ⬈| icon at the top right).

In this chapter, you have learned how to store basic data in `var`s and `val`s and seen when to use each, depending on whether you need to be able to change their values. You have seen how to declare immutable values using compile-time constants. Last, you learned how Kotlin leverages the power of type inference to save you keystrokes every time you declare a variable. You will be using all these basic tools over and over as you proceed through this book.

In the next chapter, you will learn how to represent more complex states using conditionals.

For the More Curious: Java Primitive Types in Kotlin

In Java, there are two kinds of types: reference types and primitive types. Reference types are defined in source code: A matching source code definition corresponds to the type. Java also offers primitive types (often called just "primitives"), which have no source file definition and are represented by special keywords instead.

A reference type in Java always begins with a capital letter, indicating that it is backed by a source definition for its type. Here is experiencePoints defined using a Java reference type:

```
Integer experiencePoints = 5;
```

A Java primitive type starts with a lowercase letter:

```
int experiencePoints = 5;
```

All primitives in Java have a corresponding reference type. (But not all reference types have a corresponding primitive type.) Why use one versus the other?

One reason for choosing a reference type is that there are certain features of the Java language that are only available when using reference types. Generics, for example, which you will learn about in Chapter 17, do not work with primitives. Reference types can also work with the object-oriented features of Java more readily than Java primitives. (You will learn about object-oriented programming and the object-oriented features of Kotlin in Chapter 12.)

On the other hand, primitives offer better performance and some other perks.

Unlike Java, Kotlin provides only one kind of type: reference types.

```
var experiencePoints: Int = 5
```

Kotlin made this design decision for several reasons. First, if there is no choice between kinds of types, you cannot code yourself into a corner as easily as you can with multiple kinds to choose from. For example, what if you define an instance of a primitive type, then realize later that you need to use the generic feature, which requires a reference type? Having only reference types in Kotlin means that you will never encounter this problem.

If you are familiar with Java, you may be thinking, "But primitives offer better performance than reference types!" This is true. But take another look at the experiencePoints variable in the decompiled bytecode you saw earlier:

```
int experiencePoints = 5;
```

As you can see, a primitive type was used in place of the reference type. Why is that, if Kotlin only has reference types? The Kotlin compiler will, where possible, use primitives in the Java bytecode, because they do indeed offer better performance.

Kotlin gives you the ease of reference types with the performance of primitives under the hood. In Kotlin you will find a corresponding reference type for the eight primitive types you may be familiar with in Java.

Challenge: hasSteed

Here is your first challenge: In the text adventure game, players may acquire a dragon or minotaur they can ride. Define a variable called `hasSteed` to track whether the player has acquired one. Give the variable an initial state indicating that the player does not have one yet.

Challenge: The Unicorn's Horn

Imagine this scene from the adventure game:

The hero Estragon arrives at a pub known as the Unicorn's Horn. The publican asks, "Do you need to stable a steed?"

"No," Estragon replies, "I have no steed. But I do have 50 gold pieces, and I would like a drink."

"Excellent!" says the publican. "I have mead, wine, and LaCroix. What will you have?"

For this challenge, add below your `hasSteed` variable the variables required for the scene at the Unicorn's Horn, using type inference and assigned values where possible. Add variables to hold values for the name of the pub, the name of the current publican on duty, and how much gold the player has acquired so far.

Notice that the Unicorn's Horn has a menu of drinks the hero can select from. What type might you use to represent the menu? If you need to, consult Table 2.1.

Challenge: Magic Mirror

Refreshed, Estragon is ready for a challenging quest. Are you?

The hero discovers a magic mirror that shows a player the reflection of their `playerName`. Using the `String` type's magic, transform the `playerName` string `"Estragon"` into `"nogartsE"`, a reflection of its value.

To solve this challenge, consult the documentation for `String` at `kotlinlang.org/api/latest/jvm/stdlib/kotlin/-string/index.html`. You will find that, fortunately, the actions that a particular type can perform are usually very intuitively named (hint).

3

Conditionals

In this chapter, you will learn how to define rules for when code should be executed. This language feature is called *control flow*, and it allows you to describe the conditions for when specific portions of your program should run. You will see the if/else statement and expression and the when expression, and you will learn how to write true/false tests using the comparison and logical operators. Along the way, you will also take a look at Kotlin's string templating feature.

To see these concepts in action, you will begin building a project called NyetHack, which you will work on through most of this book.

Why "NyetHack"? We are glad you asked. Perhaps you remember NetHack, a game released in 1987 by The NetHack DevTeam. NetHack was a single-player text-based fantasy game with ASCII graphics; check it out at nethack.org. You will be building elements of a similar text-based game (no awesome ASCII graphics, though – sorry). JetBrains, the creator of the Kotlin language, has offices in Russia; when you put together a text-based game like NetHack and Kotlin's Russian origins, you get NyetHack.

if/else Statements

Let's get started. Open IntelliJ and create a new project. (If you already have IntelliJ open, you can select File → New → Project...) Select the Kotlin/JVM target and name your project NyetHack.

Click on the NyetHack disclosure arrow in the project tool window and right-click the src directory to create a new Kotlin File/Class. Name your file Game. Add a **main** entry point function to Game.kt by typing "main" and pressing the Tab key. Your function should look like this:

```
fun main(args: Array<String>) {

}
```

In NyetHack, a player's condition is based on remaining health points, ranging from 0 to 100. On their quest, they may sustain injuries during combat. On the other hand, they may be in excellent condition. You want to define rules for how to describe the player's visible health condition: *If* the player's health is 100, you want to show that they are in excellent health, *else* you will let them know how hurt they are. One tool you can use to define rules like that is the if/else statement.

Within the **main** function, write your first if/else statement, as shown below. There is a lot going on in this code; we will break it down after you enter it.

Listing 3.1 Printing the player's health condition (Game.kt)

```kotlin
fun main(args: Array<String>) {
    val name = "Madrigal"
    var healthPoints = 100

    if (healthPoints == 100) {
        println(name + " is in excellent condition!")
    } else {
        println(name + " is in awful condition!")
    }
}
```

Let's go through this new code line by line. First, you define a val called name and assign it a string value representing your intrepid player's name. Next, you define a var called healthPoints and assign it an initial value of 100, a perfect score. Then, you add an if/else statement.

In your if/else statement, you begin by posing the following true/false question: "Does the player have a healthPoints score of 100?" You express this with the == *structural equality operator*. It can be read as "is equal to," so this statement reads "if healthPoints is equal to 100."

Your if statement is followed by a statement in curly braces ({}). The code within the curly braces is what you want the program to do if the if condition evaluates as the Boolean value true – in this case, if healthPoints has a value of exactly 100.

```kotlin
if (healthPoints == 100) {
    println(name + " is in excellent condition!")
}
```

Included in this statement is the familiar **println** function used to print something to the console. What to print, in the parentheses, consists of the value of name and the string " is in excellent condition!" (Note the leading space, so you do not get a result of Madrigalis in excellent condition!) In short, your if/else statement so far says that if Madrigal has 100 health points, the program should print that the hero is in excellent condition.

(While your if statement's curly braces enclose only one statement, more than one can be included if you want multiple actions to be taken when the if evaluates as true.)

Using the addition operator (+) to append a value to a string is called *string concatenation*. It is an easy way to customize what is printed to the console based on the value of a variable. Later in this chapter, you will see another, preferred way to inject values into your strings.

What if healthPoints has a value other than 100? In that case, the if evaluates as false, and the compiler will skip the expression in curly braces that follows if and move on to the else. Think of else as meaning "otherwise": If some condition is true, do this; *otherwise* do that. Like if, else is followed by one or more expressions in curly braces that tell the compiler what to do. But unlike if, else does not need to define a condition. It applies whenever the if does not, so the curly braces immediately follow the keyword.

```kotlin
else {
    println(name + " is in awful condition!")
}
```

The only difference in this call to the **println** function is in the string that follows the hero's name. Instead of reporting that the hero "is in excellent condition!", this one reports that the injured hero "is in awful condition!" (Thus far, most of the function calls that you have seen serve only to print strings out to the console. You will learn more about functions, including how to define your own, in Chapter 4.)

Putting this all together in plain English, your code says to the compiler, "If the hero has exactly 100 health points, print `Madrigal is in excellent condition!` to the console. If Madrigal does not have 100 health points, print `Madrigal is in awful condition!` to the console."

The structural equality operator, ==, is one of Kotlin's *comparison operators*. Table 3.1 lists Kotlin's comparison operators. You do not need to know all of the operators listed now, as you will learn more about them later. Return to this table when you are considering possible operators to express a condition.

Table 3.1 Comparison operators

Operator	Description
<	Evaluates whether the value on the left is less than the value on the right.
<=	Evaluates whether the value on the left is less than or equal to the value on the right.
>	Evaluates whether the value on the left is greater than the value on the right.
>=	Evaluates whether the value on the left is greater than or equal to the value on the right.
==	Evaluates whether the value on the left is equal to the value on the right.
!=	Evaluates whether the value on the left is not equal to the value on the right.
===	Evaluates whether the two instances point to the same reference.
!==	Evaluates whether the two instances do not point to the same reference.

Back to business. Run `Game.kt` by clicking the run button to the left of the **main** function. You should see the following output:

```
Madrigal is in excellent condition!
```

Since the condition you defined, `healthPoints == 100`, is true, the `if` branch in the `if/else` statement was triggered. (We use the word *branch* because the flow of your code execution will branch depending on whether your specified condition is met.) Now, try changing the `healthPoints` value to 89:

Listing 3.2 Modifying healthPoints (Game.kt)

```
fun main(args: Array<String>) {
    val name = "Madrigal"
    var healthPoints = 100
    var healthPoints = 89

    if (healthPoints == 100) {
        println(name + " is in excellent condition!")
    } else {
        println(name + " is in awful condition!")
    }
}
```

Run the program again, and you will see:

```
Madrigal is in awful condition!
```

Now, the condition you defined is false (89 is not equal to 100), so the `else` branch is triggered.

Adding more conditions

The health status code gives a crude idea of the player's condition, but it is … well, crude. If the player's healthPoints is 89, you report that they are in "awful condition," which hardly makes sense. It might be just a flesh wound, after all.

To make your if/else statement more nuanced, you can add more conditions to check for and more branches to include as possible results. You do this with else if branches, whose syntax is just like an if's, between the if and the else. Update your if/else statement to include three else if branches checking for intermediate values of healthPoints:

Listing 3.3 Checking for more player conditions (Game.kt)

```
fun main(args: Array<String>) {
    val name = "Madrigal"
    var healthPoints = 89

    if (healthPoints == 100) {
        println(name + " is in excellent condition!")
    } else if (healthPoints >= 90) {
        println(name + " has a few scratches.")
    } else if (healthPoints >= 75) {
        println(name + " has some minor wounds.")
    } else if (healthPoints >= 15) {
        println(name + " looks pretty hurt.")
    } else {
        println(name + " is in awful condition!")
    }
}
```

Your new logic reads like this:

If Madrigal has this many health points	… print this message
100	Madrigal is in excellent condition!
90-99	Madrigal has a few scratches.
75-89	Madrigal has some minor wounds.
15-74	Madrigal looks pretty hurt.
0-14	Madrigal is in awful condition!

Run the program again. Because the value of Madrigal's healthPoints is 89, neither the if nor the first else if will evaluate as true. But else if (healthPoints >= 75) is true, so you will see Madrigal has some minor wounds. in the console.

Note that the compiler evaluates the conditions of an if/else from top to bottom and stops checking conditions as soon as one evaluates as true. If none of the conditions you provide are true, the else branch will be executed.

This means that the order of the conditions matters: If you had arranged the if and else ifs from the lowest checked value to the highest, none of the else ifs would ever be executed. Any healthPoints value of 15 or higher would trigger the first condition, and any value lower than 15 would make the else ifs evaluate as false – so the else would apply. (Do not make this change to your code. It is only for illustration.)

```
fun main(args: Array<String>) {
    val name = "Madrigal"
    var healthPoints = 89

    if (healthPoints >= 15) {    // Triggered for any value of 15 or higher
        println(name + " looks pretty hurt.")
    } else if (healthPoints >= 75) {
        println(name + " has some minor wounds.")
    } else if (healthPoints >= 90) {
        println(name + " has a few scratches.")
    } else if (healthPoints == 100) {
        println(name + " is in excellent condition!")
    } else {                          // Triggered for values 0-14
        println(name + " is in awful condition!")
    }
}
```

You have added more subtlety in how the player's health is reported by including `else if` statements with more conditions to check when the initial `if` condition evaluates as false. Try varying `healthPoints`'s value to trigger the result in each branch you defined. When you are done, return `healthPoints` to a value of 89.

Nested if/else statements

In NyetHack, a player can be "blessed," which means that if they are in good health they will heal from minor injuries quickly. Your next step is to add a variable to track whether a player is blessed (what type do you think it will be?) and, if so, to change the health status message to reflect that.

Do this by nesting an `if/else` statement within one of your existing branches so that when the player's health is greater than or equal to 75 you use an additional `if/else` to check whether the player is blessed. (As you enter the changes below, do not miss the added } before the last `else if`.)

Listing 3.4 Checking for blessedness (`Game.kt`)

```
fun main(args: Array<String>) {
    val name = "Madrigal"
    var healthPoints = 89
    val isBlessed = true

    if (healthPoints == 100) {
        println(name + "is in excellent condition!")
    } else if (healthPoints >= 90) {
        println(name + " has a few scratches.")
    } else if (healthPoints >= 75) {
        if (isBlessed) {
            println(name + " has some minor wounds but is healing quite quickly!")
        } else {
            println(name + " has some minor wounds.")
        }
    } else if (healthPoints >= 15) {
        println(name + " looks pretty hurt.")
    } else {
        println(name + " is in awful condition!")
    }
}
```

31

You added a Boolean val representing whether the player is blessed and inserted an if/else statement to create a new output when a player is blessed and has between 75 and 89 health points. Recall that healthPoints has a value of 89, so you should expect to see the new message when you run the program. Run it and see. Your output should be:

```
Madrigal has some minor wounds but is healing quite quickly!
```

If you see any other output, check that your code matches Listing 3.4 exactly – in particular that healthPoints is assigned a value of 89.

Nesting conditionals allows you to create logical branches within branches so that the conditions that you check for can be precise and complex.

More elegant conditionals

If you do not keep a sharp eye on them, conditionals will explode all over the place like tribbles. Thankfully, Kotlin allows you to take advantage of conditionals' usefulness while keeping them concise and readable. Let's look at some examples.

Logical operators

In NyetHack, more complex conditions can arise that you need to check for. For example, if a player is blessed *and* their health is above 50, *or* if they are immortal, they have an aura that is visible. Otherwise, the player's aura cannot be seen by the naked eye.

You could use a series of if/else statements to determine whether a player has a visible aura, but you would end up with a lot of duplicate code and the logic of the conditions would be masked. There is a more elegant and reader-friendly way: using logical operators in a conditional.

Add a new variable and an if/else statement to print aura information to the console:

Listing 3.5 Using logical operators in a conditional (Game.kt)

```kotlin
fun main(args: Array<String>) {
    val name = "Madrigal"
    var healthPoints = 89
    val isBlessed = true
    val isImmortal = false

    // Aura
    if (isBlessed && healthPoints > 50 || isImmortal) {
        println("GREEN")
    } else {
        println("NONE")
    }

    if (healthPoints == 100) {
        ...
    }
}
```

You added a val called isImmortal to track the player's immortality (read-only because a player's immortality does not change). That part is familiar, but there are a couple of new things going on, too. First, you included a *code comment*, indicated by //.

Anything to the right of // is included in the comment and is ignored by the compiler, so you can use any syntax you want there. Comments are useful for organizing and adding information about your code, making it more readable for others (or for your future self, who may not remember all the details).

Next, you used two *logical operators* in your if. Logical operators allow you to combine comparison operators into a larger statement.

&& is the *logical 'and' operator*, and it requires that *both* the condition on its left *and* the condition on its right be true for the expression as a whole to be true. || is the *logical 'or' operator*, and it allows the expression as a whole to be true if *either* the condition on its left *or* the condition on its right (or both) is true.

Table 3.2 shows Kotlin's logical operators.

Table 3.2 Logical operators

Operator	Description
&&	Logical 'and': true if and only if both are true (false otherwise).
||	Logical 'or': true if either is true (false only if both are false).
!	Logical 'not': true becomes false, false becomes true.

One note: When operators are combined, there is an order of precedence that determines what order they are evaluated in. Operators with the same precedence are applied from left to right. You can also group operations by surrounding the operators that should be evaluated as a group in parentheses. Here is the order of operator precedence, from highest to lowest:

! (logical 'not')

< (less than), <= (less than or equal to), > (greater than), >= (greater than or equal to)

== (structural equality), != (non-equality)

&& (logical 'and')

|| (logical 'or')

Getting back to NyetHack, let's take a look at your new condition:

```
if (isBlessed && healthPoints > 50 || isImmortal) {
    println("GREEN")
}
```

Put another way, if the player is blessed *and* has more than 50 health points, *or* if the player is immortal, a green aura is visible. Madrigal is not immortal, but is blessed and has 89 health points. Thus, the first option is met, and Madrigal's aura should be visible. Run your program to see whether this is so. You should see:

```
GREEN
Madrigal has some minor wounds but is healing quite quickly!
```

Think about the nested conditional statements that would be required to express this logic without logical operators. These operators give you the tools to express complex logic clearly.

Your aura code is more clear than a set of if/else statements, but it could be even more readable. Logical operators are not only for conditionals. They can be used in many expressions, including in the declaration of a variable. Add a new Boolean variable that encapsulates the conditions for a visible aura and *refactor* (that is, rewrite) your conditional to use the new variable.

Listing 3.6 Using logical operators in the declaration of a variable (Game.kt)

```kotlin
fun main(args: Array<String>) {
    ...
    // Aura
    if (isBlessed && healthPoints > 50 || isImmortal) {
    val auraVisible = isBlessed && healthPoints > 50 || isImmortal
    if (auraVisible) {
        println("GREEN")
    } else {
        println("NONE")
    }
    ...
}
```

You have moved the condition check to a new val called auraVisible and changed your if/else statement to check its value. This is functionally equivalent to what you had written before, but now you express the rules as a value assignment instead. The name of the value clearly signifies what the rule you defined expresses in "human-readable" terms: aura visibility. This is an especially useful technique for when your program's rules become complex, and it helps to communicate what your rules mean for future readers of your code.

Run your program again to make sure it functions as before. The output should be the same.

Conditional expressions

Now the if/else statement displays the player's health status correctly – and with some subtlety.

On the other hand, it would be somewhat unwieldy to make changes to it, because each branch repeats a similar **println** statement. What if you wanted to make a change to the overall formatting of the player status display? The program in its current state would require you to hunt through each branch in the if/else statement and change each **println** function to the new format.

You can solve this by changing the if/else statement you wrote to a *conditional expression* instead. A conditional expression is like a conditional statement, except that you assign the if/else to a value that you can use later. Update the health status display code to see what this looks like.

Listing 3.7 Using a conditional expression (Game.kt)

```kotlin
fun main(args: Array<String>) {
    ...
    if (healthPoints == 100) {
    val healthStatus = if (healthPoints == 100) {
        println(name + "is in excellent condition!")
        "is in excellent condition!"
    } else if (healthPoints >= 90) {
        println(name + " has a few scratches.")
        "has a few scratches."
    } else if (healthPoints >= 75) {
        if (isBlessed) {
            println(name + " has some minor wounds but is healing quite quickly!")
            "has some minor wounds but is healing quite quickly!"
        } else {
            println(name + " has some minor wounds.")
            "has some minor wounds."
        }
    } else if (healthPoints >= 15) {
        println(name + " looks pretty hurt.")
        "looks pretty hurt."
    } else {
        println(name + " is in awful condition!")
        "is in awful condition!"
    }

    // Player status
    println(name + " " + healthStatus)
}
```

(Incidentally, if you are tired of keeping your code nicely indented as you make changes, IntelliJ is here to help. Select Code → Auto-Indent Lines and enjoy the simple pleasure of clean indents.)

Through the if/else expression, the new variable healthStatus is assigned a string value of "is in excellent condition!", etc., depending on the value of healthPoints. That is the beauty of a conditional expression. Because you can now print the player's status using the new healthStatus variable, you are able to remove six virtually identical print statements.

When you need to assign a variable based on a condition, you can likely use a conditional expression. Keep in mind, however, that conditional expressions are often most intuitive when the value being assigned from each branch is of the same type (like the healthStatus strings).

Your aura code can also be streamlined using a conditional expression. Do so now.

Listing 3.8 Improving aura code with a conditional expression (Game.kt)

```kotlin
...
// Aura
val auraVisible = isBlessed && healthPoints > 50 || isImmortal
if (auraVisible) {
    println("GREEN")
} else {
    println("NONE")
}
val auraColor = if (auraVisible) "GREEN" else "NONE"
println(auraColor)
...
```

Run your code one more time to make sure everything works as expected. You should see the same output, but your code is now more elegant and reader-friendly.

You may have noticed that you dropped the curly braces in the aura color conditional expression. Let's discuss why.

Removing braces from if/else expressions

In cases where you have a single response for the matching condition, it is valid (at least, syntactically – more on that shortly) to omit the curly braces wrapping the expression. You can only omit the {}s when a branch contains only one expression – omitting them from a branch with more than one expression will affect how the code is evaluated.

Take a look at a version of `healthStatus` without braces:

```
val healthStatus = if (healthPoints == 100) "is in excellent condition!"
    else if (healthPoints >= 90) "has a few scratches."
    else if (healthPoints >= 75)
        if (isBlessed) "has some minor wounds but is healing quite quickly!"
        else "has some minor wounds."
    else if (healthPoints >= 15) "looks pretty hurt."
    else "is in awful condition!"
```

This version of the `healthStatus` conditional expression does the same thing as the version you have in your code. It even expresses the same logic in less code. But which version do you find easier to read and understand at a glance? If you chose the version with the braces – the version in your code – you have chosen the style that the Kotlin community prefers.

We recommend that you do not omit braces for conditional statements or expressions that span more than one line. For one thing, without braces it becomes increasingly difficult to understand where a branch starts and ends with every condition that is added. For another, omitting the braces for the conditional increases the risk of a new contributor mistakenly updating the wrong branch or misunderstanding what the implementation does. It is just not worth it to save a few keystrokes.

Also, while the code above expresses the same thing with or without braces, this is not the case for every example. If you have multiple expressions on a branch and you drop the braces around the conditional, only the first expression is executed in that branch. Take this example:

```
var arrowsInQuiver = 2
if (arrowsInQuiver >= 5) {
    println("Plenty of arrows")
    println("Cannot hold any more arrows")
}
```

If the hero has five or more arrows, they have plenty and cannot hold any more. The hero has only two arrows, so nothing prints to the console. However, without the braces the logic changes:

```
var arrowsInQuiver = 2
if (arrowsInQuiver >= 5)
    println("Plenty of arrows")
    println("Cannot hold any more arrows")
```

Without the braces, the second **println** statement is no longer part of the `if` branch. While "Plenty of arrows" only prints when `arrowsInQuiver` is at least 5, "Cannot hold any more arrows" always prints – no matter how many arrows the hero is carrying.

For a one-line expression, this overall principle should inform your choice: "Which way of writing the expression is most clear for new readers to understand?" Often, for one-line expressions, removing the curly braces is more readable. For example, removing the curly braces helps to clarify a simple one-line conditional expression like your aura code, or this example:

```
val healthSummary = if (healthPoints != 100) "Need healing!" else "Looking good."
```

By the way, if you are thinking, "OK, but I still don't love the if/else syntax, even with the curly braces. It is just *ugly*!" … fear not. You are going to rewrite the health status expression one last time in a less verbose – and more legible – syntax soon.

Ranges

All the conditions that you wrote in the if/else expression for healthStatus branch off the value of an integer, healthPoints. Some branches use the structural equality operator to check whether healthPoints is equal to a value, and others use multiple comparison operators to check whether healthPoints is within a range of two numbers. There is a better alternative for the second group: Kotlin provides *ranges* to represent a linear series of values.

The .. operator, as in in 1..5, signals a range. A range includes all values from the value on the left of the .. operator to the value on the right, so 1..5 includes 1, 2, 3, 4, and 5. Ranges can also be a sequence of characters.

You use the in keyword to check whether a value is within a range. Refactor your healthStatus conditional expression to use ranges rather than comparison operators.

Listing 3.9 Refactoring healthStatus with ranges (Game.kt)

```
fun main(args: Array<String>) {
    ...
    val healthStatus = if (healthPoints == 100) {
        "is in excellent condition!"
    } else if (healthPoints >= 90) {
    } else if (healthPoints in 90..99) {
        "has a few scratches."
    } else if (healthPoints >= 75) {
    } else if (healthPoints in 75..89) {
        if (isBlessed) {
            "has some minor wounds but is healing quite quickly!"
        } else {
            "has some minor wounds."
        }
    } else if (healthPoints >= 15) {
    } else if (healthPoints in 15..74) {
        "looks pretty hurt."
    } else {
        "is in awful condition!"
    }
}
```

Bonus: Using ranges in a conditional like this solves the else if ordering issue you saw earlier in this chapter. With ranges, your branches can be in any order and the code will evaluate the same.

In addition to the .. operator, several functions exist for creating ranges. The **downTo** function creates a range that descends rather than ascends, for example. And the **until** function creates a range that excludes the upper bound of the range specified. You will see some of these functions in a challenge near the end of this chapter, and you will learn more about ranges in Chapter 10.

when Expressions

The when expression is another control flow mechanism available in Kotlin. Like if/else, the when expression allows you to write conditions to check for and will execute corresponding code when the condition evaluates as true. when provides a more concise syntax and is an especially good fit for conditionals with three or more branches.

Suppose that in NyetHack, players can be members of several different fantasy races, like orc or gnome, and those fantasy races ally with each other in factions. This when expression takes in a fantasy race and returns the name of the faction to which it belongs:

```
val race = "gnome"
val faction = when (race) {
    "dwarf" -> "Keepers of the Mines"
    "gnome" -> "Keepers of the Mines"
    "orc" -> "Free People of the Rolling Hills"
    "human" -> "Free People of the Rolling Hills"
}
```

First, a val is declared, race. Next, a second val is declared: faction, whose value is determined with a when expression. The expression checks the value of race against each of the values on the lefthand side of the -> operator (called the *arrow*), and when it finds a match it assigns faction the value on the righthand side. (-> is used differently in other languages – and, in fact, it has other uses in Kotlin, as you will see later in this book.)

By default, a when expression behaves as though there were a == equality operator between the argument you provide in parentheses and the conditions you specify in the curly braces. (An *argument* is data that is given to a piece of code as input. You will learn more about them in Chapter 4.)

In the example when expression, race is provided as the argument, so the compiler compares the value of race, which is "gnome", against the first condition to check whether they are equal. They are not, so the result of the comparison is false, and the compiler moves along to the next condition. The next comparison is true, so the value in the corresponding branch, "Keepers of the Mines", is assigned to faction.

Now that you have seen how to leverage when expressions, you can refine how the healthStatus logic is implemented. You previously used an if/else expression, but, in this case, a when expression will make your code more readable and concise. A practical rule of thumb is that a when expression should replace an if/else expression if your code includes an else if branch.

Update the healthStatus logic to use when:

Listing 3.10 Refactoring healthStatus with when (Game.kt)

```
fun main(args: Array<String>) {
    ...
    val healthStatus = if (healthPoints == 100) {
        "is in excellent condition!"
    } else if (healthPoints in 90..99) {
        "has a few scratches."
    } else if (healthPoints in 75..89) {
        if (isBlessed) {
            "has some minor wounds but is healing quite quickly!"
        } else {
            "has some minor wounds."
        }
    } else if (healthPoints in 15..74) {
        "looks pretty hurt."
    } else {
        "is in awful condition!"
    }
    val healthStatus = when (healthPoints) {
        100 -> "is in excellent condition!"
        in 90..99 -> "has a few scratches."
        in 75..89 -> if (isBlessed) {
            "has some minor wounds but is healing quite quickly!"
        } else {
            "has some minor wounds."
        }
        in 15..74 -> "looks pretty hurt."
        else -> "is in awful condition!"
    }
}
```

A when expression works similarly to an if/else expression in that you define conditions and branches that are executed if a condition is true. when is different in that it *scopes* the lefthand side of the condition automatically to whatever you provide as an argument to when. We will talk more about scoping in more depth in Chapter 4 and Chapter 12. For a quick introduction, consider the in 90..99 branch condition.

You have seen how to use the in keyword to check whether a value is within a range, and that is what you are doing here – you are checking the value of healthPoints, even though you do not mention it by name. Because the range, on the left of the ->, is scoped to the healthPoints variable, the compiler evaluates when expressions as though healthPoints were included in each branch condition.

Often, when better expresses the logic behind code. In this case, achieving the same result with an if/else expression required three else if branches. Your when expression is much cleaner.

when expressions also support greater flexibility than if/else statements in how they match branches against the conditions you define. Most of the conditions on the lefthand side of the branches evaluate to either true or false, and others fall back to a default equality check, as is the case with the 100 branch condition. A when expression can express either one interchangeably, as demonstrated above.

By the way, were you wondering about the nested if/else in one branch of your when expression? This pattern is not very common, but Kotlin's when expression gives you all of the flexibility that you need to implement it.

Run NyetHack to confirm that your refactoring of healthStatus to use a when expression did not change any logic.

String Templates

You have seen that a string can be built up with the values of variables and even the results of conditional expressions. Kotlin features *string templates* to aid in this common need and, again, make your code more readable. Templates allow you to include the value of a variable inside a string's quotation marks. Update the player status display code to use string templates, as shown below:

Listing 3.11 Using a string template (Game.kt)

```kotlin
fun main(args: Array<String>) {
    ...
    // Player status
    println(name + " " + healthStatus)
    println("$name $healthStatus")
}
```

You added the values of name and healthStatus to the player status display string by prefixing each with $. This special symbol indicates to Kotlin that you would like to template a val or var within a string you define, and it is provided as a convenience. Note that these templated values appear inside the quotation marks that define the string.

Run the program. You should see the same output you have been seeing:

```
GREEN
Madrigal has some minor wounds but is healing quite quickly!
```

Kotlin also allows you to evaluate an expression within a string and *interpolate* the result – that is, to insert the result into the string. Any expression that you add within the curly braces after a dollar-sign character (${}) will be evaluated as a part of the string. Add a report of the player's blessedness and aura color to the player status display to see how this works. Be sure to remove the existing print statement for auraColor.

Listing 3.12 Formatting the isBlessed status with a string expression (Game.kt)

```kotlin
fun main(args: Array<String>) {
    ...
    // Aura
    val auraVisible = isBlessed && healthPoints > 50 || isImmortal
    val auraColor = if (auraVisible) "GREEN" else "NONE"
    print(auraColor)
    ...
    // Player status
    println("(Aura: $auraColor) " +
            "(Blessed: ${if (isBlessed) "YES" else "NO"})")
    println("$name $healthStatus")
}
```

This new line tells the compiler to print the literal string (Blessed: and the result of the expression if (isBlessed) "YES" else "NO". Note that this one-line conditional expression takes advantage of the option to skip braces for simplicity. It is the same as:

```
if (isBlessed) {
    "YES"
} else {
    "NO"
}
```

The extra syntax adds nothing here, so doing away with it makes sense. Either way, the string template will place the result of the conditional in the string. Before you run the program to check your addition, what do you think the result will be? Run the program to confirm.

Much of the work programs do is in response to some status or action. In this chapter, you saw how to add rules for when your code will execute by using if/else and when expressions. You also saw the assignable version of if/else, the if/else conditional expression. You saw how to represent series of numbers or characters using ranges. Finally, you saw how a string expression can be used to conveniently interpolate variables and values into a string.

Be sure to save NyetHack, because you will be using it again in the next chapter – where you will learn more about functions, a way to group and reuse expressions in your program.

Challenge: Trying Out Some Ranges

Ranges are a powerful tool in Kotlin, and with some practice you will find the syntax intuitive. For this simple challenge, open the Kotlin REPL (Tools → Kotlin → REPL) and explore some range syntax, including the **toList()**, **downTo**, and **until** functions. Enter the following ranges, one by one. Before pressing Command-Return (Ctrl-Return) to execute the line and see the result, think about what you expect the result to be.

Listing 3.13 Exploring ranges (REPL)

```
1 in 1..3
(1..3).toList()
1 in 3 downTo 1
1 in 1 until 3
3 in 1 until 3
2 in 1..3
2 !in 1..3
'x' in 'a'..'z'
```

Challenge: Enhancing the Aura

Before you start this challenge or the next one, close NyetHack and create a copy of it using your file explorer. You will be making changes to your program that you will not want to keep for future chapters. Name your copy NyetHack_ConditionalsChallenges or whatever you would like. You will want to do this before starting the challenges in future chapters as well.

Currently, if an aura is displayed, it is always green. For this challenge, have the color of the player's aura reflect their current karma.

Karma has a numeric value from 0 to 20. To determine the player's karma, use the following formula:

```
val karma = (Math.pow(Math.random(), (110 - healthPoints) / 100.0) * 20 ).toInt()
```

Have the displayed aura follow these rules:

Karma value	Aura color
0-5	red
6-10	orange
11-15	purple
16-20	green

Determine the karma value with the formula above and check the player's aura color using a conditional expression. Finally, modify the player status display to report the new color if the aura is visible.

Challenge: Configurable Status Format

Currently, the player's status display is created by two calls to **println**. There is no variable that holds the value of the full display string.

The code looks like this:

```
// Player status
println("(Aura: $auraColor) " +
        "(Blessed: ${if (isBlessed) "YES" else "NO" })")
println("$name $healthStatus")
```

And it produces output like this:

```
(Aura: GREEN) (Blessed: YES)
Madrigal has some minor wounds but is healing quite quickly!
```

For this more difficult challenge, make the status line configurable with a status format string. Use the character B for blessed, A for aura color, H for healthStatus, and HP for healthPoints. For example, a status format string of:

```
val statusFormatString = "(HP)(A) -> H"
```

should generate a player status display like:

```
(HP: 100)(Aura: Green) -> Madrigal is in excellent condition!
```

4

Functions

A *function* is a reusable portion of code that accomplishes a specific task. Functions are a very important part of programming. In fact, programs are fundamentally a series of functions combined to accomplish more complex tasks.

You have worked with some functions already, like the **println** function, which is provided by the Kotlin standard library for printing data to the console. You can also define your own functions in code that you write. Some functions take in data required to perform a specific task. Some functions also return data, generating output that can be used elsewhere after the function has performed its task.

To get your function feet wet, you will start by using functions to organize NyetHack's existing code. Then, you will define your own function to add an exciting new feature to NyetHack: a fireball spell.

Extracting Code to Functions

The logic you coded into NyetHack in Chapter 3 was sound, but it would be a better practice to organize it using functions. Your first task is to reorganize your project to encapsulate much of the logic you have already written in functions. This will set the stage for adding new features to NyetHack.

Does this mean you are going to delete all your code and type the same logic in a different way? Perish the thought. IntelliJ will help you group your logic into functions easily.

Begin by opening your NyetHack project. Make sure the file Game.kt is open in the editor.

Next, select the conditional code that you defined for generating the player's healthStatus message. Click and drag the cursor, beginning with the line that defines healthStatus and ending with the closing curly brace for the when expression, like so:

```
...
val healthStatus = when (healthPoints) {
    100 -> "is in excellent condition!"
    in 90..99 -> "has a few scratches."
    in 75..89 -> if (isBlessed) {
        "has some minor wounds, but is healing quite quickly!"
    } else {
        "has some minor wounds."
    }
    in 15..74 -> "looks pretty hurt."
    else -> "is in awful condition!"
}
...
```

Control-click (right-click) on the code you selected and choose Refactor → Extract → Function...
(Figure 4.1).

Figure 4.1 Extracting logic to a function

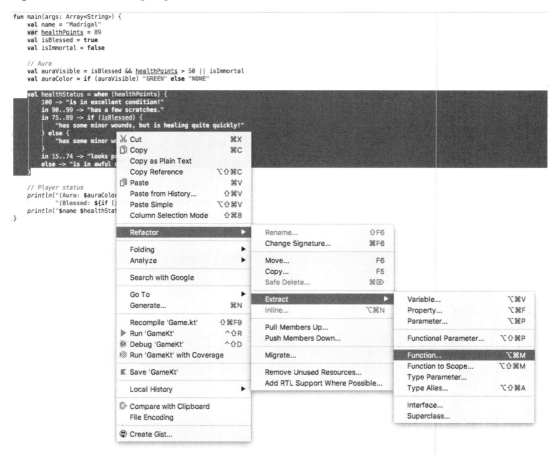

The Extract Function dialog will pop up, as in Figure 4.2:

Figure 4.2 The Extract Function dialog

We will come back to the elements of this dialog shortly. For now, enter "formatHealthStatus" for the name, as shown, and leave everything else as is. Then, click the OK button. IntelliJ will add a function definition to the bottom of Game.kt, like this:

```
private fun formatHealthStatus(healthPoints: Int, isBlessed: Boolean): String {
    val healthStatus = when (healthPoints) {
        100 -> "is in excellent condition!"
        in 90..99 -> "has a few scratches."
        in 75..89 -> if (isBlessed) {
            "has some minor wounds, but is healing quite quickly!"
        } else {
            "has some minor wounds."
        }
        in 15..74 -> "looks pretty hurt."
        else -> "is in awful condition!"
    }
    return healthStatus
}
```

Your formatHealthStatus function is surrounded by some new code. We will break this down piece by piece next.

Anatomy of a Function

Figure 4.3 shows the two primary parts of a function, the *header* and *body*, using `formatHealthStatus` as a model:

Figure 4.3 A function consists of a function header and a function body

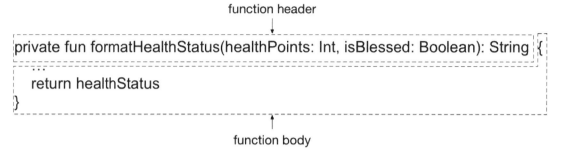

Function header

The first part of a function is the function header. The function header is made up of five parts: the visibility modifier, function declaration keyword, function name, function parameters, and return type (Figure 4.4).

Figure 4.4 Anatomy of a function header

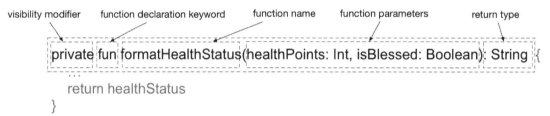

Let's look at each of those elements in some detail.

Visibility modifier

Not all functions should be *visible*, or accessible, to all other functions. Some might deal with data that should be kept private to a particular file, for example.

A function can optionally begin with a *visibility modifier* (Figure 4.5). The visibility modifier determines which other functions can "see" – and therefore use – the function.

Figure 4.5 Function visibility modifier

```
private fun formatHealthStatus(healthPoints: Int, isBlessed: Boolean): String {
    ...
    return healthStatus
}
```

By default, a function's visibility is public – meaning that all other functions (including functions defined in other files) can use the function. In other words, if you do not specify a modifier for the function, the function is considered public.

In this case, IntelliJ has determined that this function can have private visibility, since the `formatHealthStatus` function is used only within the current file, `Game.kt`. You will learn more about the available visibility modifiers and how to use them to control which functions can see the function you define in Chapter 12.

Function name declaration

After the visibility modifier (if there is one) comes the `fun` keyword, followed by a name for the function (Figure 4.6):

Figure 4.6 Function keyword and name declaration

```
private fun formatHealthStatus(healthPoints: Int, isBlessed: Boolean): String {
    ...
    return healthStatus
}
```

You specified `formatHealthStatus` for the function name in the Extract Function dialog, so IntelliJ added `fun formatHealthStatus` for the function's name declaration.

Notice that the name you chose for the function, `formatHealthStatus`, starts with a lowercase letter and uses "camel case" naming with no underscores. All of your function names should conform to this official standard naming convention.

Function parameters

Next come the function parameters (Figure 4.7):

Figure 4.7 Function parameters

```
private fun formatHealthStatus(healthPoints: Int, isBlessed: Boolean): String {
    ...
    return healthStatus
}
```

Function *parameters* specify the name and type of each input required for the function to perform its task. Functions can require zero to several or more parameters, depending on the task they are designed to perform.

For the **formatHealthStatus** function to determine the health status message it should display, the healthPoints and isBlessed variables are needed, because the when expression requires them to check its conditions. Therefore, **formatHealthStatus**'s function definition specifies that those two variables are required as parameters:

```
private fun formatHealthStatus(healthPoints: Int, isBlessed: Boolean): String {
    val healthStatus = when (healthPoints) {
        ...
        in 75..89 -> if (isBlessed) {
            ...
        } else {
            ...
        }
        ...
    }
    return healthStatus
}
```

For each parameter, the definition also specifies the type of data it requires. healthPoints must be an Int, and isBlessed must be a Boolean.

Note that function parameters are always read-only – they do not support reassignment within the function body. In other words, within the body of a function, a function parameter is a val, instead of a var.

Function return type

Many functions generate some type of output; that is their job, to send a value of some type back to where they are called. The final element of the function header is the *return type*, which defines the type of output that the function will return once it has completed its work.

The return type in **formatHealthStatus** specifies that the function sends back a String (Figure 4.8):

Figure 4.8 Function return type

```
private fun formatHealthStatus(healthPoints: Int, isBlessed: Boolean): String {
    ...
    return healthStatus
}
```

Function body

After the function header, the function body is defined within curly braces. The body is where the action the function performs takes place. It may also include a return statement that indicates what data to send back.

In this case, the extract function command moved the definition of the `healthStatus` val (the code you selected when you ran the command) into the body of the **formatHealthStatus** function.

After that is the new line `return healthStatus`. The `return` keyword indicates to the compiler that the function has finished its work and is ready to return its output data. Here, the output data is `healthStatus`, meaning that the function will return the value of the `healthStatus` variable – the string selected based on the logic in `healthStatus`'s definition.

Function scope

Notice that the declaration and assignment for the healthStatus variable occur within the function body and that its value is returned at the end of the function body:

```
private fun formatHealthStatus(healthPoints: Int, isBlessed: Boolean): String {
    val healthStatus = when (healthPoints) {
        ...
    }
    return healthStatus
}
```

The healthStatus variable is referred to as a *local variable* because it exists only in the **formatHealthStatus** function's body. Another way to put this is that the healthStatus variable exists only within the **formatHealthStatus** function's *scope*. You can think of scope as the lifespan for a variable.

Because it exists only within the function's scope, healthStatus will cease to exist once **formatHealthStatus** completes. The function returns healthStatus's value to its caller, but the variable that held the value is gone once the function completes.

The same is true of the function parameters: The variables healthPoints and isBlessed exist within the scope of the function body and cease to exist once the function completes.

In Chapter 2, you saw an example of a variable that was not local to a function or class – a *file-level variable*:

```
const val MAX_EXPERIENCE: Int = 5000

fun main(args: Array<String>) {
    ...
}
```

This file-level variable can be accessed from anywhere in the project (though a visibility modifier can be added to the declaration to change its visibility level). File-level variables remain initialized until program execution stops.

Because of the differences between local and file-level variables, the compiler enforces different requirements on when they must be assigned an initial value, or *initialized*.

File-level variables must always be assigned when they are defined, or the code will not compile. (You will see certain exceptions to this in Chapter 15.) This requirement protects you from unexpected – and unwanted – behavior, like a variable not having a value when you try to use it.

Since a local variable is more limited in where it can be used – within the scope of the function in which it is defined – the compiler is more lenient about when it must be initialized. A local variable only has to be initialized before it is used. This means that the following statement is valid:

```
fun main(args: Array<String>) {
    val name: String
    name = "Madrigal"
    var healthPoints: Int
    healthPoints = 89
    healthPoints += 3
    ...
}
```

So long as you have assigned a value before referencing the variable, the compiler permits the expression.

Calling a Function

IntelliJ not only generated the **formatHealthStatus** function, but it also added a line in place of the code it extracted:

```
fun main(args: Array<String>) {
    val name = "Madrigal"
    var healthPoints = 89
    var isBlessed = true
    ...
    val healthStatus = formatHealthStatus(healthPoints, isBlessed)
    ...
}
```

This line is a *function call*, which triggers the function to perform whatever actions are defined in its body. You call a function with its name, along with data to satisfy any parameters required by the function header.

Compare the function header for **formatHealthStatus** with its corresponding function call:

```
formatHealthStatus(healthPoints: Int, isBlessed: Boolean): String // Header
formatHealthStatus(healthPoints, isBlessed)                        // Call
```

The definition of **formatHealthStatus** shows that it requires two parameters, as discussed above. When you call **formatHealthStatus**, you include in parentheses the inputs to those parameters. The inputs are called *arguments*, and providing them to the function is called *passing in arguments*.

(A note about the terminology: While technically a parameter is what a function requires and an argument is what the caller passes in to fulfill the requirement, you will hear the two terms used interchangeably.)

Here, as the function definition specifies, you pass in the value of healthPoints (which, as required, is an Int) and the Boolean value of isBlessed.

Run NyetHack by clicking the run button, and shazam! You will see the same output you have seen before:

```
(Aura: GREEN) (Blessed: YES)
Madrigal has some minor wounds, but is healing quite quickly!
```

While the output has not changed, NyetHack's code is now more organized and maintainable.

Refactoring to Functions

Continue extracting the logic previously defined in the **main** function into separate functions by using the extract to function feature. Start by refactoring the logic for the aura color. Select the code from the line where aura visibility is defined to the end of the if/else condition that checks the Boolean to determine what value to print:

```
...
// Aura
val auraVisible = isBlessed && healthPoints > 50 || isImmortal
val auraColor = if (auraVisible) "GREEN" else "NONE"
...
```

Next, select the Extract Function command. You can Control-click (right-click) the selected code and choose Refactor → Extract → Function..., as you did before. You can also use the menus to select Refactor → Extract → Function... Or you can use the keyboard shortcut Command-Option-M (Ctrl-Alt-M). Whichever way you choose, the Extract Function dialog you saw in Figure 4.2 appears.

Give the new function the name **auraColor**.

(If you want to check the resulting code, hang tight: We will show you the full file after you extract a few more functions.)

Next, extract the logic that prints the player's status to a new function. Select the two calls to **println** in **main**:

```
...
// Player status
println("(Aura: $auraColor) " +
        "(Blessed: ${if (isBlessed) "YES" else "NO"})")
println("$name $healthStatus")
...
```

Extract them to a function called **printPlayerStatus**.

The Game.kt file now looks like this:

```kotlin
fun main(args: Array<String>) {
    val name = "Madrigal"
    var healthPoints = 89
    var isBlessed = true
    val isImmortal = false

    // Aura
    val auraColor = auraColor(isBlessed, healthPoints, isImmortal)

    val healthStatus = formatHealthStatus(healthPoints, isBlessed)

    // Player status
    printPlayerStatus(auraColor, isBlessed, name, healthStatus)

}

private fun formatHealthStatus(healthPoints: Int, isBlessed: Boolean): String {
    val healthStatus = when (healthPoints) {
        100 -> "is in excellent condition!"
        in 90..99 -> "has a few scratches."
        in 75..89 -> if (isBlessed) {
            "has some minor wounds, but is healing quite quickly!"
        } else {
            "has some minor wounds."
        }
        in 15..74 -> "looks pretty hurt."
        else -> "is in awful condition!"
    }
    return healthStatus
}

private fun printPlayerStatus(auraColor: String,
                              isBlessed: Boolean,
                              name: String,
                              healthStatus: String) {
    println("(Aura: $auraColor) " +
            "(Blessed: ${if (isBlessed) "YES" else "NO"})")
    println("$name $healthStatus")
}

private fun auraColor(isBlessed: Boolean,
                      healthPoints: Int,
                      isImmortal: Boolean): String {
    val auraVisible = isBlessed && healthPoints > 50 || isImmortal
    val auraColor = if (auraVisible) "GREEN" else "NONE"
    return auraColor
}
```

(We have broken the headers for **printPlayerStatus** and **auraColor** onto multiple lines for readability and to fit on the page.)

Run NyetHack. You should see Madrigal's familiar stats and aura color printed:

```
(Aura: GREEN) (Blessed: YES)
Madrigal has some minor wounds, but is healing quite quickly!
```

53

Writing Your Own Functions

Now that you have organized NyetHack's logic in functions, you can proceed as planned to implement the new fireball spell. At the bottom of Game.kt, define a function called **castFireball** that takes no parameters. Make its visibility private. **castFireball** should have no return statement, but it should print the results of casting the spell.

Listing 4.1 Adding a **castFireball** function (Game.kt)

```
...
private fun auraColor(isBlessed: Boolean,
                     healthPoints: Int,
                     isImmortal: Boolean): String {
    val auraVisible = isBlessed && healthPoints > 50 || isImmortal
    val auraColor = if (auraVisible) "GREEN" else "NONE"
    return auraColor
}

private fun castFireball() {
    println("A glass of Fireball springs into existence.")
}
```

Now, call **castFireball** at the bottom of the **main** function. (**castFireball** was defined without parameters, so you do not pass in any arguments to call it – hence the empty parentheses.)

Listing 4.2 Calling **castFireball** (Game.kt)

```
fun main(args: Array<String>) {
    ...
    // Player status
    printPlayerStatus(auraColor, isBlessed, name, healthStatus)

    castFireball()
}
...
```

Run NyetHack and admire your new output:

```
(Aura: GREEN) (Blessed: YES)
Madrigal has some minor wounds, but is healing quite quickly!
A glass of Fireball springs into existence.
```

Excellent – it appears the spell works as intended. Feel free to have a glass of Fireball as a celebratory measure. (On second thought, better wait until the end of this chapter.)

One fireball is fine, but two or more is a party. Your player needs to be able to cast more than one at a time.

Update the **castFireball** function to accept an Int parameter called numFireballs. In the call to **castFireball**, pass in 5 as the argument. Finally, display the number of fireballs in the message that is printed.

Listing 4.3 Adding a numFireballs parameter (Game.kt)

```kotlin
fun main(args: Array<String>) {
    ...
    // Player status
    printPlayerStatus(auraColor, isBlessed, name, healthStatus)

    castFireball()
    castFireball(5)
}
...
private fun castFireball() {
private fun castFireball(numFireballs: Int) {
    println("A glass of Fireball springs into existence.")
    println("A glass of Fireball springs into existence. (x$numFireballs)")
}
```

Run NyetHack again. You should see the following output:

```
(Aura: GREEN) (Blessed: YES)
Madrigal has some minor wounds, but is healing quite quickly!
A glass of Fireball springs into existence. (x5)
```

Functions with parameters provide a way for the caller to supply the function with input as an argument. You can use that input in your function's logic or simply print it out in a string template, as you did here with the value 5.

Default Arguments

Sometimes an argument for a function has a "usual" value. For example, with the **castFireball** function, five glasses of Fireball is excessive. Typically, only two glasses of Fireball should appear when the spell is cast. To make calling **castFireball** more efficient, you can use a *default argument* to specify this.

You saw in Chapter 2 that a var can be assigned an initial value and later reassigned. Similarly, you can assign a default value for a parameter that will be assigned if no argument is specified. Update the **castFireball** function with a default value for numFireballs:

Listing 4.4 Giving the numFireballs parameter a default value (Game.kt)

```
fun main(args: Array<String>) {
    ...
    // Player status
    printPlayerStatus(auraColor, isBlessed, name, healthStatus)

    castFireball(5)
}
...
private fun castFireball(numFireballs: Int) {
private fun castFireball(numFireballs: Int = 2) {
    println("A glass of Fireball springs into existence. (x$numFireballs)")
}
```

Now, by default, numFireballs's Int value will be 2 if no other argument is provided when calling **castFireball**. Update the **main** function, removing the Int argument in the call to **castFireball**:

Listing 4.5 Using **castFireball**'s default argument value (Game.kt)

```
fun main(args: Array<String>) {
    ...
    // Player status
    printPlayerStatus(auraColor, isBlessed, name, healthStatus)

    castFireball(5)
    castFireball()
}
...
```

Run NyetHack again. With no argument specified for **castFireball**, you will see the following output:

```
(Aura: GREEN) (Blessed: YES)
Madrigal has some minor wounds, but is healing quite quickly!
A glass of Fireball springs into existence. (x2)
```

Because you do not pass an argument for the numFireballs parameter, the default value you defined, 2, is used for the function argument.

Single-Expression Functions

Kotlin allows you to reduce the amount of code required to define a function like **castFireball** or **formatHealthStatus** that has only one expression – that is, one statement to be evaluated. For *single-expression functions*, you can omit the return type, curly braces, and return statement. Make those changes to your **castFireball** and **formatHealthStatus** functions, as shown below:

Listing 4.6 Using optional single-expression function syntax (Game.kt)

```
...
private fun formatHealthStatus(healthPoints: Int, isBlessed: Boolean): String {
    val healthStatus = when (healthPoints) {
private fun formatHealthStatus(healthPoints: Int, isBlessed: Boolean) =
        when (healthPoints) {
            100 -> "is in excellent condition!"
            in 90..99 -> "has a few scratches."
            in 75..89 -> if (isBlessed) {
                "has some minor wounds, but is healing quite quickly!"
            } else {
                "has some minor wounds."
            }
            in 15..74 -> "looks pretty hurt."
            else -> "is in awful condition!"
        }
    return healthStatus
}
...
private fun castFireball(numFireballs: Int = 2) {
private fun castFireball(numFireballs: Int = 2) =
    println("A glass of Fireball springs into existence. (x$numFireballs)")
}
```

Notice that instead of using the function body to specify the work the function will perform, with single-expression function syntax you use the assignment operator (=), followed by the expression.

This optional syntax allows you to tighten up the definition for functions with only one expression that is evaluated to perform their task. When you need the results of more than one expression, use the function definition syntax you have already seen.

From this point forward, we will favor using single-expression function syntax when possible to make the code more concise.

Unit Functions

Not all functions return a value. Some use side effects instead to do their work, like modifying the state of a variable or calling other functions that yield system output. Think about your player status and aura display code, or the **castFireball** function, for example. They define no return type and have no return statement. They use **println** to do their work.

```
private fun castFireball(numFireballs: Int = 2) =
    println("A glass of Fireball springs into existence. (x$numFireballs)")
```

In Kotlin, such functions are known as Unit functions, meaning their return type is Unit. Click on the **castFireball** function's name and press Control-Shift-P (Ctrl-P). IntelliJ will display its return type information (Figure 4.9).

Figure 4.9 **castFireball** is a Unit function

What kind of type is Unit? Kotlin uses the Unit return type to signify exactly this: a function that returns no value. If the return keyword is not used, it is implicit that the return type for that function is Unit.

Prior to Kotlin, many languages faced the problem of describing a function that does not return anything. Some languages opted for a keyword void, which said, "There is no return type; skip it, because it does not apply." This seems sound on the surface: If the function does not return anything, skip the type, since there is nothing being returned.

Unfortunately, this solution fails to account for an important feature found in modern languages: generics. Generics are a feature of modern compiled language that enable a great deal of flexibility. You will investigate generics in Kotlin, which allow you to specify functions that work with many types, in Chapter 17.

What do generics have to do with Unit and void? Languages that use the void keyword have no good way to deal with a generic function that returns nothing. void is not a type – in fact, it says, "Type information is not relevant; skip it." And there is no way to describe this "generically," so these languages miss out on being able to describe generic functions that return nothing.

Kotlin solves this problem by specifying Unit for the return type instead. Unit indicates a function that does not return anything, but at the same time it is compatible with generic functions that must have some type to work with. This is why Kotlin uses Unit: You get the best of both worlds.

Named Function Arguments

Take a look at how you call the **printPlayerStatus** function, passing arguments as parameters:

```
printPlayerStatus("NONE", true, "Madrigal", status)
```

Another way you could call the same function is:

```
printPlayerStatus(auraColor = "NONE",
                  isBlessed = true,
                  name = "Madrigal",
                  healthStatus = status)
```

This optional syntax uses *named function arguments* and is an alternative way to provide arguments to a function. In certain cases, it grants several advantages.

For example, using named arguments frees you to pass the arguments to the function in whatever order you would like. For example, you could also call **printPlayerStatus** like this:

```
printPlayerStatus(healthStatus = status,
                  auraColor = "NONE",
                  name = "Madrigal",
                  isBlessed = true)
```

When you do not use named function arguments, you must pass arguments in the order they are defined on the function header. With named function arguments, you can pass arguments independent of the function header's parameter order.

Another benefit of named function arguments is that they can bring clarity to your code. When a function requires a large number of arguments, it can become confusing to keep track of which argument provides the value for which function parameter. This is especially true if the names of the variables passed in do not match the names of the defined function parameters. Named function arguments are always named the same as the parameters they provide values for.

In this chapter, you saw how to define functions to encapsulate your code's logic. Your code has become much cleaner and better organized. You also learned a number of the conveniences built into Kotlin's function syntax to enable you to write less code that is just as descriptive: single-expression function syntax, named function arguments, and default arguments. In the next chapter, you will learn about a different kind of function available in Kotlin – anonymous functions.

Do not forget to save NyetHack and create a copy before working through the challenges below.

For the More Curious: The Nothing Type

In this chapter you learned about the Unit type and that a function of the Unit type returns no value.

Another type that is related to Unit is the Nothing type. Like Unit, Nothing indicates that a function returns no value – but there the similarity ends. Nothing lets the compiler know that a function is guaranteed to never successfully complete; the function will either throw an exception or for some other reason never return to where it was called.

What is the use of the Nothing type? One example of Nothing's use is the **TODO** function, included with the Kotlin standard library.

Take a look at **TODO** by pressing the Shift key twice to open the Search Everywhere dialog and entering its name.

```
/**
 * Always throws [NotImplementedError] stating that operation is not implemented.
 */
public inline fun TODO(): Nothing = throw NotImplementedError()
```

TODO throws an exception – in other words, it is guaranteed to never complete successfully – and returns the Nothing type.

When would you use **TODO**? The answer is in the name: It tells you what you still have "to do." Consider the following function that has yet to be implemented, and instead calls **TODO**:

```
fun shouldReturnAString(): String {
    TODO("implement the string building functionality here to return a string")
}
```

The developer knows that the **shouldReturnAString** function should return a String, but they have not yet completed the other features needed to implement it. Notice that the return type for **shouldReturnAString** is a String, but the function never actually returns anything at all. Because of **TODO**'s return value, that is perfectly fine.

TODO's Nothing return type indicates to the compiler that the function is guaranteed to cause an error, so checking the return type in the function body is not required past **TODO** because **shouldReturnAString** will never return. The compiler is happy, and the developer is able to continue feature development without completing the implementation for **shouldReturnAString** until all the details are ready.

Another feature of Nothing that is useful in development is that if you add code below the **TODO** function, the compiler will show a warning indicating that the code is unreachable (Figure 4.10):

Figure 4.10 Unreachable code

```
fun shouldReturnAString(): String {
    TODO()
    println("unreachable")
}
```

Unreachable code

Because of the Nothing type, the compiler can make this assertion: It is aware that **TODO** will not successfully complete; therefore, all code after **TODO** is unreachable.

For the More Curious: File-Level Functions in Java

All of the functions that you have written so far have been defined at the file level in Game.kt. If you are a Java developer, then this may seem surprising to you. In Java, functions and variables can only be defined within classes, a rule that Kotlin does not adhere to.

How is this possible if Kotlin code compiles to Java bytecode to run on the JVM? Does Kotlin not have to play by the same rules? A look at the decompiled Java bytecode for Game.kt should prove illuminating:

```java
public final class GameKt {
    public static final void main(...) {
        ...
    }

    private static final String formatHealthStatus(...) {
        ...
    }

    private static final void printPlayerStatus(...) {
        ...
    }

    private static final String auraColor(...) {
        ...
    }

    private static final void castFireball(...) {
        ...
    }

    // $FF: synthetic method
    // $FF: bridge method
    static void castFireball$default(...) {
        ...
    }
}
```

File-level functions are represented in Java as static methods on a class with a name based on the file in which they are declared in Kotlin. (*Method* is Java for "function.") In this case, functions and variables defined in Game.kt are defined in Java in a class called **GameKt**.

You will see how to declare functions in classes in Chapter 12, but being able to declare functions and variables outside of them gives you more flexibility to define a function that is not tied to a particular class definition. (And if you are wondering what the **castFireball$default** method in **GameKt** is all about, this is how default arguments are implemented. You will see this in more detail in Chapter 20.)

For the More Curious: Function Overloading

The **castFireball** function you defined, with its default argument for the numFireballs parameter, can be called two ways:

```
castFireball()
castFireball(numFireballs)
```

When a function has multiple implementations, like **castFireball**, it is said to be *overloaded*. Overloading is not always the result of a default argument. You can define multiple implementations with the same function name. To see what this looks like, open the Kotlin REPL (Tools → Kotlin → Kotlin REPL) and enter these function definitions:

Listing 4.7 Defining an overloaded function (REPL)

```
fun performCombat() {
    println("You see nothing to fight!")
}

fun performCombat(enemyName: String) {
    println("You begin fighting $enemyName.")
}

fun performCombat(enemyName: String, isBlessed: Boolean) {
    if (isBlessed) {
        println("You begin fighting $enemyName. You are blessed with 2X damage!")
    } else {
        println("You begin fighting $enemyName.")
    }
}
```

You have defined three implementations of **performCombat**. All are Unit functions, with no return value. One takes no arguments. One takes a single argument, the name of an enemy. And the last takes two arguments: the enemy's name and a Boolean indicating whether the player is blessed. Each function generates a different message (or messages) through calls to **println**.

When you call **performCombat**, how will the REPL know which one you want? It will evaluate the arguments you pass in and find the implementation that matches the number and type of the arguments. In the REPL, call each of the implementations of **performCombat**, as shown:

Listing 4.8 Calling the overloaded functions (REPL)

```
performCombat()
performCombat("Ulrich")
performCombat("Hildr", true)
```

Your output will read:

```
You see nothing to fight!
You begin fighting Ulrich.
You begin fighting Hildr. You are blessed with 2X damage!
```

Notice that the implementation of the overloaded function was selected based on how many arguments you provided.

For the More Curious: Function Names in Backticks

Kotlin includes a feature that might, at first glance, seem slightly peculiar: the ability to define or invoke a function named using spaces and other unusual characters, so long as they are surrounded using the backtick symbol, `` ` ``. For example, you can define a function like this:

```
fun `**~prolly not a good idea!~**`() {
    ...
}
```

And you could then invoke `` `**~prolly not a good idea!~**` `` like this:

```
`**~prolly not a good idea!~**`()
```

Why is this feature included? You should never name a function anything like `` `**~prolly not a good idea!~**` ``. (Nor with an emoji. Please backtick responsibly.) There are several valid reasons the function name backticks exist.

The first is to support Java interoperability. Kotlin includes great support for invoking methods from existing Java code within a Kotlin file. (You will tour a number of Java interoperability features in Chapter 20.) Because Kotlin and Java have different *reserved keywords*, words that are forbidden for use as function names, the function name backticks allow you to dodge any potential conflict when interoperability is important.

For example, imagine a Java method name from a legacy Java project, **is**:

```
public static void is() {
    ...
}
```

In Kotlin, **is** is a reserved keyword (the Kotlin standard library includes an **is** operator; it allows you to check the type of an instance, as you will see in Chapter 14). In Java, however, **is** is a valid method name, since no **is** keyword exists in the language. Because of the backtick feature, you are able to invoke a Java **is** method from Kotlin, like so:

```
fun doStuff() {
    `is`() // Invokes the Java `is` method from Kotlin
}
```

In this case the, backtick feature supports interoperating with a Java method that would otherwise be inaccessible due to its name.

The second reason for the feature is to support more expressive names of functions that are used in a testing file. For example, a function name like this:

```
fun `users should be signed out when they click logout`() {
    // Do test
}
```

Is more expressive and readable than this:

```
fun usersShouldBeSignedOutWhenTheyClickLogout() {
    // Do test
}
```

Using backticks to provide an expressive name for a test function is the exception to the "lowercase first letter, followed by camel case" naming standard for functions.

Challenge: Single-Expression Functions

Earlier, you saw the single-expression function syntax as a way to make functions that execute one statement more concise. Can you convert **auraColor** to use the single-expression function syntax?

Challenge: Fireball Inebriation Level

Casting fireballs does not just print a message to the console. While NyetHack fireballs are more delicious than strong, they do have an intoxicating effect on the caster. Make the **castFireball** function return a resulting inebriation value that depends on the number of fireballs cast. The inebriation value should be between 1 and 50, with 50 being the maximum level of intoxication in the game.

Challenge: Inebriation Status

Building on your last challenge, display the player's inebriation status based on the inebriation value returned from **castFireball**. Have the displayed inebriation status follow these rules:

Inebriation level	Inebriation status
1-10	tipsy
11-20	sloshed
21-30	soused
31-40	stewed
41-50	..t0aSt3d

BIG NERD RANCH
CODING BOOTCAMPS

Looking for additional support? Look into one of our coding bootcamps. Students learn from authors and full-time consultants who work on projects every day. Don't take our word for it; hear from our alumni:

LIFE CHANGING. The Big Nerd Ranch changed my life. I was working as a lawyer and writing software on the side. I wanted to transition to writing software full-time, but I didn't have the confidence to make the switch. I heard about the Big Nerd Ranch from a friend and I decided to attend a seven-day bootcamp in Atlanta. I was very nervous because I wasn't a professional software developer and I didn't have a computer science degree. The first morning, my instructor made me feel at ease. As we worked through the materials and the examples, I noticed that I knew as much or more than my peers. I took advantage of the lunch and dinner time to speak with my instructors and peers and my confidence continued to grow. I got home and, with my Big Nerd Ranch certification in hand, I applied to several software development jobs. After several offers, I closed up my law firm and started my new career as a software developer. I still work as a software developer. I even write software for some of my lawyer friends. All thanks to The Big Nerd Ranch.

—Larry Staton, Jr., Alumnus

We offer classes in Android, Kotlin, Front End, iOS, Swift, design, and more. Take $100 off your bootcamp tuition by using code BNRGUIDE100 when you register.

Alumni gain access to an exclusive developer community to network and nurture their career growth.

www.bignerdranch.com

5

Anonymous Functions and the Function Type

In the last chapter, you saw how to define functions in Kotlin by naming them and how to call them by name. In this chapter, you will see another way to define functions: anonymously. You will be taking a short break from NyetHack to work with anonymous functions in your Sandbox project, but do not worry – there is more NyetHack action in the next chapter.

Functions like the ones you saw and wrote in Chapter 4 are called *named functions*. Functions defined without a name, called *anonymous functions*, are similar, with two major differences: Anonymous functions have no name as part of their definition, and they interact with the rest of your code a little differently in that they are commonly passed to or returned from other functions. These interactions are made possible by the *function type* and *function arguments*, which you will also learn about in this chapter.

Anonymous Functions

Anonymous functions are an essential part of Kotlin. One way they are used is to allow you to easily customize how built-in functions from the Kotlin standard library work to meet your particular needs. An anonymous function lets you describe additional rules for a standard library function so that you can customize its behavior. Let's look at an example.

One of the many functions in the standard library is **count**. When called on a string, **count** returns the total number of letters in the string. The following code counts the letters in the string "Mississippi":

```
val numLetters = "Mississippi".count()
print(numLetters)
// Prints 11
```

(Here you have used *dot syntax* to invoke the **count** function. This syntax is used any time you invoke a function that is included as part of a type's definition.)

But what if you wanted to count only a specific character in "Mississippi", say the letter "s"?

For this kind of problem, the Kotlin standard library allows you to provide rules to the **count** function to determine whether a letter should be counted. You describe the rules for the function by providing an anonymous function as an argument. It looks like this:

```
val numLetters = "Mississippi".count({ letter ->
    letter == 's'
})
print(numLetters)
// Prints 4
```

Here, the Kotlin String **count** function uses an anonymous function to decide how it should count the characters in the string. Proceeding character by character, if the anonymous function evaluates as true, the count is incremented. Once it has checked every character, **count** returns the final number.

Anonymous functions let the standard library do what it does best – provide a foundation of functions and types for building great Kotlin applications – without including features that would be too specific to be considered "standard." They also have other uses, which you will see later in this chapter.

To understand how **count** works, take a closer look at Kotlin's anonymous function syntax by defining your own. You are going to write a small simulation called SimVillage, a game that allows players to serve as mayor of a virtual village.

Your first anonymous function in SimVillage will display a greeting to the player, acknowledging them as mayor of the village. (Why do this with an anonymous function? As you will see later in the chapter, this will allow you to easily pass the anonymous function to other functions.)

Open your Sandbox project, create a new file called SimVillage.kt, and give it a **main** function, as you have done before (type "main" and press the Tab key).

Define an anonymous function within the **main** function, call it, and print the result:

Listing 5.1 Defining an anonymous greeting function (SimVillage.kt)

```
fun main(args: Array<String>) {
    println({
        val currentYear = 2018
        "Welcome to SimVillage, Mayor! (copyright $currentYear)"
    }())
}
```

Just as you write a string by putting characters between opening and closing quotes, you write a function by putting an expression or statements between opening and closing curly braces. Here, you begin with a call to **println**. Inside the parentheses that enclose **println**'s argument, you define an anonymous function inside a set of curly braces. The anonymous function defines a variable and returns a greeting message string:

```
{
    val currentYear = 2018
    "Welcome to SimVillage, Mayor! (copyright $currentYear)"
}
```

Outside the anonymous function's closing brace, you call the function with a pair of empty parentheses. If you were to leave the parentheses off the end of the anonymous function, the greeting message string would not print. Just like a named function, an anonymous function does its work only when it has been called, using parentheses along with any arguments the function expects (zero, in this case):

```
{
    val currentYear = 2018
    "Welcome to SimVillage, Mayor! (copyright $currentYear)"
}()
```

Run SimVillage.kt's **main** function. You will see the following output:

```
Welcome to SimVillage, Mayor! (copyright 2018)
```

The function type

In Chapter 2, you learned about data types like Int and String. Anonymous functions also have a type, called the *function type*. Variables of the function type can hold an anonymous function as their value, and the function can then be passed around your code like any other variable.

(Do not confuse the function type with a type called Function. You define the specifics of a function using a function type declaration, which varies depending on the details of a particular function's input, output, and parameters, as you will soon see.)

Update SimVillage.kt to define a variable that holds a function, and assign it the anonymous function that displays the greeting. There is some unfamiliar syntax here, which we will explain after you enter it.

Listing 5.2 Assigning the anonymous function to a variable (SimVillage.kt)

```
fun main(args: Array<String>) {
    println({
    val greetingFunction: () -> String = {
        val currentYear = 2018
        "Welcome to SimVillage, Mayor! (copyright $currentYear)"
    }
    }()

    println(greetingFunction())
}
```

You can declare a variable with its name followed by a colon and its type. That is exactly what you have done here with greetingFunction: () -> String. And just as : Int tells the compiler what kind of data a variable can hold (an integer), the function type : () -> String tells the compiler what kind of function a variable can hold.

A function type definition consists of two parts: the function's parameters, in parentheses, followed by its return type, delimited by the arrow (->), as shown in Figure 5.1.

Figure 5.1 Function type syntax

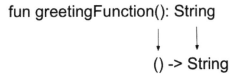

The type declaration you specified for the variable greetingFunction, () -> String, indicates to the compiler that greetingFunction can be assigned any function that accepts no arguments (indicated by the empty parentheses) and returns a String. As with any other type declaration for a variable, the compiler will ensure that the function assigned to the variable or passed as an argument is of the correct type.

Run **main**. The output is the same:

```
Welcome to SimVillage, Mayor! (copyright 2018)
```

69

Implicit returns

You may have noticed that there is no return keyword within the anonymous function you defined:

```
val greetingFunction: () -> String = {
    val currentYear = 2018
    "Welcome to SimVillage, Mayor! (copyright $currentYear)"
}
```

However, the function type you specified indicates that the function must return a String, and the compiler did not complain. And, based on the output, a string is indeed returned: the greeting to the mayor. Why, then, is there no return keyword?

Unlike a named function, an anonymous function does not require – or even allow, except in rare cases – the return keyword to output data. Anonymous functions *implicitly*, or automatically, return the last line of their function definition, allowing you to omit the return keyword.

This feature of anonymous functions is both a convenience and a necessity of the anonymous function syntax. The return keyword is prohibited in an anonymous function because it could be ambiguous to the compiler which function the return is from: the function the anonymous function was invoked within, or the anonymous function itself.

Function arguments

Like a named function, an anonymous function can accept zero, one, or multiple arguments of any type. The parameters an anonymous function accepts are indicated by type in the function type definition and then named in the anonymous function's definition.

Update the greetingFunction variable declaration to accept the player's name as an argument:

Listing 5.3 Adding a playerName parameter to the anonymous function (SimVillage.kt)

```
fun main(args: Array<String>) {
    val greetingFunction: () -> String = {
    val greetingFunction: (String) -> String = { playerName ->
        val currentYear = 2018
        "Welcome to SimVillage, Mayor! (copyright $currentYear)"
        "Welcome to SimVillage, $playerName! (copyright $currentYear)"
    }
    println(greetingFunction())
    println(greetingFunction("Guyal"))
}
```

Here you specify that the anonymous function accepts a String. You name the string parameter within the function, right after the opening brace, and follow the name with an arrow:

```
val greetingFunction: (String) -> String = { playerName ->
```

Run SimVillage.kt again. You will see that the argument you passed to the anonymous function was added to the string:

```
Welcome to SimVillage, Guyal! (copyright 2018)
```

Remember the **count** function? It takes in an anonymous function with an argument called predicate of type (Char) -> Boolean. The predicate function type takes a Char as an argument and returns a Boolean. You will see anonymous functions used to implement much of the Kotlin standard library, so it is best to familiarize yourself with their syntax.

The it keyword

When defining anonymous functions that accept exactly one argument, the it keyword is available as a convenient alternative to specifying the parameter name. Both it and a named parameter are valid when you have an anonymous function that has only one parameter.

Delete the parameter name and arrow from the beginning of the anonymous function and use the it keyword instead:

Listing 5.4 Using the it keyword (SimVillage.kt)

```
fun main(args: Array<String>) {
    val greetingFunction: (String) -> String = { playerName ->
    val greetingFunction: (String) -> String = {
        val currentYear = 2018
        "Welcome to SimVillage, $playerName! (copyright $currentYear)"
        "Welcome to SimVillage, $it! (copyright $currentYear)"
    }
    println(greetingFunction("Guyal"))
}
```

Run SimVillage.kt to confirm that it works as before.

it is convenient in that it requires no variable naming, but notice that it is not very descriptive about the data it represents. We suggest that when you are working with more complex anonymous function definitions, or with nested anonymous functions (anonymous functions within anonymous functions), you stick with naming the parameter to preserve future readers' (and your own) sanity. On the other hand, it is great for shorter expressions, like the **count** function you saw earlier, where the logic is clear even without an argument name:

```
"Mississippi".count({ it == 's' })
```

Accepting multiple arguments

While the it syntax is available for an anonymous function that accepts one argument, it is not allowed when there is more than one argument. However, anonymous functions can certainly accept multiple named arguments.

It is time for SimVillage to do something besides greet its mayor. The mayor needs to know whether the village is growing, for example. Change your anonymous function to accept a numBuildings argument, representing the number of houses or shops constructed, in addition to the player's name:

Listing 5.5 Accepting a second argument (SimVillage.kt)

```
fun main(args: Array<String>) {
    val greetingFunction: (String) -> String = {
    val greetingFunction: (String, Int) -> String = { playerName, numBuildings ->
        val currentYear = 2018
        println("Adding $numBuildings houses")
        "Welcome to SimVillage, $it! (copyright $currentYear)"
        "Welcome to SimVillage, $playerName! (copyright $currentYear)"
    }
    println(greetingFunction("Guyal"))
    println(greetingFunction("Guyal", 2))
}
```

The expression now declares two parameters, playerName and numBuildings, and accepts two arguments when called. Because there is more than one parameter defined for the expression, the it keyword is no longer available.

Run SimVillage again. This time, you will see the number of buildings constructed as well as the greeting:

```
Adding 2 houses
Welcome to SimVillage, Guyal! (copyright 2018)
```

Type Inference Support

Kotlin's type inference rules behave exactly the same with function types as they do with the types you met earlier in this book: If a variable is given an anonymous function as its value when it is declared, no explicit type definition is needed.

This means that the anonymous function you wrote earlier that accepted no arguments:

```
val greetingFunction: () -> String = {
    val currentYear = 2018
    "Welcome to SimVillage, Mayor! (copyright $currentYear)"
}
```

Could also have been written with no specified type, like this:

```
val greetingFunction = {
    val currentYear = 2018
    "Welcome to SimVillage, Mayor! (copyright $currentYear)"
}
```

Type inference is also an option when the anonymous function accepts one or more arguments, but to help the compiler infer the type of the variable, you do need to provide both the name and the type of each parameter in the anonymous function definition.

Update the greetingFunction variable to use type inference by including types for each parameter in the anonymous function.

Listing 5.6 Using type inference for greetingFunction (SimVillage.kt)

```
fun main() {
    val greetingFunction: (String, Int) -> String = { playerName, numBuildings ->
    val greetingFunction = { playerName: String, numBuildings: Int ->
        val currentYear = 2018
        println("Adding $numBuildings houses")
        "Welcome to SimVillage, $playerName! (copyright $currentYear)"
    }
    println(greetingFunction("Guyal", 2))
}
```

Run SimVillage.kt and confirm that it works just as before.

When combined with an ambiguous implicit return type, type inference may make an anonymous function difficult to read. But when your anonymous function is simple and clear, type inference is an asset for making your code more concise.

Defining a Function That Accepts a Function

You have seen that anonymous functions can customize the work of standard library functions. You can also use them in functions you write yourself.

By the way, from here on out, we will refer to anonymous functions as *lambdas* and their definitions as *lambda expressions*. We will also refer to what an anonymous function returns as a *lambda result*. This is common terminology you will encounter in the wild as well. (A bit of trivia: Why "lambda"? The term, also represented with the Greek character λ, is short for "lambda calculus" – a system of logic for expressing computations, devised in the 1930s by mathematician Alonzo Church. You use lambda calculus notation when you define an anonymous function.)

A function parameter can accept arguments of any type, including arguments that are functions. A function type parameter is defined like a parameter of any other type: You list it in the parentheses after the function name and include the type. To see how this works, you are going to add a new function to SimVillage that randomly decides how many buildings have been constructed, then invokes the lambda to display the greeting.

Add a function called **runSimulation** that accepts the `playerName` and `greetingFunction` variables. You will use a couple of standard library functions that we have provided for you to generate a random number. Finally, call the new **runSimulation** function.

Listing 5.7 Adding the **runSimulation** function (`SimVillage.kt`)

```
fun main(args: Array<String>) {
    val greetingFunction = { playerName: String, numBuildings: Int ->
        val currentYear = 2018
        println("Adding $numBuildings houses")
        "Welcome to SimVillage, $playerName! (copyright $currentYear)"
    }
    println(greetingFunction("Guyal", 2))
    runSimulation("Guyal", greetingFunction)
}

fun runSimulation(playerName: String, greetingFunction: (String, Int) -> String) {
    val numBuildings = (1..3).shuffled().last()   // Randomly selects 1, 2, or 3
    println(greetingFunction(playerName, numBuildings))
}
```

The two parameters to **runSimulation** are the player's name and `greetingFunction`, a function that accepts a `String` and `Int` and returns a `String`. **runSimulation** generates a random number and calls the function passed as `greetingFunction` with the generated number and the `playerName` (which **runSimulation** received as an argument).

Run SimVillage several times. You will see that the number of buildings constructed varies now, because **runSimulation** provides a random number to the greeting function.

Shorthand syntax

When a function accepts a function type for its last parameter, you can also omit the parentheses around the lambda argument. So this example that we showed you earlier:

```
"Mississippi".count({ it == 's' })
```

Can also be written this way, without the parentheses:

```
"Mississippi".count { it == 's' }
```

This syntax is cleaner to read and gets to the essential ingredients of your function call just a bit more quickly.

This simplification can be made only when a lambda is passed as the last argument into a function. When writing functions, declare function type parameters as the final parameter so that callers of your function can take advantage of this pattern.

In SimVillage, you can take advantage of this shorthand with the **runSimulation** function you defined. **runSimulation** expects two arguments: a string and a function. Provide the arguments that are not functions to **runSimulation** inside of parentheses. Then, list the last argument, the function, outside of the parentheses:

Listing 5.8 Passing a lambda with the shorthand syntax (SimVillage.kt)

```
fun main(args: Array<String>) {
    val greetingFunction = { playerName: String, numBuildings: Int ->
    runSimulation("Guyal") { playerName, numBuildings ->
        val currentYear = 2018
        println("Adding $numBuildings houses")
        "Welcome to SimVillage, $playerName! (copyright $currentYear)"
    }
}

fun runSimulation(playerName: String, greetingFunction: (String, Int) -> String) {
    val numBuildings = (1..3).shuffled().last()    // Randomly selects 1, 2, or 3
    println(greetingFunction(playerName, numBuildings))
}
```

Nothing changed in the implementation of **runSimulation**; all changes were on how it is called. Notice that because you are no longer assigning the lambda to a variable and are instead directly passing it to **runSimulation**, listing the types for the parameters in the lambda is no longer required.

This shorthand syntax empowers you to write cleaner code, and we will leverage it where applicable in this book.

Function Inlining

Lambdas are useful because they enable a high degree of flexibility in how your programs can be written. However, that flexibility comes at a cost.

When you define a lambda, it is represented as an object instance on the JVM. The JVM also performs memory allocations for all variables accessible to the lambda, and this behavior comes with associated memory costs. As a result, lambdas introduce memory overhead that can in turn cause a performance impact – and such performance impacts are to be avoided.

Fortunately, there is an optimization you can enable that removes the overhead when using lambdas as arguments to other functions, called *inlining*. Inlining removes the need for the JVM to use an object instance and to perform variable memory allocations for the lambda.

To inline a lambda, you mark the function that accepts the lambda using the inline keyword. Add the inline keyword to the **runSimulation** function:

Listing 5.9 Using the inline keyword (SimVillage.kt)

```
...

inline fun runSimulation(playerName: String,
                         greetingFunction: (String, Int) -> String) {
    val numBuildings = (1..3).shuffled().last()   // Randomly selects 1, 2, or 3
    println(greetingFunction(playerName, numBuildings))
}
```

Now that you have added the inline keyword, instead of invoking **runSimulation** with a lambda object instance, the compiler "copy and pastes" the function body where the call is made. Take a look at the decompiled Kotlin bytecode for SimVillage.kt's **main** function, where the (now inlined) **runSimulation** function is called:

```
    ...
    public static final void main(@NotNull String[] args) {
    Intrinsics.checkParameterIsNotNull(args, "args");
    String playerName$iv = "Guyal";
    byte var2 = 1;
    int numBuildings$iv =
        ((Number)CollectionsKt.last(CollectionsKt.shuffled((Iterable)
        (new IntRange(var2, 3)))))).intValue();
    int currentYear = 2018;
    String var7 = "Adding " + numBuildings$iv + " houses";
    System.out.println(var7);
    String var10 = "Welcome to SimVillage, " + playerName$iv + "!
        (copyright " + currentYear + ')';
    System.out.println(var10);
    }
    ...
```

Notice that instead of invoking the **runSimulation** function, the work that **runSimulation** performed with the lambda is now directly inlined into the **main** function, avoiding the need to pass any lambda at all (and so avoiding the need for a new object instance).

It is generally a good idea to mark functions that accept lambdas as arguments with the `inline` keyword. However, in a few limited instances, it is not possible. One situation where inlining is not permitted, for example, is a recursive function that accepts a lambda, since the result of inlining such a function would be an infinite loop of copying and pasting function bodies. The compiler will warn you if you try to inline a function that violates the rules.

Function References

So far, you have defined lambdas to provide a function as an argument to another function. There is another way to do so: by passing a *function reference*. A function reference converts a named function (a function defined using the `fun` keyword) to a value that can be passed as an argument. You can use a function reference anywhere you use a lambda expression.

To see a function reference, start by defining a new function, called **printConstructionCost**:

Listing 5.10 Defining the **printConstructionCost** function (SimVillage.kt)

...

```
inline fun runSimulation(playerName: String,
                    greetingFunction: (String, Int) -> String) {
    val numBuildings = (1..3).shuffled().last()    // Randomly selects 1, 2, or 3
    println(greetingFunction(playerName, numBuildings))
}

fun printConstructionCost(numBuildings: Int) {
    val cost = 500
    println("construction cost: ${cost * numBuildings}")
}
```

Now, add a function parameter to **runSimulation** called **costPrinter**, and use the value within **runSimulation** to print the construction cost for the buildings.

Listing 5.11 Adding a **costPrinter** parameter (SimVillage.kt)

...

```
inline fun runSimulation(playerName: String,
                    greetingFunction: (String, Int) -> String) {
inline fun runSimulation(playerName: String,
                    costPrinter: (Int) -> Unit,
                    greetingFunction: (String, Int) -> String) {
    val numBuildings = (1..3).shuffled().last()    // Randomly selects 1, 2, or 3
    costPrinter(numBuildings)
    println(greetingFunction(playerName, numBuildings))
}

fun printConstructionCost(numBuildings: Int) {
    val cost = 500
    println("construction cost: ${cost * numBuildings}")
}
```

To obtain a function reference, you use the :: operator with the function name you would like a reference for. Obtain a function reference for the **printConstructionCost** function and pass the reference as the argument for the new costPrinter parameter you defined on **runSimulation**:

Listing 5.12 Passing a function reference (SimVillage.kt)

```
fun main(args: Array<String>) {
    runSimulation("Guyal") { playerName, numBuildings ->
    runSimulation("Guyal", ::printConstructionCost) { playerName, numBuildings ->
        val currentYear = 2018
        println("Adding $numBuildings houses")
        "Welcome to SimVillage, $playerName! (copyright $currentYear)"
    }
}
...
```

Run SimVillage.kt. You will see that in addition to the number of buildings constructed, the total cost of the construction prints as well.

Function references are useful in a number of situations. If you have a named function that fits the needs of a parameter that requires a function argument, a function reference allows you to use it instead of defining a lambda. Or you may want to use a Kotlin standard library function as an argument to a function. You will see more examples of both of these uses of function references in Chapter 9.

Function Type as Return Type

Like any other type, the function type is also a valid return type, meaning you can define a function that returns a function.

In SimVillage, define a **configureGreetingFunction** function that configures the arguments for the lambda held by the greetingFunction variable and generates and then returns the lambda, ready for use:

Listing 5.13 Adding the **configureGreetingFunction** function (SimVillage.kt)

```
fun main(args: Array<String>) {
    runSimulation("Guyal", ::printContructionCost) { playerName, numBuildings ->
        val currentYear = 2018
        println("Adding $numBuildings houses")
        "Welcome to SimVillage, $playerName! (copyright $currentYear)"
    }
    runSimulation()
}

inline fun runSimulation(playerName: String,
                         costPrinter: (Int) -> Unit,
                         greetingFunction: (String, Int) -> String) {
    val numBuildings = (1..3).shuffled().last()    // Randomly selects 1, 2, or 3
    costPrinter(numBuildings)
    println(greetingFunction(playerName, numBuildings))
fun runSimulation() {
    val greetingFunction = configureGreetingFunction()
    println(greetingFunction("Guyal"))
}

fun configureGreetingFunction(): (String) -> String {
    val structureType = "hospitals"
    var numBuildings = 5
    return { playerName: String ->
        val currentYear = 2018
        numBuildings += 1
        println("Adding $numBuildings $structureType")
        "Welcome to SimVillage, $playerName! (copyright $currentYear)"
    }
}
```

You might think of **configureGreetingFunction** as a "function factory" – a function that sets up another function. It declares the necessary variables and assembles them in a lambda that it then returns to its caller, **runSimulation**.

Run SimVillage.kt again. The number of hospitals built is incremented and displayed:

```
Adding 6 hospitals
Welcome to SimVillage, Guyal! (copyright 2018)
```

Both numBuildings and structureType, local variables defined within **configureGreetingFunction**, were used by the lambda that **configureGreetingFunction** returns, even though they were defined in the outer function the lambda was returned from. This works because lambdas in Kotlin are what are called *closures* – they "close over" the variables in the outer scope that they are defined within. To learn more about closures, take a look at the section called *For the More Curious: Kotlin's Lambdas Are Closures*, below.

A function that accepts or returns another function is sometimes also referred to as a *higher-order function*. The terminology is borrowed from the same area of mathematics the term lambda is borrowed from. Higher-order functions are used extensively in a style of programming called *functional programming*, which you will learn about in Chapter 19.

In this chapter, you have learned how lambdas (AKA anonymous functions) are used to customize Kotlin standard library functions and how to define your own. You have also learned how functions behave like any other type in Kotlin and how they can be used as arguments or returned by functions that you define.

In the next chapter, you will see how Kotlin helps prevent programming mistakes by enforcing nullability in its type system. You will also return to NyetHack and begin building a tavern in the game.

For the More Curious: Kotlin's Lambdas Are Closures

In Kotlin, an anonymous function can modify and reference variables defined outside of its scope. This means that an anonymous function has a *reference* to the variables defined in the scope where it is itself created – as in the case of the **configureGreetingFunction** function you saw earlier.

As a demonstration of this property of anonymous functions, update the **runSimulation** function to call the function returned from **configureGreetingFunction** multiple times:

Listing 5.14 Calling **println** twice in **runSimulation** (SimVillage.kt)

```
...
fun runSimulation() {
    val greetingFunction = configureGreetingFunction()
    println(greetingFunction("Guyal"))
    println(greetingFunction("Guyal"))
}
...
```

Run SimVillage again. You will see the following output:

```
building 6 hospitals
Welcome to SimVillage, Guyal! (copyright 2018)
building 7 hospitals
Welcome to SimVillage, Guyal! (copyright 2018)
```

Though the numBuildings variable is defined outside of the anonymous function, the anonymous function has access to the variable and can modify it. Therefore, the numBuildings value increments from 6 to 7.

For the More Curious: Lambdas vs Anonymous Inner Classes

If you have not used function types before, you may wonder why you would want to use them in your program. Our answer: Function types offer increased flexibility with less boilerplate. Consider a language that does not offer function types, like Java 8.

Java 8 includes support for object-oriented programming and lambda expressions but does not include the ability to define a function as a parameter to a function or variable. Instead, Java provides anonymous inner classes – nameless classes that are defined within another class to implement a single method definition. You can pass anonymous inner classes as an instance, like a lambda. For example, in Java 8, to pass the definition for a single method, you would write:

```
Greeting greeting = (playerName, numBuildings) -> {
    int currentYear = 2018;
    System.out.println("Adding " + numBuildings + " houses");
    return "Welcome to SimVillage, " + playerName +
            "! (copyright " + currentYear + ")";
};

public interface Greeting {
    String greet(String playerName, int numBuildings);
}

greeting.greet("Guyal", 6);
```

On the surface, this seems mostly equivalent to what Kotlin provides: the ability to pass lambda expressions. But if you dig deeper, you will find that Java requires the definition of named interfaces or classes to represent the functions the lambda will define, even though instances of those types appear to be written in almost the same shorthand Kotlin allows. If you would like to simply pass a function without defining an interface, you will find Java does not support this concise syntax.

For example, take a look at the **Runnable** interface in Java:

```
public interface Runnable {
    public abstract void run();
}
```

This Java 8 lambda declaration requires an interface definition. In Kotlin, this extra effort to describe a single abstract method is not required. The following is possible in Kotlin and is functionally equivalent to the Java code:

```
fun runMyRunnable(runnable: () -> Unit) = { runnable() }
runMyRunnable { println("hey now") }
```

Combine this more precise syntax with the other features you learned about in the chapter – implicit returns, the it keyword, and the closure behavior – and you have a nice improvement on manually defining inner classes to implement a single method.

The flexibility Kotlin provides by including functions as first-class citizens frees you to spend your time on more valuable pursuits than writing boilerplate – like getting your work done.

6

Null Safety and Exceptions

Null is a special value that indicates that the value of a var or val does not exist. In many programming languages, including Java, null is a common cause of crashes, because a nonexistent value cannot be asked to do anything. Kotlin requires a specific declaration if a var or val can accept null as a value, which helps avoid this type of crash.

In this chapter, you will learn why null causes a crash, how Kotlin protects against null by default at compile time, and how to safely work with nullable values in Kotlin when you require them. You will also see how to work with what are called *exceptions* in Kotlin, indicators that something went wrong in your program.

To see these issues in action, you will be updating the NyetHack project. You will add a tavern to the game that accepts user input and attempts to fulfill custom drink requests for its choosy patrons. You will also add a dangerous sword juggling feature.

Nullability

Some elements in Kotlin can be assigned a value of null, and some cannot. We say that the former are *nullable* and the latter are *non-nullable*. For example, while you might want a variable in NyetHack that tracks a player's steed to be nullable, since not every player will ride a steed, you would not want the health points variable to be null. Every player has to have an associated health points value; it would be illogical for them not to. Its value might be 0, but 0 is not the same as null – null is the absence of any value.

Open NyetHack and create a new file called Tavern.kt. Add a **main** function, where your code will begin executing.

Before opening the tavern to custom drink requests from users, first try an experiment. Start by adding a familiar-looking var assignment to **main**, and then reassigning the variable's value to null:

Listing 6.1 Reassigning a var's value to null (Tavern.kt)

```
fun main(args: Array<String>) {
    var signatureDrink = "Buttered Ale"
    signatureDrink = null
}
```

Even before you execute this code, IntelliJ warns you with a red underline that something is amiss. Run it anyway, and you will see:

```
Null can not be a value of a non-null type String
```

Kotlin prevents the assignment of null to the signatureDrink variable, because it is a non-null type (String). A non-null type is one that does not support the assignment of null. The current definition of signatureDrink is guaranteed to be a string, rather than null.

If you have worked with Java before, this behavior is different than what you may be familiar with. In Java, the following code is permitted, for example.

```
String signatureDrink = "Buttered Ale";
signatureDrink = null;
```

Reassigning signatureDrink to a value of null is fine in Java. But what do you think would happen if you asked Java to concatenate a string to the null signatureDrink variable?

```
String signatureDrink = "Buttered Ale";
signatureDrink = null;
signatureDrink = signatureDrink + ", large";
```

In fact, this code will cause an exception that will crash the program, called a NullPointerException.

The Java code crashes because a nonexistent String has been asked to perform string concatenation. This is an impossible request. (If you are confused about why a value of null is not the same as an empty string, this example shows the difference. A value of null means that the variable does not exist. An empty string means that the variable exists and has a value of "", which could easily concatenate with ", large".)

Java and many other programming languages support exactly this pseudo-code statement: "Hey, nonexistent string, do string concatenation." In those languages, the value of any variable can be null (with the exception of primitives, which Kotlin does not support). In languages that allow null for any type, NullPointerExceptions are a common source of application crashes.

Kotlin takes the opposite position on the problem of null. Unless otherwise specified, a variable cannot be assigned a value of null. This guards against the problem of "Hey, nonexistent thing, do something" at compile time, rather than crashing at runtime.

Kotlin's Explicit Null Type

NullPointerExceptions like the one that you saw above should be avoided at all costs. Kotlin protected you by preventing you from assigning a null value to a variable of a non-nullable type. That said, nullness does still exist in Kotlin.

Here is an example, from the header for the function called **readLine**. **readLine** accepts user input from the console and returns it so that it can be used later.

```
public fun readLine(): String?
```

readLine's header looks like one that you have seen before, with one exception: the return type String?. The question mark represents a nullable version of a type. That means **readLine** will either return a value of type String, or it will return null.

Remove your earlier signatureDrink experiment and add a call to **readLine**. Store the value that is passed in to **readLine** and print it out.

Listing 6.2 Defining a nullable variable (Tavern.kt)

```
fun main(args: Array<String>) {
    var signatureDrink = "Buttered Ale"
    signatureDrink = null
    var beverage = readLine()

    println(beverage)
}
```

Run Tavern.kt. Nothing will happen initially, because it is waiting for your input. Click in the console, type the name of your preferred beverage, and press Return. The name that you entered will be echoed back to you in the console.

(What if you entered no beverage name and just pressed Return? Would that assign beverage a null value? No. It would assign the variable the value of the empty string, which would then be echoed back to you.)

Recall that a variable of type String? can hold either a string value or null. This means that assigning beverage to a null value will indeed compile. Try it out:

Listing 6.3 Reassigning a variable to null (Tavern.kt)

```
fun main(args: Array<String>) {
    var beverage = readLine()
    beverage = null

    println(beverage)
}
```

Run Tavern.kt and, as before, enter your beverage of choice. This time, no matter what you enter, the value printed to the console will be null. No beverage for you – but no error, either.

Before moving on, comment out the reassignment to null so that your tavern will actually serve customers. IntelliJ provides a shortcut for commenting out a line of code: Click anywhere in the line and press Command-/ (Ctrl-/). Commenting out this line of code instead of deleting it will give you the option to toggle the nullness of beverage by uncommenting the line (using the same keybinding). This way, you can easily test the strategies for handling nullness outlined in this chapter.

Listing 6.4 Restoring service (Tavern.kt)

```kotlin
fun main(args: Array<String>) {
    var beverage = readLine()
    beverage = null
//    beverage = null

    println(beverage)
}
```

Compile Time vs Runtime

Kotlin is a *compiled language*, meaning that your program is translated into machine-language instructions prior to execution by a special program, called the *compiler*. During this step, the compiler ensures that certain requirements are met by your code before the instructions are generated. For example, the compiler checks whether null is assigned to a nullable type. As you have seen, if you attempt to assign null to a non-nullable type, Kotlin will refuse to compile your program.

Errors caught at compile time are called *compile-time errors*, and they are one of the advantages of working with Kotlin. It may sound odd to say that errors are an advantage, but having the compiler check your work during development – before you allow others to run your program and tell you about your mistakes – makes it much easier to track down problems.

On the other hand, a *runtime error* is a mistake that happens after the program has compiled and is already running, because the compiler was unable to discover it. For example, because Java lacks any distinction between nullable and non-nullable types, the Java compiler cannot tell you that there is a problem if you ask a variable with a value of null to perform work. Code like that compiles just fine in Java, but it will crash at runtime.

Generally speaking, compile-time errors are preferable to runtime errors. Finding out about a problem while you are writing code is better than finding out later. And finding out after your program has been released? That is the worst.

Null Safety

Because Kotlin distinguishes between nullable and non-nullable types, the compiler is aware of the possibly dangerous situation of asking a variable defined as a nullable type to do something when the variable might not exist. To shield against these dangers, Kotlin will prevent you from calling functions on a value defined as nullable until you have accepted responsibility for this unsafe situation.

To see what this looks like in practice, try to call a function on beverage. This is a fancy tavern, and, as such, all drink names should be capitalized. Try to call **capitalize** on beverage. (You will see more String functions in Chapter 7.)

Listing 6.5 Using a nullable variable (Tavern.kt)

```
fun main(args: Array<String>) {
    var beverage = readLine()
    var beverage = readLine().capitalize()
//  beverage = null

    println(beverage)
}
```

Run Tavern.kt. You might expect that the result of this code will be a fancily capitalized version of the drink that you order. But when you execute the code, you will see a compile-time error instead:

```
Only safe (?.) or non-null asserted (!!.) calls
are allowed on a nullable receiver of type String?
```

Kotlin did not allow you to call the **capitalize** function, because you did not deal with the possibility of beverage being null. Even though you assign beverage to a non-null value via the console at its declaration, its type remains nullable. Kotlin has prevented you at compile time from potentially causing a runtime error, because the compiler was aware of your mistake with the nullable type.

By now you are likely thinking, "So how do I deal with the possibility of null? I have important drink name fancying-up to do." You have a number of choices for safely working with a nullable type in Kotlin, and in a moment we will give you three options, plus some extras.

First, though, consider option zero: Use a non-nullable type, if at all possible. Non-nullable types are easier to reason about because they guarantee that they contain a value that can have functions called on it. So ask yourself, "Why do I need a nullable type here? Would a non-nullable type work just as well?" Often, you simply do not need null – and when you do not need it, avoiding it is the safest course.

Option one: the safe call operator

Sometimes, nothing but a nullable type will do. For example, when you are working with a variable from code you do not control, you cannot be sure that it will not return null. In cases like that, your first option is to use the *safe call operator* (`?.`) in your function call. Try it out in `Tavern.kt`:

Listing 6.6 Using the safe call operator (`Tavern.kt`)

```
fun main(args: Array<String>) {
    var beverage = readLine().capitalize()
    var beverage = readLine()?.capitalize()
//  beverage = null

    println(beverage)
}
```

Notice that Kotlin does not generate an error this time. When the compiler encounters the safe call operator, it knows to check for a null value. If it finds one, it skips over the call and does not evaluate it, instead returning null. Here, if beverage is non-null, a capitalized version is returned. (Try it and see.) If beverage *is* null, **capitalize** is not called, because it would not be safe to do so. (Try that, too.)

The safe call operator ensures that a function is called if and only if the variable it acts on is not null, thus preventing a null pointer exception. We say, using the example above, that **capitalize** is called "safely," because the risk of a null pointer exception no longer exists.

Using safe calls with let

Safe calls allow you to call a single function on a nullable type, but what if you want to perform additional work, like creating a new value or calling other functions if the variable is not null? One way to achieve this is to use the safe call operator with the function **let**. **let** can be called on any value, and its purpose is to allow you to define a variable or variables for a given scope that you provide. (Recall that you learned about function scope in Chapter 4.)

Because **let** provides its own function scope, you can use a safe call with **let** to scope multiple expressions that each require the variable that they are called on to be non-null. You will learn more details about working with **let** in Chapter 9, but for now adapt your beverage implementation to get a sneak preview:

Listing 6.7 Using **let** with the safe call operator (`Tavern.kt`)

```
fun main(args: Array<String>) {
    var beverage = readLine()?.capitalize()
    var beverage = readLine()?.let {
        if (it.isNotBlank()) {
            it.capitalize()
        } else {
            "Buttered Ale"
        }
    }
//  beverage = null

    println(beverage)
}
```

Here, you define beverage as a nullable variable, as before. But this time you assign its value to the result of safely calling **let** on it. When beverage is not null and **let** is invoked, everything within the anonymous function passed to **let** is evaluated: The input from **readLine** is checked to see whether it is blank; if it is not blank it is capitalized, and if it is blank, then a fallback beverage name, "Buttered Ale", is returned instead. Both **isNotBlank** and **capitalize** require the beverage name to be non-null, which is guaranteed by **let**.

let provides a number of conveniences, two of which you take advantage of here. As you define beverage, you use the convenience value it, provided by **let**. You saw it in Chapter 5. Within **let**, it is a reference to the variable on which **let** is called, and is guaranteed to be non-null. You call **isNotBlank** and **capitalize** on it – a non-null form of beverage.

The second **let** convenience is behind the scenes: **let** returns the results of your expression implicitly, so you can (and do) assign that result to a variable once it has completed evaluating the expression you define.

Run Tavern.kt with the reassignment to null commented out, then uncommented. When beverage is not null, **let** is invoked, capitalization happens, and the result is printed. When beverage is null, the contents of the **let** function are not evaluated, and beverage remains null.

Option two: the double-bang operator

The double-bang operator (!!.) can also be used to call a function on a nullable type. But be forewarned: This is a much more drastic option than the safe call operator and should generally not be used. Visually, the !!. should look very loud in your code, because it is a dangerous option. If you use !!., you are proclaiming to the compiler: "If I ask a nonexistent thing to do something, I DEMAND that you throw a null pointer exception!!" (By the way, its official name is the *non-null assertion operator*, but it is more often called the double-bang operator.)

While we generally advise against the double-bang operator, strap on your safety goggles and try it out:

Listing 6.8 Using the double-bang operator (Tavern.kt)

```kotlin
fun main(args: Array<String>) {
    var beverage = readLine()?.let {
        if (it.isNotBlank()) {
            it.capitalize()
        } else {
            "Buttered Ale"
        }
    }
    var beverage = readLine()!!.capitalize()
//    beverage = null

    println(beverage)
}
```

beverage = readLine()!!.capitalize() means, "I don't care whether beverage is null; capitalize it anyway!" If beverage is indeed null, a KotlinNullPointerException is thrown.

There are situations where using the double-bang operator is appropriate. Perhaps you do not have control over the type of a variable, but you are sure that it will never be null. As long as you are confident that the variable you are using will not be null when you use it, then !!. may be an option for you. You will see an example of an appropriate use of !!. later in this chapter.

Option three: checking whether a value is null with if

A third option for working safely with null values is to check whether a value is null as a condition for executing an `if` branch. Recall Table 3.1 in Chapter 3, which lists the comparison operators available in Kotlin. The `!=` operator evaluates whether the value on the left is not equal to the value on the right, and you can use it to check that a value is not null. Try it out in the tavern:

Listing 6.9 Using `!=` `null` for null checking (Tavern.kt)

```
fun main(args: Array<String>) {
    var beverage = readLine()!!.capitalize()
    var beverage = readLine()
//   beverage = null

    if (beverage != null) {
        beverage = beverage.capitalize()
    } else {
        println("I can't do that without crashing - beverage was null!")
    }

    println(beverage)
}
```

Now, if beverage is null, you will get the following output, and no error.

```
I can't do that without crashing - beverage was null!
```

Using the safe call operator should be favored before using `value != null` as a means to guard against null, since it is a more flexible tool to solve generally the same problem, but in less code. For example, the safe call operator can be chained on to subsequent function calls with ease:

```
beverage?.capitalize()?.plus(", large")
```

Notice that you did not have to use the `!!.` operator when referencing beverage in `beverage = beverage.capitalize()`. The Kotlin compiler recognizes that beverage must be non-null as a condition for that branch, and it can deduce that a second null check is unnecessary. This feature – the compiler tracking conditions within an `if` expression – is an example of *smart casting*.

When would you use an `if/else` statement for null checking? This option is best for times when you have some complex logic that you would only like to be evaluated if a variable is null. An `if/else` statement allows you to represent that complex logic in a readable form.

The null coalescing operator

Another way to check for null values is to use Kotlin's *null coalescing operator* `?:` (also known as the "Elvis operator" due to its semblance to Elvis Presley's iconic hairstyle). This operator says, "If the thing on the lefthand side of me is null, do the thing on the righthand side instead."

Add a default beverage choice to your tavern using the null coalescing operator. If `beverage` is null, then print out the house specialty, `Buttered Ale`.

Listing 6.10 Using the null coalescing operator (`Tavern.kt`)

```
fun main(args: Array<String>) {
    var beverage = readLine()
//    beverage = null

    if (beverage != null) {
        beverage = beverage.capitalize()
    } else {
        println("I can't do that without crashing – beverage was null!")
    }

    println(beverage)
    val beverageServed: String = beverage ?: "Buttered Ale"
    println(beverageServed)
}
```

Most often in this book, we exclude the type of a variable if it can be inferred by the Kotlin compiler. We include it here to illuminate the role of the null coalescing operator.

If `beverage` is non-null, then it will be assigned to `beverageServed`. If `beverage` is null, then `"Buttered Ale"` is assigned. Either way, `beverageServed` is assigned a value of type `String`, not `String?`. This is great – the beverage served to the user is now guaranteed to be non-null.

Think of the null coalescing operator as ensuring that a value is not null by providing a default (and not null) value to be assigned if the first option turns out to be null. Null coalescing can be used to clean up values that might be null so that you can have peace of mind as you work with them.

Run `Tavern.kt`. As long as `beverage` is not null, you will see your capitalized drink order. When `beverage` is null, you will see the following printed to the console instead.

```
I can't do that without crashing – beverage was null!
Buttered Ale
```

The null coalescing operator can also be used in conjunction with the **let** function in place of an if/ else statement. Compare this code, which is the result of Listing 6.9:

```
var beverage = readLine()
    if (beverage != null) {
        beverage = beverage.capitalize()
    } else {
        println("I can't do that without crashing - beverage was null!")
    }
```

With this:

```
var beverage = readLine()
beverage?.let {
    beverage = it.capitalize()
} ?: println("I can't do that without crashing - beverage was null!")
```

This code is functionally equivalent to the code in Listing 6.9. If beverage is null, then "I can't do that without crashing - beverage was null!" is printed to the console. Otherwise, beverage is capitalized.

So, should you replace your existing if/else statements with this style? That is not a question that we can answer for you, because the choice is a stylistic one. We tend to opt for if/else statements in this type of scenario, and you will see them throughout this book. We prefer their readability. If you or your team disagree, that is OK – either syntax is valid.

Exceptions

Like many other languages, Kotlin also includes *exceptions* to indicate that something went wrong in your program. This is important, because the world of NyetHack is a place in which things can indeed go wrong.

Let's see some examples. Start by creating a new file in NyetHack called SwordJuggler.kt and adding a **main** function.

Against your better judgment, a group of tavern attendees has convinced you to juggle some swords. You will keep track of the number of swords that you are juggling with a nullable integer. Why a nullable integer? If swordsJuggling is null, then you lack proficiency in sword juggling and your journey in NyetHack may be cut short.

Begin by adding variables for the number of swords you are juggling as well as your juggling proficiency. You can represent sword juggling proficiency using the same randomness mechanism that you wrote in Chapter 5. If you are a proficient juggler, print the number of swords juggled to the console.

Listing 6.11 Adding sword juggling logic (SwordJuggler.kt)

```kotlin
fun main(args: Array<String>) {
    var swordsJuggling: Int? = null
    val isJugglingProficient = (1..3).shuffled().last() == 3
    if (isJugglingProficient) {
        swordsJuggling = 2
    }

    println("You juggle $swordsJuggling swords!")
}
```

Run SwordJuggler. You have a 1 in 3 chance of being proficient with juggling swords – not bad for a first-timer. If your proficiency check passes, then you will see You juggle 2 swords! printed to the console. If your check fails, then you will see You juggle null swords! instead.

Printing the value of swordsJuggling is not an inherently dangerous operation. You can print null to the console, and your program will continue running. It is time to ratchet up the danger. Add another sword using the **plus** function and the !!. operator.

Listing 6.12 Adding a third sword (SwordJuggler.kt)

```kotlin
fun main(args: Array<String>) {
    var swordsJuggling: Int? = null
    val isJugglingProficient = (1..3).shuffled().last() == 3
    if (isJugglingProficient) {
        swordsJuggling = 2
    }

    swordsJuggling = swordsJuggling!!.plus(1)

    println("You juggle $swordsJuggling swords!")
}
```

Using the !!. operator on a nullable variable *is* a dangerous operation. One-third of the time, your sword-juggling proficiency enables you juggle a third sword. The other two-thirds of the time, your program crashes.

When an exception occurs, it must be dealt with, or execution of the program will be halted. An exception that is not dealt with is called an *unhandled exception*. And halting the execution of the program is known by the ugly name *crash*.

Test your luck by running SwordJuggler a couple of times. If your application crashes, you will see a KotlinNullPointerException, and the rest of the code (the **println** statement) will not execute.

When there is the possibility of a variable being null, there is the possibility of a KotlinNullPointerException. This is one of the reasons Kotlin makes variables non-nullable by default.

Throwing an exception

Similar to many other languages, Kotlin allows you to manually signal that an exception has occurred. You do this with the `throw` operator, and it is called *throwing* an exception. There are many more exceptions that can be thrown in addition to the null pointer exception that you just saw.

Why would you want to throw an exception? It is all in the name – exceptions are used to represent exceptional state. If something in your code has gone extraordinarily wrong, then throwing an exception signals that the issue must be handled before execution continues.

One of the more common exceptions that you will see is called an `IllegalStateException`. `IllegalStateException` is a vague name, to be sure – it means that your program has reached some state that you have deemed illegal. This is useful, because you can pass `IllegalStateException` a string to print out when the exception is thrown to provide more information about what went wrong.

The world of NyetHack may be expansive and mysterious, but the tavern has its share of good people. One particular merrymaker recognizes your lack of sword-juggling proficiency and steps in before you can do anything dangerous. Add a function called **proficiencyCheck** to SwordJuggler, and call it in **main**. If `swordsJuggling` is null, interject by throwing an `IllegalStateException` before any dangerous operations can be performed.

Listing 6.13 Throwing an `IllegalStateException` (SwordJuggler.kt)

```
fun main(args: Array<String>) {
    var swordsJuggling: Int? = null
    val isJugglingProficient = (1..3).shuffled().last() == 3
    if (isJugglingProficient) {
        swordsJuggling = 2
    }

    proficiencyCheck(swordsJuggling)
    swordsJuggling = swordsJuggling!!.plus(1)

    println("You juggle $swordsJuggling swords!")
}

fun proficiencyCheck(swordsJuggling: Int?) {
    swordsJuggling ?: throw IllegalStateException("Player cannot juggle swords")
}
```

Run this code a couple of times to see the different results.

Here, you signaled that the state of the program is an illegal one – `swordsJuggling` should not be null, lest you put yourself at risk. This signal decrees that anyone that would like to work with the `swordsJuggling` variable must handle the exceptional state stemming from its nullability. It is loud, but that is a good thing, as it increases the likelihood that you will notice the exceptional state during development – before it causes a crash for your user. And because you provided an error message to the `IllegalStateException`, you know exactly why your program crashed.

When you throw an exception, you are not limited to Kotlin's built-in types. You can define your own custom exceptions to represent a state that is specific to your application.

Custom exceptions

You have now seen how to use the throw operator to signal that an exception has occurred. The exception you just threw, IllegalStateException, indicates that an illegal state has occurred and gives you the opportunity to add more information by passing a string to be printed when the exception is thrown.

To add more detail to your exception, you can create a custom exception for the particular problem. To define a custom exception, you define a new *class* that inherits from some other exception. Classes allow you to define the "things" in your program – monsters, weapons, food, tools, and so on. You will learn lots more about classes in Chapter 12, so do not worry about the details of the syntax now.

Define a custom exception called UnskilledSwordJugglerException in SwordJuggler.kt.

Listing 6.14 Defining a custom exception (SwordJuggler.kt)

```
fun main(args: Array<String>) {
    ...
}

fun proficiencyCheck(swordsJuggling: Int?) {
    swordsJuggling ?: throw IllegalStateException("Player cannot juggle swords")
}

class UnskilledSwordJugglerException() :
        IllegalStateException("Player cannot juggle swords")
```

UnskilledSwordJugglerException is a custom exception that acts as an IllegalStateException with a specific message.

You can throw this new, custom exception in the same way that you threw IllegalStateException, using the throw operator. Throw your custom exception in SwordJuggler.kt.

Listing 6.15 Throwing a custom exception (SwordJuggler.kt)

```
fun main(args: Array<String>) {
    ...
}

fun proficiencyCheck(swordsJuggling: Int?) {
    swordsJuggling ?: throw IllegalStateException("Player cannot juggle swords")
    swordsJuggling ?: throw UnskilledSwordJugglerException()
}

class UnskilledSwordJugglerException() :
        IllegalStateException("Player cannot juggle swords")
```

UnskilledSwordJugglerException is a custom error intended to be thrown when swordsJuggling is null. Nothing about the code used to define this exception specifies when it is thrown – that is your responsibility.

Custom exceptions are flexible and useful. Not only can you use them to print custom messages, but you also can add functionality to be executed when the exception is thrown. And they reduce duplication, as you can reuse them across your codebase.

Handling exceptions

Exceptions are disruptive, and they should be – they represent a state that is unrecoverable unless it is handled. Kotlin allows you to specify how to handle exceptions by defining a try/catch statement around the code that might cause one. The syntax of try/catch is similar to the syntax for if/else. To see what it looks like, use try/catch in SwordJuggler.kt to protect against the dangerous operation that you performed, as shown:

Listing 6.16 Adding a try/catch statement (SwordJuggler.kt)

```
fun main(args: Array<String>) {
    var swordsJuggling: Int? = null
    val isJugglingProficient = (1..3).shuffled().last() == 3
    if (isJugglingProficient) {
        swordsJuggling = 2
    }

    try {
        proficiencyCheck(swordsJuggling)
        swordsJuggling = swordsJuggling!!.plus(1)
    } catch (e: Exception) {
        println(e)
    }

    println("You juggle $swordsJuggling swords!")
}

fun proficiencyCheck(swordsJuggling: Int?) {
    swordsJuggling ?: throw UnskilledSwordJugglerException()
}

class UnskilledSwordJugglerException() :
        IllegalStateException("Player cannot juggle swords")
```

When you define a try/catch statement, you declare what will happen in the event that some value is not null and what will happen if it is null. In the try block, you "try" to use a variable. If no exception occurs, the try statement executes and the catch statement does not. This branching logic is akin to a conditional. In this case, you try to add another sword to be juggled using the !!. operator.

In the catch block, you define what will happen if some expression in the try block causes an exception. The catch block takes a specific type of exception to protect as an argument. In this case, you catch any exception of type Exception.

catch blocks can include all sorts of logic, but this example keeps it simple. Here, you use the catch block to simply print the name of the exception.

Within the try block, each line of code is executed in the order it is declared. In this case, if swordsJuggling is non-null, the **plus** function will add 1 to swordsJuggling without issue, and the following statement will be printed to the console:

    You juggle 3 swords!

If you are not fortunate enough to be proficient with sword juggling, then swordsJuggling will be null. As such, **proficiencyCheck** will throw an UnskilledSwordJugglerException. But because you handled the exception with a try/catch statement, program execution will continue and the catch block will run, printing the following output to the console:

```
UnskilledSwordJugglerException: Player cannot juggle swords
You juggle null swords!
```

Note that both the name of the exception and `You juggle null swords!` was printed. This is significant, because the latter string is printed after the `try`/`catch` block executes. An unhandled exception will crash your program, halting execution. Because you handled the exception using a `try`/`catch` block, code execution can continue as if a dangerous operation never caused an issue.

Run `SwordJuggler.kt` several times to see both outcomes.

Preconditions

Unexpected values can cause your program to behave in unintended ways. As a developer, you will spend plenty of time validating input to ensure you are working with the values you intend. Some sources of exceptions are common, like unexpected null values. To make it easier to validate input and debug to avoid certain common issues, Kotlin provides some convenience functions as part of its standard library. They allow you to use a built-in function to throw an exception with a custom message.

These functions are called *precondition functions*, because they allow you to define preconditions – conditions that must be true before some piece of code is executed.

For example, you have seen a number of ways in this chapter to guard against the `KotlinNullPointerException` and other exceptions. One last option is to use a precondition function like **checkNotNull**, which checks whether a value is null and returns the value, if it is not null, or throws an `IllegalStateException` if it is null. Try replacing your thrown `UnskilledSwordJugglerException` with a precondition function:

Listing 6.17 Using a precondition function (`SwordJuggler.kt`)

```
fun main(args: Array<String>) {
    var swordsJuggling: Int? = null
    val isJugglingProficient = (1..3).shuffled().last() == 3
    if (isJugglingProficient) {
        swordsJuggling = 2
    }

    try {
        proficiencyCheck(swordsJuggling)
        swordsJuggling = swordsJuggling!!.plus(1)
    } catch (e: Exception) {
        println(e)
    }

    println("You juggle $swordsJuggling swords!")
}

fun proficiencyCheck(swordsJuggling: Int?) {
    swordsJuggling ?: throw UnskilledSwordJugglerException()
    checkNotNull(swordsJuggling, { "Player cannot juggle swords" })
}

class UnskilledSwordJugglerException() :
        IllegalStateException("Player cannot juggle swords")
```

checkNotNull makes explicit that swordsJuggling must not be null past a certain point in your code execution. If it is null when passed to **checkNotNull**, then a thrown IllegalStateException makes it clear that the current state is unacceptable. **checkNotNull** takes two arguments: The first is a value to check for nullness, and the second is an error message to be printed to the console in the event that the first argument is null.

Precondition functions are a great way to communicate requirements before some bit of code is executed. They can be cleaner than manually throwing your own exception, because the condition to be satisfied is included in the name of the function. In this case, while the outcome is the same – you can be assured that either swordsJuggling will not be null or that a custom exception message will print – **checkNotNull** is more clear than the earlier throw UnskilledSwordJugglerException.

Kotlin includes five preconditions in the standard library; this variety differentiates them from other types of null checks. The five precondition functions are shown in Table 6.1:

Table 6.1 Kotlin precondition functions

Function	Description
checkNotNull	Throws an IllegalStateException if argument is null. Otherwise returns the non-null value.
require	Throws an IllegalArgumentException if argument is false.
requireNotNull	Throws an IllegalArgumentException if argument is null. Otherwise returns the non-null value.
error	Throws an IllegalArgumentException with a provided message if argument is null. Otherwise returns the non-null value.
assert	Throws an AssertionError if argument is false and the assertion compiler flag is enabled.[a]

[a]The details of enabling assertions are outside the scope of this book. If you are interested, see kotlinlang.org/api/latest/jvm/stdlib/kotlin/assert.html and docs.oracle.com/cd/E19683-01/806-7930/assert-4/index.html.

require is a particularly useful precondition. Functions can leverage **require** to communicate bounds for the arguments passed to them. Take a look at a function using **require** to make the requirements for the swordsJuggling parameter explicit:

```
fun juggleSwords(swordsJuggling: Int) {
    require(swordsJuggling >= 3, { "Juggle at least 3 swords to be exciting." })
    // Juggle
}
```

To put on a good show, the player must juggle at least three swords. Using **require** at the top of the function declaration makes this clear to whoever calls **juggleSwords**.

Null: What Is It Good For?

This chapter has taken a largely anti-null stance. We view this stance to be a noble one, but in the wild world of software engineering, representing state using null is common.

Why? Null is often used in Java and languages of its ilk as an initial value for variables. For example, think of a variable declared to hold a person's name. There are common first names for human beings, but no name can be considered a *default*. Null is often used as an initial value for variables that have no natural default value. In fact, in many languages, you can define a variable without assigning it a value, and its value will default to null.

This mentality of defaulting to null can lead to null pointer exceptions, which can be common in other languages. One way that you can work around nullness is to provide better initializers. Not every type has a natural initial value, but the String in our name example does – an empty string. An empty string tells you as much as a null initializer would: This value is not yet initialized. Therefore, you can represent an uninitialized state without resorting to null checks in your code.

The other way to work with nullness is to accept it and to use the strategies outlined in this chapter to work with nullable types. Whether you use the safe call operator to protect yourself against null pointer exceptions or the null coalescing operator to provide your own default value, working with null is a reasonable expectation of you as a Kotlin developer.

Nullness – the absence of a value – is a real-world phenomenon. Being able to represent nullness in Kotlin is important for that reason. When you represent it in your code or call into someone else's code that relies on nullness, do so wisely.

In this chapter, you have learned how Kotlin handles problems related to nullness. You have seen that you must explicitly define when you support nullability, because values are by default non-nullable. And you learned that you should favor types that do not support null when possible, because they let the compiler help prevent runtime errors.

You have also seen how to work safely with nullable types when you absolutely must have them – by using the safe call operator or null coalescing operator, or by explicitly checking whether the value is null. You also saw the `let` function and how it can be used in conjunction with the safe call operator to evaluate expressions safely on a nullable variable. Finally, you learned about exceptions, how to deal with them using the `try/catch` syntax that Kotlin provides, and how to define preconditions to catch exceptional states before they cause a crash.

In the next chapter you will learn more about working with strings in Kotlin as you continue to build NyetHack's tavern.

For the More Curious: Checked vs Unchecked Exceptions

In Kotlin, all exceptions are *unchecked*. This means that the Kotlin compiler does not force you to wrap all code that could produce an exception in a `try/catch` statement.

Compare this with Java, for example, which supports a mixture of both checked and unchecked exception types. With a checked exception, the compiler checks that the exception is guarded against, requiring you add a `try/catch` to your program.

This *sounds* reasonable. But in practice, the idea of checked exceptions does not hold up as well as the inventors thought it would. Often, checked exceptions are caught (because the compiler requires the checked exception to be handled) and then simply ignored, just to allow the program to compile. This is called "swallowing an exception," and it makes your program very hard to debug because it suppresses the information that anything went wrong in the first place. In most cases, ignoring the problem at compile time leads to more errors at runtime.

Unchecked exceptions have won out in modern languages because experience has shown that checked exceptions lead to more problems than they solve: code duplication, difficult-to-understand error recovery logic, and swallowed exceptions with no record of an error even taking place.

For the More Curious: How Is Nullability Enforced?

Kotlin has strict patterns around nullness when compared to languages like Java. This is a boon when working exclusively in Kotlin, but how is this pattern implemented? Do Kotlin's rules still protect you when interoperating with a less strict language like Java? Think back to the **printPlayerStatus** function from Chapter 4.

```
fun printPlayerStatus(auraColor: String,
                      isBlessed: Boolean,
                      name: String,
                      healthStatus: String) {
    ...
}
```

printPlayerStatus takes in parameters of Kotlin types String and Boolean.

If you are calling this function from Kotlin, then the function signature is clear – auraColor, name, and healthStatus must be of type String, which is not nullable, and isBlessed must be of type Boolean, which is also not nullable. However, because Java does not have the same rules regarding nullability, a String in Java could potentially be null.

How does Kotlin maintain a null-safe environment? Answering that question requires a dive into the decompiled Java bytecode:

```
public static final void printPlayerStatus(@NotNull String auraColor,
                                           boolean isBlessed,
                                           @NotNull String name,
                                           @NotNull String healthStatus) {
    Intrinsics.checkParameterIsNotNull(auraColor, "auraColor");
    Intrinsics.checkParameterIsNotNull(name, "name");
    Intrinsics.checkParameterIsNotNull(healthStatus, "healthStatus");
    ...
}
```

There are two mechanisms for ensuring that non-null parameters do not accept null arguments. First, note the @NotNull annotations on each of the non-primitive parameters to **printPlayerStatus**. These annotations serve as a signal to callers of this Java method that the annotated parameters should not take null arguments. isBlessed does not require a @NotNull annotation, because booleans are represented as primitive types in Java and, as such, cannot be null.

@NotNull annotations can be found in many Java projects, but they are particularly useful for those calling Java methods from Kotlin, as the Kotlin compiler uses them to determine whether a Java method parameter is nullable. You will learn more about Kotlin's interoperability with Java in Chapter 20.

The Kotlin compiler goes a step further in guaranteeing that auraColor, name, and healthStatus will not be null: using a method called **Intrinsics.checkParameterIsNotNull**. This method is called on each non-nullable parameter and will throw an IllegalArgumentException if a null value manages to be passed as an argument.

In short, any function that you declare in Kotlin will play by Kotlin's rules about nullness, even when represented as Java code on the JVM.

So there you have it – you are doubly protected from a null pointer exception when writing functions that take values of non-null types in Kotlin, even when interoperating with languages that are less strict about nullness.

7
Strings

In programming, textual data is represented by *strings* – ordered sequences of characters. You have already used Kotlin's strings, like the string you formatted and displayed in SimVillage:

```
"Welcome to SimVillage, Mayor! (copyright 2018)"
```

In this chapter you will see more of what strings can do, using a variety of functions for the String type from the Kotlin standard library. In the process, you will upgrade NyetHack's tavern to allow customers to order from the menu, an essential feature of any tavern worth its salt.

Extracting Substrings

To allow tavern customers to place an order, you will look at two ways to extract one string from another: the functions **substring** and **split**.

substring

Your first task is to write a function that allows a player to place an order with the tavern master. Open Tavern.kt in the NyetHack project, add a variable to hold the name of the tavern, and add a new function called **placeOrder**.

Within the new **placeOrder** function, use String's **indexOf** and **substring** functions to extract the tavern master's name from the TAVERN_NAME string and display it. (We will walk through each line of **placeOrder** after you add it.) Also, remove the old beverage code from the previous exercise. The tavern will feature more than beverage items, and Buttered Ale is no longer lawful to serve in the realm anyway.

Listing 7.1 Extracting the tavern master's name (Tavern.kt)

```
const val TAVERN_NAME = "Taernyl's Folly"

fun main(args: Array<String>) {
    var beverage = readLine()
    // beverage = null

    if (beverage != null) {
        beverage = beverage.capitalize()
    } else {
        println("I can't do that without crashing - beverage was null!")
    }

    val beverageServed: String = beverage ?: "Buttered Ale"
    println(beverageServed)
    placeOrder()
}

private fun placeOrder() {
    val indexOfApostrophe = TAVERN_NAME.indexOf('\'')
    val tavernMaster = TAVERN_NAME.substring(0 until indexOfApostrophe)
    println("Madrigal speaks with $tavernMaster about their order.")
}
```

Run Tavern.kt. You will see the output Madrigal speaks with Taernyl about their order.

Let's go line by line to see how **placeOrder** extracted the tavern master's name from the name of the tavern.

First, you use String's **indexOf** function to get the *index* of the first apostrophe in the String:

```
    val indexOfFirstApostrophe = TAVERN_NAME.indexOf('\'')
```

An index is an integer that corresponds to the position of a character in the string. The index starts at 0 for the first character. The next character has the index 1, the next 2, and so forth.

The Char type, defined within single quotes, is used to represent the individual characters in a string. Passing a Char to **indexOf** tells the function to locate the first instance of the Char and return its index. The argument you provide **indexOf** is '\'', so the **indexOf** function scans through the string until it finds a match and returns the index for the apostrophe character.

What is the \ doing in that argument? The apostrophe character is also the single quotation mark that signals a character literal. If you entered your argument as ''', the compiler would read the apostrophe in the middle as a single quotation mark enclosing an empty character literal. You need to let the compiler know that you are specifying the apostrophe character instead, and you do this with the \ *escape character*, which distinguishes between certain characters and special meanings they have to the compiler.

Table 7.1 lists the escape sequences (consisting of \ and the character being escaped) and their meanings to the compiler:

Table 7.1 Escape sequences

Escape sequence	Meaning
\t	Tab character
\b	Backspace character
\n	Newline character
\r	Carriage return
\"	Double quotation mark
\'	Single quotation mark/apostrophe
\\	Backslash
\$	Dollar sign
\u	Unicode character

Once you have the index of the first apostrophe in the string, you use string's **substring** function, which returns a new string from an existing string using parameters you provide:

```
val tavernMaster = TAVERN_NAME.substring(0 until indexOfFirstApostrophe)
```

substring accepts an IntRange (a type that represents a range of integers) that determines the indices of the characters to extract. In this case, the range starts with the first character and ends with the character before the first apostrophe (recall that **until** creates a range that excludes the specified upper bound).

This sets the value of the variable tavernMaster to the string consisting of the characters from the beginning of the TAVERN_NAME string to just before the first apostrophe – in other words, "Taernyl".

Finally, you used string templating (as you saw in Chapter 3) to interpolate the variable tavernMaster in the output by prefixing the variable with $:

```
println("Madrigal speaks with $tavernMaster about their order.")
```

split

The tavern's menu data will be represented as a string and stored in the following format, separated by commas: type of drink, drink name, and price (in gold). For example:

```
shandy,Dragon's Breath,5.91
```

Your next task is to allow the **placeOrder** function to accept tavern menu data and display the name, type, and price of the item the customer has ordered. Update the **placeOrder** function to accept tavern menu data, passing some menu data where **placeOrder** is called.

(Note that from here forward we will show additions to a line of code in the existing line, rather than showing the line deleted and re-entered with the change.)

Listing 7.2 Passing tavern data to **placeOrder** (Tavern.kt)

```
const val TAVERN_NAME = "Taernyl's Folly"

fun main(args: Array<String>) {
    placeOrder("shandy,Dragon's Breath,5.91")
}

private fun placeOrder(menuData: String) {
    val indexOfApostrophe = TAVERN_NAME.indexOf('\'')
    val tavernMaster = TAVERN_NAME.substring(0 until indexOfApostrophe)
    println("Madrigal speaks with $tavernMaster about their order.")
}
```

Next, to extract the individual parts of the menu data for display, you are going to use String's **split** function, which creates a series of substrings using a delimiter you provide. Add the **split** function to **placeOrder**:

Listing 7.3 Splitting the menu data (Tavern.kt)

```
...

private fun placeOrder(menuData: String) {
    val indexOfApostrophe = TAVERN_NAME.indexOf('\'')
    val tavernMaster = TAVERN_NAME.substring(0 until indexOfApostrophe)
    println("Madrigal speaks with $tavernMaster about their order.")

    val data = menuData.split(',')
    val type = data[0]
    val name = data[1]
    val price = data[2]
    val message = "Madrigal buys a $name ($type) for $price."
    println(message)
}
```

split accepts a delimiter character to look for and returns a list of the resulting substrings with the delimiter omitted. (Lists, which you will learn about in Chapter 10, hold a series of elements.) In this case, **split** returns a list of strings in the order it found them. You use indices in square brackets, officially known as the *indexed access operator*, to extract the first, second, and third strings from the list and assign them as the values of the variables type, name, and price.

Finally, as before, you include the strings in a message using string interpolation.

Run `Tavern.kt`. This time, you will see the drink order printed, including the item type and price.

```
Madrigal speaks with Taernyl about their order.
Madrigal buys a Dragon's Breath (shandy) for 5.91.
```

Because **split** returns a list, it also supports simplified syntax called *destructuring* – a feature that allows you to declare and assign multiple variables in a single expression. Update **placeOrder** to use destructuring syntax instead of individual assignments.

Listing 7.4 Destructuring the menu data (`Tavern.kt`)

```
...

private fun placeOrder(menuData: String) {
    val indexOfApostrophe = TAVERN_NAME.indexOf('\'')
    val tavernMaster = TAVERN_NAME.substring(0 until indexOfApostrophe)
    println("Madrigal speaks with $tavernMaster about their order.")

    val data = menuData.split(',')
    val type = data[0]
    val name = data[1]
    val price = data[2]
    val (type, name, price) = menuData.split(',')
    val message = "Madrigal buys a $name ($type) for $price."
    println(message)
}
```

Destructuring can often be used to simplify the assignment of variables. Any time the result is a list, a destructuring assignment is allowed. In addition to `List`, other types that support destructuring include `Maps` and `Pairs` (both of which you will learn about in Chapter 11), as well as data classes.

Run `Tavern.kt` again. The results should be the same.

String Manipulation

Whoever drinks a Dragon's Breath enjoys not only a delightful sensory experience but also gains elite programming abilities as well as DragonSpeak, an ancient tongue similar to 1337Sp34k.

For example, the following utterance:

```
A word of advice: Don't drink the Dragon's Breath
```

Translates to this in DragonSpeak:

```
A w0rd 0f 4dv1c3: D0n't dr1nk th3 Dr4g0n's Br34th
```

The `String` type includes functions for manipulating the values of a string. To add a DragonSpeak translator to NyetHack's tavern, you are going to use `String`'s **replace** function, which, as the name suggests, replaces characters based on rules you specify. **replace** accepts a regular expression (more on that in a moment) to determine what characters it should act on and calls an anonymous function that you define to determine what to replace the matched characters with.

Add a new function called **toDragonSpeak** that accepts a phrase and returns a DragonSpeak translation. Also, add a phrase to **printOrder** and call **toDragonSpeak** on it.

Listing 7.5 Defining the **toDragonSpeak** function (Tavern.kt)

```
const val TAVERN_NAME = "Taernyl's Folly"

fun main(args: Array<String>) {
    placeOrder("shandy,Dragon's Breath,5.91")
}

private fun toDragonSpeak(phrase: String) =
    phrase.replace(Regex("[aeiou]")) {
        when (it.value) {
            "a" -> "4"
            "e" -> "3"
            "i" -> "1"
            "o" -> "0"
            "u" -> "|_|"
            else -> it.value
        }
    }

private fun placeOrder(menuData: String) {
    ...
    println(message)

    val phrase = "Ah, delicious $name!"
    println("Madrigal exclaims: ${toDragonSpeak(phrase)}")
}
```

Run Tavern.kt. This time, you will notice Madrigal's speech has taken on the very distinctive drawl of DragonSpeak:

```
Madrigal speaks with Taernyl about their order.
Madrigal buys a Dragon's breath (shandy) for 5.91
Madrigal exclaims: Ah, d3l1c10|_|s Dr4g0n's Br34th!
```

Here you used a combination of features available on String to generate the DragonSpeak version of the phrase.

The version of the **replace** function you used accepts two arguments. The first argument is a *regular expression* that determines which characters you want to replace. A regular expression, or *regex*, defines a search pattern for characters you want to look for. The second argument is an anonymous function that defines what you want to replace each matching character with.

Take a look at the first argument that you provided to **replace**, the regular expression that determines which characters to select for replacement:

```
phrase.replace(Regex("[aeiou]")) {
    ...
}
```

Regex accepts a pattern argument, "[aeiou]", that defines the characters you want to match and replace. Kotlin uses the same regular expression patterns as Java. You can read the documentation for the supported regular expression pattern syntax at docs.oracle.com/javase/8/docs/api/java/util/regex/Pattern.html.

After defining the characters you want **replace** to match, you define what you want to replace those characters with, using an anonymous function.

```
phrase.replace(Regex("[aeiou]")) {
    when (it.value) {
        "a" -> "4"
        "e" -> "3"
        "i" -> "1"
        "o" -> "0"
        "u" -> "|_|"
        else -> it.value
    }
}
```

The argument received by the anonymous function gives the value of the each match found by the regular expression you defined and returns the new value for the match.

Strings are immutable

A clarification regarding the "replacing" of the characters performed by **toDragonSpeak**: If you were to print the phrase variable from Listing 7.5 before and after calling **replace** on it, you would find that the variable's value does not actually change.

In reality, the **replace** function does not "replace" any part of the phrase variable. Instead, **replace** creates a new string. It uses the old string's value as an input and chooses characters for the new string using the expression you provide.

Whether they are defined with var or val, all strings in Kotlin are actually immutable (as they are in Java). Though the variables that hold the value for the String can be reassigned if the string is a var, the string instance itself can never be changed. Any function that appears to change the value of a string (like **replace**) actually creates a new string with the changes applied to it.

String Comparison

What if a player were to order something other than Dragon's Breath? **toDragonSpeak** would still be called. This is not what you want.

Add a conditional to Tavern.kt's **placeOrder** function to skip calling **toDragonSpeak** if the player did not order Dragon's Breath:

Listing 7.6 Comparing strings in **placeOrder** (Tavern.kt)

...

```
private fun placeOrder(menuData: String) {
    ...
    val phrase = "Ah, delicious $name!"
    println("Madrigal exclaims: ${toDragonSpeak(phrase)}")

    val phrase = if (name == "Dragon's Breath") {
        "Madrigal exclaims ${toDragonSpeak("Ah, delicious $name!")}"
    } else {
        "Madrigal says: Thanks for the $name."
    }
    println(phrase)
}
```

Comment out your Dragon's Breath order in the **main** function – we will return to it soon – and add a new call to **placeOrder** with different menu data.

Listing 7.7 Changing the menu data (Tavern.kt)

```
const val TAVERN_NAME = "Taernyl's Folly"

fun main(args: Array<String>) {
    placeOrder("shandy,Dragon's Breath,5.91")
//  placeOrder("shandy,Dragon's Breath,5.91")
    placeOrder("elixir,Shirley's Temple,4.12")
}
...
```

Run Tavern.kt. You will see the following output:

```
Madrigal speaks with Taernyl about their order.
Madrigal buys a Shirley's Temple (elixir) for 4.12
Madrigal says: Thanks for the Shirley's Temple.
```

You checked the *structural equality* of name and "Dragon's Breath" using the structural equality operator, ==. You have seen this operator before, used with numeric values. When used with strings, it checks that the characters in each string match one another and are in the same order.

There is another way to check the equality of two variables: comparing *referential equality*, which means checking that two variables share the same reference to a type instance – in other words, that two variables point to the same object on the heap. Referential equality is checked using ===.

Referential comparison is not usually what you want. You generally do not care whether strings are different instances, only that they have the same characters in the same sequence (i.e., that the structures of two separate type instances are identical).

If you are familiar with Java, the string comparison behavior using == is different than what you may have expected, because Java uses the == symbol for referential comparison. To compare strings structurally in Java, you use the function **equals**.

In this chapter, you have learned more about how to work with strings in Kotlin. You saw how to use the **indexOf** function to find the specific index of a character and regular expressions to search through strings for patterns that you define. You learned about destructuring syntax, which allows you to declare multiple variables and assign their values in a single expression, and you also learned that Kotlin uses structural comparison when using the == operator.

In the next chapter, you will learn about working with numbers in Kotlin by building out the strongbox for the tavern so that gold and silver can change hands.

For the More Curious: Unicode

As you have learned, a string consists of an ordered sequence of characters, and a character is an instance of the Char type. Specifically, a Char is a *Unicode character*. The Unicode character encoding system is designed to support "the interchange, processing, and display of the written texts of the diverse languages and technical disciplines of the modern world" (unicode.org).

This means the individual characters in a string can be any of a diverse palette of characters and symbols – 136,690 of them (and growing) – including characters from the alphabet of any language in the world, icons, glyphs, emoji, and more.

To declare a character, you have two options. Both are wrapped in single quotes. For characters on your keyboard, the simplest option is the character itself in the single quotes:

```
val capitalA: Char = 'A'
```

But not all 136,690 characters are included on your keyboard. The other way to represent a character is with its Unicode character code, preceded by the Unicode character escape sequence \u:

```
val unicodeCapitalA: Char = '\u0041'
```

There is a key for the letter "A" on your keyboard, but there is not one for the ॐ symbol. To represent it in your program, your only choice is to use its character code in single quotes. If you want to try it out, create a new Kotlin file in your project. Enter the code below into the file and run it. (Delete the file when you are done by right-clicking on it in the project tool window and selecting Delete.)

Listing 7.8 Om... (scratch file)

```
fun main(args: Array<String>) {
    val omSymbol = '\u0950'
    print(omSymbol)
}
```

You will see the ॐ symbol printed in the console.

For the More Curious: Traversing a String's Characters

The String type includes other functions that move through the sequence of characters one at a time, as **indexOf** and **split** do. For example, you can print each character of the tavern data, one character at a time, using String's **forEach** function. This call:

```
"Dragon's Breath".forEach {
    println("$it\n")
}
```

Would generate the following output:

```
D
r
a
g
o
n
'
s

B
r
e
a
t
h
```

Many of these functions are also available on the List type, just as the majority of the functions for traversing lists that you will learn about in Chapter 10 are also available for strings. In many ways, a Kotlin String behaves like a list of characters.

Challenge: Improving DragonSpeak

Currently, **toDragonSpeak** only works on lowercase letters. For example, the following exclamation would not be rendered correctly as DragonSpeak output:

```
DRAGON'S BREATH: IT'S GOT WHAT ADVENTURERS CRAVE!
```

Improve the **toDragonSpeak** function to work with capital letters.

8

Numbers

Kotlin has a variety of types for dealing with numbers and numeric computations. Multiple types are available for each of the two main varieties of numbers that Kotlin can work with: whole-number integers and numbers with decimals. In this chapter, you will see how Kotlin handles both varieties as you update NyetHack to implement the player's purse and allow money to change hands at the tavern.

Numeric Types

All numeric types in Kotlin, as in Java, are *signed*, meaning they can represent both positive and negative numbers. In addition to whether they support decimal values, the numeric types differ in the number of bits they are allocated in memory and, consequently, their minimum and maximum values.

Table 8.1 shows some of the numeric types in Kotlin, the number of bits for each type, and the maximum and minimum value the type supports. (We will explain these details in a moment.)

Table 8.1 Commonly used numeric types

Type	Bits	Max Value	Min Value
Byte	8	127	-128
Short	16	32767	-32768
Int	32	2147483647	-2147483648
Long	64	9223372036854775807	-9223372036854775808
Float	32	3.4028235E38	1.4E-45
Double	64	1.7976931348623157E308	4.9E-324

What is the relationship between a type's bit size and its maximum and minimum values? Computers store integers in binary form with a fixed number of bits ("bit" is short for "binary digit," by the way). A bit is represented by a single 0 or 1.

To represent a number, Kotlin assigns a finite number of bits, depending on the numeric type chosen. The leftmost bit position represents the sign (the positive or negative nature of the number). The remaining bit positions each represent a power of 2, with the rightmost position being 2^0. To compute the value of a binary number, add up each of the powers of 2 whose bit is a 1.

Figure 8.1 shows the example of the number 42 in binary form.

Figure 8.1 42 in binary

$$\boxed{1}\ \boxed{0}\ \boxed{1}\ \boxed{0}\ \boxed{1}\ \boxed{0} = 2^1 + 2^3 + 2^5 = 2 + 8 + 32 = 42$$
$$2^5\ 2^4\ 2^3\ 2^2\ 2^1\ 2^0$$

Since Int is 32 bit, the largest number that can be stored in an Int is represented, in its binary form, with 31 1s. Adding up all those powers of 2 yields a total of 2,147,483,647, the largest value an Int in Kotlin can hold.

Because the number of bits determines the maximum and minimum value a numeric type can represent, the difference between the types is the number of bits available to represent the number. Since Long uses 64 bits instead of 32, a Long can hold an exponentially larger number (2^{63}).

A note about the types Short and Byte. The long and short of it (sorry) is that neither Short or Byte is commonly used when representing conventional numbers. They are used for specialized cases and to support interoperability with legacy Java programs. For example, you might work with Byte when reading a stream of data from a file or processing graphics (a color pixel is often represented as three bytes: one for each color in RGB). You will sometimes see Short used when interacting with native code for CPUs that do not support 32 bit instructions. However, for most purposes, whole numbers are represented with Int or, when a greater value is needed, Long.

Integers

You learned in Chapter 2 that an integer is a number that does not have a decimal point – a whole number – and is represented in Kotlin with the Int type. Int is good for representing a quantity or count of "things": the remaining pints of mead, the number of tavern patrons, or the count of gold and silver coins a player possesses.

Time to do some coding. Open Tavern.kt and add Int variables to represent the current gold and silver in the player's purse. Uncomment the call to **placeOrder** to pass the menu data for an order of Dragon's Breath and remove your order of a Shirley's Temple.

Also, add a placeholder **performPurchase** function that will handle the logic for making a purchase and a function to display the player's current purse balance. Call the new **performPurchase** in **placeOrder**.

Listing 8.1 Setting up the player's purse (`Tavern.kt`)

```kotlin
const val TAVERN_NAME = "Taernyl's Folly"

var playerGold = 10
var playerSilver = 10

fun main(args: Array<String>) {
//  placeOrder("shandy,Dragon's Breath,5.91")
    placeOrder("elixir,Shirley's Temple,4.12")
}

fun performPurchase() {
    displayBalance()
}

private fun displayBalance() {
    println("Player's purse balance: Gold: $playerGold , Silver: $playerSilver")
}

private fun toDragonSpeak(phrase: String) =
        ...
        }

private fun placeOrder(menuData: String) {
    val indexOfApostrophe = TAVERN_NAME.indexOf('\'')
    val tavernMaster = TAVERN_NAME.substring(0 until indexOfApostrophe)
    println("Madrigal speaks with $tavernMaster about their order.")

    val (type, name, price) = menuData.split(',')
    val message = "Madrigal buys a $name ($type) for $price."
    println(message)

    performPurchase()

    val phrase = if (name == "Dragon's Breath") {
        "Madrigal exclaims ${toDragonSpeak("Ah, delicious $name!")}"
    } else {
        "Madrigal says: Thanks for the $name."
    }
    println(phrase)
}
```

Notice that you used an `Int` to represent the player's gold and silver quantities. The max quantity of gold and silver in the player's purse (and in the known NyetHack universe) will be much less than 2,147,483,647, the max value for an `Int`.

Go ahead and run `Tavern.kt`. You have not yet implemented the logic for showing that the player has paid for an item, so this time Madrigal gets their order on the house:

```
Madrigal speaks with Taernyl about their order.
Madrigal buys a Dragon's Breath (shandy) for 5.91.
Player's purse balance: Gold: 10 , Silver: 10
Madrigal exclaims: Ah, d3l1c10|_|s Dr4g0n's Br34th!
```

Decimal Numbers

Take another look at the `menuData` string for the tavern:

    "shandy,Dragon's Breath,5.91"

Madrigal needs to pay 5.91 gold for the Dragon's Breath, so `playerGold` should decrease by 5.91 when the drink is ordered.

Numeric values with decimal places are represented with the `Float` or `Double` type. Update `Tavern.kt` so that a double with the value for the item is passed to the **performPurchase** function:

Listing 8.2 Passing the price information (`Tavern.kt`)

```kotlin
const val TAVERN_NAME = "Taernyl's Folly"
...

fun performPurchase(price: Double) {
    displayBalance()
    println("Purchasing item for $price")
}
...

private fun placeOrder(menuData: String) {
    ...

    val (type, name, price) = menuData.split(',')
    val message = "Madrigal buys a $name ($type) for $price."
    println(message)

    performPurchase(price)
    ...
}
```

Converting a String to a Numeric Type

If you were to run `Tavern.kt` right now, you would see a compilation error. This is because the price variable that you are currently passing to **performPurchase** is a string, and the function expects a double. To the human eye, "5.91" might look like a number, but the Kotlin compiler sees it differently, because it was split from the `menuData` string.

The good news is that Kotlin includes functions that convert strings to different types – including numbers. Some of the most commonly used of these conversion functions are:

- **toFloat**
- **toDouble**
- **toDoubleOrNull**
- **toIntOrNull**
- **toLong**
- **toBigDecimal**

Attempting to convert a string of the wrong format will throw an exception. For example, calling **toInt** on a string with the value "5.91" would throw an exception, since the decimal portion of the string value would not fit into an `Int`.

Because of the possibility of exceptions when converting between different numeric types, Kotlin also provides the safe conversion functions **toDoubleOrNull** and **toIntOrNull**. When the number does not convert correctly, a null value is returned instead of an exception. You could use the null coalescing operator with **toIntOrNull**, for example, to provide a default value:

```
val gold: Int = "5.91".toIntOrNull() ?: 0
```

Update **placeOrder** to convert the string argument to **performPurchase** to a double.

Listing 8.3 Converting the price argument to a double (Tavern.kt)

```
...
private fun placeOrder(menuData: String) {
    val indexOfApostrophe = TAVERN_NAME.indexOf('\'')
    val tavernMaster = TAVERN_NAME.substring(0 until indexOfApostrophe)
    println("Madrigal speaks with $tavernMaster about their order.")

    val (type, name, price) = menuData.split(',')
    val message = "Madrigal buys a $name ($type) for $price."
    println(message)

    performPurchase(price.toDouble())
    ...
}
```

Converting an Int to a Double

Now to take the gold out of the player's purse. The purse contains whole gold and silver coins, but the price of a menu item is represented in gold as a double.

To do the sale, you first need to convert the player's gold and silver to a single double so that the item price can be subtracted. Add a new variable to **performPurchase** to track the player's total purse. One gold is worth 100 silver, so divide the player's silver by 100 and add the result to the quantity of gold to get the total value. The totalPurse and price variables are of the same type, Double, so subtract the price from the purse and assign the result to a new variable.

Listing 8.4 Subtracting the price from the player's purse (Tavern.kt)

```
...
fun performPurchase(price: Double) {
    displayBalance()
    val totalPurse = playerGold + (playerSilver / 100.0)
    println("Total purse: $totalPurse")
    println("Purchasing item for $price")

    val remainingBalance = totalPurse - price
}
...
```

First, you do the calculation for getting the totalPurse and print the result. Notice that the division to convert playerSilver for totalPurse includes a decimal point for the divisor – 100.0, not 100.

If you were to divide playerSilver, an Int, by 100, also an Int, Kotlin would not give you 0.10, a Double. Instead, you would get another Int – 0, in fact – that loses the decimal result you are looking for. (Try it in the REPL.)

Because both numbers in the operation are integers, Kotlin performs integer arithmetic, which does not support a result with a decimal.

To get a decimal result, you need Kotlin to perform floating-point arithmetic, which you achieve by including in the operation at least one type that supports a decimal. Try the calculation in the REPL again, but this time add a decimal to either number to indicate that floating-point arithmetic should be used and the result should be a Double (0.1).

With the player's purse converted to totalPurse, you next subtract the price of the Dragon's Breath from the converted purse value:

```
val remainingBalance = totalPurse - price
```

To see the result of this calculation, enter 10.1 - 5.91 in the REPL. If you have not worked with numeric types in another programming language, the result might be surprising.

You might have assumed a result of 4.19, but what you get is 4.1899999999999995. This result is due to the way computers represent fractional quantities: by using a *floating point*. A floating point, meaning a decimal that can be positioned at an arbitrary place ("float"), is an *approximation* of a real number. A floating point number approximates its value to support both precision (the ability to represent a wide range of numbers with varying levels of decimal places) and performance (speedy calculations).

How precisely you represent a number with a fractional portion depends on the type of calculation required. For example, if you were programming the mainframe for the central bank of NyetHack, processing a high volume of financial transactions and involved fractional computations, you would represent those transactions using a very high level of precision, at the cost of some processing time. Generally speaking, for this sort of financial calculation you would use a type called BigDecimal to specify the precision and rounding of the floating point calculations. (This is the same BigDecimal type that you may be familiar with from Java.)

For your tavern simulation, however, you can accept the very small degree of imprecision in Double.

Formatting a Double

Rather than working with 4.1899999999999995 pieces of gold, you will round the value up to 4.19. String's **format** function can be used to round a double to a precision that you define. Update the **performPurchase** function to format the remaining balance amount:

Listing 8.5 Formatting a double (Tavern.kt)

```
...
fun performPurchase(price: Double) {
    displayBalance()
    val totalPurse = playerGold + (playerSilver / 100.0)
    println("Total purse: $totalPurse")
    println("Purchasing item for $price")

    val remainingBalance = totalPurse - price
    println("Remaining balance: ${"%.2f".format(remainingBalance)}")
}
...
```

The gold remaining in the purse is interpolated into the string using $, as you have seen before. But what follows the $ is not simply the name of the variable – it is an expression in curly braces. Within the braces is a call to **format** with remainingBalance passed in as the argument.

The call to **format** also specifies a format string, "%.2f". A format string uses a special sequence of characters to define how you want to format data. The particular format string you defined specifies that you want to round the floating point number up to the second decimal place. Then you pass the value or values to format as an argument to the **format** function.

Kotlin's format strings use the same style as the standard format strings in Java, C/C++, Ruby, and many other languages. For details on format string specification, take a look at the Java API documentation at docs.oracle.com/javase/8/docs/api/java/util/Formatter.html.

Run Tavern.kt. You will see that Madrigal now pays for the Dragon's Breath:

```
Madrigal speaks with Taernyl about their order.
Madrigal buys a Dragon's Breath (shandy) for 5.91.
Player's purse balance: Gold: 10 , Silver: 10
Total purse: 10.1
Purchasing item for 5.91
Remaining balance: 4.19
Madrigal exclaims Ah, d3l1c10|_|s Dr4g0n's Br34th!
```

Converting a Double to an Int

Now that the player's remaining balance has been calculated, all that is left to do is to convert the remaining balance back to gold and silver amounts. Update the **performPurchase** function to convert the player's total purse value to gold and silver. (Make sure to add the import kotlin.math.roundToInt statement at the top of the file.)

Listing 8.6 Converting to silver and gold (Tavern.kt)

```
import kotlin.math.roundToInt
const val TAVERN_NAME = "Taernyl's Folly"
...

fun performPurchase(price: Double) {
    displayBalance()
    val totalPurse = playerGold + (playerSilver / 100.0)
    println("Total purse: $totalPurse")
    println("Purchasing item for $price")

    val remainingBalance = totalPurse – price
    println("Remaining balance: ${"%.2f".format(remainingBalance)}")

    val remainingGold = remainingBalance.toInt()
    val remainingSilver = (remainingBalance % 1 * 100).roundToInt()
    playerGold = remainingGold
    playerSilver = remainingSilver
    displayBalance()
}
...
```

Here, you used two of the conversion functions available on Double. Calling **toInt** on a Double results in dropping any fractional value from the double. Another term for this is *loss of precision*. Some portion of the original data is lost, because you asked for an integer representation of a double that included a fractional quantity, and the integer representation is less precise.

Note that calling **toInt** on a double is different than calling **toInt** on a string like "5.91", which would result in an exception being thrown. The difference is that converting a string to a double requires parsing the string to turn it into a numeric type, whereas a type that is already numeric, like Double or Int, does not require any parsing.

In this case, remainingBalance is 4.1899999999999995, so calling **toInt** results in the integer 4. This is the amount of gold the player has remaining.

Next, you convert the fractional portion of the total value to silver:

```
val remainingSilver = (remainingBalance % 1 * 100).roundToInt()
```

Here, you use the *modulus operator* (%, also known as the *remainder operator*), which finds the remainder when one number is divided by another. % 1 has the effect of stripping the whole-number portion of remainingBalance (the portion that can be evenly divided by 1), leaving the decimal value. Finally, you multiply the remainder by 100 to convert to silver and call **roundToInt** on the result, 18.99999999999995. **roundToInt** rounds to the nearest integer, so you are left with 19 silver.

Run Tavern.kt again to see the smooth operation of your Tavern:

```
Madrigal speaks with Taernyl about their order.
Madrigal buys a Dragon's Breath (shandy) for 5.91.
Player's purse balance: Gold: 10 , Silver: 10
Total purse: 10.1
Purchasing item for 5.91
Remaining balance: 4.19
Player's purse balance: Gold: 4 , Silver: 19
Madrigal exclaims Ah, d3l1c10|_|s Dr4g0n's Br34th!
```

In this chapter you have worked with Kotlin's numeric types and learned how Kotlin handles the two major categories of numbers: whole numbers and decimal point numbers. You have also learned how to convert between the different types and what each type supports. In the next chapter, you will learn about Kotlin's standard functions – a set of utility functions available for use with all types.

For the More Curious: Bit Manipulation

Earlier, you saw that numbers have a binary representation. You can get the binary representation for a number at any time. For example, you could ask for the binary representation of the integer 42 with:

```
Integer.toBinaryString(42)
101010
```

Kotlin includes functions for performing operations on the binary representation of a value, called bitwise operations – including operations you may be familiar with from other languages, such as Java. Table 8.2 shows commonly used binary operations available in Kotlin.

Table 8.2 Binary operations

Function	Description	Example
`Integer.toBinaryString`	Converts an integer to binary representation.	`Integer.toBinaryString(42)` `// 101010`
`shl(bitcount)`	Shifts bits left by bitcount.	`42.shl(2)` `// 10101000`
`shr(bitcount)`	Shifts bits right by bitcount.	`42.shr(2)` `// 1010`
`inv()`	Inverts bits.	`42.inv()` `// 11111111111111111111111111010101`
`xor(number)`	Compares two binary representations and performs a logical 'exclusive or' operation on the corresponding bit positions, returning 1 for each bit position that has a 1 in one input but not the other.	`42.xor(33)` `// 001011`
`and(number)`	Compares two binary representations and performs a logical 'and' operation on the corresponding bit positions, returning 1 for each bit position that has a 1 in both inputs.	`42.and(10)` `// 1010`

Challenge: Remaining Pints

When a Dragon's Breath is sold, it is drafted from the cask, which holds 5 gallons. Assuming an order is one pint (.125 gallons), track the remaining quantity of Dragon's Breath. Display the number of pints left in the cask after 12 pints have been sold.

Challenge: Handling a Negative Balance

Currently, Madrigal can place an order no matter how little gold and silver is in their purse – even if there is none. This is an unsustainable business model for Taernyl's Folly. In this challenge you will correct that.

Update the code for **performPurchase** to determine whether the purchase can be performed. If it cannot, no money should change hands, and instead of the message "Madrigal buys a Dragon's Breath (shandy) for 5.91", a message from the bartender explaining that the customer is short on gold should be printed. To simulate multiple orders, call **performPurchase** several times in the **placeOrder** function.

Challenge: Dragoncoin

A new currency is sweeping the land: dragoncoin – instant, secure, and anonymous to spend at any tavern. Assuming the current valuation is 1.43 gold per dragoncoin, represent the player's purchase in dragoncoin instead of silver and gold. Tavern prices remain defined in gold prices. Your player starts the game with 5 dragoncoin. For a single purchase of Dragon's Breath that costs 5.91 gold, make sure the player's remaining dragoncoin balance is .8671 after the purchase.

9

Standard Functions

Standard functions are general utility functions in the Kotlin standard library that accept lambdas to specify their work. In this chapter you will meet the six most commonly used standard functions – `apply`, `let`, `run`, `with`, `also`, and `takeIf` – and see examples of what they can do.

This is not a hands-on chapter, and you will not be adding to NyetHack or Sandbox. As always, however, we encourage you to experiment with the code examples in the REPL.

In this chapter we will refer to an instance of a type using the term *receiver*. This is because Kotlin's standard functions are *extension functions* under the hood, and *receiver* is the term for the subject of an extension function. You will learn about extensions, which are a flexible way to define functions for use with different types, in Chapter 18.

apply

First on our tour of the standard functions is `apply`. `apply` can be thought of as a configuration function: It allows you to call a series of functions on a receiver to configure it for use. After the lambda provided to `apply` executes, `apply` returns the configured receiver.

`apply` can be used to reduce the amount of repetition when configuring an object for use. Here is an example of configuring a file instance without `apply`:

```
val menuFile = File("menu-file.txt")
menuFile.setReadable(true)
menuFile.setWritable(true)
menuFile.setExecutable(false)
```

Using `apply`, the same configuration can be achieved with less repetition:

```
val menuFile = File("menu-file.txt").apply {
    setReadable(true)
    setWritable(true)
    setExecutable(false)
}
```

`apply` allows you to drop the variable name from every function call performed to configure the receiver. This is because `apply` scopes each function call within the lambda to the receiver it is called on.

This behavior is sometimes referred to as *relative scoping*, because all the function calls within the lambda are now called relative to the receiver. Another way to say this is that they are *implicitly called* on the receiver:

```
val menuFile = File("menu-file.txt").apply {
    setReadable(true)   // Implicitly, menuFile.setReadable(true)
    setWritable(true)   // Implicitly, menuFile.setWritable(true)
    setExecutable(false)  // Implicitly, menuFile.setExecutable(false)
}
```

let

Another commonly used standard function is **let**, which you encountered in Chapter 6. **let** scopes a variable to the lambda provided and makes the keyword it, which you learned about in Chapter 5, available to refer to it. Here is an example of **let**, which squares the first number in a list:

```
val firstItemSquared = listOf(1,2,3).first().let {
    it * it
}
```

Without **let**, you would need to assign the first element to a variable to do the multiplication:

```
val firstElement = listOf(1,2,3).first()
val firstItemSquared = firstElement * firstElement
```

When combined with other Kotlin syntax, **let** provides additional benefits. You saw in Chapter 6 that the null coalescing operator and **let** can be combined to work on a nullable type. Consider the following example that customizes a greeting message depending on whether a player is recognized by the tavern master:

```
fun formatGreeting(vipGuest: String?): String {
    return vipGuest?.let {
        "Welcome, $it. Please, go straight back - your table is ready."
    } ?: "Welcome to the tavern. You'll be seated soon."
}
```

Since the vipGuest string is nullable, it is important to deal with the possibility of null before calling functions on it. Using the safe call operator means that **let** executes if and only if the string is non-null – and, if **let** is executed, that means that the it argument is non-null.

Compare **formatGreeting** using **let** with a version that does not use **let**:

```
fun formatGreeting(vipGuest: String?): String {
    return if (vipGuest != null) {
        "Welcome, $vipGuest. Please, go straight back - your table is ready."
    } else {
        "Welcome to the tavern. You'll be seated shortly."
    }
}
```

This version of **formatGreeting** is functionally equivalent, but slightly more verbose. The if/else structure uses the full vipGuest variable name twice: once in the condition and once to create the resulting string. **let**, on the other hand, allows a fluent or *chainable* style that only requires the variable name to be used one time.

let can be called on any kind of receiver and returns the result of evaluating the lambda you provide. Here, **let** is called on a nullable string, vipGuest. The lambda passed to **let** accepts the receiver it is called on as its only argument. You can therefore access the argument using the it keyword.

Several differences between **let** and **apply** are worth mentioning: As you saw, **let** passes the receiver to the lambda you provide, but **apply** passes nothing. Also, **apply** returns the current receiver once the anonymous function completes. **let**, on the other hand, returns the last line of the lambda (the lambda result).

Standard functions like **let** can also be used to reduce the risk of accidentally changing a variable, because the argument **let** passes to the lambda is a read-only function parameter. You will see an example of this application of standard functions in Chapter 12.

run

Next up on our tour of the standard functions is **run**. **run** is similar to **apply** in that it provides the same relative scoping behavior. However, unlike **apply**, **run** does not return the receiver.

Say you wanted to check whether a file contains a particular string:

```
val menuFile = File("menu-file.txt")
val servesDragonsBreath = menuFile.run {
    readText().contains("Dragon's Breath")
}
```

The **readText** function is implicitly performed on the receiver – the File instance. This is just like the **setReadable**, **setWriteable**, and **setExecutable** functions you saw with **apply**. However, unlike **apply**, **run** returns the lambda result – here, a true or false value.

run can also be used to execute a function reference on a receiver. You used function references in Chapter 5; here is an example that shows their use with **run**:

```
fun nameIsLong(name: String) = name.length >= 20

"Madrigal".run(::nameIsLong)  // False
"Polarcubis, Supreme Master of NyetHack".run(::nameIsLong) // True
```

While code like this is equivalent to nameIsLong("Madrigal"), the benefits of using **run** become clear when there are multiple function calls: Chained calls using **run** are easier to read and follow than nested function calls. For example, consider the following code that checks whether a player's name is 10 characters or longer, formats a message depending on the result, and prints the result.

```
fun nameIsLong(name: String) = name.length >= 20
fun playerCreateMessage(nameTooLong: Boolean): String {
    return if (nameTooLong) {
        "Name is too long. Please choose another name."
    } else {
        "Welcome, adventurer"
    }
}

"Polarcubis, Supreme Master of NyetHack"
    .run(::nameIsLong)
    .run(::playerCreateMessage)
    .run(::println)
```

Compare the calls chained with **run** to calling the three functions using nested syntax:

```
println(playerCreateMessage(nameIsLong("Polarcubis, Supreme Master of NyetHack")))
```

The nested function calls are more difficult to understand because they require the reader to work from the inside out, rather than the more familiar top to bottom.

Note that there is a second flavor of **run** that is not called on a receiver. This form is far less commonly seen, but we include it here for completeness:

```
val status = run {
    if (healthPoints == 100) "perfect health" else "has injuries"
}
```

with

with is a variant of **run**. It behaves identically, but it uses a different calling convention. Unlike the standard functions you have seen so far, **with** requires its argument to be accepted as the first parameter rather than calling the standard function on a receiver type:

```
val nameTooLong = with("Polarcubis, Supreme Master of NyetHack") {
    length >= 20
}
```

Instead of calling **with** on the string, as in "Polarcubis, Supreme Master of NyetHack".run, the string is passed as the first (in this case, only) argument to **with**.

This is inconsistent with the way you work with the rest of the standard functions, making it a less favorable choice than **run**. In fact, we recommend avoiding **with** and using **run** instead. We are including **with** here so that if you encounter it in the wild you will know what it means (and possibly consider replacing it with **run**).

also

The **also** function works very similarly to the **let** function. Just like **let**, **also** passes the receiver you call it on as an argument to a lambda you provide. But there is one major difference between **let** and **also**: **also** returns the receiver, rather than the result of the lambda.

This makes **also** especially useful for adding multiple side effects from a common source. In the example below, **also** is called twice to organize two different operations: One prints the filename, and the other assigns a variable, fileContents, with the contents of the file.

```
var fileContents: List<String>
File("file.txt")
        .also {
            print(it.name)
        }.also {
            fileContents = it.readLines()
        }
}
```

Since **also** returns the receiver instead of the result of the lambda, you can continue to chain additional function calls on to the original receiver.

takeIf

The last stop on our tour of the standard functions is **takeIf**. **takeIf** works a bit differently than the other standard functions: It evaluates a condition provided in a lambda, called a *predicate*, that returns either true or false depending on the conditions defined. If the condition evaluates as true, the receiver is returned from **takeIf**. If the condition is false, null is returned instead.

Consider the following example, which reads a file if and only if it is readable and writable.

```
val fileContents = File("myfile.txt")
        .takeIf { it.canRead() && it.canWrite() }
        ?.readText()
```

Without **takeIf**, this would be more verbose:

```
val file = File("myfile.txt")
val fileContents = if (file.canRead() && file.canWrite()) {
    file.readText()
} else {
    null
}
```

The **takeIf** version does not require the temporary variable file, nor does it need to specify the possibility of a null return. **takeIf** is useful for checking that some condition required for assigning a variable or proceeding with work is true before continuing. Conceptually, **takeIf** is similar to an if statement, but with the advantage of being directly callable on an instance, often allowing you to remove a temporary variable assignment.

takeUnless

We said that the tour was over, but there is a complementary function to **takeIf** that we should mention, if only to warn you away from it: **takeUnless**. The **takeUnless** function is exactly like **takeIf** except that it returns the original value if the condition you define is *false*. This example reads the file if it is not hidden (and returns null otherwise):

```
val fileContents = File("myfile.txt").takeUnless { it.isHidden }?.readText()
```

We recommend that you limit the use of **takeUnless**, especially for more complicated condition-checking, because it takes longer for human readers of your program to interpret. Compare the "understandability" of these two phrases:

- "Return the value if the condition is true" – **takeIf**
- "Return the value unless the condition is true" – **takeUnless**

If you found yourself having to pause slightly for the second phrase, you are like us: **takeUnless** seems to be a less natural way of describing the logic you want to express.

For simple conditions (as in the example above), **takeUnless** is not problematic. But with more complicated examples, we find **takeUnless** is harder to parse (for human brains, anyway).

Using Standard Library Functions

Table 9.1 summarizes the Kotlin standard library functions discussed in this chapter:

Table 9.1 Standard functions

Function	Passes receiver to lambda as argument?	Provides relative scoping?	Returns
`let`	Yes	No	Lambda result
`apply`	No	Yes	Receiver
`run`[a]	No	Yes	Lambda result
`with`[b]	No	Yes	Lambda result
`also`	Yes	No	Receiver
`takeIf`	Yes	No	Nullable version of receiver
`takeUnless`	Yes	No	Nullable version of receiver

[a]The non-receiver version of `run` (less commonly used) passes no receiver, performs no relative scoping, and returns the lambda result.

[b]`with` is not called on the receiver like this: "hello.with {..}". Instead, it treats the first argument as the receiver, the second being the lambda, like this: with("hello"){..}. It is the only standard function that works this way, which is why we recommend avoiding it.

In this chapter, you saw how to simplify your code using standard functions. They give you the ability to write code that is not only concise but also has the unique feel of Kotlin. We will use standard functions in the rest of this book where applicable.

In Chapter 2, you saw how to represent data using variables. In the next chapter, you will learn how to represent series of data with variables of Kotlin's List and Set collection types.

10

Lists and Sets

Working with a group of related values is an essential part of many programs. For example, your program might manage lists of books, travel destinations, menu items, or tavern patron check balances. *Collections* allow you to conveniently work with those groups of values and pass them as arguments to functions.

You will see the most commonly used collection types in the next two chapters: List, Set, and Map. Like the other variable types you learned about in Chapter 2, lists, sets, and maps come in two distinct varieties: mutable and read-only. In this chapter, we will focus on lists and sets.

You are going to use collections to upgrade NyetHack's tavern. When your work is finished, the tavern will sport a full menu of items for purchase – along with a bustling scene of patrons eager to spend their gold.

Lists

You worked indirectly with a list in Chapter 7, when you used the **split** function to extract three elements from the menu data. Lists hold an ordered collection of values and allow duplicate values.

Begin your tavern simulation in Tavern.kt by adding a list of patrons, using the **listOf** function. **listOf** returns a read-only list (more on that shortly) populated with the elements you provide for the argument. Create your list with three patron names:

Listing 10.1 Creating a list of patrons (Tavern.kt)

```
import kotlin.math.roundToInt
const val TAVERN_NAME = "Taernyl's Folly"

var playerGold = 10
var playerSilver = 10
val patronList: List<String> = listOf("Eli", "Mordoc", "Sophie")

fun main(args: Array<String>) {
    placeOrder("shandy,Dragon's Breath,5.91")

    println(patronList)
}
...
```

Up to now, you have been creating variables of various types by simply declaring them. But collections require two steps: creating the collection (here, the list to hold the patrons) and adding contents to it (the patron names). Kotlin provides functions, like **listOf**, that do both at once.

Now that you have a list, let's take a closer look at the `List` type.

Though type inference does work with lists, you included the type information – `val patronList: List<String>` – to make it visible for discussion. Notice the diamond braces in `List<String>`. `<String>` is known as a *parameterized type*, and it tells the compiler about the type that the contents of the list will be – in this case, `Strings`. Changing the type parameter changes what the compiler allows the list to hold.

If you tried to put an integer in the `patronList`, the compiler would not allow it. Try adding a number to the list you defined:

Listing 10.2 Adding an integer to a list of strings (`Tavern.kt`)

```
...
var patronList: List<String> = listOf("Eli", "Mordoc", "Sophie", 1)
...
```

IntelliJ warns you that the integer does not conform to the expected type, `String`. Type parameters are used with `List` because `List` is a *generic type*. This means that a list can hold any type of data, including textual data like strings (as in the case of `patronList`) or characters, numeric data like integers or doubles, or even a new type that you define. (You will learn more about generics in Chapter 17.)

Undo your last change, either with IntelliJ's undo command (Command-z [Ctrl-z]) or by deleting the integer:

Listing 10.3 Correcting the list contents (`Tavern.kt`)

```
...
var patronList: List<String> = listOf("Eli", "Mordoc", "Sophie", 1)
...
```

Accessing a list's elements

Recall from your work with the **split** function in Chapter 7 that you can access any element of a list using the element's index and the [] operator. Lists are *zero-indexed*, so `"Eli"` is at index 0, and `"Sophie"` is at index 2.

Change `Tavern.kt` to print only the first patron. Also, remove the explicit type information from `patronList`. Now that you have seen the parameterized type that this `List` uses, you can return to using type inference for cleaner code.

Listing 10.4 Accessing the first patron (`Tavern.kt`)

```
import kotlin.math.roundToInt
const val TAVERN_NAME = "Taernyl's Folly"

var playerGold = 10
var playerSilver = 10
val patronList: List<String> = listOf("Eli", "Mordoc", "Sophie")

fun main(args: Array<String>) {
    placeOrder("shandy,Dragon's Breath,5.91")

    println(patronList[0])
}
...
```

Run `Tavern.kt`. You will see the first patron, `Eli`, printed.

`List` also provides other convenience index access functions, like accessing the first or last element:

```
patronList.first() // Eli
patronList.last() // Sophie
```

Index boundaries and safe index access

Accessing an element by index requires care, because attempting to access an element at an index that does not exist – say, the fourth item from a list that contains only three – causes an `ArrayIndexOutOfBoundsException` exception.

Try this in the Kotlin REPL. (You can copy the first line from `Tavern.kt`.)

Listing 10.5 Accessing a nonexistent index (REPL)

```
val patronList = listOf("Eli", "Mordoc", "Sophie")
patronList[4]
```

The result is `java.lang.ArrayIndexOutOfBoundsException: 4`.

Because accessing an element by an index can throw an exception, Kotlin provides safe index access functions that allow you to deal with the problem differently. Instead of throwing an exception if the index is out of bounds, some other result will occur.

For example, one of these safe index access functions, **getOrElse**, takes two arguments: The first is the requested index (in parentheses, not square brackets). The second is a lambda that generates a default value, instead of an exception, if the requested index does not exist.

Try it out in the REPL:

Listing 10.6 Testing **getOrElse** (REPL)

```
val patronList = listOf("Eli", "Mordoc", "Sophie")
patronList.getOrElse(4) { "Unknown Patron" }
```

This time, the result is `Unknown Patron`. The anonymous function was used to provide a default value, since the requested index does not exist.

Another safe index access function, **getOrNull**, returns null instead of throwing an exception. When you use **getOrNull**, you must decide what to do with the null value, as you saw in Chapter 6. One option is to coalesce the null value to a default. Try using **getOrNull** with the null coalescing operator in the REPL.

Listing 10.7 Testing **getOrNull** (REPL)

```
val fifthPatron = patronList.getOrNull(4) ?: "Unknown Patron"
fifthPatron
```

Again, the result is `Unknown Patron`.

Checking the contents of a list

The tavern has dark corners and secret back rooms. Fortunately, the keen-eyed tavern master keeps diligent records of which patrons have left or entered in the patron list. If you ask whether a particular patron is present, the tavern master can tell you by looking at the list.

Update `Tavern.kt` to use the **contains** function to check whether a particular patron is present:

Listing 10.8 Checking for a patron (`Tavern.kt`)

```
...
fun main(args: Array<String>) {
    if (patronList.contains("Eli")) {
        println("The tavern master says: Eli's in the back playing cards.")
    } else {
        println("The tavern master says: Eli isn't here.")
    }

    placeOrder("shandy,Dragon's Breath,5.91")

    println(patronList[0])
}
...
```

Run `Tavern.kt`. Because `patronList` does contain `"Eli"`, you will see `The tavern master says: Eli's in the back playing cards.` in the console above the output from your **placeOrder** call.

Note that the **contains** function performs a structural comparison for the elements in the list, like the structural equality operator.

You can also use the **containsAll** function to check whether several patrons are present at once. Update the code to ask the tavern master whether both Sophie and Mordoc are present:

Listing 10.9 Checking for multiple patrons (`Tavern.kt`)

```
...
fun main(args: Array<String>) {
    if (patronList.contains("Eli")) {
        println("The tavern master says: Eli's in the back playing cards. ")
    } else {
        println("The tavern master says: Eli isn't here.")
    }

    if (patronList.containsAll(listOf("Sophie", "Mordoc"))) {
        println("The tavern master says: Yea, they're seated by the stew kettle.")
    } else {
        println("The tavern master says: Nay, they departed hours ago.")
    }

    placeOrder("shandy,Dragon's Breath,5.91")
}
...
```

Run `Tavern.kt`. You will see the following printed:

```
The tavern master says: Eli's in the back playing cards.
The tavern master says: Yea, they're seated by the stew kettle.
...
```

Changing a list's contents

If a patron shows up or leaves halfway through the night, the watchful tavern master needs to add or remove the patron's name from the patronList variable. Currently, that is not possible.

listOf returns a read-only list that does not allow changes to its contents: You cannot add, remove, update, or replace entries. Read-only lists are a good idea, because they prevent unfortunate mistakes – like kicking a patron out into the cold by accidentally removing them from the list.

The read-only nature of the list has nothing to do with the val or var keyword you used to define the list variable. Changing the variable declaration for patronList from val (as it is defined now) to var would not change the list from read-only to writable. Instead, it would allow you to reassign the patronList variable to hold a new, different list.

List mutability is defined by the *type* of the list and refers to whether you can modify the elements in the list. Since patrons come and go from the tavern freely, the type of patronList needs to be changed to allow updates. In Kotlin, a modifiable list is known as a *mutable list*, and you use the mutableListOf function to create one.

Update Tavern.kt to use **mutableListOf** instead of **listOf**. Mutable lists come with a variety of functions for adding, removing, and updating items. Simulate several patrons coming and going by using the **add** and **remove** functions:

Listing 10.10 Making the patron list mutable (Tavern.kt)

```
...
val patronList = listOf("Eli", "Mordoc", "Sophie")
val patronList = mutableListOf("Eli", "Mordoc", "Sophie")

fun main(args: Array<String>) {
    ...
    placeOrder("shandy,Dragon's Breath,5.91")

    println(patronList)
    patronList.remove("Eli")
    patronList.add("Alex")
    println(patronList)
}
...
```

Run Tavern.kt. You will see the following printed to the console:

```
...
Madrigal exclaims Ah, d3l1c10|_|s Dr4g0n's Br34th!
[Eli, Mordoc, Sophie]
[Mordoc, Sophie, Alex]
```

The read-only nature of the list has nothing to do with the val or var keyword you used to define the list variable. Changing the variable declaration for patronList from val (as it is defined now) to var would not change the list from read-only to writable. Instead, you would be able to reassign the patronList variable to hold a new, different list.

List mutability is defined by the *type* of the list and refers to whether you can modify the elements in the list. When you need to be able to modify the elements in a list, use a MutableList. Otherwise, it is a good idea to restrict mutability by using List.

133

Note that the new element was added at the end of the list. You can also add a patron at a particular position in the list. For example, if a VIP comes into the tavern, the tavern master can prioritize their place in line.

Add a VIP patron – coincidentally also with the name Alex – to the beginning of the patron list. (This Alex is well-known around town and enjoys perks like getting a pint of Dragon's Breath before everyone else, much to the chagrin of the other Alex.) List supports multiple elements with the same value, such as two patrons with the same name, so adding another Alex is no problem for the list.

Listing 10.11 Adding another Alex (Tavern.kt)

```
...
val patronList = mutableListOf("Eli", "Mordoc", "Sophie")

fun main(args: Array<String>) {
    ...
    placeOrder("shandy,Dragon's Breath,5.91")

    println(patronList)
    patronList.remove("Eli")
    patronList.add("Alex")
    patronList.add(0, "Alex")
    println(patronList)
}
...
```

Run Tavern.kt again. You will see the following printed:

```
...
[Eli, Mordoc, Sophie]
[Alex, Mordoc, Sophie, Alex]
```

To change patronList from a read-only list to a mutable list, you changed your code to use **mutableListOf** instead of **listOf**. List also provides functions for moving between read-only and mutable versions on the fly: **toList** and **toMutableList**. For example, you could create a read-only version of the mutable patronList using **toList**:

```
val patronList = mutableListOf("Eli", "Mordoc", "Sophie")
val readOnlyPatronList = patronList.toList()
```

Say that the famous Alex would prefer to go by Alexis. Respect this wish by modifying patronList using the set operator ([]=) to reassign the string at the first index in the list.

Listing 10.12 Modifying a mutable list using the set operator (Tavern.kt)

```
...
val patronList = mutableListOf("Eli", "Mordoc", "Sophie")

fun main(args: Array<String>) {
    ...
    placeOrder("shandy,Dragon's Breath,5.91")

    println(patronList)
    patronList.remove("Eli")
    patronList.add("Alex")
    patronList.add(0, "Alex")
    patronList[0] = "Alexis"
    println(patronList)
}
...
```

Run `Tavern.kt`. You will see that `patronList` has been updated with Alexis' preferred name.

```
...
[Eli, Mordoc, Sophie]
[Alexis, Mordoc, Sophie, Alex]
```

Functions that change the contents of a mutable list are called *mutator functions*. Table 10.1 lists the most commonly used mutator functions for lists.

Table 10.1 Mutable list mutator functions

Function	Description	Example(s)
[]= (set operator)	Sets the value at the index; throws an exception if the index does not exist.	```val patronList = mutableListOf("Eli", "Mordoc", "Sophie") patronList[4] = "Reggie" IndexOutOfBoundsException```
add	Adds an element to the end of the list, resizing it by one element.	```val patronList = mutableListOf("Eli", "Mordoc", "Sophie") patronList.add("Reggie") [Eli, Mordoc, Sophie, Reggie] patronList.size 4```
add (at index)	Adds an element to the list at a particular index, resizing the list by one element. Throws an exception if the index does not exist.	```val patronList = mutableListOf("Eli", "Mordoc", "Sophie") patronList.add(0, "Reggie") [Reggie, Eli, Mordoc, Sophie] patronList.add(5, "Sophie") IndexOutOfBoundsException```
addAll	Adds all of another collection with contents of the same type to the list.	```val patronList = mutableListOf("Eli", "Mordoc", "Sophie") patronList.addAll(listOf("Reginald", "Alex")) [Eli, Mordoc, Sophie, Reginald, Alex]```
+= (plus assign operator)	Adds an element or collection of elements to the list.	```mutableListOf("Eli", "Mordoc", "Sophie") += "Reginald" [Eli, Mordoc, Sophie, Reginald] mutableListOf("Eli", "Mordoc", "Sophie") += listOf("Alex", "Shruti") [Eli, Mordoc, Sophie, Alex, Shruti]```
-= (minus assign operator)	Removes an element or collection of elements from the list.	```mutableListOf("Eli", "Mordoc", "Sophie") -= "Eli" [Mordoc, Sophie] val patronList = mutableListOf("Eli", "Mordoc", "Sophie") patronList -= listOf("Eli", Mordoc") [Sophie]```
clear	Removes all the elements from the list.	```mutableListOf("Eli", "Mordoc", Sophie").clear() []```
removeIf	Removes elements from the list based on a predicate lambda.	```val patronList = mutableListOf("Eli", "Mordoc", "Sophie") patronList.removeIf { it.contains("o") } [Eli]```

Iteration

The tavern master makes a point of greeting each patron, as it is just good business to do so. Lists include built-in support for a variety of functions that allow you to perform an action for each element of their contents. This concept is called *iteration*.

One way to iterate through a list is a for loop. Its logic is, "for each element in the list, do something." You give the element a name, and the Kotlin compiler will automatically detect its type for you.

Update Tavern.kt to print a greeting for each patron. (Also, remove the code from earlier that modifies and prints patronList to tidy up your console output.)

Listing 10.13 Iterating over the patronList with for (Tavern.kt)

```
...
fun main(args: Array<String>) {
    ...
    placeOrder("shandy,Dragon's Breath,5.91")

    println(patronList)
    patronList.remove("Eli")
    patronList.add("Alex")
    patronList.add(0, "Alex")
    patronList[0] = "Alexis"
    println(patronList)
    for (patron in patronList) {
        println("Good evening, $patron")
    }
}
...
```

Run Tavern.kt, and the tavern master will greet each patron by name:

```
...
Good evening, Eli
Good evening, Mordoc
Good evening, Sophie
```

In this case, because patronList is of type MutableList<String>, patron will be of type String. Within the block of the for loop, any code that you apply to patron will be applied to all elements in patronList.

In some languages, Java included, the default for loop syntax requires you to work with indices of the array or collection you are iterating through. This is often cumbersome, but it can be useful. The syntax is verbose and not very readable, but you do get a great amount of control over how you iterate.

In Kotlin, all for loops rely on iteration to do their work. If you are familiar with Java or C#, this is equivalent to the foreach loops found in those languages.

For those familiar with Java, it can be surprising to find that the common Java expression for(int i = 0; i < 10; i++) { ... } is not possible in Kotlin. Instead, a for loop is written for(i in 1..10) { ... }. However, at the bytecode level, the compiler will optimize a Kotlin for loop to use the Java version, when possible, to improve performance.

Note the in keyword:

```
for (patron in patronList) { ... }
```

in specifies the object being iterated over in a for loop.

The for loop is simple and readable, but if you prefer a more functional style to your code, then a loop using the **forEach** function is also an option.

The **forEach** function traverses each element in the list – one by one, from left to right – and passes each element to the anonymous function you provide as an argument.

Replace your for loop with the **forEach** function.

Listing 10.14 Iterating over the patronList with **forEach** (Tavern.kt)

```
...
fun main(args: Array<String>) {
    ...
    placeOrder("shandy,Dragon's Breath,5.91")

    for (patron in patronList) {
        println("Good evening, $patron")
    }
    patronList.forEach { patron ->
        println("Good evening, $patron")
    }
}
...
```

Run Tavern.kt, and you will see the same output as before. The for loop and the **forEach** function are functionally equivalent.

Kotlin's for loop and **forEach** function handle indexing behind the scenes. If you also want access to the index of each element in a list as you iterate, use **forEachIndexed**. Update Tavern.kt to use **forEachIndexed** to display each patron's position in line:

Listing 10.15 Displaying line position with **forEachIndexed** (Tavern.kt)

```
...
fun main(args: Array<String>) {
    ...
    placeOrder("shandy,Dragon's Breath,5.91")

    patronList.forEachIndexed { index, patron ->
        println("Good evening, $patron – you're #${index + 1} in line.")
    }
}
...
```

Run `Tavern.kt` again to see the patrons and their positions:

```
...
Good evening, Eli – you're #1 in line.
Good evening, Mordoc – you're #2 in line.
Good evening, Sophie – you're #3 in line.
```

The `forEach` and `forEachIndexed` functions are also available on certain other types in Kotlin. This category of types is called `Iterable`, and `List`, `Set`, `Map`, `IntRange` (ranges like `0..9`, which you saw in Chapter 3), and other collection types belong to the `Iterable` category. An iterable supports iteration – in other words, it allows traversing the elements it holds, performing some action for each element.

Time to get the tavern simulation going. Have each patron place an order for a Dragon's Breath. To do so, move the call to `placeOrder` within the lambda that you passed to the `forEachIndexed` function so that it will be called for each patron in the list. Now that patrons other than Madrigal will be ordering, update `placeOrder` to accept the name of the patron placing the order.

Also, comment out the call to `performPurchase` in `placeOrder`. (You will add it back in the next chapter.)

Listing 10.16 Simulating several orders (`Tavern.kt`)

```
...
fun main(args: Array<String>) {
    ...
    placeOrder("shandy,Dragon's Breath,5.91")

    patronList.forEachIndexed { index, patron ->
        println("Good evening, $patron – you're #${index + 1} in line.")
        placeOrder(patron, "shandy,Dragon's Breath,5.91")
    }
}
...

private fun placeOrder(patronName: String, menuData: String) {
    val indexOfApostrophe = TAVERN_NAME.indexOf('\'')
    val tavernMaster = TAVERN_NAME.substring(0 until indexOfApostrophe)
    println("Madrigal speaks with $tavernMaster about their order.")
    println("$patronName speaks with $tavernMaster about their order.")

    val (type, name, price) = menuData.split(',')
    val message = "Madrigal buys a $name ($type) for $price."
    val message = "$patronName buys a $name ($type) for $price."
    println(message)

//  performPurchase(price.toDouble())
    performPurchase(price.toDouble())

    val phrase = if (name == "Dragon's Breath") {
        "Madrigal exclaims: ${toDragonSpeak("Ah, delicious $name!")}"
        "$patronName exclaims: ${toDragonSpeak("Ah, delicious $name!")}"
    } else {
        "Madrigal says: Thanks for the $name."
        "$patronName says: Thanks for the $name."
    }
    println(phrase)
}
```

Run `Tavern.kt` and watch the tavern spring to life as the three patrons excitedly place their orders for Dragon's Breath:

```
The tavern master says: Eli's in the back playing cards.
The tavern master says: Yea, they're seated by the stew kettle.
Good evening, Eli - you're #1 in line.
Eli speaks with Taernyl about their order.
Eli buys a Dragon's Breath (shandy) for 5.91.
Eli exclaims: Ah, d3l1c10|_|s Dr4g0n's Br34th!
Good evening, Mordoc - you're #2 in line.
Mordoc speaks with Taernyl about their order.
Mordoc buys a Dragon's Breath (shandy) for 5.91.
Mordoc exclaims: Ah, d3l1c10|_|s Dr4g0n's Br34th!
Good evening, Sophie - you're #3 in line.
Sophie speaks with Taernyl about their order.
Sophie buys a Dragon's Breath (shandy) for 5.91.
Sophie exclaims: Ah, d3l1c10|_|s Dr4g0n's Br34th!
```

`Iterable` collections support a variety of functions that let you define an action to perform for each item in the collection. You will learn more about `Iterables` and the other iteration functions in Chapter 19.

Reading a File into a List

Variety is the spice of life – and the tavern master knows that patrons expect a variety of items on the menu. Currently, Dragon's Breath is the only item for sale. Time to fix that by loading up some menu items for patrons to choose from.

To save you some typing, we have provided you with predefined menu data in a text file you can load into NyetHack. The file contains several menu items in the same format as your current Dragon's Breath menu data.

Start by creating a new folder for data: Right-click the NyetHack project in the project tool window and choose New → Directory (Figure 10.1). Name the directory `data`.

Figure 10.1 Creating a new directory

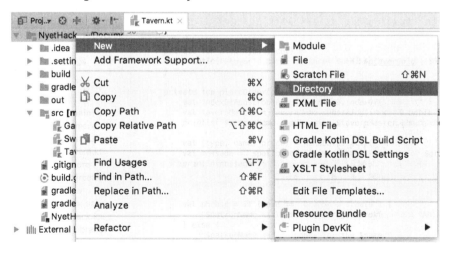

Next, download the menu data from bignerdranch.com/solutions/tavern-menu-data.txt and save it to the data folder you created in a file called tavern-menu-items.txt.

Now you can update Tavern.kt to read the text from that file into a string and call **split** on the resulting string. Make sure to include the java.io.File statement at the very top of Tavern.kt.

Listing 10.17 Reading menu data from a file (Tavern.kt)

```
import java.io.File
...
val patronList = mutableListOf("Eli", "Mordoc", "Sophie")
val menuList = File("data/tavern-menu-items.txt")
                    .readText()
                    .split("\n")
...
```

You used the java.io.File type to work with a particular file by providing a file path.

The **readText** function on File returns the contents of the file as a String. Then you use the **split** function (as you did in Chapter 7) to return a list, splitting on the newline character (represented by the escape sequence '\n').

Now, call **forEachIndexed** on menuList to print out each entry in the List along with its index.

Listing 10.18 Printing the diversified menu (Tavern.kt)

```
...
fun main(args: Array<String>) {
    ...
    patronList.forEachIndexed { index, patron ->
        println("Good evening, $patron - you're #${index + 1} in line.")
        placeOrder(patron, "shandy,Dragon's Breath,5.91")
    }

    menuList.forEachIndexed { index, data ->
        println("$index : $data")
    }
}
...
```

Run Tavern.kt. You will see the menu data that was loaded into the List:

```
...
0 : shandy,Dragon's Breath,5.91
1 : elixir,Shirley's Temple,4.12
2 : meal,goblet of LaCroix,1.22
3 : desert dessert,pickled camel hump,7.33
4 : elixir,iced boilermaker,11.22
```

Now that the `menuList` is loaded, have each patron choose randomly from the menu when placing their order:

Listing 10.19 Placing random orders (`Tavern.kt`)

```
...
fun main(args: Array<String>) {
    ...
    patronList.forEachIndexed { index, patron ->
        println("Good evening, $patron - you're #${index + 1} in line.")
        placeOrder(patron, "shandy,Dragon's Breath,5.91")
        placeOrder(patron, menuList.shuffled().first())
    }

    menuList.forEachIndexed { index, data ->
        println("$index : $data")
    }
}
...
```

Run `Tavern.kt`. You will see each patron place an order for a random item on the menu.

Destructuring

A list also offers the ability to destructure up to the first five elements it contains. Destructuring, as you saw in Chapter 7, allows you to declare and assign multiple variables in a single expression. You are using this destructuring declaration to separate the elements of the menu data:

```
val (type, name, price) = menuData.split(',')
```

This declaration assigns the first three elements in the list returned by the **split** function to string values named `type`, `name`, and `price`.

By the way, you can also selectively destructure elements from a list by using the symbol _ to skip unwanted elements. Say, for example, that the tavern master would like to hand out medals to the best sword jugglers in the realm but has misplaced the silver medal. If you wanted to destructure only the first and third value in the result from splitting the patron list, you could do so with:

```
val (goldMedal, _, bronzeMedal) = patronList
```

Sets

Lists, as you have seen, allow duplicate elements (and are ordered, so duplicates – and other elements – can be identified by their position). But sometimes you want a collection that guarantees that its items are unique. For that, you use a `Set`.

`Sets` are like `Lists` in many ways. They use the same iteration functions, and `Set` also comes in read-only and mutable flavors.

But there are two major differences between lists and sets: The elements of a set are unique, and a set does not provide index-based mutators, because the items in a set are not guaranteed to be in any particular order. (That said, you can still read an element at a particular index, which we will discuss shortly.)

Creating a set

Just as you can create a list using the **listOf** function, you can create a Set using the **setOf** function. Try creating a set in the REPL:

Listing 10.20 Creating a set (REPL)

```
val planets = setOf("Mercury", "Venus", "Earth")
planets
["Mercury", "Venus", "Earth"]
```

If you try to create the planets set with a duplicate, only one of the duplicate items will remain in the set:

Listing 10.21 Trying to create a set with a duplicate (REPL)

```
val planets = setOf("Mercury", "Venus", "Earth", "Earth")
planets
["Mercury", "Venus", "Earth"]
```

The duplicate element "Earth" was dropped from the set.

As with a List, you can check whether a set contains a particular element using **contains** and **containsAll**. Try the **contains** function in the REPL:

Listing 10.22 Checking planets (REPL)

```
planets.contains("Earth")
true
```

```
planets.contains("Pluto")
false
```

Set does not index its contents – meaning it provides no built-in [] operator to access elements using an index. However, you can still request an element at a particular index, using functions that use iteration to accomplish the task. Enter the following into the REPL to read the third planet in the set with the **elementAt** function:

Listing 10.23 Finding the third planet (REPL)

```
val planets = setOf("Mercury", "Venus", "Earth")
planets.elementAt(2)
Earth
```

While this works, using index-based access with a set is an order of magnitude slower than index-based access with a list, because of the way **elementAt** works under the hood. When you call the **elementAt** function on the set, the set iterates to the index you provide, one element at a time. This means that for a large set, requesting an element at a high index would be slower than accessing an element by index in a list. For this reason, if you want index-based access, you probably want a List, not a Set.

Also, while Set does have a mutable version (which you will soon see), no mutator functions are available that rely on indices (like List's **add(index, element)** function).

Having said that, Set does provide the very useful feature of eliminating duplicate elements. So what is a programmer who wants unique elements *and* high-performance, index-based access to do? Use both:

Create a Set to eliminate duplicates and convert it a to a List when index-based access or mutator functions are needed.

This is exactly what you will do to develop a more elaborate patron name list for your tavern simulation.

Adding elements to a set

To add some diversity to the tavern, you will randomly generate patron names, using lists of first and last names. Update Tavern.kt with a list of last names and use **forEach** to generate 10 random combinations of first names (from patronList) and last names. (Recall that ranges are iterable.)

Remove the two calls to **forEachIndexed** that created patron greetings and menu orders. You will be iterating over a list of unique patrons soon instead.

Listing 10.24 Generating 10 random patrons (Tavern.kt)

```
...
val patronList = mutableListOf("Eli", "Mordoc", "Sophie")
val lastName = listOf("Ironfoot", "Fernsworth", "Baggins")
val menuList = File("data/tavern-menu-items.txt")
                            .readText()
                            .split("\n")

fun main(args: Array<String>) {
    ...
    patronList.forEachIndexed { index, patron ->
        println("Good evening, $patron - you're #${index + 1} in line.")
        placeOrder(patron, menuList.shuffled().first())
    }

    menuList.forEachIndexed { index, data ->
        println("$index : $data")
    }
    (0..9).forEach {
        val first = patronList.shuffled().first()
        val last = lastName.shuffled().first()
        val name = "$first $last"
        println(name)
    }
}
...
```

Run Tavern.kt. You will see 10 random patron names in the output. They will not necessarily match the ones below, but they will be similar – and you should see some duplicate first and last name combinations:

```
...
Eli Baggins
Eli Baggins
Eli Baggins
Eli Ironfoot
Sophie Baggins
Sophie Fernsworth
Sophie Baggins
Eli Ironfoot
Eli Ironfoot
Sophie Fernsworth
```

Your tavern simulation requires unique patron names, because soon you will associate gold balances with each patron's unique name in the tavern ledger. A duplicate patron name could lead to a case of mistaken identity.

To remove the duplicate names from your list, you will add each name to a set. Any duplicate elements will be dropped, and you will be left with only the unique elements.

Define an empty mutable set and add the randomly generated patron names to it:

Listing 10.25 Ensuring uniqueness using a set (Tavern.kt)

```
...
val lastName = listOf("Ironfoot", "Fernsworth", "Baggins")
val uniquePatrons = mutableSetOf<String>()
val menuList = File("data/tavern-menu-items.txt")
                            .readText()
                            .split("\n")

fun main(args: Array<String>) {
    ...
    (0..9).forEach {
        val first = patronList.shuffled().first()
        val last = lastName.shuffled().first()
        val name = "$first $last"
        println(name)
        uniquePatrons += name
    }
    println(uniquePatrons)
}
...
```

Note that you cannot rely on type inference for uniquePatrons, because you declare it as an empty set. You must specify the type of elements it can hold: **mutableSetOf<String>**. Then, you use the += operator to add name to uniquePatrons, iterating 10 times.

Run Tavern.kt again. You will see that only unique values are held in the set, and consequently you will have fewer than 10 patron names.

```
...
[Eli Fernsworth, Eli Ironfoot, Sophie Baggins, Mordoc Baggins, Sophie Fernsworth]
```

While MutableSet supports adding and removing elements, like MutableList, it does not provide index-based mutator functions. Table 10.2 shows some of the most commonly used MutableSet mutator functions.

Table 10.2 Mutable set mutator functions

Function	Description	Example(s)
add	Adds the value to the set.	mutableSetOf(1,2).add(3) *[1,2,3]*
addAll	Adds all elements from another collection to the set.	mutableSetOf(1,2).addAll(listOf(1,5,6)) *[1,2,5,6]*
+= (plus assign operator)	Adds the value(s) to the set.	mutableSetOf(1,2) += 3 *[1,2,3]*
-= (minus assign operator)	Removes the value(s) from the set.	mutableSetOf(1,2,3) -= 3 *[1,2]* mutableSetOf(1,2,3) -= listOf(2,3) *[1]*
remove	Removes the element from the set.	mutableSetOf(1,2,3).remove(1) *[2,3]*
removeAll	Removes all elements in another collection from the set.	mutableSetOf(1,2).removeAll(listOf(1,5,6)) *[2]*
clear	Removes all elements from the set.	mutableSetOf(1,2).clear() *[]*

while Loops

Now that you have a unique list of patrons, you will have them randomly place their orders from the menu. In this section, however, you will use a different control flow mechanism for looping through a collection: a while loop.

for loops are a useful form of control flow when you want to run some code for each element in series. But they are not as good at representing state that cannot be iterated through. That is where while loops are useful.

A while loop's logic is, "While some condition is true, execute the code in this block." You are going to generate exactly 10 orders by using a var to keep track of how many orders have been generated and a while loop to continue generating orders until 10 have been placed.

Update `Tavern.kt` to iterate through the set and have a total of 10 orders placed using a `while` loop:

Listing 10.26 Unique patrons placing random orders (`Tavern.kt`)

```
...
fun main(args: Array<String>) {
    ...
    println(uniquePatrons)

    var orderCount = 0
    while (orderCount <= 9) {
        placeOrder(uniquePatrons.shuffled().first(),
                menuList.shuffled().first())
        orderCount++
    }
}
...
```

The *increment operator* (++) adds 1 to the value of `orderCount` during each iteration.

Run `Tavern.kt`. This time, you will see 10 random orders placed by the patrons you generated, along the lines of:

```
Sophie Ironfoot speaks with Taernyl about their order.
Sophie Ironfoot buys a Dragon's Breath (shandy) for 5.91.
Sophie Ironfoot exclaims: Ah, d3l1c10|_|s Dr4g0n's Br34th!
Mordoc Fernsworth speaks with Taernyl about their order.
Mordoc Fernsworth buys a Dragon's Breath (shandy) for 5.91.
Mordoc Fernsworth exclaims: Ah, d3l1c10|_|s Dr4g0n's Br34th!
Eli Baggins speaks with Taernyl about their order.
Eli Baggins buys a pickled camel hump (desert dessert) for 7.33.
Eli Baggins says: Thanks for the pickled camel hump.
...
```

A `while` loop requires you to maintain your own counter to manage its state. You start with an `orderCount` value of 0 and increment each time that you loop. `while` loops are more flexible than `for` loops in that they can represent state that is not purely based on iteration. Here, you are doing so by incrementing the `orderCount` counter.

You can represent more complex state by combining `while` loops with other forms of control flow, like the conditionals you saw in Chapter 3. Consider this Boolean example:

```
var isTavernOpen = true
val isClosingTime = false
while (isTavernOpen == true) {
    if (isClosingTime) {
        isTavernOpen = false
    }

    println("Having a grand old time!")
}
```

In this example, the `while` loop continues to loop as long as `isTavernOpen` is true, keeping track of state represented by a `Boolean`. This is very powerful – but can also be dangerous. Consider what would happen if `isTavernOpen` was never false. This `while` loop would loop forever, and the program would "hang," or continue to execute indefinitely. Take care when using `while` loops for this reason.

The break Expression

One way to exit a while loop is by changing the state it depends on. Another way to break out of a loop is the break expression. Consider the above example in which a while loop runs while isTavernOpen is true. Instead of changing isTavernOpen's value to false to end the loop, a break expression would halt the loop immediately:

```
var isTavernOpen = true
val isClosingTime = false
while (isTavernOpen == true) {
    if (isClosingTime) {
        break
    }

    println("Having a grand old time!")
}
```

Without break, "Having a grand old time!" would print one more time after the value of isClosingTime changes. With break, the grand old times are interrupted as execution breaks out of the loop immediately.

Note that break does not stop execution of your program entirely. Rather, it simply breaks out of the loop from which it is called, and program execution continues. break can be used to jump out of any loop or conditional, which can be quite useful.

Collection Conversion

In NyetHack, you create a mutable set of unique patron names by feeding the elements from a list into it, one by one. You can also convert a list to a set, or vice versa, using the **toSet** and **toList** functions (or their mutable cousins: **toMutableSet** and **toMutableList**). A common trick is to call **toSet** to drop the non-unique elements in a list. (Try these experiments in the REPL.)

Listing 10.27 Converting a list to a set (REPL)

```
listOf("Eli Baggins", "Eli Baggins", "Eli Ironfoot").toSet()
[Eli Baggins, Eli Ironfoot]
```

If you want quick index-based access after converting a list to a set to remove duplicates, you can convert the set back to a list:

Listing 10.28 Converting a set back to a list (REPL)

```
val patrons = listOf("Eli Baggins", "Eli Baggins", "Eli Ironfoot")
            .toSet()
            .toList()
[Eli Baggins, Eli Ironfoot]
patrons[0]
Eli Baggins
```

The need to remove duplicates and resume index-based access is so common that Kotlin provides a function on List called **distinct** that calls **toSet** and **toList** internally:

Listing 10.29 Calling **distinct** (REPL)

```
val patrons = listOf("Eli Baggins", "Eli Baggins", "Eli Ironfoot").distinct()
[Eli Baggins, Eli Ironfoot]
patrons[0]
Eli Baggins
```

Sets are useful for representing series of data where each element is unique. In the next chapter, you will complete your tour of the Kotlin collection types by learning about maps as you finish the tavern simulation.

For the More Curious: Array Types

If you have worked with Java, you know that it supports primitive definitions of arrays – different from the reference types like List and Set that you worked with in this chapter. Kotlin also includes a number of reference types, called Arrays, that compile down to Java primitive arrays. Arrays are included primarily to support interoperability between Kotlin and Java.

Suppose you had a Java method that you wanted to call from Kotlin that looked like this:

```
static void displayPlayerAges(int[] playerAges) {
    for(int i = 0; i < ages.length; i++) {
        System.out.println("age: " + ages[i]);
    }
}
```

Notice that the parameter expected by **displayPlayerAges** is int[] playerAges, a Java primitive array of int primitives. To call the Java **displayPlayerAges** method from Kotlin, you would write the following:

```
val playerAges: IntArray = intArrayOf(34, 27, 14, 52, 101)
displayPlayerAges(playerAges)
```

Notice the IntArray type and the **intArrayOf** function that was called. Like a List, an IntArray represents a series of elements – specifically integers. Unlike a List, an IntArray is backed by a primitive type when compiled to bytecode. When the Kotlin code is compiled, the bytecode that is generated will exactly match the expected primitive int array required for the Java **displayPlayerAges** method to be invoked.

It is also possible to convert a Kotlin collection to the required Java primitive array type using built-in conversion functions. For example, you could convert a list of integers to an IntArray using the **toIntArray** function provided by List. This would allow you to convert a collection to an int array only at the point that you need to provide a primitive array to a Java function:

```
val playerAges: List<Int> = listOf(34, 27, 14, 52, 101)
displayPlayerAges(playerAges.toIntArray())
```

Table 10.3 shows the array types and the functions that create them.

Table 10.3 Array types

Array type	Creation function
IntArray	**intArrayOf**
DoubleArray	**doubleArrayOf**
LongArray	**longArrayOf**
ShortArray	**shortArrayOf**
ByteArray	**byteArrayOf**
FloatArray	**floatArrayOf**
BooleanArray	**booleanArrayOf**
Array[a]	**arrayOf**

[a]Array compiles to a primitive array that holds any reference type.

As a general rule, stick with the collection types like List unless you have a compelling reason to do otherwise – like the need to interoperate with Java code. A Kotlin collection is a better choice in most cases because collections provide the concept of "read-only-ness" versus "mutability" and support a more robust set of features.

For the More Curious: Read-Only vs Immutable

Throughout this book, we have favored the terms "read-only" over "immutable," with few exceptions – but we have not explained why. Now is the time. "Immutable" means "unchangeable," and we think it is a misleading label for Kotlin collections (and certain other types) because they can, indeed, change. Let's look at some examples using lists.

Here are declarations of two Lists. They are read-only – declared with val. The element each one happens to contain is a mutable list.

```
val x = listOf(mutableListOf(1,2,3))
val y = listOf(mutableListOf(1,2,3))

x == y
true
```

So far, so good. It appears that x and y were assigned with the same value, and the List API does not expose any functions for adding, removing, or reassigning a particular element.

However, the lists contain mutable lists, and *their* contents *can* be modified:

```
val x = listOf(mutableListOf(1,2,3))
val y = listOf(mutableListOf(1,2,3))
x[0].add(4)

x == y
false
```

The structural comparison between x and y now evaluates as false, because the contents of x mutated. Should an immutable ("unchangeable") list behave this way? In our opinion, it should not.

Here is another example:

```
var myList: List<Int> = listOf(1,2,3)
(myList as MutableList)[2] = 1000
myList
[1, 2, 1000]
```

In this example, myList was cast to the MutableList type – meaning that the compiler was instructed to treat myList as a mutable list, despite the fact that it was created with **listOf**. (You will read about casting in depth in Chapter 14 and Chapter 16.) This cast has the effect of allowing a change to the value of the third item in myList. Again, not the behavior we expect of something labeled "unchangeable."

A List in Kotlin does not enforce immutability – it is up to you to use it in an immutable fashion. A Kotlin List's "immutability" is only skin deep – and whatever you wind up calling it, remember that.

Challenge: Formatted Tavern Menu

First impressions go a long way, and one of the first things a patron will see is the tavern menu. For this challenge, generate a more elegant version of the menu to kick it up a notch. Show the item names capitalized and uniformly aligned. Include the prices, aligned by their decimal points. Format the whole menu in a pleasing block.

The output should resemble the following:

```
*** Welcome to Taernyl's Folly ***

Dragon's Breath..............5.91
Shirley's Temple.............4.12
Goblet of LaCroix............1.22
Pickled Camel Hump...........7.33
Iced Boilermaker............11.22
```

Hint: You will need to calculate the amount of padding for each line by using the longest string from the list of menu items.

Challenge: Advanced Formatted Tavern Menu

Building on the previous menu formatting code, generate a menu that additionally groups the elements to be listed by their type. The output should resemble the following:

```
*** Welcome to Taernyl's Folly ***
          ~[shandy]~
Dragon's Breath..............5.91
          ~[elixir]~
Iced Boilermaker............11.22
Shirley's Temple.............4.12
          ~[meal]~
Goblet of LaCroix............1.22
      ~[desert dessert]~
Pickled Camel Hump...........7.33
```

11

Maps

The third commonly used type of collection in Kotlin is Map. The Map type has a lot in common with the List and Set types: All three group a series of elements, are read-only by default, use parameterized types to tell the compiler the type of their contents, and support iteration.

Where Map is different from List and Set is that its elements consist of key-value pairs that you define, and instead of index-based access using an integer, a map provides key-based access using a type that you specify. Keys are unique and identify the values in the map; the values, on the other hand, do not need to be unique. In this way, Map shares another feature with Set: The keys of a map are guaranteed to be unique, just like the elements of a set.

Creating a Map

Like lists and sets, maps are created using functions: **mapOf** and **mutableMapOf**. In Tavern.kt, create a map representing the amount of gold each patron's purse contains. (We will explain the argument syntax shortly.)

Listing 11.1 Creating a read-only map (Tavern.kt)

```
...
var uniquePatrons = mutableSetOf<String>()
val menuList = File("data/tavern-menu-items.txt")
                            .readText()
                            .split("\n")
val patronGold = mapOf("Eli" to 10.5, "Mordoc" to 8.0, "Sophie" to 5.5)

fun main(args: Array<String>) {
    ...
    println(uniquePatrons)

    var orderCount = 0
    while (orderCount <= 9) {
        placeOrder(uniquePatrons.shuffled().first(),
                menuList.shuffled().first())
        orderCount++
    }

    println(patronGold)
}
...
```

While the keys in a map must all be of the same type, and the values must be of the same type, the keys and values can be of different types. Here you have a map with string keys and double values. You are using type inference, but if you had wanted to include explicit type information, it would look like this: val patronGold: Map<String, Double>.

Run Tavern.kt to see the map printed. Notice that when a map is printed, it is shown in curly braces, while lists and sets are both shown in square brackets.

```
The tavern master says: Eli's in the back playing cards.
The tavern master says: Yea, they're seated back by the stew kettle.
...
{Eli=10.5, Mordoc=8.0, Sophie=5.5}
```

You used **to** to define each entry (key and value) in the map:

```
...
mapOf("Eli" to 10.75, "Mordoc" to 8.25, "Sophie" to 5.50)
```

to may look like a keyword, but in fact it is a special type of function that allows you to drop the dot and the parentheses around its arguments. You will learn more about this in Chapter 18. The **to** function converts the values on its lefthand and righthand sides into a Pair – a type for representing a group of two elements.

Maps are built using key-value Pairs. In fact, another way you could have defined the entries for the map is as follows. (Try it in the REPL.)

Listing 11.2 Defining a map using the Pair type (REPL)

```
val patronGold = mapOf(Pair("Eli", 10.75),
    Pair("Mordoc", 8.00),
    Pair("Sophie", 5.50))
```

However, building a map using the **to** function is cleaner than this syntax.

We have said that the keys in a map must be unique. What if you tried adding a duplicate entry to the map? In the REPL, add another pair with "Sophie" for the key:

Listing 11.3 Adding a duplicate key (REPL)

```
val patronGold = mutableMapOf("Eli" to 5.0, "Sophie" to 1.0)
patronGold += "Sophie" to 6.0
println(patronGold)
{Eli=5.0, Sophie=6.0}
```

You used Map's plus assign operator (+=) to add a pair with a duplicate key into the map. Since the key "Sophie" was already in the map, the existing pair was replaced with the new one. You see the same behavior if you try to include duplicate keys when initializing a map:

```
println(mapOf("Eli" to 10.75,
        "Mordoc" to 8.25,
        "Sophie" to 5.50,
        "Sophie" to 6.25))
{Eli=10.5, Mordoc=8.0, Sophie=6.25}
```

Accessing Map Values

You access a value in a map using its key. For the `patronGold` map, you will use the string key to access the patron's gold balance value.

Listing 11.4 Accessing individual gold balances (Tavern.kt)

```
...

fun main(args: Array<String>) {
    ...
    println(uniquePatrons)

    var orderCount = 0
    while (orderCount <= 9) {
        placeOrder(uniquePatrons.shuffled().first(),
                menuList.shuffled().first())
        orderCount++
    }

    println(patronGold)
    println(patronGold["Eli"])
    println(patronGold["Mordoc"])
    println(patronGold["Sophie"])
}
```

Run `Tavern.kt` to print the balances for the three patrons you added to the map:

```
...
10.5
8.0
5.5
```

Note that the output includes only the values, not the keys.

As with other collections, Kotlin provides functions for accessing the values stored in a map. Table 11.1 shows some of the common map accessor functions and their behaviors.

Table 11.1 Map accessor functions

Function	Description	Example
[] (get/index operator)	Gets the value for a key; returns null if the key does not exist.	`patronGold["Reginald"]` `null`
getValue	Gets the value for a key; throws an exception if the key provided is not in the map.	`patronGold.getValue("Reggie")` `NoSuchElementException`
getOrElse	Gets the value for the key or returns a default using an anonymous function.	`patronGold.getOrElse("Reggie") {"No such patron"}` `No such patron`
getOrDefault	Gets the value for the key or returns a default using a value you provide.	`patronGold.getOrDefault("Reginald", 0.0)` `0.0`

Adding Entries to a Map

Your map of patron gold values represents the purses of Eli, Mordoc, and Sophie, but it does not include the purse values for the patrons you dynamically generated. Time to fix that by replacing patronGold with a MutableMap.

Make the patronGold map mutable. Then iterate through the uniquePatrons set, adding an entry to the map for each patron with a value of 6.0 gold. Also, remove the map entry look-ups that you performed, since the keys are no longer just first names.

Listing 11.5 Populating the mutable map (Tavern.kt)

```kotlin
import java.io.File
import kotlin.math.roundToInt
const val TAVERN_NAME: String = "Taernyl's Folly"

var playerGold = 10
var playerSilver = 10
val patronList = mutableListOf("Eli", "Mordoc", "Sophie")
val lastName = listOf("Ironfoot", "Fernsworth", "Baggins")
val uniquePatrons = mutableSetOf<String>()
val menuList = File("data/tavern-menu-items.txt")
        .readText()
        .split("\n")
val patronGold = mapOf("Eli" to 10.5, "Mordoc" to 8.0, "Sophie" to 5.5)
val patronGold = mutableMapOf<String, Double>()

fun main(args: Array<String>) {
    ...
    println(uniquePatrons)
    uniquePatrons.forEach {
        patronGold[it] = 6.0
    }

    var orderCount = 0
    while (orderCount <= 9) {
        placeOrder(uniquePatrons.shuffled().first(),
                menuList.shuffled().first())
        orderCount++
    }

    println(patronGold)
    println(patronGold["Eli"])
    println(patronGold["Mordoc"])
    println(patronGold["Sophie"])
}
...
```

You have added an entry for each unique patron to the map, with a value of 6.0 gold for each, by iterating over uniquePatrons. (Remember the it keyword? Here, it refers to an element in uniquePatrons.)

Table 11.2 shows some of the commonly used functions for modifying the contents of a mutable map.

Table 11.2 Mutable map mutator functions

Function	Description	Example

=
(assignment operator)
	Adds or updates the value in the map for the key specified.	```val patronGold = mutableMapOf("Mordoc" to 6.0)```
		```patronGold["Mordoc"] = 5.0```
		{Mordoc=5.0}

+=
(plus assign operator)
	Adds or updates an entry or entries in the map based on the entry or map specified.	```val patronGold = mutableMapOf("Mordoc" to 6.0)```
		```patronGold += "Eli" to 5.0```
		{Mordoc=6.0, Eli=5.0}
		
		```val patronGold = mutableMapOf("Mordoc" to 6.0)```
		```patronGold += mapOf("Eli" to 7.0,```
		``` "Mordoc" to 1.0,```
		``` "Jebediah" to 4.5)```
		{Mordoc=1.0, Eli=7.0, Jebediah=4.5}

put	Adds or updates the value in the map for the key specified.	```val patronGold = mutableMapOf("Mordoc" to 6.0)```
		```patronGold.put("Mordoc", 5.0)```
		{Mordoc=5.0}

putAll	Adds all of the key-value pairs provided to the map.	```val patronGold = mutableMapOf("Mordoc" to 6.0)```
		```patronGold.putAll(listOf("Jebediah" to 5.0,```
		``` "Sahara" to 6.0))```
		```patronGold["Jebediah"]```
		5.0
		
		```patronGold["Sahara"]```
		6.0

getOrPut	Adds an entry for the key if it does not exist already and returns the result; otherwise returns the existing entry.	```val patronGold = mutableMapOf<String, Double>()```
		```patronGold.getOrPut("Randy"){5.0}```
		5.0
		
		```patronGold.getOrPut("Randy"){10.0}```
		5.0

remove	Removes an entry from the map and returns the value.	```val patronGold = mutableMapOf("Mordoc" to 5.0)```
		```val mordocBalance = patronGold.remove("Mordoc")```
		{}
		
		```print(mordocBalance)```
		5.0

–
(minus operator)
	Returns a new map, excluding the entries specified.	```val newPatrons = mutableMapOf("Mordoc" to 6.0,```
		``` "Jebediah" to 1.0) - "Mordoc"```
		{Jebediah=1.0}

–=
(minus assign operator)
	Removes entry or map of entries from the map.	```mutableMapOf("Mordoc" to 6.0,```
		``` "Jebediah" to 1.0) -= "Mordoc"```
		{Jebediah=1.0}

clear	Removes all entries from the map.	```mutableMapOf("Mordoc" to 6.0,```
		``` "Jebediah" to 1.0).clear()```
		{}

Modifying Map Values

To complete the transaction, the price of the item should be deducted from the patron's purse. The patronGold map associates gold balance values with a given patron's name as a key. You will modify the gold balance value for a patron to record the patron's new balance once the purchase is completed.

Your **performPurchase** and **displayBalance** functions are tied to Madrigal's purse and get into details of gold and silver pieces that are not needed here. Delete them and the playerGold and playerSilver variables, which are only used in those functions. Then define a new **performPurchase** function to handle a patron purchase. (You will define a new function to display patron balances soon.)

To update the value after the purchase is made, the function will get it from the patronGold map using the patron's name. Call the new **performPurchase** function after the patron speaks to Taernyl, the tavern master, about their order (do not forget to uncomment the call).

Listing 11.6 Updating the values in patronGold (Tavern.kt)

```kotlin
import java.io.File
import kotlin.math.roundToInt
const val TAVERN_NAME: String = "Taernyl's Folly"

var playerGold = 10
var playerSilver = 10
val patronList = mutableListOf("Eli", "Mordoc", "Sophie")
...
fun performPurchase(price: Double) {
    displayBalance()
    val totalPurse = playerGold + (playerSilver / 100.0)
    println("Total purse: $totalPurse")
    println("Purchasing item for $price")

    val remainingBalance = totalPurse - price
    println("Remaining balance: ${"%.2f".format(remainingBalance)}")

    val remainingGold = remainingBalance.toInt()
    val remainingSilver = (remainingBalance % 1 * 100).roundToInt()
    playerGold = remainingGold
    playerSilver = remainingSilver
    displayBalance()
}

private fun displayBalance() {
    println("Player's purse balance: Gold: $playerGold , Silver: $playerSilver")
}

fun performPurchase(price: Double, patronName: String) {
    val totalPurse = patronGold.getValue(patronName)
    patronGold[patronName] = totalPurse - price
}

private fun toDragonSpeak(phrase: String) =
        ...
        }

private fun placeOrder(patronName: String, menuData: String) {
    ...
    println(message)
    performPurchase(price.toDouble(), patronName)

    val phrase = if (name == "Dragon's Breath") {
    ...
}
...
```

Run `Tavern.kt`. You will continue to see ten random orders along the lines of:

```
The tavern master says: Eli's in the back playing cards.
The tavern master says: Yea, they're seated by the stew kettle.
Mordoc Fernsworth speaks with Taernyl about their order.
Mordoc Fernsworth buys a goblet of LaCroix (meal) for 1.22.
Mordoc Fernsworth says: Thanks for the goblet of LaCroix.
...
```

You have updated the patron's gold balance, and only one task remains – reporting the patrons' gold balances after they make their purchases. You will do this by iterating through your map using **forEach**.

Add a new function to `Tavern.kt` called **displayPatronBalances** that iterates through the map, printing the final gold balance (formatted to the second decimal place, as you did in Chapter 8) for each patron. Call it after the simulation completes in the **main** function.

Listing 11.7 Displaying patron balances (`Tavern.kt`)

```kotlin
...
fun main(args: Array<String>) {
    ...
    var orderCount = 0
    while (orderCount <= 9) {
        placeOrder(uniquePatrons.shuffled().first(),
                menuList.shuffled().first())
        orderCount++
    }

    displayPatronBalances()
}

private fun displayPatronBalances() {
    patronGold.forEach { patron, balance ->
        println("$patron, balance: ${"%.2f".format(balance)}")
    }
}
...
```

Run Tavern.kt, sit back, and watch as the patrons of Taernyl's Folly chat with the tavern master, order off the menu, and pay for their items:

```
The tavern master says: Eli's in the back playing cards.
The tavern master says: Yea, they're seated by the stew kettle.
Mordoc Ironfoot speaks with Taernyl about their order.
Mordoc Ironfoot buys a iced boilermaker (elixir) for 11.22.
Mordoc Ironfoot says: Thanks for the iced boilermaker.
Sophie Baggins speaks with Taernyl about their order.
Sophie Baggins buys a Dragon's Breath (shandy) for 5.91.
Sophie Baggins exclaims: Ah, d3l1c10|_|s Dr4g0n's Br34th!
Sophie Ironfoot speaks with Taernyl about their order.
Sophie Ironfoot buys a pickled camel hump (desert dessert) for 7.33.
Sophie Ironfoot says: Thanks for the pickled camel hump.
Eli Fernsworth speaks with Taernyl about their order.
Eli Fernsworth buys a Dragon's Breath (shandy) for 5.91.
Eli Fernsworth exclaims: Ah, d3l1c10|_|s Dr4g0n's Br34th!
Sophie Fernsworth speaks with Taernyl about their order.
Sophie Fernsworth buys a iced boilermaker (elixir) for 11.22.
Sophie Fernsworth says: Thanks for the iced boilermaker.
Sophie Fernsworth speaks with Taernyl about their order.
Sophie Fernsworth buys a Dragon's Breath (shandy) for 5.91.
Sophie Fernsworth exclaims: Ah, d3l1c10|_|s Dr4g0n's Br34th!
Sophie Fernsworth speaks with Taernyl about their order.
Sophie Fernsworth buys a pickled camel hump (desert dessert) for 7.33.
Sophie Fernsworth says: Thanks for the pickled camel hump.
Mordoc Fernsworth speaks with Taernyl about their order.
Mordoc Fernsworth buys a Shirley's Temple (elixir) for 4.12.
Mordoc Fernsworth says: Thanks for the Shirley's Temple.
Sophie Baggins speaks with Taernyl about their order.
Sophie Baggins buys a goblet of LaCroix (meal) for 1.22.
Sophie Baggins says: Thanks for the goblet of LaCroix.
Mordoc Fernsworth speaks with Taernyl about their order.
Mordoc Fernsworth buys a iced boilermaker (elixir) for 11.22.
Mordoc Fernsworth says: Thanks for the iced boilermaker.
Mordoc Ironfoot, balance: -5.22
Sophie Baggins, balance: -1.13
Eli Fernsworth, balance: 0.09
Sophie Fernsworth, balance: -18.46
Sophie Ironfoot, balance: -1.33
Mordoc Fernsworth, balance: -9.34
```

In the last two chapters, you learned how to work with Kotlin's List, Set, and Map collection types. Table 11.3 compares their features.

Table 11.3 Kotlin collections summary

Collection type	Ordered?	Unique?	Stores	Supports destructuring?
List	Yes	No	Elements	Yes
Set	No	Yes	Elements	No
Map	No	Keys	Key-value pairs	No

Since collections are read-only by default, you must explicitly create a mutable collection (or convert a read-only collection to be mutable) to modify its contents – preventing you from accidentally adding or removing elements.

In the next chapter, you will learn how to apply object-oriented programming principles as you define your own classes within NyetHack.

Challenge: Tavern Bouncer

A patron without any gold should not be allowed to place an order. In fact, they should not be allowed to loiter in the tavern – the tavern bouncer should see to that. If a patron lacks sufficient funds, boot them out onto the mean streets of NyetHack by removing them from uniquePatrons and the patronGold map.

12

Defining Classes

The object-oriented programming paradigm has been around since the 1960s and continues to be popular because it provides a set of useful tools for simplifying the structure of a program. Central to the object-oriented style are *classes*, definitions of the unique categories of "things" your code represents. Classes define what sort of data those things will consist of and what kind of work they can do.

To make NyetHack object-oriented, you will start by identifying the unique types of things that will exist in the world and defining classes for them. In this chapter, you will add a custom **Player** class to NyetHack, which you will use to represent a NyetHack player's particular characteristics.

Defining a Class

A class can be defined in its own file or alongside other elements, like functions or variables. Defining a class in its own file gives it room to grow as the program scales up over time, and that is what you will do in NyetHack. Create a new Player.kt file and declare your first class with the class keyword:

Listing 12.1 Defining the **Player** class (Player.kt)

```
class Player
```

A class is often declared in a file matching its name, but it does not have to be. You can define multiple classes in the same file – and you may want to if you have multiple classes used for a similar purpose.

With that, your class is defined. Now all you have to do is give it some work to do.

Constructing Instances

A class declaration is like a blueprint. Blueprints contain the details for how to construct a building, but they are not a building. Your **Player** class declaration works similarly: So far, a player has not been constructed – you have only created the (so far, quite sparse) blueprint.

When you start a new game of NyetHack, the **main** function is called, and one of the first things that you will want to do is create a player character to play the game. To construct a player so that it can be used in NyetHack, you must *instantiate* it – create an *instance* of it – by calling its *constructor*. In Game.kt, where variables are declared in the **main** function, instantiate a **Player**, as shown:

Listing 12.2 Instantiating a **Player** (Game.kt)

```
fun main(args: Array<String>) {
    val name = "Madrigal"
    var healthPoints = 89
    val isBlessed = true
    val isImmortal = false

    val player = Player()

    // Aura
    val auraColor = auraColor(isBlessed, healthPoints, isImmortal)

    // Player status
    val healthStatus = formatHealthStatus(healthPoints, isBlessed)
    printPlayerStatus(auraColor, isBlessed, name, healthStatus)

    castFireball()
}
...
```

You called **Player**'s *primary constructor* by suffixing the **Player** class name with parentheses. This constructs an instance of the **Player** class. The player variable is now said to "contain an instance of the **Player** class."

A constructor does what its name says: It constructs. Specifically, it constructs an instance and prepares it for use. The syntax for calling a constructor is a lot like calling a function: It uses parentheses to capture arguments for its parameters. You will see other ways instances can be constructed in Chapter 13.

Now that you have an instance of **Player**, what can you do with it?

Class Functions

Class definitions can specify two types of content: *behavior* and *data*. In NyetHack, a player can take various actions: perform combat, move, cast the fireball spell, or check their inventory, for example. You define behavior for a class by adding function definitions to its class body. Functions defined within a class are called *class functions*.

You already have some player behaviors that are defined in Game.kt. Now, you are going to reorganize your code to bring class-specific elements into the class definition.

Begin by adding the **castFireball** function to **Player**:

Listing 12.3 Defining a class function (Player.kt)

```
class Player {
    fun castFireball(numFireballs: Int = 2) =
            println("A glass of Fireball springs into existence. (x$numFireballs)")
}
```

(You might notice that this implementation of **castFireball** does not have a private keyword. We will explain that in a moment.)

Here, you define a *class body* for **Player** with curly braces. The class body holds definitions for the class's behavior and data, much like the actions of a function are defined within the function body.

In Game.kt, remove the definition of **castFireball** and add a call to it as a class function in **main**:

Listing 12.4 Calling a class function (Game.kt)

```
fun main(args: Array<String>) {
    var healthPoints = 89
    val isBlessed = true
    val isImmortal = false

    val player = Player()
    player.castFireball()

    // Aura
    val auraColor = auraColor(isBlessed, healthPoints, isImmortal)

    // Player status
    val healthStatus = formatHealthStatus(healthPoints, isBlessed)
    printPlayerStatus(auraColor, isBlessed, player.name, healthStatus)

    castFireball()
}
...
private fun castFireball(numFireballs: Int = 2) =
        println("A glass of Fireball springs into existence. (x$numFireballs)")
```

Grouping the logic about the "things" in your code using classes keeps your code organized at scale. As NyetHack grows, you will add more classes, each with its own responsibilities.

Run Game.kt and confirm that the player summons a glass of Fireball.

Why move **castFireball** to **Player**? In NyetHack, summoning a glass of Fireball is something that a player does: It cannot happen without an instance of **Player**, and it is performed by the particular player on which **castFireball** is called. Defining **castFireball** as a class function, so that it is called on an instance of the class, reflects this logic. Later in this chapter, you will move other functions associated with NyetHack's player into the **Player** class as well.

Visibility and Encapsulation

Adding behavior to a class with class functions (and data with class properties, as you will see in a moment) builds a description of what that class can do and be, and that description is visible to anyone with an instance of that class.

By default, any function or property without a visibility modifier is public – meaning it is accessible from any file or function in your program. Since you now include no visibility modifier on **castFireball**, it can be called from everywhere.

In some cases, like with **castFireball**, you want other parts of your code to be able to access your class properties or call your class functions. But you might have other class functions or properties you do not want to be called from elsewhere in your codebase.

As the number of classes in your program grows, so does your codebase's complexity. Hiding the implementation details that do not need to be visible from other parts of your codebase helps to ensure that the logic of your code is clear and concise. That is where visibility comes into play.

While a public class function can be invoked anywhere in the program, a private class function cannot be invoked outside of the class on which it is defined. This idea of restricting visibility to certain class functions or properties drives a concept in object-oriented programming known as *encapsulation*. Encapsulation says that a class should selectively expose functions and properties to define how other objects interact with it. Anything that is not essential to expose, including implementation details of exposed functions and properties, should be kept private.

For example, if **castFireball** is called from Game.kt, Game.kt does not care about how **castFireball** is implemented. It only cares that a glass of Fireball is summoned. So while the function itself may be exposed, the details of its implementation should not matter to the caller.

In fact, it could be dangerous if code in Game.kt could alter values that **castFireball** depends on to do its work – like the number of glasses of Fireball to create, or the Fireball intensity level.

In short: When building classes, expose only what you need to.

Table 12.1 lists the available visibility modifiers:

Table 12.1 Visibility modifiers

Modifier	Description
public (default)	The function or property will be accessible by code outside of the class. By default, functions and properties without a visibility modifier are public.
private	The function or property will be accessible only within the same class.
protected	The function or property will be accessible only within the same class or its subclass.
internal	The function or property will be accessible within the same module.

We will discuss the protected keyword in Chapter 14.

If you are familiar with Java, notice that the package private visibility level is not included in Kotlin. We will explain why in the section called *For the More Curious: Package Private* at the end of this chapter.

Class Properties

Class function definitions describe the behavior associated with a class. Data definitions, better known as *class properties*, are the attributes required to represent the specific state or characteristics of a class. For example, **Player**'s class properties could represent a player's name, current health points, race, alignment, gender, and other attributes.

Currently, you define a name for a player in the **main** function, but your new class definition is a better place for it. Update Player.kt with a name property. (The value for name may look sloppy, but there is a method to our madness – enter it as shown.)

Listing 12.5 Defining the name property (Player.kt)

```
class Player {
    val name = "madrigal"

    fun castFireball(numFireballs: Int = 2) =
            println("A glass of Fireball springs into existence. (x$numFireballs)")
}
```

You add the name property to the **Player** class body, including it as relevant data a **Player** instance contains. Notice that name is defined as a val. Like variables, properties can represent either read-only or mutable data using the val and var keywords, respectively. We will talk more about property mutability later in this chapter.

Now, remove the name declaration from Game.kt:

Listing 12.6 Removing name from **main** (Game.kt)

```
fun main(args: Array<String>) {
    val name = "Madrigal"
    var healthPoints = 89
    ...
}
...
```

You might notice that IntelliJ is now warning you about a problem in Game.kt (Figure 12.1).

Figure 12.1 Unresolved reference error

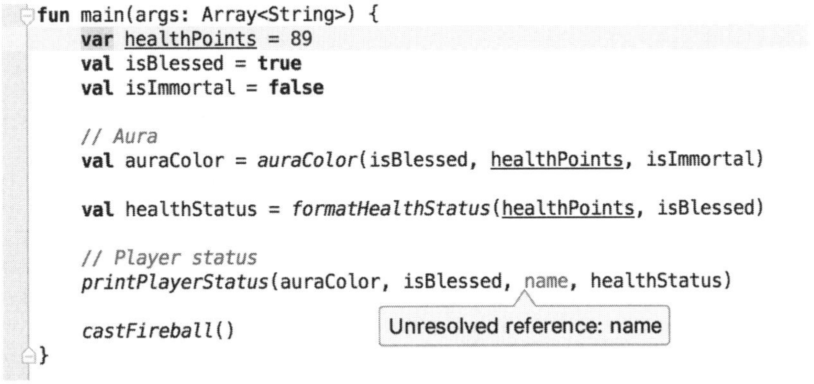

```
fun main(args: Array<String>) {
    var healthPoints = 89
    val isBlessed = true
    val isImmortal = false

    // Aura
    val auraColor = auraColor(isBlessed, healthPoints, isImmortal)

    val healthStatus = formatHealthStatus(healthPoints, isBlessed)

    // Player status
    printPlayerStatus(auraColor, isBlessed, name, healthStatus)

    castFireball()          Unresolved reference: name
}
```

Now that name is a property of **Player**, you will need to update **printPlayerStatus** to access it from the instance of the **Player** class. Use dot syntax to pass the player variable's name property to **printPlayerStatus**:

Listing 12.7 Resolving the reference to **Player**'s name property (Game.kt)

```
fun main(args: Array<String>) {
    ...

    // Player status
    printPlayerStatus(auraColor, isBlessed, player.name, healthStatus)
}
...
```

Run Game.kt. The player status, including the name, prints as before, but now you access the name property from the instance of the **Player** class rather than from a local variable in **main**.

When an instance of a class is constructed, all of its properties must have values. This means that, unlike other variables, class properties must be assigned an initial value. For example, the following code is invalid, because name is not assigned at declaration:

```
class Player {
    var name: String
}
```

We will explore the nuances of class and property initialization in Chapter 13.

Later in this chapter, you will refactor NyetHack to move the other data belonging to the **Player** class into the class definition.

Property getters and setters

Properties model the characteristics of each instance of a class. They also provide a way for other entities to interface with the data that the class keeps track of, represented in a compact and concise syntax. This interaction happens through getters and setters.

For each property you define, Kotlin will generate a *field*, a *getter*, and, if needed, a *setter*. A field is where the data for a property is stored. You cannot directly define a field on a class. Kotlin encapsulates the fields for you, protecting the data in the field and exposing it via getters and setters. A property's getter specifies how the property is read. Getters are generated for every property. A setter defines how a property's value is assigned, so it is generated only when a property is writable – in other words, when the property is a var.

Imagine that you are in a restaurant where the menu advertises spaghetti, among other foods. You order spaghetti, and the waiter serves you spaghetti dressed up with spaghetti sauce and cheese. You do not have access to the kitchen, and the waiter handles everything behind the scenes for you, even adding spaghetti sauce and cheese to your order of spaghetti. You are like the caller, and the waiter is the getter.

As a patron of this restaurant, you do not want the responsibility of boiling water when you order spaghetti. Rather, you simply want to order spaghetti and have it brought to you. And the restaurant does not want you in the kitchen, nosing around in the ingredients and putting together dishes in your own way. This is encapsulation at work.

Although default getters and setters are provided automatically by Kotlin, you can define your own custom getters and setters when you want to specify how the data will be read or written. This is called *overriding* the getter or setter.

To see how getter overriding works, add a getter to name that ensures that its value is capitalized when it is accessed.

Listing 12.8 Defining a custom getter (Player.kt)

```kotlin
class Player {
    val name = "madrigal"
        get() = field.capitalize()

    fun castFireball(numFireballs: Int = 2) =
            println("A glass of Fireball springs into existence. (x$numFireballs)")
}
```

When you define a custom getter for a property, you change how the property works when it is accessed. Because name contains a proper noun, you always want it to be capitalized when you reference it. This custom getter makes sure of that.

Run Game.kt and confirm that Madrigal now prints with capital "M."

The field keyword here points to the backing field that Kotlin manages for your property automatically. The backing field is the data that the getters and setters use to read and write the data that represents the property. It is like the ingredients in the restaurant kitchen – the caller never sees the backing field directly, only the data as presented by the getter. In fact, a field is only accessible within a getter or a setter.

When the capitalized version of name is returned, the backing field is not modified. If the value assigned to name is not capitalized, as in your code, it remains lowercase after the getter does its work.

A setter, on the other hand, *does* modify the backing field of the property on which it is declared. Add a setter to name that uses the **trim** function to remove any leading and trailing spaces from the value it is passed.

Listing 12.9 Defining a custom setter (Player.kt)

```kotlin
class Player {
    val name = "madrigal"
        get() = field.capitalize()
        set(value) {
            field = value.trim()
        }

    fun castFireball(numFireballs: Int = 2) =
            println("A glass of Fireball springs into existence. (x$numFireballs)")
}
```

There is a problem with adding a setter to this property, which IntelliJ is warning you about (Figure 12.2):

Figure 12.2 `val` properties are read-only

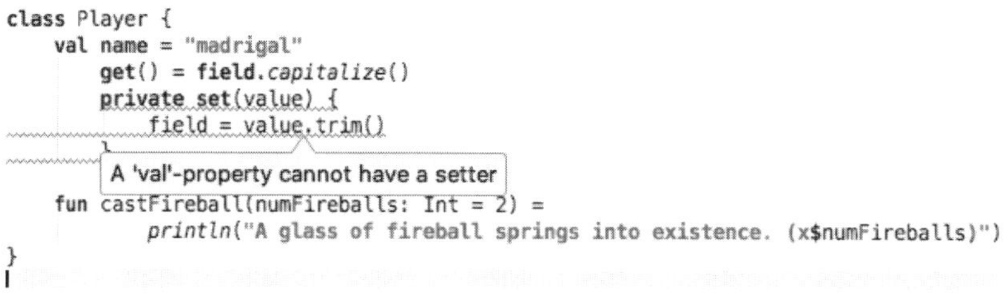

```
class Player {
    val name = "madrigal"
        get() = field.capitalize()
        private set(value) {
            field = value.trim()
        }
```
A 'val'-property cannot have a setter
```
    fun castFireball(numFireballs: Int = 2) =
            println("A glass of fireball springs into existence. (x$numFireballs)")
}
```

Because you defined the name property as a `val`, it is read-only and cannot be modified, even with a setter. This protects your `val`s from being modified without your consent.

IntelliJ's complaint underscores an important point about setters: They are triggered when the value of a property is set. It is not logical (and, in fact, it is an error) to define a setter for a `val` property, because if the value is read-only, the setter can never do its job.

You want to be able to change the player's name, so change the name property from a `val` to a `var`. (Note that from this point forward, we will show all changes to the code inline when possible.)

Listing 12.10 Making name mutable (`Player.kt`)

```
class Player {
    ~~val~~var name = "madrigal"
        get() = field.capitalize()
        set(value) {
            field = value.trim()
        }

    fun castFireball(numFireballs: Int = 2) =
            println("A glass of Fireball springs into existence. (x$numFireballs)")
}
```

Now, name can be modified according to the rules outlined in its custom setter, and IntelliJ's warnings disappear accordingly.

Property getters are called using the same access syntax as the other variables that you have seen. Property setters are called using the assignment operator that you have used to assign values to variables. In the Kotlin REPL, try changing a player's name from outside of the **Player** class.

Listing 12.11 Changing a player's name (REPL)

```
val player = Player()
player.name = "estragon "
print(player.name + "TheBrave")
EstragonTheBrave
```

Here you can see the effect of both the getter and the setter on the new value for name.

Assigning new values to class properties changes the state of the class on which they are assigned. If name were still a val, then the example that you just tried in the REPL would result in the following error message:

```
error: val cannot be reassigned
```

(If you try this, you will need to reload the REPL with the Build and restart button to the left so that the change to **Player** is recognized.)

Property visibility

Properties are different from variables defined locally within a function. When a property is defined, it is defined at the class level. As such, it may be accessible to other classes, if its visibility allows. Over-permissive visibility can cause problems: If other classes have access to a **Player**'s data, then any class in your application could make changes to that instance of **Player** at will.

Properties provide fine-grained control around reading and modifying data through their getters and setters. All properties have getters – and all var properties have setters – whether you define custom behavior for them or not. By default, the visibility of a property's getter and setter match the visibility of the property itself. So if you have a public property, both its getter and setter are public.

What if you want to expose access to a property but do not want to expose its setter? You can define the visibility of the setter separately. Make the name property's setter private:

Listing 12.12 Hiding name's setter (Player.kt)

```
class Player {
    var name = "madrigal"
        get() = field.capitalize()
        private set(value) {
            field = value.trim()
        }

    fun castFireball(numFireballs: Int = 2) =
            println("A glass of Fireball springs into existence. (x$numFireballs)")
}
```

Now, name can be accessed from anywhere in NyetHack, but it can only be modified from within **Player**. This technique is quite useful if you want to control whether certain properties can be modified by other parts of your application.

A getter or a setter's visibility cannot be more permissive than the property on which it is defined. You can restrict access to a property via a getter or a setter, but they are not intended for making properties more visible.

Remember that properties must be assigned when declared. This rule is especially important when your class has a public property. If an instance of the **Player** class is referenced elsewhere in your codebase, then whoever makes that reference must be assured that when they reference Player.name, a value for name exists.

Computed properties

Earlier, we said that when you define a property, a field is always generated to store the value the property encapsulates. That is true ... except in a particular case: *computed properties*. A computed property is a property that is specified with an overridden **get** and/or **set** operator in a way that makes a field unnecessary. In such cases, Kotlin will not generate a field.

In the REPL, create a **Dice** class with a computed rolledValue property:

Listing 12.13 Defining a computed property (REPL)

```
class Dice() {
    val rolledValue
        get() = (1..6).shuffled().first()
}
```

Now, take it for a roll:

Listing 12.14 Accessing the computed property (REPL)

```
val myD6 = Dice()
myD6.rolledValue
6
myD6.rolledValue
1
myD6.rolledValue
4
```

The value is different each time the rolledValue property is accessed. This is because the value is computed each time the variable is accessed. It has no initial or default value – and no backing field to hold a value.

You will look more carefully at how val and var properties are implemented and what bytecode is emitted by the compiler when you specify them in the section called *For the More Curious: A Closer Look at var and val Properties* near the end of this chapter.

Refactoring NyetHack

You have learned about class functions, properties, and encapsulation, and you have done some of the work to apply these concepts to NyetHack. It is time to finish the job and thoroughly clean up NyetHack's code.

You will be moving chunks of code from one file to another. It helps to see the two files side by side. Fortunately, IntelliJ provides this feature.

With `Game.kt` open, right-click on the Player.kt tab at the top of the editor and select Split Vertically (Figure 12.3).

Figure 12.3 Splitting the editor vertically

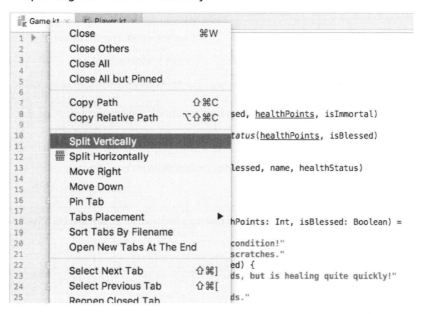

You now have another editor pane to work in (Figure 12.4). (You can drag tabs between editor panes to configure your editor experience to your liking.)

Figure 12.4 Two panes

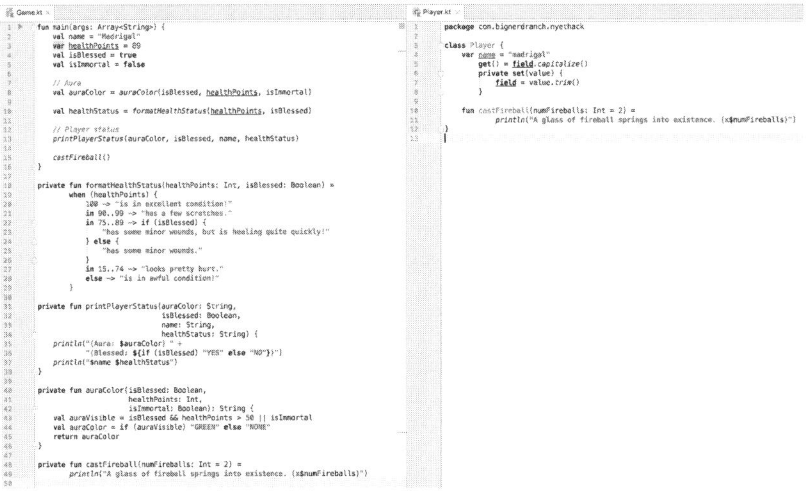

This is a complex refactor, but by the end of this section **Player** will expose a selective API and encapsulate the implementation details that other components do not need to know about. In short: It is for a good cause.

First, locate the variables declared in Game.kt's **main** function that make sense as properties of **Player**. These include healthPoints, isBlessed, and isImmortal. Refactor them to become properties of **Player**.

Listing 12.15 Removing variables from **main** (Game.kt)

```
fun main(args: Array<String>) {
    var healthPoints = 89
    val isBlessed = true
    val isImmortal = false

    val player = Player()
    player.castFireball()
    ...
}
...
```

As you add them to Player.kt, be sure that the variables are all defined inside the **Player** class's body.

Listing 12.16 Adding properties to **Player** (Player.kt)

```
class Player {
    var name = "madrigal"
        get() = field.capitalize()
        private set(value) {
            field = value.trim()
        }

    var healthPoints = 89
    val isBlessed = true
    val isImmortal = false

    fun castFireball(numFireballs: Int = 2) =
            println("A glass of Fireball springs into existence. (x$numFireballs)")
}
```

These changes will result in a number of errors in Game.kt. Hang tight; by the time you are finished, all the errors will be taken care of.

healthPoints and isBlessed will be accessed from Game.kt. But isImmortal is never accessed from outside of **Player**, so it behooves you to make isImmortal private. Encapsulate the property by making it private to ensure that other classes will not have access to it.

Listing 12.17 Encapsulating isImmortal within **Player** (Player.kt)

```
class Player {
    var name = "madrigal"
        get() = field.capitalize()
        private set(value) {
            field = value.trim()
        }

    var healthPoints = 89
    val isBlessed = true
    private val isImmortal = false

    fun castFireball(numFireballs: Int = 2) =
            println("A glass of Fireball springs into existence. (x$numFireballs)")
}
```

Next, review the functions declared in Game.kt. **printPlayerStatus** prints out the textual interface for the game, so it is appropriate for it to be declared in Game.kt. But **auraColor** and **formatHealthStatus** both relate directly to the player, rather than the gameplay. Therefore, those two functions belong in the class definition rather than in **main**.

Move **auraColor** and **formatHealthStatus** into **Player**.

Listing 12.18 Removing functions from **main** (Game.kt)

```kotlin
fun main(args: Array<String>) {
    ...
}

private fun formatHealthStatus(healthPoints: Int, isBlessed: Boolean) =
        when (healthPoints) {
            100 -> "is in excellent condition!"
            in 90..99 -> "has a few scratches."
            in 75..89 -> if (isBlessed) {
                "has some minor wounds, but is healing quite quickly!"
            } else {
                "has some minor wounds."
            }
            in 15..74 -> "looks pretty hurt."
            else -> "is in awful condition!"
        }

private fun printPlayerStatus(auraColor: String,
                              isBlessed: Boolean,
                              name: String,
                              healthStatus: String) {
    println("(Aura: $auraColor) " +
            "(Blessed: ${if (isBlessed) "YES" else "NO"})")
    println("$name $healthStatus")
}

private fun auraColor(isBlessed: Boolean,
                      healthPoints: Int,
                      isImmortal: Boolean): String {
    val auraVisible = isBlessed && healthPoints > 50 || isImmortal
    val auraColor = if (auraVisible) "GREEN" else "NONE"
    return auraColor
}
```

Again, make sure the refactored functions are inside the class's body.

Listing 12.19 Adding class functions to **Player** (Player.kt)

```kotlin
class Player {
    var name = "madrigal"
        get() = field.capitalize()
        private set(value) {
            field = value.trim()
        }

    var healthPoints = 89
    val isBlessed = true
    private val isImmortal = false

    private fun auraColor(isBlessed: Boolean,
                          healthPoints: Int,
                          isImmortal: Boolean): String {
        val auraVisible = isBlessed && healthPoints > 50 || isImmortal
        val auraColor = if (auraVisible) "GREEN" else "NONE"
        return auraColor
    }

    private fun formatHealthStatus(healthPoints: Int, isBlessed: Boolean) =
            when (healthPoints) {
                100 -> "is in excellent condition!"
                in 90..99 -> "has a few scratches."
                in 75..89 -> if (isBlessed) {
                    "has some minor wounds, but is healing quite quickly!"
                } else {
                    "has some minor wounds."
                }
                in 15..74 -> "looks pretty hurt."
                else -> "is in awful condition!"
            }

    fun castFireball(numFireballs: Int = 2) =
            println("A glass of Fireball springs into existence. (x$numFireballs)")
}
```

That takes care of the cutting and pasting, but there is work left to do in both Game.kt and Player.kt. For now, turn your attention to **Player**.

(If you split your editor earlier, you can un-split it now by closing all the files open in a pane. Close files by clicking the X in their tab [Figure 12.5] or by pressing Command-W [Ctrl-W].)

Figure 12.5 Closing a tab in IntelliJ

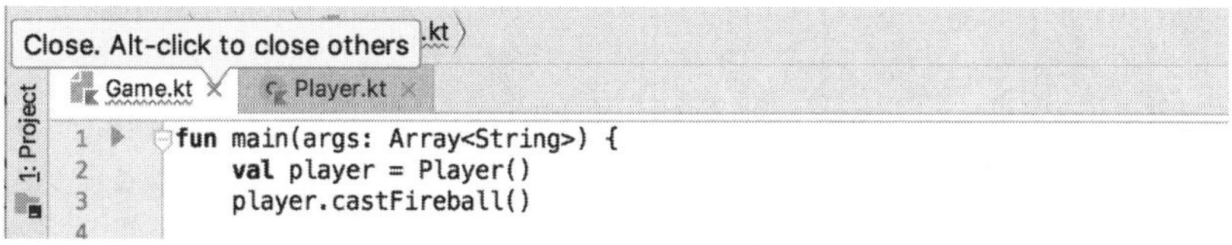

In Player.kt, notice that the functions previously declared in Game.kt that were moved to **Player** – **auraColor** and **formatHealthStatus** – take in values that are now properties of **Player** – isBlessed, healthPoints, and isImmortal. When the functions were defined in Game.kt, they were outside of **Player**'s class scope. But because they are now class functions on **Player**, they have access to all of the properties declared in **Player**.

This means that the class functions in **Player** no longer need any of their parameters, as they can all be accessed from within the **Player** class.

Modify the function headers to remove their parameters.

Listing 12.20 Removing unnecessary parameters from class functions (Player.kt)

```
class Player {
    var name = "madrigal"
        get() = field.capitalize()
        private set(value) {
            field = value.trim()
        }

    var healthPoints = 89
    val isBlessed = true
    private val isImmortal = false

    private fun auraColor(isBlessed: Boolean,
                          healthPoints: Int,
                          isImmortal: Boolean): String {
        val auraVisible = isBlessed && healthPoints > 50 || isImmortal
        val auraColor = if (auraVisible) "GREEN" else "NONE"
        return auraColor
    }

    private fun formatHealthStatus(healthPoints: Int, isBlessed: Boolean) =
            when (healthPoints) {
                100 -> "is in excellent condition!"
                in 90..99 -> "has a few scratches."
                in 75..89 -> if (isBlessed) {
                    "has some minor wounds, but is healing quite quickly!"
                } else {
                    "has some minor wounds."
                }
                in 15..74 -> "looks pretty hurt."
                else -> "is in awful condition!"
            }

    fun castFireball(numFireballs: Int = 2) =
            println("A glass of Fireball springs into existence. (x$numFireballs)")
}
```

Before this change, a reference to healthPoints within the **formatHealthStatus** function would be a reference to **formatHealthStatus**'s parameter, because that reference was scoped to the function. Without a variable named healthPoints within the function scope, the next most local scope is at the class level, where the healthPoints property is defined.

Next, notice that the two class functions are defined as private. This was not a problem when they were defined in the same file from which they were accessed. But now that they are private to the **Player** class, they are not visible to other classes. These functions should not be encapsulated, so make them visible by removing the private keyword from **auraColor** and **formatHealthStatus**.

Listing 12.21 Making class functions public (Player.kt)

```kotlin
class Player {
    var name = "madrigal"
        get() = field.capitalize()
        private set(value) {
            field = value.trim()
        }

    var healthPoints = 89
    val isBlessed = true
    private val isImmortal = false

    private fun auraColor(): String {
        ...
    }

    private fun formatHealthStatus() = when (healthPoints) {
        ...
    }

    fun castFireball(numFireballs: Int = 2) =
            println("A glass of Fireball springs into existence. (x$numFireballs)")
}
```

At this point, your properties and functions are declared in the correct places, but their invocation syntax in Game.kt is no longer correct, for three reasons:

1. **printPlayerStatus** no longer has access to the variables that it needs to do its job, because those variables are now properties of **Player**.

2. Now that functions like **auraColor** are class functions declared in **Player**, they need to be called on an instance of **Player**.

3. **Player**'s class functions need to be called with their new, parameterless signatures.

Refactor **printPlayerStatus** to take a **Player** as an argument that can be used to access any properties necessary and to call the new, parameterless versions of **auraColor** and **formatHealthStatus**.

Listing 12.22 Calling class functions (Game.kt)

```
fun main(args: Array<String>) {
    val player = Player()
    player.castFireball()

    // Aura
    val auraColor = player.auraColor(~~isBlessed, healthPoints, isImmortal~~)

    // Player status
    ~~val healthStatus = formatHealthStatus(healthPoints, isBlessed)~~
    printPlayerStatus(player~~auraColor, isBlessed, player.name, healthStatus~~)

    // Aura
    player.auraColor(~~isBlessed, healthPoints, isImmortal~~)
}

private fun printPlayerStatus(player: Player~~auraColor: String,~~
                              ~~isBlessed: Boolean,~~
                              ~~name: String,~~
                              ~~healthStatus: String~~) {
    println("(Aura: ${player.auraColor()}) " +
            "(Blessed: ${if (player.isBlessed) "YES" else "NO"})")
    println("${player.name} ${player.formatHealthStatus()}")
}
```

This change to **printPlayerStatus**'s header keeps it clean from the implementation details of **Player**. Compare these two signatures:

```
printPlayerStatus(player: Player)

printPlayerStatus(auraColor: String,
                  isBlessed: Boolean,
                  name: String,
                  healthStatus: String)
```

Which is cleaner to call? The latter requires the caller to know quite a lot about the implementation details of **Player**. The former simply requires an instance of **Player**. Here you see one of the benefits of object-oriented programming: Since the data is now a part of the **Player** class, it can be referenced without having to explicitly pass it to and from each function.

Take a step back and assess what you have accomplished in this refactor. The **Player** class now owns all the data and behaviors specific to a player entity in the game. It deliberately exposes three properties and three functions and encapsulates all other implementation details as private concerns that only the **Player** class should have access to. These functions advertise capabilities of the player: The player can provide a health status, the player can tell you their aura color, etc.

As your applications grow in scale, keeping scope manageable is imperative. By embracing object-oriented programming, you subscribe to the idea that each object should hold its own responsibilities and expose only the properties and functions that other functions and classes should see. Now, **Player** exposes what it means to be a player of NyetHack, and Game.kt holds the game loop in a much more readable **main** function.

Run Game.kt to confirm that everything works as it did before. And pat yourself on the back for completing that refactor. In the chapters to come, you will build on this solid foundation for NyetHack, adding complexity and features that rely on the object-oriented programming paradigm.

In the next chapter, you will add more ways to instantiate **Player** as you learn about initialization. But before growing your application further, it is a good time to learn about packages.

Using Packages

A package is like a folder for similar elements that helps give a logical grouping to the files in your project. For example, the `kotlin.collections` package contains classes to create and manage lists and sets. Packages allow you to organize your project as it becomes more complex, and they also prevent naming collisions.

Create a package by right-clicking your src directory and selecting New → Package. When prompted, name your package com.bignerdranch.nyethack. (You can name a package anything you like, but we prefer this reverse-DNS style that scales with the number of applications that you write.)

The package you created, `com.bignerdranch.nyethack`, is the top-level package for NyetHack. Including your files within a top-level package will prevent any naming collisions with types that you define and types defined elsewhere – for instance, in external libraries or modules. As you add more files, you can create additional packages to keep the files organized.

Notice that the new `com.bignerdranch.nyethack` package (which resembles a folder) is displayed in the project tool window. Add your source files (`Game.kt`, `Player.kt`, `SwordJuggler.kt`, and `Tavern.kt`) to your new package by dragging them into the package (Figure 12.6).

Figure 12.6 The `com.bignerdranch.nyethack` package

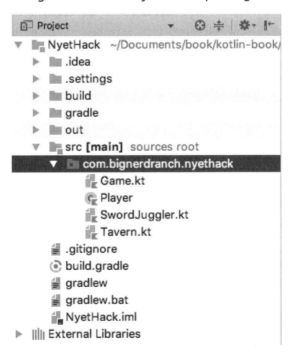

Organizing code using classes, files, and packages will help you to make sure that your code is clear as your application grows in complexity.

181

For the More Curious: A Closer Look at var and val Properties

In this chapter you learned that the var and val keywords are used when specifying a class property – var for writable, and val for read-only.

You may be wondering how a Kotlin class property works, under the hood, when targeting the JVM.

To understand how class properties are implemented, it is helpful to look at the decompiled JVM bytecode – specifically, to compare the bytecode generated for a single property depending on how it is specified. Create a new file called Student.kt. (You will delete this file after this exercise.)

First, define a class with a var property (which allows both reading and writing the class property).

Listing 12.23 Defining a **Student** class (Student.kt)

```
class Student(var name: String)
```

The name property in this example is defined in **Student**'s primary constructor. You will learn more about constructors in Chapter 13, but for now, just think of the constructor as providing a way to customize how your class is built. In this case, the constructor gives you a way to specify the name of the student.

Now, take a look at the resulting decompiled bytecode (Tools → Kotlin → Show Kotlin Bytecode):

```
public final class Student {
  @NotNull
  private String name;

  @NotNull
  public final String getName() {
     return this.name;
  }

  public final void setName(@NotNull String var1) {
     Intrinsics.checkParameterIsNotNull(var1, "<set-?>");
     this.name = var1;
  }

  public Student(@NotNull String name) {
     Intrinsics.checkParameterIsNotNull(name, "name");
     super();
     this.name = name;
  }
}
```

Four elements of the **Student** class were generated in bytecode when you defined the name var on the class: a name field (where name's data will be stored), a getter method, a setter method, and finally a constructor assignment for the field, where the name field is initialized with the **Student**'s name constructor argument.

Now try changing the property from a var to a val:

Listing 12.24 Changing the var to a val (Student.kt)

```
class Student(varval name: String)
```

And observe the resulting decompiled bytecode. (The strike-through here is to emphasize what is missing.)

```
public final class Student {
  @NotNull
  private String name;

  @NotNull
  public final String getName() {
     return this.name;
  }

  public final void setName(@NotNull String var1) {
     Intrinsics.checkParameterIsNotNull(var1, "<set ?>");
     this.name = var1;
  }

  public Student(@NotNull String name) {
     Intrinsics.checkParameterIsNotNull(name, "name");
     super();
     this.name = name;
  }
}
```

The difference between using the var keyword and val keyword for the property is the absence of a setter.

You also learned in this chapter that you can define a custom getter or setter for a property. What happens in bytecode when you define a computed property, with a custom getter and no field for storing the data? Try it with the **Student** class you defined:

Listing 12.25 Making name a computed property (Student.kt)

```
class Student(val name: String) {
    val name: String
        get() = "Madrigal"
}
```

Now take a look at the resulting decompiled bytecode:

```
public final class Student {
    @NotNull
    private String name;

    @NotNull
    public final String getName() {
       return this.name;
       return "Madrigal"
    }

    public final void setName(@NotNull String var1) {
       Intrinsics.checkParameterIsNotNull(var1, "<set ?>");
       this.name = var1;
    }

    public Student(@NotNull String name) {
       Intrinsics.checkParameterIsNotNull(name, "name");
       super();
       this.name = name;
    }
}
```

Only one element was generated in the bytecode this time – a getter. The compiler was able to determine that no field was required, since no data from a field was read or written.

This particular feature of properties – computing a value, rather than reading a field's state – is another reason we use the terms "writable" and "read-only" rather than "mutable" and "immutable." Look again at the **Dice** class you defined in the REPL earlier:

```
class Dice() {
    val rolledValue
        get() = (1..6).shuffled().first()
}
```

The result of reading **Dice**'s rolledValue property is a random value ranging from 1 to 6, determined each time the property is accessed – hardly the definition of "immutable."

When you are done exploring the bytecode, close Student.kt and delete it by Control-clicking (right-clicking) on the filename in the project tool window and selecting Delete.

For the More Curious: Guarding Against Race Conditions

When a class property is both nullable and mutable, you must ensure that it is non-null before referencing it. For example, consider the following code that checks whether a player is wielding a weapon (since the player may have been disarmed or dropped their weapon) and, if so, prints its name:

```
class Weapon(val name: String)
class Player {
    var weapon: Weapon? = Weapon("Ebony Kris")

    fun printWeaponName() {
        if (weapon != null) {
            println(weapon.name)
        }
    }
}

fun main(args: Array<String>) {
    Player().printWeaponName()
}
```

You may be surprised to learn that this code does not compile. Check out the error to see why (Figure 12.7):

Figure 12.7 Smart cast to 'Weapon' is impossible

```
class Weapon(val name: String)
class Player {
    var weapon: Weapon? = Weapon( name: "Ebony Kris")

    fun printWeaponName() {
        if (weapon != null) {
            println(weapon.name)
```

Smart cast to 'Weapon' is impossible, because 'weapon' is a mutable property that could have been changed by this time

```
    }
```

The compiler prevents the code from compiling because of the possibility of what is known as a *race condition*. A race condition occurs when some other part of your program simultaneously modifies the state of your code in a manner that leads to unpredictable results.

Here, the compiler sees that although weapon is checked for a null value, there is still a possibility of the **Player**'s weapon property being replaced with a null value between the time that check passed and the time the name of the weapon is printed.

Therefore, unlike in other cases where weapon could be smart cast within the null check, the compiler balks because it cannot safely say that weapon will never be null.

One way to fix this problem is to use a standard function like **also**, which you read about in Chapter 9, to guard against null:

```
class Player {
    var weapon: Weapon? = Weapon("Ebony Kris")

    fun printWeaponName() {
        weapon?.also {
            println(it.name)
        }
    }
}
```

This code compiles, thanks to the **also** standard function. Instead of referring to the class property, it, the argument to **also**, is a local variable that exists only within the scope of the anonymous function. Therefore, the it variable is guaranteed to not be changed by another part of your program. The smart cast issue is avoided entirely, because instead of dealing with the original nullable property, this code uses a read-only, non-nullable local variable (since **also** is called after the safe call operator: weapon?.also).

For the More Curious: Package Private

Recall from earlier in the chapter the discussion about public and private visibility levels. As you learned, a Kotlin class, function, or property is public by default (without a visibility modifier), which means it is usable by any other class, function, or property in the project.

If you are familiar with Java, you may have noticed that the default access level differs from that of Kotlin: By default, Java uses package private visibility, which means that methods, fields, and classes with no visibility modifier are usable from classes belonging to the same package only. Kotlin opted out of supporting package private visibility because it accomplishes little. In practice, it is easily circumvented by creating a matching package and adding a class to it.

On the other hand, a visibility level Kotlin provides that Java does not is the internal visibility level. Internal visibility marks a function, class, or property as public to other functions, classes, and properties within the same *module*. A module is a discrete unit of functionality that can be run, tested, and debugged independently.

Modules include such things as source code, build scripts, unit tests, deployment descriptors, and so on. NyetHack is one module within your project, and an IntelliJ project can contain multiple modules. Modules can also depend on other modules for source files and resources.

Internal visibility is useful for sharing classes within a module while disallowing access from other modules, which makes it a great choice for building libraries in Kotlin.

13

Initialization

In the last chapter, you saw how to define classes that represent real-world objects. In NyetHack, a player is defined in part by its properties and by its behavior. For all the complexity that can be represented using class properties and functions, you have seen very little so far of how instances of classes come to be.

Think back to how **Player** was defined in the last chapter.

```
class Player {
    ...
}
```

Player's class header is quite simple, and, as such, instantiating **Player** was also simple.

```
fun main(args: Array<String>) {
    val player = Player()
    ...
}
```

Recall that when you call a class's constructor, an instance of that class is created – a process known as instantiation. This chapter covers the ways classes and their properties can be *initialized*. When you initialize a variable, property, or class instance, you assign it an initial value to make it ready for use. You will see more constructors, learn about property initialization, and even learn how to bend the rules with late and lazy initialization.

A note about terminology: Technically, an object is *instantiated* when memory is allocated for it, and it is *initialized* when it is assigned a value. However, in practice the terms are often used slightly differently. Often, *initialization* is used to mean "everything required to make a variable, property, or class instance ready to use," while *instantiation* tends to be limited to "creating an instance of a class." In this book, we follow this more typical usage.

Constructors

Player now contains behavior and data you defined. For example, you specified an isImmortal property:

```
val isImmortal = false
```

You used a val because once the player is created, their immortality should never be reassigned. But this property declaration means that, at the moment, no player can be immortal: There is currently no way to initialize isImmortal to any value other than false.

This is where a *primary constructor* comes into play. A constructor allows its caller to specify the initial values that an instance of a class will require in order to be constructed. Those values are then available for assignment to the properties defined within the class.

Primary constructors

Like a function, a constructor defines expected parameters that must be provided as arguments. To specify what is needed for a **Player** instance to work correctly, you are going to define the primary constructor in **Player**'s header. Update Player.kt to provide initial values for each of **Player**'s properties using temporary variables.

Listing 13.1 Defining a primary constructor (Player.kt)

```
class Player(_name: String,
            _healthPoints: Int,
            _isBlessed: Boolean,
            _isImmortal: Boolean) {
    var name = "Madrigal"_name
        get() = field.capitalize()
        private set(value) {
            field = value.trim()
        }

    var healthPoints = 89_healthPoints
    val isBlessed = true_isBlessed
    private val isImmortal = false_isImmortal
    ...
}
```

(Why prepend these variable names with underscores? Temporary variables, including parameters that you do not need to reference more than once, are often given a name starting with an underscore to signify that they are single-use.)

Now, to create an instance of **Player**, you provide arguments that match the parameters you added to the constructor. Instead of hardcoding the value for the player's name property, for example, you pass an argument to **Player**'s primary constructor. Change the call to **Player**'s constructor in **main** to reflect this.

Listing 13.2 Calling the primary constructor (Game.kt)

```
fun main(args: Array<String>) {
    val player = Player("Madrigal", 89, true, false)
    ...
}
```

Consider how much functionality the primary constructor has added to **Player**: Before, a player of NyetHack was always named Madrigal, was never immortal, and so on. Now, a player can be named anything, and the door to immortality is open – none of **Player**'s data is hardcoded.

Run Game.kt to confirm that the output has not changed.

Defining properties in a primary constructor

Notice the one-to-one relationship between the constructor parameters in **Player** and the class properties: You have a parameter and a class property for each property to be specified when the player is constructed.

For properties that use the default getter and setter, Kotlin allows you to specify both in one definition, rather than having to assign them using temporary variables. name uses a custom getter and setter, so it cannot take advantage of this feature, but **Player**'s other properties can.

Update the **Player** class to define healthPoints, isBlessed, and isImmortal as properties in **Player**'s primary constructor. (Do not neglect to delete the underscores before the names of the variables.)

Listing 13.3 Defining properties in the primary constructor (Player.kt)

```
class Player(_name: String,
            var _healthPoints: Int,
            val _isBlessed: Boolean,
            private val _isImmortal: Boolean) {
    var name = _name
        get() = field.capitalize()
        private set(value) {
            field = value.trim()
        }

    var healthPoints = _healthPoints
    val isBlessed = _isBlessed
    private val isImmortal = _isImmortal
    ...
}
```

For each constructor parameter, you specify whether it is writable or read-only. By specifying the parameters with val or var keywords in the constructor, you define properties for the class, whether they are val or var properties, and the parameters the constructor will expect arguments for. You also implicitly assign each property to the value passed to it as an argument.

Duplication of code makes it harder to make changes. Generally, we prefer this way of defining class properties because it leads to less duplication. You were not able to use this syntax for name, because of its custom getter and setter, but in other cases, defining a property in a primary constructor is often the most straightforward choice.

Secondary constructors

Constructors come in two flavors: primary and secondary. When you specify a primary constructor, you say, "These parameters are required for any instance of this class." When you specify a secondary constructor, you provide alternative ways to construct the class (while still meeting the requirements of the primary constructor).

A secondary constructor must either call the primary constructor, providing it all of the arguments it requires, or call through to another secondary constructor – which follows the same rule. For example, say you know that in most cases a player will begin with 100 health points, will be blessed, and will be mortal. You can define a secondary constructor to provide that configuration. Add a secondary constructor to **Player**:

Listing 13.4 Defining a secondary constructor (`Player.kt`)

```
class Player(_name: String,
             var healthPoints: Int
             val isBlessed: Boolean
             private val isImmortal: Boolean) {
    var name = _name
        get() = field.capitalize()
        private set(value) {
            field = value.trim()
        }

    constructor(name: String) : this(name,
            healthPoints = 100,
            isBlessed = true,
            isImmortal = false)
    ...
}
```

You can define multiple secondary constructors for different combinations of parameters. This secondary constructor calls through to the primary constructor with a certain set of parameters. The this keyword in this case refers to the instance of the class for which this constructor is defined. Specifically, this is calling into another constructor defined in the class – the primary constructor.

Because this secondary constructor provides default values for healthPoints, isBlessed, and isImmortal, you do not need to pass arguments for those parameters when calling it. Call **Player**'s secondary constructor from Game.kt instead of its primary constructor.

Listing 13.5 Calling a secondary constructor (`Game.kt`)

```
fun main(args: Array<String>) {
    val player = Player("Madrigal", 89, true, false)
    ...
}
```

You can also use a secondary constructor to define initialization logic – code that will run when your class is instantiated. For example, add an expression that reduces the player's health points value to 40 if their name is Kar.

Listing 13.6 Adding logic to a secondary constructor (`Player.kt`)

```
class Player(_name: String,
             var healthPoints: Int
             val isBlessed: Boolean
             private val isImmortal: Boolean) {
    var name = _name
        get() = field.capitalize()
        private set(value) {
            field = value.trim()
        }

    constructor(name: String) : this(name,
            healthPoints = 100,
            isBlessed = true,
            isImmortal = false) {
        if (name.toLowerCase() == "kar") healthPoints = 40
    }
    ...
}
```

Although they are useful for defining alternative logic to be run on instantiation, secondary constructors cannot be used to define properties like primary constructors can. Class properties must be defined in the primary constructor or at the class level.

Run Game.kt to see that Madrigal is still blessed and has health points, showing that **Player**'s secondary constructor was called from Game.kt.

Default arguments

When defining a constructor, you can also specify default values that should be assigned if an argument is not provided for a specific parameter. You have seen these default arguments in the context of functions, and they work the same way with both primary and secondary constructors. For example, set the default value for healthPoints with a default parameter value of 100 in the primary constructor, as follows:

Listing 13.7 Defining a default argument in a constructor (Player.kt)

```
class Player(_name: String,
            var healthPoints: Int = 100
            val isBlessed: Boolean
            private val isImmortal: Boolean) {
    var name = _name
        get() = field.capitalize()
        private set(value) {
            field = value.trim()
        }

    constructor(name: String) : this(name,
            healthPoints = 100,
            isBlessed = true,
            isImmortal = false) {
        if (name.toLowerCase() == "kar") healthPoints = 40
    }
    ...
}
```

Because you added a default argument value to the healthPoints parameter in the primary constructor, you removed the healthPoints argument passed from **Player**'s secondary constructor to its primary constructor. This gives you another way to instantiate **Player**: with or without an argument for healthPoints.

```
// Player constructed with 64 health points using the primary constructor
Player("Madrigal", 64, true, false)

// Player constructed with 100 health points using the primary constructor
Player("Madrigal", true, false)

// Player constructed with 100 health points using the secondary constructor
Player("Madrigal")
```

Named arguments

The more default arguments you use, the more options you have for calling your constructor. More options can open the door for more ambiguity, so Kotlin provides named constructor arguments, just like the named arguments that you have used to call functions.

Compare the following two options for constructing an instance of **Player**:

```
val player = Player(name = "Madrigal",
        healthPoints = 100,
        isBlessed = true,
        isImmortal = false)

val player = Player("Madrigal", 100, true, false)
```

Which option do you find to be more readable? If you chose the first, we agree with your judgment.

Named argument syntax lets you include the parameter name for each argument to improve readability. This is especially useful when you have multiple parameters of the same type: If you see "true" and "false" both passed into the **Player** constructor, named arguments will help you determine which value corresponds to which parameter. This reduced ambiguity leads to another benefit: Named arguments allow you to specify the arguments to a function or constructor in any order. If parameters are unnamed, then you need to refer to the constructor to know their order.

You may have noticed that the secondary constructor you wrote for **Player** used named arguments, similar to the ones that you saw in Chapter 4.

```
constructor(name: String) : this(name,
        healthPoints = 100,
        isBlessed = true,
        isImmortal = false)
```

When you have more than a few arguments to provide to a constructor or function, we recommend using named parameters. They make it easier for readers to keep track of which argument is being passed as which parameter.

Initializer Blocks

In addition to the primary and secondary constructors, you can also specify an *initializer block* for a class in Kotlin. The initializer block is a way to set up variables or values as well as perform validation – like checking to make sure that the arguments to the constructor are valid ones. The code it holds is executed when the class is constructed.

For example, players have certain requirements as they are constructed: A player must begin the game with at least one health point. Their name must not be blank.

Use an initializer block, denoted by the init keyword, to enforce these requirements with preconditions.

Listing 13.8 Defining an initializer block (Player.kt)

```kotlin
class Player(_name: String,
            var healthPoints: Int = 100
            val isBlessed: Boolean
            private val isImmortal: Boolean) {
    var name = _name
        get() = field.capitalize()
        private set(value) {
            field = value.trim()
        }

    init {
        require(healthPoints > 0, { "healthPoints must be greater than zero." })
        require(name.isNotBlank(), { "Player must have a name." })
    }

    constructor(name: String) : this(name,
            isBlessed = true,
            isImmortal = false) {
        if (name.toLowerCase() == "kar") healthPoints = 40
    }
    ...
}
```

If either of these preconditions fails, then an IllegalArgumentException is thrown. (You can test this by passing **Player** different parameters in the Kotlin REPL.)

These requirements would be difficult to encapsulate in a constructor or a property declaration. The code in the initializer block will be called when the class is instantiated – no matter which constructor for the class is called, primary or secondary.

Property Initialization

So far, you have seen a property initialized in two ways – either assigned to a value passed as an argument, or defined *inline* in a primary constructor.

A property can (and must) be initialized with any value of its type, including function return values. Let's look at an example.

Your hero can come from one of any number of exotic locales in the world of NyetHack. Define a new String property called hometown to hold the name of a player's town of origin.

Listing 13.9 Defining the hometown property (Player.kt)

```kotlin
class Player(_name: String,
            var healthPoints: Int = 100
            val isBlessed: Boolean
            private val isImmortal: Boolean) {
    var name = _name
        get() = field.capitalize()
        private set(value) {
            field = value.trim()
        }

    val hometown: String

    init {
        require(healthPoints > 0, { "healthPoints must be greater than zero." })
        require(name.isNotBlank(), { "Player must have a name" })
    }
    ...
}
```

You have defined hometown, but you have not yet satisfied the Kotlin compiler. Defining the name and type of a property is not enough – you must assign an initial value when defining a property. Why? Kotlin's null safety rules. Without an initial value, a property could be null, which would be illegal if the property is of a non-nullable type.

One way to put a bandage on this problem would be to initialize hometown as an empty string:

```kotlin
val hometown = ""
```

This compiles, but it is not the ideal solution because "" is not a town in NyetHack. Instead, add a new function called **selectHometown** that returns a random town from a file containing towns. You will use this function to assign an initial value to hometown.

Listing 13.10 Defining the **selectHometown** function (Player.kt)

```
import java.io.File

class Player(_name: String,
             var healthPoints: Int = 100
             val isBlessed: Boolean
             private val isImmortal: Boolean) {
    var name = _name
        get() = field.capitalize()
        private set(value) {
            field = value.trim()
        }

    val hometown: String = selectHometown()
    ...
    private fun selectHometown() = File("data/towns.txt")
            .readText()
            .split("\n")
            .shuffled()
            .first()
}
```

(Notice that you need to import java.io.File into Player.kt to access the **File** class.)

You will need to add a towns.txt file to your existing data directory to hold this list of towns. You can find the file at bignerdranch.com/solutions/towns.txt.

Test out your hometown property by using it in the name property's getter. To differentiate your hero from all of the other Madrigals in the world, your hero should be addressed by a name that includes their hometown.

Listing 13.11 Using the hometown property (Player.kt)

```
class Player(_name: String,
             var healthPoints: Int = 100
             val isBlessed: Boolean
             private val isImmortal: Boolean) {
    var name = _name
        get() = "${field.capitalize()} of $hometown"
        private set(value) {
            field = value.trim()
        }

    val hometown = selectHometown()
    ...
    private fun selectHometown() = File("data/towns.txt")
            .readText()
            .split("\n")
            .shuffled()
            .first()
}
```

Run Game.kt. Whenever your hero is addressed by name, they will be differentiated via their hometown:

```
A glass of Fireball springs into existence. Delicious! (x2)
(Aura: GREEN) (Blessed: YES)
Madrigal of Tampa is in excellent condition!
```

If your property requires complex initialization logic – multiple expressions, for example – consider pulling this initialization logic into a function or an initializer block.

The rule that states that properties must be assigned on declaration does not apply to variables in a smaller scope, like a function. For example:

```
class JazzPlayer {
    fun acquireMusicalInstrument() {
        val instrumentName: String
        instrumentName = "Oboe"
    }
}
```

Because `instrumentName` is assigned a value before it can be referenced, this code compiles.

Properties have more strict rules on initialization because they can be accessed from other classes if they are public. Variables local to a function, on the other hand, are scoped to the function in which they are defined and cannot be accessed from outside of it.

Initialization Order

You have seen how to initialize properties or add logic to the initialization of properties in various ways – inline in a primary constructor, initialized at declaration, initialized in a secondary constructor, or initialized in an initializer block. It is possible for the same property to be referenced in multiple initializers, so the order in which they are executed is important.

To take a closer look, it is helpful to examine the resulting field initialization order and method invocations in the decompiled Java bytecode. Consider the following, which defines a **Player** class and constructs an instance of it:

```
class Player(_name: String, val health: Int) {

    val race = "DWARF"
    var town = "Bavaria"
    val name = _name
    val alignment: String
    private var age = 0

    init {
        println("initializing player")
        alignment = "GOOD"
    }

    constructor(_name: String) : this(_name, 100) {
        town = "The Shire"
    }

}

fun main(args: Array<String>) {
    Player("Madrigal")
}
```

Notice that this **Player** class is constructed by calling `Player("Madrigal")`, the secondary constructor.

Figure 13.1 shows this **Player** class on the left. The abbreviated decompiled Java bytecode on the right shows the resulting initialization order:

Figure 13.1 Initialization order for the **Player** class (decompiled bytecode)

```
Player("Madrigal")
```

```
class Player(_name: String, val health: Int) {
    val race = "DWARF"
    var town = "Bavaria"
    val name = _name
    val alignment: String
    private var age = 0

    init {
        println("initializing player")
        alignment = "GOOD"
    }

    constructor(_name: String) : this(_name, health: 100) {
        town = "The Shire"
    }
}
```

```
public final class Player {
    private final String race;
    private String town;
    private final String name;
    private final String alignment;
    private int age;
    private final int health;

    public Player(String _name, int health) {
        this.health = health;
        this.race = "DWARF";
        this.town = "Bavaria";
        this.name = _name;
        String var3 = "initializing player";
        System.out.println(var3);
        this.alignment = "GOOD";
    }

    public Player(String _name) {
        this(_name, health: 100);
        this.town = "The Shire";
    }
}
```

The resulting initialization order is as follows:

1. the primary constructor's inline properties (val health: Int)

2. required class-level property assignments (val race = "DWARF", val town = "Bavaria", val name = _name)

3. init block property assignments and function calls (alignment = "GOOD", **println** function)

4. secondary constructor property assignments and function calls (town = "The Shire")

The initialization order of the init block (item 3) and the class-level property assignments (item 2) depends on the order they are specified in. If the init block were defined before the class property assignments, it would be initialized second, followed by the class property assignments.

Note that one property is not assigned in the constructor – age – even though it is assigned at the class property level. Because its value is 0 (Java's primitive int default value), the assignment is not required and the compiler optimizes initialization by skipping it.

Delaying Initialization

Wherever it is declared, a class property must be initialized when the class instance is constructed. This rule is an important part of Kotlin's null safety system, because it means that all non-nullable properties of a class are initialized with a non-null value when the constructor for that class is called. When you instantiate an object, you can immediately reference any property on that object, from within or outside of the class.

Despite its importance, you can bend this rule. Why would you? You do not always have control over how or when a constructor is called. One such case is in the Android framework.

Late initialization

On Android, a class called **Activity** represents a screen in your application. You do not have control over when the constructor of your **Activity** is called. Instead, the earliest point of code execution you have is in a function called **onCreate**. If you cannot initialize your properties at instantiation time, when can you?

This is where *late initialization* becomes important – and more than just a simple bending of Kotlin's rules on initialization.

Any var property declaration can be appended with the lateinit keyword, and the Kotlin compiler will let you put off initializing the property until you assign it.

```
class Player {
    lateinit var alignment: String

    fun determineFate() {
        alignment = "Good"
    }

    fun proclaimFate() {
        if (::alignment.isInitialized) println(alignment)
    }
}
```

This is useful but must be regarded with care. As long as you initialize your late-initialized variable before it is accessed, then there is no problem. But if you reference your late-initialized property before it has been initialized, then you will be greeted with an unpleasant UninitializedPropertyAccessException.

You could implement this pattern using a nullable type instead, but you would then be required to handle your property's nullability throughout your codebase, which is burdensome. Late-initialized variables function just like other variables once assigned.

The lateinit keyword functions as a contract that you make with yourself: "I take responsibility for initializing this variable before it is accessed." Kotlin does provide a way to check whether a late-initialized variable has been initialized: the **isInitialized** check shown in the example above. You can check **isInitialized** when there is any uncertainty about whether the lateinit variable is initialized to avoid an UninitializedPropertyAccessException.

However, **isInitialized** should be used sparingly – it should not be added to every lateinit, for example. If you are using **isInitialized** a lot, it is likely an indicator that you should be using a nullable type instead.

Lazy initialization

Late initialization is not the only way to delay initialization. You can also hold off on initializing a variable until it is accessed for the first time. This concept is known as *lazy initialization*, and despite the name, it can actually make your code more efficient.

Most of the properties that you have initialized in this chapter have been pretty lightweight – single objects, like a String. Many classes, however, are more complex. They may require the instantiation of multiple objects, or they may involve some more computationally intensive task when being initialized, like reading from a file. If your property triggers a large number of these sorts of tasks, or if your class does not require access to a property right away, then lazy initialization could be a good choice.

Lazy initialization is implemented in Kotlin using a mechanism known as a *delegate*. Delegates define templates for how a property is initialized.

You use a delegate with the by keyword. The Kotlin standard library includes some delegates that are already implemented for you, and **lazy** is one of them. Lazy initialization takes a lambda in which you define any code that you wish to execute when your property is initialized.

Player's hometown property reads from a file as a part of its initialization. You might not access hometown right away, so it is more efficient to wait to initialize until hometown is needed. Lazily initialize hometown in **Player**. (Some of these changes are tricky to see. You need to delete the =, add by lazy, and add curly braces around selectHometown().)

Listing 13.12 Lazily initializing hometown (Player.kt)

```
class Player(_name: String,
            var healthPoints: Int = 100
            val isBlessed: Boolean
            private val isImmortal: Boolean) {
    var name = _name
        get() = "${field.capitalize()} of $hometown"
        private set(value) {
            field = value.trim()
        }

    val hometown ➡by lazy { selectHometown() }
    ...
    private fun selectHometown() = File("towns.txt")
            .readText()
            .split("\n")
            .shuffled()
            .first()
}
```

In this lambda, the result of **selectHometown** is implicitly returned and assigned to hometown.

hometown remains uninitialized until it is referenced for the first time. At that point, all of the code in **lazy**'s lambda is executed. Importantly, this code is only executed once – the first time that the delegated property (hometown, here) is accessed in name's getter. Future access to the lazy property will use a cached result instead of performing the expensive computation again.

Lazy initialization is useful, but it can be a bit verbose, so stick to using lazy initialization for more computationally needy tasks.

And with that, you have seen what there is to see when it comes to initializing an object in Kotlin. Most often, your experience will be quite straightforward: You call a constructor, and you get a reference to an instance of a class to do with what you will. That said, you have other options when initializing an object in Kotlin, and understanding those options can help you write clean, efficient code.

In the next chapter you will learn about inheritance, an object-oriented principle that allows you to share data and behavior between related classes.

For the More Curious: Initialization Gotchas

You saw earlier in the chapter that order is important when using initializer blocks – you must ensure that all properties used in the block are initialized before the initializer block is defined. Take a look at the following code that shows this initializer block ordering problem:

```
class Player() {
    init {
        val healthBonus = health.times(3)
    }

    val health = 100
}

fun main(args: Array<String>) {
    Player()
}
```

This code would not compile, because the health property is not initialized at the point that it is used by the init block. As we mentioned earlier, when a property is used within an init block, the property initialization must happen before it is accessed. When health is defined before the initializer block, the code compiles:

```
class Player() {
    val health = 100

    init {
        val healthBonus = health.times(3)
    }
}

fun main(args: Array<String>) {
    Player()
}
```

There are a couple of similar, but more subtle, scenarios that trip up unwary programmers. For example, in the following code, a name property is declared, then a **firstLetter** function reads the first character from the property:

```
class Player() {
    val name: String

    private fun firstLetter() = name[0]

    init {
        println(firstLetter())
        name = "Madrigal"
    }
}

fun main(args: Array<String>) {
    Player()
}
```

This code will compile, because the compiler sees that the name property is initialized in the init block, a legal place to assign an initial value. But running this code would result in a null pointer exception, because the **firstLetter** function (which uses the name property) is called before the name property is assigned an initial value in the init block.

The compiler does not inspect the order properties are initialized in compared to the functions that use them within the init block. When defining an init block that calls functions that access properties, it is up to you to ensure that you have initialized those properties before calling the functions. When name is assigned before **firstLetter** is called, the code compiles *and* will run without error:

```
class Player() {
    val name: String

    private fun firstLetter() = name[0]

    init {
        name = "Madrigal"
        println(firstLetter())
    }
}

fun main(args: Array<String>) {
    Player()
}
```

One more tricky scenario is shown in the following code, in which two properties are initialized:

```
class Player(_name: String) {
    val playerName: String = initPlayerName()
    val name: String = _name

    private fun initPlayerName() = name
}

fun main(args: Array<String>) {
    println(Player("Madrigal").playerName)
}
```

Again, this code compiles, since the compiler sees that all properties have been initialized. But running the code would result in the unsatisfying output null.

What is the problem here? When playerName is initialized with the **initPlayerName** function, the compiler assumes that name is initialized, but when **initPlayerName** is called, name is actually not yet initialized.

In this case, once again, order matters. The initialization order of the two properties must be reversed. With that done, the **Player** class compiles and returns a non-null name value:

```
class Player(_name: String) {
    val name: String = _name
    val playerName: String = initPlayerName()

    private fun initPlayerName() = name
}

fun main(args: Array<String>) {
    println(Player("Madrigal").playerName)
}
```

Challenge: The Riddle of Excalibur

As you learned in Chapter 12, you can specify your own getter and setter for a property. Now that you have seen how properties and their classes are initialized, we have a riddle for you.

Every great sword has a name. Define a class called **Sword** in the Kotlin REPL that reflects this truth.

Listing 13.13 Defining **Sword** (REPL)

```
class Sword(_name: String) {
    var name = _name
        get() = "The Legendary $field"
        set(value) {
            field = value.toLowerCase().reversed().capitalize()
        }
}
```

What is printed when you instantiate a **Sword** and reference name? (Try to answer for yourself before you check the REPL.)

Listing 13.14 Referencing name (REPL)

```
val sword = Sword("Excalibur")
println(sword.name)
```

What is printed when you reassign name?

Listing 13.15 Reassigning name (REPL)

```
sword.name = "Gleipnir"
println(sword.name)
```

Finally, add an initializer block to **Sword** that assigns name.

Listing 13.16 Adding an initializer block (REPL)

```
class Sword(_name: String) {
    var name = _name
        get() = "The Legendary $field"
        set(value) {
            field = value.toLowerCase().reversed().capitalize()
        }

    init {
        name = _name
    }
}
```

What is printed when you instantiate **Sword** and reference name now?

Listing 13.17 Referencing name again (REPL)

```
val sword = Sword("Excalibur")
println(sword.name)
```

This challenge will test your knowledge of both initializers and custom property getters and setters.

14

Inheritance

Inheritance is an object-oriented principle you can use to define hierarchical relationships between types. In this chapter you will use inheritance to share data and behavior between related classes.

To get a handle on inheritance, consider an example outside of programming. Cars and trucks have much in common: They each have wheels, an engine, etc. They also have some different features. Using inheritance, you could define the things that they have in common in a shared class, Vehicle, so that you do not have to implement Wheel and Engine and so on in both Car and Truck. Car and Truck would inherit those shared features, and each would then define its unique features as well.

In NyetHack, you have defined what it means to be a **Player** in the game. In this chapter, you will put inheritance to work by adding a series of rooms to NyetHack so that your player has places to go.

Defining the Room Class

Begin by creating a new file in NyetHack called Room.kt. Room.kt will contain a new class called **Room** that will represent one square in NyetHack's coordinate plane. Later, you will define a particular kind of room in a class that inherits qualities from **Room**.

To begin, **Room** will have one property – name – and two functions, **description** and **load**. **description** returns a String describing the room. **load** returns a String that will be printed to the console when you enter the room. These are features you want for every room in NyetHack.

Add the **Room** class definition to Room.kt, as shown:

Listing 14.1 Declaring the **Room** class (Room.kt)

```
class Room(val name: String) {
    fun description() = "Room: $name"

    fun load() = "Nothing much to see here..."
}
```

To test your new **Room** class, create a **Room** instance when the game starts in **main** and print the result of its **description** function.

Listing 14.2 Printing the room description (Game.kt)

```
fun main(args: Array<String>) {
    val player = Player("Madrigal")
    player.castFireball()

    var currentRoom = Room("Foyer")
    println(currentRoom.description())
    println(currentRoom.load())

    // Player status
    printPlayerStatus(player)
}
...
```

Run Game.kt. You should see the following output to the console.

```
A glass of Fireball springs into existence. Delicious! (x2)
Room: Foyer
Nothing much to see here...
(Aura: GREEN) (Blessed: YES)
Madrigal of Tampa is in excellent condition!
```

So far, so good … but kind of boring. Who wants to hang out in a foyer? It is time for Madrigal of Tampa to go places.

Creating a Subclass

A *subclass* shares all properties with the class it inherits from, commonly known as the parent class or *superclass*.

For example, citizens of NyetHack will need a town square. A town square is a type of **Room** with special features only town squares will have – like a customized loading message when players enter. To create the **TownSquare** class, you will subclass **Room**, since they have common features, and then describe how **TownSquare** differs from **Room**.

But before defining a **TownSquare** class, you first need to make a change to the **Room** class so that it can be subclassed.

Not every class you write is intended to be part of a hierarchy, and, in fact, classes are closed – meaning they prohibit subclassing – by default. For a class to be subclassed, it must be marked with the open keyword.

Add the open keyword to **Room** so that it can be subclassed.

Listing 14.3 Making the **Room** class open for subclassing (Room.kt)

```
open class Room(val name: String) {
    fun description() = "Room: $name"

    fun load() = "Nothing much to see here..."
}
```

Now that **Room** is marked open, create a **TownSquare** class in Room.kt by subclassing the **Room** class using the : operator, like so:

Listing 14.4 Declaring the **TownSquare** class (Room.kt)

```
open class Room(val name: String) {
    fun description() = "Room: $name"

    fun load() = "Nothing much to see here..."
}

class TownSquare : Room("Town Square")
```

The **TownSquare** class declaration includes the class name to the left of the : operator and a constructor invocation to the right. The constructor invocation indicates which constructor to call for **TownSquare**'s parent and what arguments to pass to it. In this case, a **TownSquare** is a version of **Room** with the specific name "Town Square".

But you want more from your town square than just a name. Another way for you to differentiate a subclass from its parent is through *overriding*. Recall from Chapter 12 that a class uses properties to represent data and functions to represent behavior. Subclasses can override, or provide custom implementations for, both.

Room has two functions, **description** and **load**. **TownSquare** should provide its own implementation of **load** to express the joy that comes with your hero entering the town square.

Override **load** in **TownSquare** using the override keyword:

Listing 14.5 Declaring the **TownSquare** class (Room.kt)

```
open class Room(val name: String) {
    fun description() = "Room: $name"

    fun load() = "Nothing much to see here..."
}

class TownSquare : Room("Town Square") {
    override fun load() = "The villagers rally and cheer as you enter!"
}
```

When you override **load**, IntelliJ complains about your override keyword (Figure 14.1):

Figure 14.1 **load** cannot be overridden

IntelliJ is right, as always: There is a problem. In addition to **Room** being marked open, **load** must also be marked open for you to override it.

Mark the **load** function in the **Room** class as a function that can be overridden.

Listing 14.6 Declaring an open function (Room.kt)

```kotlin
open class Room(val name: String) {
    fun description() = "Room: $name"

    open fun load() = "Nothing much to see here..."
}

class TownSquare : Room("Town Square") {
    override fun load() = "The villagers rally and cheer as you enter!"
}
```

Now, instead of printing a default statement (Nothing much to see here...), an instance of **TownSquare** will display the cheering villagers when the hero enters and **load** is called.

In Chapter 12, you saw how to control the visibility of properties and functions using visibility modifiers. Properties and functions are public by default. You can also make them visible only within the class where they are defined by setting visibility to private.

Protected visibility is a third option that restricts visibility to the class in which a property or function is defined *or* to any subclasses of that class.

Add a new protected property called dangerLevel to **Room**.

Listing 14.7 Declaring a protected property (Room.kt)

```kotlin
open class Room(val name: String) {
    protected open val dangerLevel = 5

    fun description() = "Room: $name\n" +
            "Danger level: $dangerLevel"

    open fun load() = "Nothing much to see here..."
}

class TownSquare : Room("Town Square") {
    override fun load() = "The villagers rally and cheer as you enter!"
}
```

dangerLevel holds a rating of how dangerous a room is on a scale of 1 to 10. It is printed to the console so that the player knows what level of suspense to expect in each room. The average danger level is 5, so that is the default value assigned to the **Room** class.

Subclasses of **Room** can modify dangerLevel to reflect how dangerous (or not) a particular room is, but dangerLevel should otherwise be encapsulated to **Room** and its subclasses. This scenario is perfect for the protected keyword: You want to expose a property only to the class where the property is defined and its subclasses.

To override the dangerLevel property in **TownSquare**, you use the override keyword, just as you did with the **load** function.

The danger level of a NyetHack town square is three points below average. To express this logic, you need to be able to reference the average danger level of a **Room**. You can reference a class's superclass using the super keyword. From there, you have access to any public or protected properties or functions, including, in this case, dangerLevel.

Override dangerLevel in **TownSquare** to indicate that the danger level of a town square is three points below the average room.

Listing 14.8 Overriding dangerLevel (Room.kt)

```kotlin
open class Room(val name: String) {
    protected open val dangerLevel = 5

    fun description() = "Room: $name\n" +
            "Danger level: $dangerLevel"

    open fun load() = "Nothing much to see here..."
}

class TownSquare : Room("Town Square") {
    override val dangerLevel = super.dangerLevel - 3

    override fun load() = "The villagers rally and cheer as you enter!"
}
```

Subclasses are not limited to overriding the properties and functions of their superclass. They can also define their own.

NyetHack town squares, for example, are unique among rooms in that they have bells that chime to announce important happenings. Add a private function called **ringBell** and a private variable called bellSound to **TownSquare**. bellSound holds a string representing the sound that the bell makes, and **ringBell**, called in the **load** function, returns a string to announce your entry to the town square.

Listing 14.9 Adding a new property and function to a subclass (Room.kt)

```kotlin
open class Room(val name: String) {
    protected open val dangerLevel = 5

    fun description() = "Room: $name\n" +
            "Danger level: $dangerLevel"

    open fun load() = "Nothing much to see here..."
}

class TownSquare : Room("Town Square") {
    override val dangerLevel = super.dangerLevel - 3
    private var bellSound = "GWONG"

    override fun load() = "The villagers rally and cheer as you enter!\n${ringBell()}"

    private fun ringBell() = "The bell tower announces your arrival. $bellSound"
}
```

TownSquare includes properties and functions defined both in **TownSquare** and in **Room**. **Room**, however, does not include all properties and functions declared in **TownSquare**, so it does not have access to **ringBell**.

Test the **load** function by updating the currentRoom variable in Game.kt to create an instance of **TownSquare**.

Listing 14.10 Calling subclass function implementation (Game.kt)

```
fun main(args: Array<String>) {
    val player = Player("Madrigal")
    player.castFireball()

    var currentRoom: Room = Room("Foyer")TownSquare()
    println(currentRoom.description())
    println(currentRoom.load())

    // Player status
    printPlayerStatus(player)
}
...
```

Run Game.kt again. You should see the following output to the console:

```
A glass of Fireball springs into existence. Delicious! (x2)
Room: Town Square
Danger level: 2
The villagers rally and cheer as you enter!
The bell tower announces your arrival. GWONG
(Aura: GREEN) (Blessed: YES)
Madrigal of Tampa is in excellent condition!
```

Notice that the currentRoom variable's type in Game.kt is still **Room**, despite the fact that the instance itself is a **TownSquare**, and its **load** function has been changed substantially from **Room**'s implementation. You explicitly declared the type of currentRoom to be **Room** so that it can hold any type of **Room**, even though you assigned currentRoom with a **TownSquare** constructor.

Since **TownSquare** subclasses **Room**, this is completely valid syntax.

You can also subclass a subclass, creating a deeper hierarchy. If you created a subclass of **TownSquare** called **Piazza**, then **Piazza** would also be of type **TownSquare** and of type **Room**. The only limit to the number of levels that you can subclass is what makes sense for the organization of your codebase. (And, of course, your imagination.)

The different versions of **load**, based on the class they are called on, are an example of a concept in object-oriented programming called *polymorphism*.

Polymorphism is a strategy for simplifying the structure of your program. It allows you to reuse functions for common sets of features across groups of classes (like what happens when a player enters a room) and also to customize the behavior for the unique needs of a class (like the cheering crowd in **TownSquare**). When you subclassed **Room** to define **TownSquare**, you defined a new **load** implementation that overrides **Room**'s version. Now, when currentRoom's **load** function is called, **TownSquare**'s version of **load** will be used – and no changes to Game.kt were required.

Consider the following function header.

```
    fun drawBlueprint(room: Room)
```

drawBlueprint accepts a **Room** as its parameter. It can also accept any subclass of **Room**, because any subclass will have at least the capabilities that **Room** does. Polymorphism allows you to write functions that care only about what a class can do, not how it is implemented.

Opening up functions to be overridden is useful – but it does come with a side effect. When you override a function in Kotlin, the overriding function in the subclass is, by default, open to being overridden (as long as the subclass is marked open).

What if you do not want this to be the case? In the **TownSquare** example, say that you wanted any subclass of **TownSquare** to be able to customize its description but not how it loads.

The final keyword allows you to specify that a function cannot be overridden. Open **TownSquare** and make its **load** function final so that no one can override the fact that villagers cheer when you enter a town square.

Listing 14.11 Declaring a function to be final (Room.kt)

```kotlin
open class Room(val name: String) {
    protected open val dangerLevel = 5

    fun description() = "Room: $name\n" +
            "Danger level: $dangerLevel"

    open fun load() = "Nothing much to see here..."
}

open class TownSquare : Room("Town Square") {
    override val dangerLevel = super.dangerLevel - 3
    private var bellSound = "GWONG"

    final override fun load() =
            "The villagers rally and cheer as you enter!\n${ringBell()}"

    private fun ringBell() = "The bell tower announces your arrival. $bellSound"
}
```

Now, any subclass of **TownSquare** could provide an overriding function for **description** but not **load**, thanks to the final keyword.

As you saw when you first tried to override **load**, functions are final by default unless they are inherited from an open class. Adding the final keyword to an inherited function will ensure that it cannot be overridden, even if the class in which it is defined is open.

You have now seen how to use inheritance to share data and behavior between classes. You have also seen how to use open, final, and override to customize what can and cannot be shared. By requiring the explicit use of the open and override keywords, Kotlin requires you to opt in to inheritance. This reduces the chances of exposing classes that were not meant to be subclassed and prevents you – or others – from overriding functions that were never meant to be overridden.

Type Checking

NyetHack is not a terribly complex program. But a production codebase can include many classes and subclasses. Despite your best efforts at clear naming, you may find yourself from time to time unsure of the type of a variable at runtime. The **is** operator is a useful tool that lets you query whether an object is of a certain type.

Try this out in the Kotlin REPL. Instantiate a **Room**. (You may need to import **Room** into the REPL.)

Listing 14.12 Instantiating a **Room** (REPL)

```
var room = Room("Foyer")
```

Next, query whether room is an instance of the **Room** class using the **is** operator.

Listing 14.13 Checking room is Room (REPL)

```
room is Room
true
```

The type of the object on the lefthand side of the **is** operator is checked against the type on the righthand side. The expression returns a Boolean: true if the types match, false otherwise.

Try another query: Check whether room is an instance of the **TownSquare** class.

Listing 14.14 Checking room is TownSquare (REPL)

```
room is TownSquare
false
```

room is of type **Room**, which is a parent class to **TownSquare**. But room is not itself a **TownSquare**.

Try another variable – this time, a **TownSquare**.

Listing 14.15 Checking townSquare is TownSquare (REPL)

```
var townSquare = TownSquare()
townSquare is TownSquare
true
```

Listing 14.16 Checking townSquare is Room (REPL)

```
townSquare is Room
true
```

townSquare is of type **TownSquare** and also of type **Room**. This, remember, is the idea that makes polymorphism possible.

If you need to know the type of a variable, type checking is a straightforward way to find out. You can build branching logic using type checking and conditionals – but be sure to bear in mind how polymorphism will affect that logic.

For example, create a when expression in the Kotlin REPL that returns **Room** or **TownSquare** depending on the type of a variable.

Listing 14.17 Type checking as a branching condition (REPL)

```
var townSquare = TownSquare()
var className = when(townSquare) {
    is TownSquare -> "TownSquare"
    is Room -> "Room"
    else -> throw IllegalArgumentException()
}
print(className)
```

The first branch in this when expression evaluates as true, because townSquare is of type **TownSquare**. The second branch is also true, because townSquare is also of type **Room** – but that does not matter, because the first branch was already satisfied.

Run this code, and *TownSquare* is printed to the console.

Now reverse the order of the branches:

Listing 14.18 Type checking with reversed conditions (REPL)

```
var townSquare = TownSquare()
var className = when(townSquare) {
    is TownSquare -> "TownSquare"
    is Room -> "Room"
    is TownSquare -> "TownSquare"
    else -> throw IllegalArgumentException()
}
print(className)
```

Run this code, and this time *Room* is printed to the console, because the first branch evaluates to true.

When branching conditionally on object type, order matters.

The Kotlin Type Hierarchy

Every class in Kotlin descends from a common superclass, known as **Any**, without you having to explicitly subclass it in your code (Figure 14.2).

Figure 14.2 **TownSquare** type hierarchy

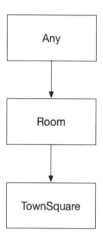

For example, a **Room** and a **Player** are both implicitly children of **Any**, which is why you can define functions that will accept either of them as parameters. If you have worked with Java, this is similar to how classes in Java subclass the **java.lang.Object** class implicitly.

Consider the following example of a function called **printIsSourceOfBlessings**. **printIsSourceOfBlessings** takes in an argument of type **Any** and uses type checking to branch conditionally on the type of the argument passed to it. It finishes by printing a statement based on the result. There are some new concepts in this code that we will discuss over the next couple of sections.

```
fun printIsSourceOfBlessings(any: Any) {
    val isSourceOfBlessings = if (any is Player) {
        any.isBlessed
    } else {
        (any as Room).name == "Fount of Blessings"
    }

    println("$any is a source of blessings: $isSourceOfBlessings")
}
```

In NyetHack, only two things are a source of blessings: a blessed player or the room called Fount of Blessings.

Because every object is a subclass of **Any**, you can pass arguments of whatever type you want to **printIsSourceOfBlessings**. This flexibility is useful, but it comes at the cost of not being able to immediately work with the argument. This example employs *type casting* to get a handle on the slippery **Any** argument.

Type casting

A type check may not always return a useful answer. For example, the any parameter in the **printIsSourceOfBlessings** function tells you that the argument passed will be of type **Any**, but the **Any** type is unspecific about what you can do with that argument.

Type casting allows you to treat an object as if it were an instance of a different type. This gives you the power to do anything with an object that you would do with an object of the type you specify (such as call functions on it).

In the **printIsSourceOfBlessings** function, the conditional expression uses a type check to see whether any is of type **Player**. If it is not, then the code on the else branch will be executed.

The else branch references a name variable:

```
fun printIsSourceOfBlessings(any: Any) {
    val isSourceOfBlessings = if (any is Player) {
        any.isBlessed
    } else {
        (any as Room).name == "Fount of Blessings"
    }

    println("$any is a source of blessings: $isSourceOfBlessings")
}
```

The **as** operator denotes a type cast. This cast says, "Treat any as if it were of type **Room** for the purposes of this expression." The expression in this case is a reference to **Room**'s name property, so that it can be compared against the string "Fount of Blessings".

Casting is powerful and comes with great responsibility; you have to use it safely. An example of a safe cast would be casting from an Int to a more precise number type like Long.

The cast in **printIsSourceOfBlessings** works – but it is not safe. Why not? **Room**, **Player**, and **TownSquare** are the only three classes in NyetHack, so isn't it valid to assume that if any is not of type **Player**, then it must be of type **Room**?

It is – at the moment. But what happens when a new class is added to NyetHack?

Your cast will fail if the type being cast to is incompatible with the type being cast from. A String has nothing to do with an Int, for example, so a cast from String to Int would cause a ClassCastException that may crash your program. (Bear in mind that a cast is different from a conversion. Some strings can be converted to integers; no String can be cast to an Int.)

Casts allow you to *attempt* to cast any variable to any type, but it is up to you to make sure that you are confident in the type of what you are casting from and casting to. If you must make an unsafe cast, then surrounding it with a try/catch block is a good idea. It is best, however, to avoid type casting unless you are sure that the cast will succeed.

Smart casting

One way to be sure that a cast will succeed is by first checking the type of the variable being cast. Return to the first branch of the conditional expression in **printIsSourceOfBlessings**.

```
fun printIsSourceOfBlessings(any: Any) {
    val isSourceOfBlessings = if (any is Player) {
        any.isBlessed
    } else {
        (any as Room).name == "Fount of Blessings"
    }

    println("$any is a source of blessings: $isSourceOfBlessings")
}
```

The condition for entering this branch is for any to be of type **Player**. Inside the branch, a reference to the isBlessed property is made on any. isBlessed is a property defined on **Player**, not **Any**, so how is this possible without a cast?

There is, in fact, a cast happening here – a smart cast. You previously saw smart casts in action in Chapter 6.

The Kotlin compiler is smart enough to recognize that if the any is Player type check is successful for a branch, then any can be treated as a **Player** within that branch. Because it knows that casting any to **Player** will always succeed in this branch, the compiler lets you drop the cast syntax and just reference isBlessed, a **Player** property, on any.

Smart casting is an example of how the intelligence of the Kotlin compiler results in a more concise syntax.

In this chapter you have seen how to use subclassing to share behavior between classes. In the next chapter, you will work with more types of classes, including data classes, enums, and object – Kotlin's single-instance class – as you add a game loop to NyetHack.

For the More Curious: Any

When you print the value of a variable to the console, a function called **toString** is called to determine what that value looks like in the console. For some types, this is easy – for example, the value of a string makes sense to represent a String value. For other types, this is a bit less clear.

Any provides abstract definitions for common functions like **toString**, which are backed by an implementation found on the platform that your project targets.

A peek at the source for the **Any** class yields the following:

```
/**
 * The root of the Kotlin class hierarchy.
 * Every Kotlin class has [Any] as a superclass.
 */
public open class Any {
    public open operator fun equals(other: Any?): Boolean
    public open fun hashCode(): Int
    public open fun toString(): String
}
```

Notice that no definition of the **toString** function is contained in the class definition. So where is it defined, and what is returned when the **toString** function for, say, a **Player** is called?

Recall that the last line of **printIsSourceOfBlessings** prints to the console:

```
fun printIsSourceOfBlessings(any: Any) {
    val isSourceOfBlessings = if (any is Player) {
        any.isBlessed
    } else {
        (any as Room).name == "Fount of Blessings"
    }

    println("$any is a source of blessings: $isSourceOfBlessings")
}
```

The result of calling **printIsSourceOfBlessings** and passing it a blessed player looks something like this:

```
Player@71efa55d is a source of blessings: true
```

Player@71efa55d is the result of the default implementation of **toString** on the **Any** class. Kotlin uses the JVM's **java.lang.Object.toString** implementation because you targeted the JVM for compilation. You can override **toString** in your **Player** class to return something more human-readable.

The **Any** type is one of the ways that Kotlin allows for platform independence – it provides an abstraction above the class that represents a common superclass on each specific platform, like the JVM. So while **Any**'s **toString** implementation is **java.lang.Object.toString** when targeting the JVM, it could be something entirely different when compiling down to JavaScript. This abstraction means that you do not need to know the details of each platform that your code could be run on. Instead, you can simply rely on the **Any** type.

15

Objects

In the last three chapters, you learned how to leverage object-oriented programming principles to build meaningful relationships between objects. Despite the variety in how they can be initialized, all of the classes that you have worked with thus far have been declared with the same class keyword. This chapter introduces *object declarations* as well as other types of classes: *nested classes*, *data classes*, and *enum classes*. As you will see, each has its own declaration syntax and unique characteristics.

By the end of this chapter, your hero will be able to walk from room to room around the world of NyetHack, thanks to all the work you have put into the game. And your program will be well organized to support further enhancements coming in later chapters.

The object Keyword

In Chapter 13, you learned about constructing classes. A class constructor returns an instance of a class, and you can call the constructor any number of times to create any number of instances.

For example, NyetHack can have any number of players, because **Player**'s constructor can be called as many times as you would like. For **Player**, this is desirable, because the world of NyetHack is big enough for multiple players.

But suppose you wanted a **Game** class to keep track of the state of the game. Having multiple instances of **Game** would be a problem, because they could each hold their own states, which could potentially get out of sync with each other.

If you need to hold on to a single instance with state that is consistent throughout the time that your program is running, consider defining a *singleton*. With the object keyword, you specify that a class will be limited to a single instance – a singleton. The first time you access an object, it is instantiated for you. That same instance will persist as long as your program is running, and each subsequent access will then return the original instance.

There are three ways to use the object keyword: *object declarations*, *object expressions*, and *companion objects*. We will outline the uses for each in the next three sections.

Object declarations

Object declarations are useful for organization and state management, especially when you need to maintain some state consistently throughout the lifespan of your program. You are going to define a **Game** object to do just that.

Defining a **Game** class using an object declaration will also give you a convenient place to define a game loop and will allow you to clean up the **main** function in Game.kt. And breaking code out into classes and object declarations furthers your quest for a codebase that remains organized at scale.

Define a **Game** object in Game.kt using an object declaration.

Listing 15.1 Declaring the **Game** object (Game.kt)

```
fun main(args: Array<String>) {
    ...
}

private fun printPlayerStatus(player: Player) {
    println("(Aura: ${player.auraColor()}) " +
            "(Blessed: ${if (player.isBlessed) "YES" else "NO"})")
    println("${player.name} ${player.formatHealthStatus()}")
}

object Game {

}
```

The **main** function in Game.kt should now serve exclusively to kick off gameplay. All game logic will be encapsulated in the **Game** object, of which there will be only one instance.

Because an object declaration is instantiated for you, you do not add a custom constructor with code to be called at initialization. Instead, you need an initializer block for any code that you want to be called when your object is initialized. Add one to the **Game** object with a greeting to be printed to the console when the object is instantiated.

Listing 15.2 Adding an init block to **Game** (Game.kt)

```
fun main(args: Array<String>) {
    ...
}

private fun printPlayerStatus(player: Player) {
    println("(Aura: ${player.auraColor()}) " +
            "(Blessed: ${if (player.isBlessed) "YES" else "NO"})")
    println("${player.name} ${player.formatHealthStatus()}")
}

object Game {
    init {
        println("Welcome, adventurer.")
    }
}
```

Run Game.kt. Your welcome message does not print, because **Game** has not been initialized. And **Game** has not been initialized because it has not been referenced yet.

An object declaration is referenced by one of its properties or functions. To trigger **Game**'s initialization, you will define and call a function called **play**. **play** will serve as the home of the game loop for NyetHack.

Add **play** to **Game** and call it from **main**. When you call a function defined in an object declaration, you call it using the name of the object in which it is defined — not on an instance of a class, as you do for other class functions.

Listing 15.3 Calling a function defined on an object declaration (Game.kt)

```kotlin
fun main(args: Array<String>) {
    ...
    // Player status
    printPlayerStatus(player)

    Game.play()
}

private fun printPlayerStatus(player: Player) {
    println("(Aura: ${player.auraColor()}) " +
            "(Blessed: ${if (player.isBlessed) "YES" else "NO"})")
    println("${player.name} ${player.formatHealthStatus()}")
}

object Game {
    init {
        println("Welcome, adventurer.")
    }

    fun play() {
        while (true) {
            // Play NyetHack
        }
    }
}
```

The **Game** object will do more than encapsulate the game state; it will also hold the game loop in order to take commands from the player. Your game loop takes the form of a while loop that will make NyetHack more interactive. The while loop has a simple condition: true. This will keep the game loop running as long as your application is running.

For now, **play** does not do anything. Eventually, it will define NyetHack's gameplay in terms of rounds: For each round, the player's status and other information describing the world will be printed to the console. Then, user input will be accepted via the **readLine** function.

Take a look at the game logic that is in **main** and think about where it should go in **Game**. For example, you will not want to create a new **Player** instance or a new currentRoom at the beginning of each round, so these aspects of game logic belong in **Game**, but not in **play**. Declare player and currentRoom as private properties of **Game**.

Next, move the call to **castFireball** to **Game**'s initializer block for a fun start to each game of NyetHack, and move the definition of **printPlayerStatus** to **Game** as well. Make **printPlayerStatus** private, like player and currentRoom, to encapsulate it within **Game**.

Listing 15.4 Encapsulating properties and functions within the object declaration (Game.kt)

```
fun main(args: Array<String>) {
    val player = Player("Madrigal")
    player.castFireball()

    var currentRoom: Room = TownSquare()
    println(currentRoom.description())
    println(currentRoom.load())

    // Player status
    printPlayerStatus(player)

    Game.play()
}

private fun printPlayerStatus(player: Player) {
    println("(Aura: ${player.auraColor()}) " +
            "(Blessed: ${if (player.isBlessed) "YES" else "NO"})")
    println("${player.name} ${player.formatHealthStatus()}")
}

object Game {
    private val player = Player("Madrigal")
    private var currentRoom: Room = TownSquare()

    init {
        println("Welcome, adventurer.")
        player.castFireball()
    }

    fun play() {
        while (true) {
            // Play NyetHack
        }
    }

    private fun printPlayerStatus(player: Player) {
        println("(Aura: ${player.auraColor()}) " +
                "(Blessed: ${if (player.isBlessed) "YES" else "NO"})")
        println("${player.name} ${player.formatHealthStatus()}")
    }
}
```

Moving code from the **main** function in Game.kt to the **play** function in **Game** keeps the code that is essential for setting up the game loop encapsulated within **Game**.

What is left in **main**? Three sets of information are printed: currentRoom's description and load statement and the player's status. These things should be printed at the beginning of each round of gameplay, so move them to the game loop. Leave the call to **Game.play** in **main**.

Listing 15.5 Printing status in the game loop (Game.kt)

```
fun main(args: Array<String>) {
    println(currentRoom.description())
    println(currentRoom.load())

    // Player status
    printPlayerStatus(player)

    Game.play()
}

object Game {
    private val player = Player("Madrigal")
    private var currentRoom: Room = TownSquare()

    init {
        println("Welcome, adventurer.")
        player.castFireball()
    }

    fun play() {
        while (true) {
            // Play NyetHack
            println(currentRoom.description())
            println(currentRoom.load())

            // Player status
            printPlayerStatus(player)
        }
    }

    private fun printPlayerStatus(player: Player) {
        println("(Aura: ${player.auraColor()}) " +
                "(Blessed: ${if (player.isBlessed) "YES" else "NO"})")
        println("${player.name} ${player.formatHealthStatus()}")
    }
}
```

If you were to run Game.kt right now, it would loop indefinitely, as there is nothing to stop the loop. The last step for the game loop, at least for now, is to accept user input from the console using the **readLine** function. You may remember **readLine** from Chapter 6: It pauses execution while it waits for user input in the console. Once the return character is received, it resumes execution, returning the input that was collected.

Add a call to **readLine** in your game loop to accept user input.

Listing 15.6 Accepting user input (Game.kt)

```
...
object Game {
    ...
    fun play() {
        while (true) {
            println(currentRoom.description())
            println(currentRoom.load())

            // Player status
            printPlayerStatus(player)

            print("> Enter your command: ")
            println("Last command: ${readLine()}")
        }
    }
    ...
}
```

Try running Game.kt now and entering a command:

```
Welcome, adventurer.
A glass of Fireball springs into existence. Delicious! (x2)
Room: Town Square
Danger level: 2
The villagers rally and cheer as you enter!
The bell tower announces your arrival. GWONG
(Aura: GREEN) (Blessed: YES)
Madrigal of Tampa is in excellent condition!
> Enter your command: fight
Last command: fight
Room: Town Square
Danger level: 2
The villagers rally and cheer as you enter!
The bell tower announces your arrival. GWONG
(Aura: GREEN) (Blessed: YES)
Madrigal of Tampa is in excellent condition!
> Enter your command:
```

Did you notice that the entered text is displayed back to you? Excellent – new input is being scanned into the game.

Object expressions

Defining a class using the class keyword is useful in that it establishes a new concept in your codebase. By writing a class called **Room**, you communicate that rooms exist in NyetHack. And by writing a subclass of **Room** called **TownSquare**, you establish that there can be specific types of rooms called town squares.

But defining a new, named class is not always necessary. Perhaps you need a class instance that is a variation of an existing class and will be used for a one-off purpose. In fact, it will be so temporary that it does not even require a name.

This is another use for the `object` keyword: an object expression. Look at the following example:

```
val abandonedTownSquare = object : TownSquare() {
    override fun load() = "You anticipate applause, but no one is here..."
}
```

This object expression is a subclass of **TownSquare** where no one cheers your entrance. In the body of this declaration, the properties and functions defined in **TownSquare** can be overridden – and new properties and functions can be added – to define the data and behavior of the anonymous class.

This class still adheres to the rules of the `object` keyword in that there will only ever be one instance of it alive at a time, but it is significantly smaller in scope than a named singleton. As a side effect, an object expression takes on some of the attributes of where it is declared. If declared at the file level, an object expression is initialized immediately. If declared within another class, it is initialized when its enclosing class is initialized.

Companion objects

If you would like to tie the initialization of an object to a class instance, there is another option for you: a companion object. A companion object is declared within another class declaration using the `companion` modifier. A class can have no more than one companion object.

There are two cases in which a companion object will be initialized. First, a companion object is initialized when its enclosing class is initialized. This makes it a good place for singleton data that has a contextual connection to a class definition. Second, a companion object is initialized when one of its properties or functions is accessed directly.

Because a companion object is still an object declaration, you do not need an instance of a class to use any of the functions or properties defined in it. Take a look at the following example of a companion object defined within a class called **PremadeWorldMap**:

```
class PremadeWorldMap {
    ...
    companion object {
        private const val MAPS_FILEPATH = "nyethack.maps"

        fun load() = File(MAPS_FILEPATH).readBytes()
    }
}
```

PremadeWorldMap has a companion object with one function called **load**. If you were to call **load** from elsewhere in your codebase, you would do so without needing an instance of **PremadeWorldMap**, like so:

```
PremadeWorldMap.load()
```

The contents of this companion object will not be loaded until either **PremadeWorldMap** is initialized or **load** is called. And no matter how many times **PremadeWorldMap** is instantiated, there will only ever be one instance of its companion object.

Understanding the differences in how and when object declarations, object expressions, and companion objects are instantiated is key in understanding when to use each of them effectively. And using them effectively helps you write well-organized code that scales well.

Nested Classes

Not all classes defined within other classes are declared without a name. You can also use the `class` keyword to define a named class *nested* inside of another class. In this section, you will define a new `GameInput` class nested within the `Game` object.

Now that you have defined a game loop, you will want to apply some control over the user input passed to your game. NyetHack is a text adventure, driven by the user entering commands to the `readLine` function. There are two things you need to ensure about the user's commands: First, that they are valid commands. Second, that commands with multiple parts, like "move east," are handled correctly. You want "move" to trigger a **move** function and "east" to provide the **move** function a direction to move in.

You are going to address these two requirements next, starting with separating multipart commands. The `GameInput` class will provide a place for the logic that delineates command and argument.

Create a private class within the `Game` object to provide this abstraction:

Listing 15.7 Defining a nested class (Game.kt)

```
...
object Game {
    ...
    private class GameInput(arg: String?) {
        private val input = arg ?: ""
        val command = input.split(" ")[0]
        val argument = input.split(" ").getOrElse(1, { "" })
    }
}
```

Why nest `GameInput` privately within `Game`? The `GameInput` class is only relevant to `Game`; it does not need to be accessed from anywhere else in NyetHack. Making `GameInput` a private, nested class means that `GameInput` can be used within `Game` but does not clutter the rest of your API.

You define two properties on the `GameInput` class: one for the command, and the other for the argument. To do this, you call **split** to break the input apart at the space character, then **getOrElse** to attempt to fetch the second item in **split**'s resulting list. If the index you provide to **getOrElse** does not exist, **getOrElse** returns an empty string as a default.

Now you can separate multipart commands. It is time to make sure the user has entered a valid command.

To filter user input, you will use a when expression to build a whitelist of valid commands in **Game**. Any good whitelist starts by locking out invalid input. Add a **commandNotFound** function to **GameInput** that returns a String to be printed when invalid input is entered.

Listing 15.8 Defining a function in a nested class (Game.kt)

```
...
object Game {
    ...
    private class GameInput(arg: String?) {
        private val input = arg ?: ""
        val command = input.split(" ")[0]
        val argument = input.split(" ").getOrElse(1, { "" })

        private fun commandNotFound() = "I'm not quite sure what you're trying to do!"
    }
}
```

Next, add another function to **GameInput** called **processCommand**. **processCommand** should return the result of a when expression that branches off of the command entered by the user. Be sure to sanitize the user's input by calling **toLowerCase** on the entered command.

Listing 15.9 Defining the **processCommand** function (Game.kt)

```
...
object Game {
    ...
    private class GameInput(arg: String?) {
        private val input = arg ?: ""
        val command = input.split(" ")[0]
        val argument = input.split(" ").getOrElse(1, { "" })

        fun processCommand() = when (command.toLowerCase()) {
            else -> commandNotFound()
        }

        private fun commandNotFound() = "I'm not quite sure what you're trying to do!"
    }
}
```

Now, it is time to put **GameInput** to work. Replace your **readLine** call in **Game.play** with a version that uses your **GameInput** class.

Listing 15.10 Using **GameInput** (Game.kt)

```
...
object Game {
    ...
    fun play() {
        while (true) {
            println(currentRoom.description())
            println(currentRoom.load())

            // Player status
            printPlayerStatus(player)

            print("> Enter your command: ")
            println("Last command: ${readLine()}")
            println(GameInput(readLine()).processCommand())
        }
    }
    ...
}
```

Run Game.kt. Now, any input that you enter triggers the **commandNotFound** response:

```
Welcome, adventurer.
A glass of Fireball springs into existence. Delicious! (x2)
Room: Town Square
Danger level: 2
The villagers rally and cheer as you enter!
The bell tower announces your arrival. GWONG
(Aura: GREEN) (Blessed: YES)
Madrigal of Tampa is in excellent condition!
> Enter your command: fight
I'm not quite sure what you're trying to do!
Room: Town Square
Danger level: 2
The villagers rally and cheer as you enter!
The bell tower announces your arrival. GWONG
(Aura: GREEN) (Blessed: YES)
Madrigal of Tampa is in excellent condition!
> Enter your command:
```

This is progress: You have restricted input to only the commands specified on a small (empty, for now) whitelist. Later in this chapter, you will add the "move" command, and **GameInput** will become a bit more useful.

But before they can move around the world of NyetHack, your hero needs a world that consists of more than one town square.

Data Classes

Step one in building a world for your hero is to establish a coordinate system to move around on. The coordinate system will use cardinal directions to communicate direction as well as a class to represent change in direction, called **Coordinate**.

Coordinate is a simple type and a good candidate to be defined as a *data class*. As the name suggests, data classes are classes designed specifically for holding data, and they come with some powerful data manipulation benefits, as you will see shortly.

Create a new file called Navigation.kt and add **Coordinate** as a data class, using the data keyword. **Coordinate** should have three properties:

- x, an Int val defined in the primary constructor for the x coordinate
- y, an Int val defined in the primary constructor for the y coordinate
- isInBounds, a Boolean val representing whether both of the coordinate values are positive

Listing 15.11 Defining a data class (Navigation.kt)

```
data class Coordinate(val x: Int, val y: Int) {
    val isInBounds = x >= 0 && y >= 0
}
```

A coordinate should never have an x or y position less than 0, so you add a property to the coordinate class that will return whether the current position is out of bounds. You will later check the isInBounds property of the **Coordinate** when attempting to update the currentRoom to determine whether the

Coordinate is a valid direction to move. For example, if a player at the top of the game map tries to move north, your isInBounds check will block this.

To keep track of where the player is on the world map, add a property called currentPosition to the Player class.

Listing 15.12 Tracking player position (Player.kt)

```
class Player(_name: String,
             var healthPoints: Int = 100,
             val isBlessed: Boolean,
             private val isImmortal: Boolean) {
    var name = _name
        get() = "${field.capitalize()} of $hometown"
        private set(value) {
            field = value.trim()
        }

    val hometown by lazy { selectHometown() }
    var currentPosition = Coordinate(0, 0)
    ...
}
```

Recall from Chapter 14 that all classes in Kotlin inherit from the same class, Any. Defined on Any are a series of functions that you can call on any instance. These functions include toString, equals, and hashCode, which improves the speed a value can be retrieved with a key when using a Map.

Any provides default implementations for all of these functions, but, as you have seen before, they are often not very reader friendly. Data classes provide implementations for these functions that may work better for your project. In this section, we will walk through two of those functions and some of the other benefits of using data classes to represent data in your codebase.

toString

The default toString implementation for a class is not very human readable. Take Coordinate, for example. If Coordinate were defined as a normal class, calling toString on a Coordinate would return something like this:

    Coordinate@3527c201

You are looking at a reference to where this Coordinate was allocated space in memory. If you are wondering why you would care about the details of Coordinate's memory allocation, that is a sensible question. Most often, you do not care.

You can override toString in your class to provide your own implementation, just like any other open function. But data classes save you that work by providing their own default implementation. For Coordinate, that implementation looks like this:

    Coordinate(x=1, y=0)

Because x and y are properties declared in Coordinate's primary constructor, they are used to represent Coordinate in textual form. (isInBounds is not included because it was not defined in Coordinate's primary constructor.) A data class's toString implementation is considerably more useful than the default implementation on Any.

equals

The next function that data classes provide an implementation for is **equals**. If **Coordinate** were defined as a normal class, what would be the result of the following expression?

```
Coordinate(1, 0) == Coordinate(1, 0)
```

You may be surprised, but the answer is false. Why?

By default, objects are compared by their references, because that is the default implementation of the **equals** function in **Any**. Because these two coordinates are separate instances, they will have different references and will not be equal.

Perhaps you would want to consider two players to be equal if they have the same name. You can provide your own equality check by overriding **equals** in your class to determine equality based on a comparison of properties, not memory references. You have seen that classes like String do this to compare equality based on value.

Again, data classes take care of this for you by providing an implementation of **equals** that bases equality on all of the properties declared in the primary constructor. With **Coordinate** defined as a data class, Coordinate(1, 0) == Coordinate(1, 0) yields a result of true, because the values of the two instances' x properties are equal, as are the values of their y properties.

copy

In addition to giving you more usable default implementations of functions on **Any**, data classes also provide a function that makes it easy to create a new copy of an object.

Say that you want to create a new instance of **Player** that has all of the same property values as another player except for isImmortal. If **Player** were a data class, then copying a **Player** instance would be as simple as calling **copy** and passing arguments for any properties that you would like to change.

```
val mortalPlayer = player.copy(isImmortal = false)
```

Data classes save you the work of implementing this **copy** function on your own.

Destructuring declarations

Another benefit of data classes is that they automatically enable your class's data to be destructured.

The examples of destructuring you have seen up to this point have involved things like the list output from **split**. Under the hood, destructuring declarations depend on the declaration of functions with names like **component1**, **component2**, etc., each declared for some piece of data that you would like to return. Data classes automatically add these functions for you for each property defined in their primary constructor.

There is nothing magic about a class supporting destructuring; a data class simply does the extra work required to make the class "destructurable" for you. You can make any class support destructuring by adding component operator functions to it, like so:

```
class PlayerScore(val experience: Int, val level:Int ){
    operator fun component1() = experience
    operator fun component2() = level
}

val (experience, level) = PlayerScore(1250, 5)
```

By declaring **Coordinate** to be a data class, you are able to retrieve the properties defined in **Coordinate**'s primary constructor like so:

```
val (x, y) = Coordinate(1, 0)
```

In this example, x has a value of 1, because **component1** returns the value of the first property declared in **Coordinate**'s primary constructor. y has a value of 0, because **component2** returns the value of the second property declared in **Coordinate**'s primary constructor.

These features all weigh in favor of using data classes to represent simple objects that hold data, like **Coordinate**. Classes that are often compared or copied or have their contents printed out are especially ripe for being made data classes.

However, there are also some limitations and requirements on data classes. Data classes:

- must have a primary constructor with at least one parameter

- require their primary constructor parameters to be marked either val or var

- cannot be abstract, open, sealed, or inner

If your class does not require the **toString**, **copy**, **equals**, or **hashCode** functions, a data class offers no benefits. And if you require a customized **equals** function – one that uses only certain properties rather than all properties for the comparison, for example – a data class is not the right tool, because it includes all properties in the **equals** function it automatically generates.

You will learn about overriding **equals** and other functions in your own types later in this chapter, in the section called *Operator Overloading*, and about a shortcut IntelliJ provides for overriding **equals** in the section called *For the More Curious: Defining Structural Comparison*.

Enumerated Classes

Enumerated classes, or "enums," are a special type of class useful for defining a collection of constants, known as *enumerated types*.

In NyetHack, you will use an enum to represent the set of four possible directions a player can move in – the four cardinal directions. Add an enum called **Direction** to Navigation.kt.

Listing 15.13 Defining an enum (Navigation.kt)

```
enum class Direction {
    NORTH,
    EAST,
    SOUTH,
    WEST
}

data class Coordinate(val x: Int, val y: Int) {
    val isInBounds = x >= 0 && y >= 0
}
```

Enums are more descriptive than other types of constants, like strings. You can reference enumerated types using the name of the enum class, a dot, and the name of the type, like so:

```
Direction.EAST
```

And enums can represent more than simple naming constants. To use **Direction** to represent character movement in NyetHack, you will tie each **Direction** type to the **Coordinate** change when the player moves in that direction.

Moving in the game world should modify the player's x and y position according to the direction moved. For example, if a player moves to the east, the x position should change by 1 and the y by 0. If the player moves to the south, the x position should change by 0 and the y by 1.

Add a primary constructor to the **Direction** enum that defines a coordinate property. Because you add a parameter to the constructor of the enum, you will have to call that constructor when defining each enumerated type in **Direction**, providing a **Coordinate** for each one.

Listing 15.14 Defining an enum constructor (Navigation.kt)

```
enum class Direction(private val coordinate: Coordinate) {
    NORTH(Coordinate(0, -1)),
    EAST(Coordinate(1, 0)),
    SOUTH(Coordinate(0, 1)),
    WEST(Coordinate(-1, 0))
}

data class Coordinate(val x: Int, val y: Int) {
    val isInBounds = x >= 0 && y >= 0
}
```

Enums, like other classes, can also hold function declarations.

Add a function called **updateCoordinate** to **Direction** to change the player's location based on their movement. (Note that you need to add a semicolon to separate your enumerated type declarations from your function declarations.)

Listing 15.15 Defining a function in an enum (Navigation.kt)

```
enum class Direction(private val coordinate: Coordinate) {
    NORTH(Coordinate(0, -1)),
    EAST(Coordinate(1, 0)),
    SOUTH(Coordinate(0, 1)),
    WEST(Coordinate(-1, 0));

    fun updateCoordinate(playerCoordinate: Coordinate) =
            Coordinate(playerCoordinate.x + coordinate.x,
                    playerCoordinate.y + coordinate.y)
}

data class Coordinate(val x: Int, val y: Int) {
    val isInBounds = x >= 0 && y >= 0
}
```

You call functions on enumerated types, not on the enum class itself, so calling **updateCoordinate** will look something like this:

```
Direction.EAST.updateCoordinate(Coordinate(1, 0))
```

Operator Overloading

You have seen that Kotlin's built-in types come with a range of available operations and that some types tailor those operations based on the data they represent. Take the **equals** function and its associated == operator: You can use them to check whether two instances of a numeric type have the same value, whether two strings hold the same sequence of characters, and whether instances of a data class have the same values for properties in the primary constructor. Similarly, the **plus** function and + operator add two numeric values together, append one string to the end of another, and add the elements of one list to another.

When you create your own types, the Kotlin compiler does not automatically know how to apply the built-in operators to them. What does it mean to ask whether one **Player** is equal to another, for example? When you want to use built-in operators with your custom types, you have to override the operators' functions to tell the compiler how to implement them for your type. This is known as *operator overloading*.

You saw operator overloading used extensively in Chapter 10 and Chapter 11. Rather than having to directly call a function called **get** to retrieve an element from a list, you were able to use the index access operator, [], to index into a collection. Kotlin's concise syntax is built on small improvements like this (spellList[3] instead of spellList.get(3)).

Coordinate is a prime candidate for improvement via operator overloading. You move your hero through the world by adding the properties of two **Coordinate** instances together. Instead of having to define that work in **Direction**, you can overload the **plus** operator on **Coordinate**.

Make it so in Navigation.kt, prepending the function declaration with the operator modifier.

Listing 15.16 Overloading the **plus** operator (Navigation.kt)

```
enum class Direction(private val coordinate: Coordinate) {
    NORTH(Coordinate(0, -1)),
    EAST(Coordinate(1, 0)),
    SOUTH(Coordinate(0, 1)),
    WEST(Coordinate(-1, 0));

    fun updateCoordinate(playerCoordinate: Coordinate) =
            Coordinate(playerCoordinate.x + coordinate.x,
                    playerCoordinate.y + coordinate.y)
}

data class Coordinate(val x: Int, val y: Int) {
    val isInBounds = x >= 0 && y >= 0

    operator fun plus(other: Coordinate) = Coordinate(x + other.x, y + other.y)
}
```

Now, you can simply use the addition operator (+) to add two **Coordinate** instances together. Do so now in **Direction**.

Listing 15.17 Using an overloaded operator (`Navigation.kt`)

```
enum class Direction(private val coordinate: Coordinate) {
    NORTH(Coordinate(0, -1)),
    EAST(Coordinate(1, 0)),
    SOUTH(Coordinate(0, 1)),
    WEST(Coordinate(-1, 0));

    fun updateCoordinate(playerCoordinate: Coordinate) =
            Coordinate(playerCoordinate.x + coordinate.x,
                    playerCoordinate.y + coordinate.y)
            coordinate + playerCoordinate
}

data class Coordinate(val x: Int, val y: Int) {
    val isInBounds = x >= 0 && y >= 0

    operator fun plus(other: Coordinate) = Coordinate(x + other.x, y + other.y)
}
```

Table 15.1 shows some commonly used operators you can override:

Table 15.1 Common operators

Operator	Function name	Purpose
+	plus	Adds an object to another.
+=	plusAssign	Adds an object to another and assigns the result to the first.
==	equals	Returns true if two objects are equal, false otherwise.
>	compareTo	Returns true if the object on the lefthand side is greater than the object on the righthand side, false otherwise.
[]	get	Returns the element in a collection at a given index.
..	rangeTo	Creates a range object.
in	contains	Returns true if an object exists within a collection.

These operators can be overloaded on any class, but make sure to do so only when it makes sense. While you can assign logic to the addition operator on the **Player** class, what does "Player plus Player" mean? Ask yourself this question before overloading an operator.

By the way, if you override **equals** yourself, you should also override a function called **hashCode**. An example of overriding both of these functions using an IntelliJ command as a shortcut is shown in the section called *For the More Curious: Defining Structural Comparison* near the end of this chapter. More detailed discussion of why and how **hashCode** should be overridden is outside the scope of this book; if you are interested, see kotlinlang.org/api/latest/jvm/stdlib/kotlin/-any/hash-code.html.

Exploring the World of NyetHack

Now that you have built a game loop and established a cardinal direction system on a coordinate plane, it is time to put your knowledge to the test and add more rooms to explore in NyetHack.

To set up a map of the world, you need a list that will hold all of the rooms. In fact, since players can move in two dimensions, you need a list containing two lists of rooms. The first list of rooms will hold the Town Square (where the player begins), Tavern, and Back Room, from west to east. The second list of rooms will hold the Long Corridor and the Generic Room. These lists will be held in a third list representing the y coordinate, called worldMap.

Add a worldMap property to **Game** with a series of rooms for your hero to explore.

Listing 15.18 Defining a world map in NyetHack (Game.kt)

```
...
object Game {
    private val player = Player("Madrigal")
    private var currentRoom: Room = TownSquare()

    private var worldMap = listOf(
            listOf(currentRoom, Room("Tavern"), Room("Back Room")),
            listOf(Room("Long Corridor"), Room("Generic Room")))
    ...
}
```

Figure 15.1 shows the grid of rooms that can be explored in NyetHack.

Figure 15.1 NyetHack world map

Town Square	Tavern	Back Room
Long Corridor	Generic Room	

With the rooms in place, it is time to add the "move" command and give the player the ability to step out into the mysterious land of NyetHack. Add a function called **move** that takes in a direction input as a String. There is a lot going in **move**; we will explain it after you enter it.

Listing 15.19 Defining the **move** function (Game.kt)

```
...
object Game {
    private var currentRoom: Room = TownSquare()
    private val player = Player("Madrigal")

    private var worldMap = listOf(
            listOf(currentRoom, Room("Tavern"), Room("Back Room")),
            listOf(Room("Long Corridor"), Room("Generic Room")))
    ...
    private fun move(directionInput: String) =
            try {
                val direction = Direction.valueOf(directionInput.toUpperCase())
                val newPosition = direction.updateCoordinate(player.currentPosition)
                if (!newPosition.isInBounds) {
                    throw IllegalStateException("$direction is out of bounds.")
                }

                val newRoom = worldMap[newPosition.y][newPosition.x]
                player.currentPosition = newPosition
                currentRoom = newRoom
                "OK, you move $direction to the ${newRoom.name}.\n${newRoom.load()}"
            } catch (e: Exception) {
                "Invalid direction: $directionInput."
            }
}
```

move returns a String based on the result of a try/catch expression. In the try block, you use the **valueOf** function to match the user's input. **valueOf** is a function available on all enum classes that returns an enumerated type with a name that matches the String value that you pass to it. If you call Direction.valueOf("EAST"), then Direction.EAST will be returned. If you pass a value that does not match one of the enumerated types, then an IllegalArgumentException is thrown.

That exception will be caught by the catch block. (In fact, it will catch any type of exception thrown in the try block.)

If execution continues past the **valueOf** call, then a check to make sure that the player is still in bounds is made. If not, then an IllegalStateException is thrown, which is also caught by the catch block.

If the player moves in a valid direction, then your next step is to query worldMap for a room at the new position. You saw how to index into a collection in Chapter 10, and here, you are doing so twice. The first indexing, worldMap[newPosition.y], returns a list from the list of lists called worldMap. The second indexing, [newPosition.x], returns a **Room** inside the list returned in the first indexing. If a room does not exist for the coordinate queried, then an ArrayIndexOutOfBoundsException is thrown and, yes, caught by the catch block.

If all that code executes without throwing an exception, then the player's currentPosition property is updated and you return some text to print out as a part of NyetHack's text interface.

The **move** function should be called when the player enters the "move" command, which you will now implement using the **GameInput** class you wrote earlier in this chapter:

Listing 15.20 Defining the **processCommand** function (Game.kt)

```
...
object Game {
    ...
    private class GameInput(arg: String?) {
        private val input = arg ?: ""
        val command = input.split(" ")[0]
        val argument = input.split(" ").getOrElse(1, { "" })

        fun processCommand() = when (command.toLowerCase()) {
            "move" -> move(argument)
            else -> commandNotFound()
        }

        private fun commandNotFound() = "I'm not quite sure what you're trying to do!"
    }
}
```

Try running Game.kt and moving around the world. You should see some output like the following:

```
Welcome, adventurer.
A glass of Fireball springs into existence. Delicious! (x2)
Room: Town Square
Danger level: 2
The villagers rally and cheer as you enter!
The bell tower announces your arrival. GWONG
(Aura: GREEN) (Blessed: YES)
Madrigal of Tampa is in excellent condition!
> Enter your command: move east
OK, you move EAST to the Tavern.
Nothing much to see here...
Room: Tavern
Danger level: 5
Nothing much to see here...
(Aura: GREEN) (Blessed: YES)
Madrigal of Tampa is in excellent condition!
> Enter your command:
```

And that is it – you are now able to walk around the world of NyetHack. In this chapter, you learned how to use several variants of classes. Beyond the class keyword, you can use object declarations, data classes, and enum classes to represent data. Using the right tool for the job will make the relationships among objects in your code more straightforward.

In the next chapter, you will learn about interfaces and abstract classes – mechanisms for defining protocols that your classes must adhere to – as you add the thrill of combat to NyetHack.

For the More Curious: Defining Structural Comparison

Imagine a **Weapon** class that has name and type properties:

```
open class Weapon(val name: String, val type: String)
```

Suppose you would like two individual weapon instances to be considered structurally equal, using the structural equality operator (==), if the values of their names and types are structurally equal. By default, as we said earlier in this chapter, == checks referential equality for objects, so this expression would evaluate as false:

```
open class Weapon(val name: String, val type: String)
println(Weapon("ebony kris", "dagger") == Weapon("ebony kris", "dagger")) // False
```

You saw in this chapter that data classes provide a solution to this problem – an implementation of **equals** that bases equality on all of the properties declared in the primary constructor. But **Weapon** is not (and cannot be) a data class, because it is intended to be the base class for other weapon variations (hence the open keyword). Data classes are not permitted to be superclasses.

However, as we discussed in the section called *Operator Overloading*, you can provide your own implementation of **equals** and **hashCode** to specify how instances of your class should be compared structurally.

This need is so common that IntelliJ has a Generate task for adding the function overrides via its Code → Generate command, which brings up the Generate dialog (Figure 15.2):

Figure 15.2 The Generate dialog

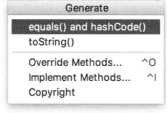

When generating **equals** and **hashCode** overrides, you can select the properties that should be used when you compare two instances of your object structurally (Figure 15.3):

Figure 15.3 Generating **equals** and **hashCode** overrides

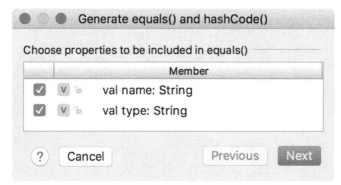

IntelliJ adds the **equals** and **hashCode** functions to the class based on the choices made:

```kotlin
open class Weapon(val name:String, val type: String) {
    override fun equals(other: Any?): Boolean {
        if (this === other) return true
        if (javaClass != other?.javaClass) return false

        other as Weapon

        if (name != other.name) return false
        if (type != other.type) return false

        return true
    }

    override fun hashCode(): Int {
        var result = name.hashCode()
        result = 31 * result + type.hashCode()
        return result
    }
}
```

With these overrides in place, comparing two weapons would result in true as long as their names and types are the same:

```kotlin
println(Weapon("ebony kris", "dagger") == Weapon("ebony kris", "dagger")) // True
```

Notice that the overridden **equals** function that was generated sets up a structural comparison between the properties selected in the Generate command:

```kotlin
...
if (name != other.name) return false
if (type != other.type) return false
return true
...
```

If any of the properties are not structurally equal, then the comparison results in false. Otherwise, true is returned.

As we mentioned earlier, whenever you define structural comparison, you also provide a **hashCode** definition. **hashCode** improves performance – how quickly a value can be retrieved with a key when using a Map type, for example – and is tied to the uniqueness of a class instance.

For the More Curious: Algebraic Data Types

Algebraic data types (or ADTs, for short) allow you to represent a closed set of possible subtypes that can be associated with a given type. Enum classes are a simple form of ADT.

Imagine a **Student** class that has three possible associated states, depending on the student's enrollment status: NOT_ENROLLED, ACTIVE, or GRADUATED.

Using the enum class that you learned about in this chapter, you could model the three states for the **Student** class as follows:

```
enum class StudentStatus {
    NOT_ENROLLED,
    ACTIVE,
    GRADUATED
}

class Student(var status: StudentStatus)

fun main(args: Array<String>) {
    val student = Student(StudentStatus.NOT_ENROLLED)
}
```

And you could write a function that generates a student message using the student's status:

```
fun studentMessage(status: StudentStatus): String {
    return when (status) {
        StudentStatus.NOT_ENROLLED -> "Please choose a course."
    }
}
```

One of the benefits of enums and other ADTs is that the compiler can check to ensure that you handled all possibilities, because an ADT is a closed set of possible types. The implementation for **studentMessage** does not handle the ACTIVE or GRADUATED types, so the compiler would give an error (Figure 15.4):

Figure 15.4 Add necessary branches

```
fun studentMessage(studentStatus: StudentStatus): String {
    return when (studentStatus) {
```
'when' expression must be exhaustive, add necessary 'ACTIVE', 'GRADUATED' branches or 'else' branch instead
```
    }
```

The compiler is satisfied when all types are addressed either explicitly or through an else branch:

```
fun studentMessage(status: StudentStatus): String {
    return when (studentStatus) {
        StudentStatus.NOT_ENROLLED -> "Please choose a course."
        StudentStatus.ACTIVE -> "Welcome, student!"
        StudentStatus.GRADUATED -> "Congratulations!"
    }
}
```

For more complex ADTs, you can use Kotlin's *sealed classes* to implement more sophisticated definitions. Sealed classes let you specify an ADT similar to an enum, but with more control over the specific subtypes than an enum provides.

For example, imagine that when a student is active, the student is also assigned a course ID. You could add a course ID property to the enum definition, but it would be used only in the ACTIVE case – leading to two unneeded null states for the property:

```
enum class StudentStatus {
    NOT_ENROLLED,
    ACTIVE,
    GRADUATED;
    var courseId: String? = null // Used for ACTIVE only
}
```

A better solution would be to use a sealed class to model the student statuses:

```
sealed class StudentStatus {
    object NotEnrolled : StudentStatus()
    class Active(val courseId: String) : StudentStatus()
    object Graduated : StudentStatus()
}
```

The **StudentStatus** sealed class has a limited number of subclasses that must be defined within the same file where **StudentStatus** is defined – otherwise it is ineligible for subclassing. Defining a sealed class instead of an enum to represent the possible states allows you to specify a limited set of **StudentStatus**es that the compiler can check in a when (as in the case of the enum), but with more control over the declaration of the subclasses.

The object keyword is used for the statuses that require no course ID, since there will never be any variation on their instances, and the class keyword is used for the ACTIVE class because it will have different instances, since the course ID will change depending on the student.

Using the new sealed class in the when would allow you to now read the courseId from the ACTIVE class, accessible through smart casting:

```
fun main(args: Array<String>) {
    val student = Student(StudentStatus.Active("Kotlin101"))
    studentMessage(student.status)
}

fun studentMessage(status: StudentStatus): String {
    return when (status) {
        is StudentStatus.NotEnrolled -> "Please choose a course!"
        is StudentStatus.Active -> "You are enrolled in: ${status.courseId}"
        is StudentStatus.Graduated -> "Congratulations!"
    }
}
```

Challenge: "Quit" Command

Players will most likely want to quit NyetHack at some point, and currently NyetHack offers no way to do that. Your challenge is to fix this. When a user enters "quit" or "exit," NyetHack should display a farewell message to the adventurer and terminate. Hint: Remember that, currently, your `while` loop executes forever – a significant part of solving this puzzle is to end that loop conditionally.

Challenge: Implementing a World Map

Remember when we said NyetHack would not feature awesome ASCII graphics? Once you successfully complete this challenge, it will!

Players sometimes get lost in the expansive world of NyetHack, and fortunately you have the power to give them a magic map of the realm. Implement a "map" command that displays the player's current position in the game world. For a player currently at the tavern, the game interaction should resemble the following:

```
> Enter your command: map
O X O
O O
```

The X represents the room the player is currently in.

Challenge: Ring the Bell

Add a "ring" command to NyetHack so that you can ring the bell as many times as you would like from within the town square.

Hint: You will have to make the **ringBell** function public.

16

Interfaces and Abstract Classes

In this chapter you will see how to define and use *interfaces* and *abstract classes* in Kotlin.

An interface allows you to specify common properties and behavior that are supported by a subset of classes in your program – without being required to specify how they will be implemented. This capability – the *what* without the *how* – is useful when inheritance is not the right relationship for classes in a program. Using an interface, a group of classes can have properties or functions in common without sharing a superclass or subclassing one another.

You will also work with a type of class called an abstract class, a hybrid between the features of interfaces and classes. Abstract classes are similar to interfaces in that they can specify the *what* without the *how*, but they are different in that they can also define constructors and act as a superclass.

These new concepts will allow you to add an exciting feature to NyetHack: Now that your hero can walk around, you will add a combat system to deal with the evildoers your hero encounters.

Defining an Interface

To define how combat is performed, you will first create an interface that specifies the functions and properties used for entities in the game when performing combat. Your player will face goblins, but you will define a combat system that can be applied to any type of creature – not just goblins.

Create a new file called Creature.kt in the com.bignerdranch.nyethack package (remember that this pattern is to avoid naming collisions), and define a **Fightable** interface, using the keyword interface:

Listing 16.1 Defining an interface (Creature.kt)

```
interface Fightable {
    var healthPoints: Int
    val diceCount: Int
    val diceSides: Int
    val damageRoll: Int

    fun attack(opponent: Fightable): Int
}
```

Your interface declaration defines things that are common to any entity that can fight in NyetHack. Fightable creatures use the number of dice, the number of sides on each die, and the damage roll – the sum of the numbers rolled on the dice – to determine the amount of damage dealt to an enemy. Fightable creatures must also have healthPoints and an implementation for a function called **attack**.

The four properties in **Fightable** have no initializers, and the **attack** function has no function body. An interface is not concerned with providing initializers or function bodies. Remember – interfaces only specify the what, not the how.

Note that the **Fightable** interface is also the type of the opponent parameter that the **attack** function accepts. An interface can be used as a type for a parameter, just as a class can be used as a parameter type.

When a function specifies a parameter type, that function cares about what the argument can do, not how the behavior is implemented. This is one of the strengths of an interface – you can create a set of requirements that is shared between classes that otherwise have nothing in common.

Implementing an Interface

To use an interface, we say that you "implement" it on a class. There are two parts to this: First, you declare that the class implements the interface. Then, you must ensure that the class provides implementations for all of the properties and functions specified in the interface.

Use the : operator to implement the **Fightable** interface on **Player**.

Listing 16.2 Implementing an interface (`Player.kt`)

```
class Player(_name: String,
        override var healthPoints: Int = 100,
        var isBlessed: Boolean = false,
        private var isImmortal: Boolean) : Fightable {
    ...
}
```

When you add the **Fightable** interface to **Player**, IntelliJ indicates that functions and properties are missing. Warning you that properties and functions have yet to be implemented on **Player** helps you adhere to **Fightable**'s rules, and IntelliJ will also help you implement everything that is required by the interface.

Right-click on **Player** and select Generate... → Implement Methods..., then select diceCount, diceSides, and **attack** in the Implement Members dialog (Figure 16.1). (You will deal with damageRoll in the next section.)

Figure 16.1 Implementing **Fightable** members

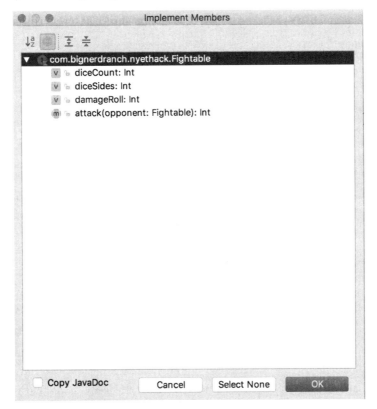

You should see the following code added to the **Player** class:

```
class Player(_name: String,
        override var healthPoints: Int = 100,
        var isBlessed: Boolean = false,
        private var isImmortal: Boolean) : Fightable {

    override val diceCount: Int
        get() = TODO("not implemented")
        //To change initializer of created properties use
        //File | Settings | File Templates.

    override val diceSides: Int
        get() = TODO("not implemented")
        //To change initializer of created properties use
        //File | Settings | File Templates.

    override fun attack(opponent: Fightable): Int {
        TODO("not implemented")
        //To change body of created functions use
        //File | Settings | File Templates.
    }
    ...
}
```

The function implementations added to **Player** are just stubs. You will provide more realistic implementations for them next. (By the way, you might recall the **TODO** function from the discussion of the Nothing type in Chapter 4. Here it is in action – or, perhaps, in *anticipation*.) Once you implement these properties and functions, **Player** will satisfy the **Fightable** interface and can be used in combat.

Notice that the property and function implementations all use the override keyword. This may surprise you – after all, you are not replacing an implementation for these properties in **Fightable**. However, all implementations of interface properties and functions must be marked with override.

On the other hand, the open keyword is not required on function declarations in an interface. This is because all properties and functions you add to an interface must be open implicitly, since they would serve no purpose otherwise. After all, an interface outlines the what, and the how must be provided in the classes that implement it.

Replace the **TODO** calls in diceCount, diceSides, and **attack** with appropriate values and functionality.

Listing 16.3 Stubbing out an interface implementation (Player.kt)

```kotlin
class Player(_name: String,
        override var healthPoints: Int = 100,
        var isBlessed: Boolean = false,
        private var isImmortal: Boolean) : Fightable {

    override val diceCount: Int = 3
        get() = TODO("not implemented")
        //To change initializer of created properties use
        //File | Settings | File Templates.

    override val diceSides: Int = 6
        get() = TODO("not implemented")
        //To change initializer of created properties use
        //File | Settings | File Templates.

    override fun attack(opponent: Fightable): Int {
        TODO("not implemented")
        //To change body of created functions use
        //File | Settings | File Templates.
        val damageDealt = if (isBlessed) {
            damageRoll * 2
        } else {
            damageRoll
        }
        opponent.healthPoints -= damageDealt
        return damageDealt
    }
    ...
}
```

diceCount and diceSides are implemented with integers. **Player**'s **attack** function takes the result from damageRoll (which is not yet fleshed out) and doubles it if the player is blessed. It then takes that value and subtracts it from opponent's healthPoints property – which opponent is guaranteed to have, no matter what its class is, because it implements **Fightable**. That is the beauty of an interface.

Default Implementations

We have said several times now that interfaces focus on the what and not the how. You can, however, provide a default implementation for property getters and functions in an interface. Classes that implement the interface then have the option of using the default or defining their own implementation.

Provide a default getter for damageRoll in **Fightable**. This getter should return the sum of all the dice rolls to determine how much damage is dealt in a round of combat.

Listing 16.4 Defining a default getter implementation (`Creature.kt`)

```
interface Fightable {
    var healthPoints: Int
    val diceCount: Int
    val diceSides: Int
    val damageRoll: Int
        get() = (0 until diceCount).map {
            Random().nextInt(diceSides + 1)
        }.sum()

    fun attack(opponent: Fightable): Int
}
```

Now that damageRoll has a default getter, any class that implements the **Fightable** interface can opt out of providing a value for the damageRoll property – in which case the property's value will be assigned based on the default implementation.

Not every property or function needs a unique implementation in every class, so providing a default implementation is a good way to reduce duplication in your code.

Abstract Classes

Abstract classes provide another way to enforce structure in your classes. An abstract class is never instantiated. Its purpose is to provide function implementations through inheritance to subclasses that *are* instantiated.

An abstract class is defined by prepending the abstract keyword to a class definition. In addition to function implementations, abstract classes can include *abstract functions* – function declarations without implementations.

It is time to give the player something to fight in NyetHack. Add an abstract class called **Monster** to Creature.kt. **Monster** implements the **Fightable** interface, and therefore needs a healthPoints property and an **attack** function. (What about the other **Fightable** properties? We will return to those in a moment.)

Listing 16.5 Defining an abstract class (`Creature.kt`)

```
interface Fightable {
    var healthPoints: Int
    val diceCount: Int
    val diceSides: Int
    val damageRoll: Int
        get() = (0 until diceCount).map {
            Random().nextInt(diceSides + 1)
        }.sum()

    fun attack(opponent: Fightable): Int
}

abstract class Monster(val name: String,
                       val description: String,
                       override var healthPoints: Int) : Fightable {

    override fun attack(opponent: Fightable): Int {
        val damageDealt = damageRoll
        opponent.healthPoints -= damageDealt
        return damageDealt
    }
}
```

You define **Monster** as an abstract class because it is meant as a foundation for more specific creatures in the game. You will never create an instance of **Monster** – and could not if you tried. Instead, you will create instances of **Monster** subclasses: more specific monsters, like goblins, wraiths, and dragons, that are concrete versions of an abstract monster.

Defining **Monster** as an abstract class provides a template for what it means to be a monster in NyetHack: A monster must have a name and a description, and it must satisfy the criteria of the **Fightable** interface.

Now, create the first concrete version of the **Monster** abstract class – the **Goblin** subclass – in Creature.kt.

Listing 16.6 Subclassing an abstract class (`Creature.kt`)

```
interface Fightable {
    ...
}

abstract class Monster(val name: String,
                       val description: String,
                       override var healthPoints: Int) : Fightable {

    override fun attack(opponent: Fightable): Int {
        val damageDealt = damageRoll
        opponent.healthPoints -= damageDealt
        return damageDealt
    }
}

class Goblin(name: String = "Goblin",
             description: String = "A nasty-looking goblin",
             healthPoints: Int = 30) : Monster(name, description, healthPoints) {

}
```

Because **Goblin** is a subclass of **Monster**, it has all of the properties and functions that **Monster** does.

If you attempted to compile your code at this point, compilation would fail. This is because both diceCount and diceSides are specified as requirements of the **Fightable** interface, but they are not implemented in **Monster** (and have no default implementation).

Monster does not have to include all the requirements of the **Fightable** interface, even though it implements it, because it is an abstract class and will never be instantiated. Its subclasses, however, must implement all requirements of **Fightable**, either through inheritance from **Monster** or on their own.

Satisfy the requirements defined on the **Fightable** interface by adding them to **Goblin**:

Listing 16.7 Implementing properties in the subclass of an abstract class (Creature.kt)

```kotlin
interface Fightable {
    ...
}

abstract class Monster(val name: String,
                       val description: String,
                       override var healthPoints: Int) : Fightable {
    ...
}

class Goblin(name: String = "Goblin",
             description: String = "A nasty-looking goblin",
             healthPoints: Int = 30) : Monster(name, description, healthPoints) {

    override val diceCount = 2
    override val diceSides = 8
}
```

A subclass shares all functionality with its superclass, by default. This is true no matter what kind of class the superclass is. If a class implements an interface, then its subclass must also satisfy the requirements of the interface.

You may have noticed the similarity between abstract classes and interfaces: Both can define functions and properties that do not require an implementation. What, then, is the difference between the two?

For one thing, an interface cannot specify a constructor. For another, a class can *extend* (or subclass) only one abstract class, but it can implement many interfaces. A good rule of thumb is this: When you need a category of behavior or properties that objects have in common that does not fit using inheritance, use an interface. If, on the other hand, inheritance makes sense – but you do not want a concrete parent class – then an abstract class may make sense. (And if you want to be able to construct your parent class, then a regular class is still your best bet.)

Combat in NyetHack

Adding combat to NyetHack will put to use all that you have learned about object-oriented programming.

Each room in NyetHack will contain a monster for your hero to vanquish in the most graphic way that you know how: by nullifying it.

Add a monster property of nullable type **Monster?** to the **Room** class, and initialize it by assigning it a **Goblin**. Update **Room**'s description to let the player know whether the room has a monster to fight.

Listing 16.8 Adding a monster to each room (Room.kt)

```
open class Room(val name: String) {
    protected open val dangerLevel = 5
    var monster: Monster? = Goblin()

    fun description() = "Room: $name\n" +
            "Danger level: $dangerLevel\n" +
            "Creature: ${monster?.description ?: "none."}"

    open fun load() = "Nothing much to see here..."
}
```

If a **Room**'s monster is null, then it has been bested. Otherwise, your hero still has a foe to defeat.

You initialized monster, a property of type **Monster?**, with an object of type **Goblin**. A room can host any subclass of **Monster**, and **Goblin** is a subclass of **Monster** – this is polymorphism at work. If you were to create another class that subclasses **Monster**, then it could also be used in a room in NyetHack.

Now, it is time to add a "fight" command to use **Room**'s new monster property. Add a private function called **fight** to **Game**.

Listing 16.9 Defining the **fight** function (Game.kt)

```
...
object Game {
    ...
    private fun move(directionInput: String) = ...

    private fun fight() = currentRoom.monster?.let {
            while (player.healthPoints > 0 && it.healthPoints > 0) {
                Thread.sleep(1000)
            }

            "Combat complete."
    } ?: "There's nothing here to fight."

    private class GameInput(arg: String?) {
        ...
    }
}
```

fight first checks to see whether the current room's monster is null. If it is, then there is nothing to fight, and a corresponding message is returned. If there is a monster to fight, then – as long as the player and the monster still have at least 1 health point – a round of combat is performed.

That round of combat is represented by the next private function you will add, called **slay**. **slay** calls the **attack** function on the monster and on the player. The same **attack** function can be called on both **Monster** and **Player**, because they both implement the **Fightable** interface.

Listing 16.10 Defining the **slay** function (Game.kt)

```
...
object Game {
    ...
    private fun fight() = ...

    private fun slay(monster: Monster) {
        println("${monster.name} did ${monster.attack(player)} damage!")
        println("${player.name} did ${player.attack(monster)} damage!")

        if (player.healthPoints <= 0) {
            println(">>>> You have been defeated! Thanks for playing. <<<<")
            exitProcess(0)
        }

        if (monster.healthPoints <= 0) {
            println(">>>> ${monster.name} has been defeated! <<<<")
            currentRoom.monster = null
        }
    }

    private class GameInput(arg: String?) {
        ...
    }
}
```

As specified by the condition of the while loop in **fight**, combat rounds repeat until either the player or the monster runs out of health points.

If the player's healthPoints value reaches 0, then the game ends, which you achieve with a call to **exitProcess**. **exitProcess** is a Kotlin standard library function that terminates the running instance of the JVM. To access this function, you will have to import **kotlin.system.exitProcess**.

If the monster's healthPoints value reaches 0, then the monster is nullified in dramatic fashion.

Call **slay** from **fight**.

Listing 16.11 Calling the **slay** function (Game.kt)

```
...
object Game {
    ...
    private fun move(directionInput: String) = ...

    private fun fight() = currentRoom.monster?.let {
            while (player.healthPoints > 0 && it.healthPoints > 0) {
                slay(it)
                Thread.sleep(1000)
            }

            "Combat complete."
        } ?: "There's nothing here to fight."

    private fun slay(monster: Monster) {
        ...
    }

    private class GameInput(arg: String?) {
        ...
    }
}
```

After a round of combat, **Thread.sleep** is called for 1 second. **Thread.sleep** is a heavy-handed function that pauses execution for a given length of time, in this case 1,000 milliseconds (or 1 second). We do not recommend using **Thread.sleep** throughout a production codebase, but in this case, it is a handy way to create time between combat rounds in NyetHack.

Once the condition of the while loop is no longer satisfied, "Combat complete." is returned to be printed to the console.

Test your new combat system by adding a "fight" command to **GameInput** that calls the **fight** function.

Listing 16.12 Adding the fight command (Game.kt)

```
...
object Game {
    ...

    private class GameInput(arg: String?) {
        private val input = arg ?: ""
        val command = input.split(" ")[0]
        val argument = input.split(" ").getOrElse(1, { "" })

        fun processCommand() = when (command.toLowerCase()) {
            "fight" -> fight()
            "move" -> move(argument)
            else -> commandNotFound()
        }

        private fun commandNotFound() = "I'm not quite sure what you're trying to do!"
    }
}
```

Run `Game.kt`. Try moving from screen to screen and using the "fight" command in different rooms. The randomness that you introduced in the `damageRoll` property on the **Fightable** interface means that you will have a different experience each time that you walk into a new room and pick a fight.

```
Welcome, adventurer.
A glass of Fireball springs into existence. Delicious! (x2)
Room: Town Square
Danger level: 2
Creature: A nasty-looking goblin
(Aura: GREEN) (Blessed: YES)
Madrigal of Tampa is in excellent condition!
> Enter your command: fight
Goblin did 11 damage!
Madrigal of Tampa did 14 damage!
Goblin did 8 damage!
Madrigal of Tampa did 14 damage!
Goblin did 7 damage!
Madrigal of Tampa did 10 damage!
>>>> Goblin has been defeated! <<<<
Combat complete.
Room: Town Square
Danger level: 2
Creature: none.
(Aura: GREEN) (Blessed: YES)
Madrigal of Tampa looks pretty hurt.
> Enter your command:
```

In this chapter, you leveraged interfaces to define what a creature needs to engage in combat, and you used abstract classes to create a base class for all monsters in the world of NyetHack. These tools will help you create relationships that focus on what a class can do rather than how it does it.

Many of the object-oriented concepts that you have learned about in the past several chapters return to this common goal: Leverage the tools of the Kotlin framework to create scalable codebases that only expose what they need to and encapsulate the rest.

In the next chapter, you will learn about generics, a feature that allows you to specify classes that work with many types.

17

Generics

You learned in Chapter 10 that a list can hold any type: integers, strings, or even new types that you have defined:

```
val listOfInts: List<Int> = listOf(1,2,3)
val listOfStrings: List<String> = listOf("string one", "string two")
val listOfRooms: List<Room> = listOf(Room(), TownSquare())
```

Lists can hold any type because of *generics*, a type system feature that allows both functions and types to work with types that are not yet known to you or the compiler. Generics greatly expand the reusability of your class definitions, because they allow your definitions to work with many types.

In this chapter, you will learn how to create your own generic classes and functions that work with generic type parameters. You will be working in your Sandbox project to model a generic **LootBox** class that can hold virtual rewards of any kind you can imagine.

Defining Generic Types

A *generic type* is a class that accepts an input of any type in its constructor. You are going to begin by defining your own generic type.

Open the Sandbox project and add a new file called Generics.kt. Within Generics.kt, define a **LootBox** class that specifies a *generic type parameter* for use with its contents and contains a private property called loot that is assigned the item.

Listing 17.1 Creating a generic type (Generics.kt)

```
class LootBox<T>(item: T) {
    private var loot: T = item
}
```

You define the **LootBox** class and make it generic by specifying a generic type parameter for use with the class, written as T and specified within diamond braces (< >) like other type parameters. The generic type parameter, T, is a placeholder for the item's type.

The **LootBox** class accepts an item of any type as a primary constructor value (item: T) and assigns the value to the private property loot, also of type T.

Note that the generic type parameter is usually represented with a single letter T, short for "type," though any letter or word can be used. We suggest you generally stick with T, since it is what is commonly used in other languages that support generics and is therefore the most readable choice.

Time to put the new **LootBox** class to the test. Add a **main** function, define a couple kinds of loot, and place an instance of each new item in its very own loot box.

Listing 17.2 Defining loot boxes (`Generics.kt`)

```
class LootBox<T>(item: T) {
    private var loot: T = item
}

class Fedora(val name: String, val value: Int)

class Coin(val value: Int)

fun main(args: Array<String>) {
    val lootBoxOne: LootBox<Fedora> = LootBox(Fedora("a generic-looking fedora", 15))
    val lootBoxTwo: LootBox<Coin> = LootBox(Coin(15))
}
```

You have created two different kinds of loot (fedoras and coins, both highly desirable virtual rewards) and two different kinds of loot boxes to hold them.

Since you made the **LootBox** class generic, you are able to use just one class definition to support different kinds of loot boxes: ones that hold fedoras, ones that hold coins, and so on.

Notice the type signature for each **LootBox** variable:

```
val lootBoxOne: LootBox<Fedora> = LootBox(Fedora("a generic-looking fedora", 15))
val lootBoxTwo: LootBox<Coin> = LootBox(Coin(15))
```

The diamond braces on the type signature for the variable show what type of loot a particular **LootBox** instance is capable of holding.

Generic types, like other types in Kotlin, support type inference. We have included the type explicitly for illustration, but it could have been omitted since each variable is initialized with a value. In your own code, you typically will omit the type information when it is not needed; feel free to delete it here, if you prefer.

Generic Functions

Generic type parameters also work with functions. That is good news, since there is currently no way for a player to retrieve loot from a loot box.

Time to fix that. Add a function that lets a player fetch the item if and only if the box is open. Track whether the box is open by adding an open property.

Listing 17.3 Adding a **fetch** function (`Generics.kt`)

```
class LootBox<T>(item: T) {
    var open = false
    private var loot: T = item

    fun fetch(): T? {
        return loot.takeIf { open }
    }
}
```

Here you define a generic function, **fetch**, that returns T – the generic type parameter specified on the **LootBox** class, which is a placeholder for the type of item.

Note that if **fetch** were defined outside of **LootBox**, type T would not be available, since T is tied to the **LootBox** class definition. However, a function does not require a class to use a generic type parameter, as you will see in the next section.

Try fetching the contents of lootBoxOne in the **main** function using the new **fetch** function, first with the box closed:

Listing 17.4 Testing the generic **fetch** function (Generics.kt)

```
...

fun main(args: Array<String>) {
    val lootBoxOne: LootBox<Fedora> = LootBox(Fedora("a generic-looking fedora", 15))
    val lootBoxTwo: LootBox<Coin> = LootBox(Coin(15))

    lootBoxOne.fetch()?.run {
        println("You retrieve $name from the box!")
    }
}
```

You use the standard function **run** (which you learned about in Chapter 9) to print the name of lootBoxOne's contents, if it is non-null.

Recall that **run** scopes everything within the lambda it accepts to the receiver instance it is called on – so $name accesses **Fedora**'s name property.

Run Generics.kt. There will be no output. You could not take the loot, because the loot box was closed. Now, open the loot box and run Generics.kt again.

Listing 17.5 Opening the box (Generics.kt)

```
...

fun main(args: Array<String>) {
    val lootBoxOne: LootBox<Fedora> = LootBox(Fedora("a generic-looking fedora", 15))
    val lootBoxTwo: LootBox<Coin> = LootBox(Coin(15))

    lootBoxOne.open = true
    lootBoxOne.fetch()?.run {
        println("You retrieve a $name from the box!")
    }
}
```

This time, when you run Generics.kt you will see the name of the loot found:

```
You retrieve a generic-looking fedora from the box!
```

Multiple Generic Type Parameters

A generic function or type can also support multiple generic type parameters. Suppose you want a second **fetch** function that accepts a loot-modification function, allowing you to convert the loot to some other new type, perhaps a coin, when you fetch it. The value of the coin returned depends on the value of the original loot – and a lootModFunction higher-order function that is passed to **fetch** will determine that.

Add a new **fetch** function to LootBox that accepts a loot-modification function.

Listing 17.6 Using multiple generic type parameters (Generics.kt)

```
class LootBox<T>(item: T) {
    var open = false
    private var loot: T = item

    fun fetch(): T? {
        return loot.takeIf { open }
    }

    fun <R> fetch(lootModFunction: (T) -> R): R? {
        return lootModFunction(loot).takeIf { open }
    }
}
...
```

Here, you add a new generic type parameter to the function, R, short for "return," since the generic type parameter will be used for **fetch**'s return type. You place the generic type parameter in diamond braces directly before the function name: fun <R> fetch. **fetch** returns a value of type R?, a nullable version of R.

You also specify that the lootModFunction (via its function type declaration, (T) -> R) accepts an argument of type T and returns a result of type R. Try out the new **fetch** function that you defined – this time, passing a loot-modification function as an argument.

Listing 17.7 Passing the loot-modification function as an argument (Generics.kt)

```
...

fun main(args: Array<String>) {
    val lootBoxOne: LootBox<Fedora> = LootBox(Fedora("a generic-looking fedora", 15))
    val lootBoxTwo: LootBox<Coin> = LootBox(Coin(15))

    lootBoxOne.open = true
    lootBoxOne.fetch()?.run {
        println("You retrieve $name from the box!")
    }

    val coin = lootBoxOne.fetch() {
        Coin(it.value * 3)
    }
    coin?.let { println(it.value) }
}
```

The new version of the **fetch** function you defined returns the type of the lambda you provide it, R. You return a **Coin?** from the lambda, so the type of R in this case is **Coin?**. But the new version of `fetch` is more flexible than returning a coin every time – whatever you return from the lambda, the `fetch` function will return that same type, since the type of R depends on what is returned from the anonymous function.

`lootBoxOne` holds an item of type **Fedora**. However, your new `fetch` function returns a **Coin?**, instead of a **Fedora?**. The new generic type parameter that you added, R, makes this possible.

The `lootModFunction` you pass to `fetch` calculates a value for the coin by looking at the value of the loot in the box and multiplying it by 3.

Run `Generics.kt`. This time you will see the name of the loot found along with the value of the coin returned from the loot box: the value of the original item (a fedora) multiplied by 3:

```
You retrieve a generic-looking fedora from the box!
45
```

Generic Constraints

What if you wanted to ensure that the loot box was only used to hold loot, and not something else? You can specify a generic type constraint to enforce exactly that.

Start by changing the **Coin** and **Fedora** classes to be subclasses of a new top-level **Loot** class:

Listing 17.8 Adding a superclass (Generics.kt)

```
class LootBox<T>(item: T) {
    var open = false
    private var loot: T = item

    fun fetch(): T? {
        return loot.takeIf { open }
    }

    fun <R> fetch(lootModFunction: (T) -> R): R? {
        return lootModFunction(loot).takeIf { open }
    }
}

open class Loot(val value: Int)

class Fedora(val name: String, val value: Int) : Loot(value)

class Coin(val value: Int) : Loot(value)
...
```

Now, add a generic type constraint to **LootBox**'s generic type parameter to allow only descendants of the **Loot** class to be used with **LootBox**:

Listing 17.9 Constraining the generic parameter to **Loot** only (Generics.kt)

```
class LootBox<T : Loot>(item: T) {
    ...
}
...
```

Here, you add a constraint to the generic type T, specified as : Loot. Now, only items that are descendants of the **Loot** class can be added to the loot box.

You might be wondering, "Why is T still needed here? Why not just use the type **Loot**?" By using T, **LootBox** allows you to access the specific kind of **Loot** while allowing the contents to be any kind of **Loot**. So, rather than the **LootBox** containing **Loot**, the **LootBox** can contain a **Fedora** – and the **Fedora**'s specific type is tracked with T.

If you used **Loot** for the type, that would constrain **LootBox** to accept descendants of **Loot**, but it would also discard the information that a **Fedora** was in the box. Using **Loot** for the type, for example, the following would not compile:

```
val lootBox: LootBox<Loot> = LootBox(Fedora("a dazzling fuschia fedora", 15))
val fedora: Fedora = lootBox.item // Type mismatch – Required: Fedora, Found: Loot
```

It would no longer be possible to see that the **LootBox** contained anything other than **Loot**. By using a type constraint, it is possible to constrain the contents to **Loot** and also preserve the specific subtype of the loot in the box.

vararg and get

Your **LootBox** can now hold any kind of **Loot**, but it cannot hold more than one item at a time. What if you want to hold multiple items of **Loot** in your **LootBox**?

To do so, modify **LootBox**'s primary constructor with the vararg keyword, which allows a variable number of arguments to be passed to the constructor.

Listing 17.10 Adding vararg (Generics.kt)

```
class LootBox<T : Loot>(vararg item: T) {
    ...
}
...
```

Now that you have added the vararg keyword to **LootBox**, its item variable will be treated as an Array of elements instead of a single element when it is initialized, and **LootBox** can accept multiple items passed into the constructor. (Recall from Chapter 10 that Array is a collection type.)

Update the loot variable and the **fetch** function to account for this change by indexing into the loot array:

Listing 17.11 Indexing into the loot array (Generics.kt)

```
class LootBox<T : Loot>(vararg item: T) {
    var open = false
    private var loot: TArray<out T> = item

    fun fetch(item: Int): T? {
        return loot[item].takeIf { open }
    }

    fun <R> fetch(item: Int, lootModFunction: (T) -> R): R? {
        return lootModFunction(loot[item]).takeIf { open }
    }
}
...
```

Notice the out keyword that you added for the new loot variable's type signature. The out keyword is required here because it is part of the return type for any variable marked as a vararg. You will learn more about this keyword, and its partner in, shortly.

Try out the new and improved **LootBox** in **main**. Pass another fedora into the loot box (get creative with the second fedora's name, if you like). Then fetch the two items from lootBoxOne, one in each call to **fetch**:

Listing 17.12 Testing the new **LootBox** (Generics.kt)

```
...
fun main(args: Array<String>) {
    val lootBoxOne: LootBox<Fedora> = LootBox(Fedora("a generic-looking fedora", 15),
                                            Fedora("a dazzling magenta fedora", 25))
    val lootBoxTwo: LootBox<Coin> = LootBox(Coin(15))

    lootBoxOne.open = true
    lootBoxOne.fetch(1)?.run {
        println("You retrieve $name from the box!")
    }

    val coin = lootBoxOne.fetch(0) {
        Coin(it.value * 3)
    }
    coin?.let { println(it.value) }
}
```

Run Generics.kt again. You will see the name of the second item in lootBoxOne and the value of the first item (multiplied by 3):

```
You retrieve a dazzling magenta fedora from the box!
45
```

Another way to provide index access to the loot array is to have **LootBox** implement an operator function: the **get** function, which enables the [] operator. (You saw operator overloading in Chapter 15.)

Update **LootBox** to include a **get** operator implementation:

Listing 17.13 Adding a **get** operator to **LootBox** (Generics.kt)

```
class LootBox<T : Loot>(vararg item: T) {
    var open = false
    private var loot: Array<out T> = item

    operator fun get(index: Int): T? = loot[index].takeIf { open }

    fun fetch(item: Int): T? {
        return loot[item].takeIf { open }
    }

    fun <R> fetch(item: Int, lootModFunction: (T) -> R): R? {
        return lootModFunction(loot[item]).takeIf { open }
    }
}
...
```

Now, use the new **get** operator in your **main** function:

Listing 17.14 Using **get** (Generics.kt)

```
...
fun main(args: Array<String>) {
    ...
    coin?.let { println(it.value) }

    val fedora = lootBoxOne[1]
    fedora?.let { println(it.name) }
}
```

get gives you a shorthand for fetching loot at a particular index. Run Generics.kt again – you will see the name of the second fedora in lootBoxOne printed after the output from before.

```
You retrieve a dazzling magenta fedora from the box!
45
a dazzling magenta fedora
```

in and out

To further customize your generic type parameters, Kotlin provides the keywords in and out. To see how they work, create a simple generic **Barrel** class in a new file called Variance.kt:

Listing 17.15 Defining **Barrel** (Variance.kt)

```
class Barrel<T>(var item: T)
```

To experiment with Barrel, add a **main** function. In **main**, define a **Barrel** to hold a **Fedora** and another **Barrel** to hold **Loot**:

Listing 17.16 Defining **Barrel**s in **main** (Variance.kt)

```
class Barrel<T>(var item: T)

fun main(args: Array<String>) {
    var fedoraBarrel: Barrel<Fedora> = Barrel(Fedora("a generic-looking fedora", 15))
    var lootBarrel: Barrel<Loot> = Barrel(Coin(15))
}
```

While a **Barrel<Loot>** can hold any kind of loot, the particular instance defined here happens to hold a **Coin** (which, remember, is a subclass of **Loot**).

Now, assign fedoraBarrel to lootBarrel:

Listing 17.17 Attempting to reassign lootBarrel (Variance.kt)

```
class Barrel<T>(var item: T)

fun main(args: Array<String>) {
    var fedoraBarrel: Barrel<Fedora> = Barrel(Fedora("a generic-looking fedora", 15))
    var lootBarrel: Barrel<Loot> = Barrel(Coin(15))

    lootBarrel = fedoraBarrel
}
```

You may be surprised to find that the assignment was not allowed by the compiler (Figure 17.1):

Figure 17.1 Type mismatch

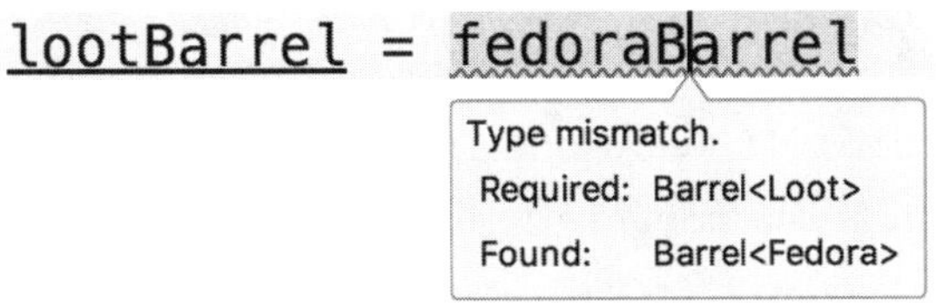

```
lootBarrel = fedoraBarrel
```

Type mismatch.
Required: Barrel<Loot>
Found: Barrel<Fedora>

It might seem like the assignment should have been possible. **Fedora** is, after all, a descendant of **Loot**, and assigning a variable of the **Loot** type an instance of **Fedora** is possible:

```
var loot: Loot = Fedora("a generic-looking fedora", 15) // No errors
```

To understand why the assignment fails, let's walk through what could happen if it succeeded.

If the compiler allowed you to assign the fedoraBarrel instance to the lootBarrel variable, lootBarrel would then point to fedoraBarrel, and it would be possible to interface with fedoraBarrel's item as **Loot**, instead of **Fedora** (because of lootBarrel's type, Barrel<Loot>).

For example, a coin is valid **Loot**, so it would be possible to assign a coin to lootBarrel.item (which points to fedoraBarrel). Do so in Variance.kt:

Listing 17.18 Assigning a coin to lootBarrel.item (Variance.kt)

```
class Barrel<T>(var item: T)

fun main(args: Array<String>) {
    var fedoraBarrel: Barrel<Fedora> = Barrel(Fedora("a generic-looking fedora", 15))
    var lootBarrel: Barrel<Loot> = Barrel(Coin(15))

    lootBarrel = fedoraBarrel
    lootBarrel.item = Coin(15)
}
```

Now, suppose you tried to access fedoraBarrel.item, expecting a fedora:

Listing 17.19 Accessing fedoraBarrel.item (Variance.kt)

```
class Barrel<T>(var item: T)

fun main(args: Array<String>) {
    var fedoraBarrel: Barrel<Fedora> = Barrel(Fedora("a generic-looking fedora", 15))
    var lootBarrel: Barrel<Loot> = Barrel(Coin(15))

    lootBarrel = fedoraBarrel
    lootBarrel.item = Coin(15)
    val myFedora: Fedora = fedoraBarrel.item
}
```

The compiler would then be faced with a type mismatch – fedoraBarrel.item is not a **Fedora**, it is a **Coin** – and you would be faced with a ClassCastException. This is the problem that arises, and the reason the assignment is not allowed by the compiler.

It is also why the in and out keywords exist.

In the **Barrel** class's definition, add the out keyword and change item from a var to a val:

Listing 17.20 Adding out (Variance.kt)

```
class Barrel<out T>(~~var~~val item: T)
...
```

Next, delete the line that assigned `Coin` to item (which is no longer allowed, since item is a val) and change the assignment of myFedora to lootBarrel.item instead of fedoraBarrel.item.

Listing 17.21 Changing the assignment (`Variance.kt`)

```kotlin
class Barrel<out T>(val item: T)

fun main(args: Array<String>) {
    var fedoraBarrel: Barrel<Fedora> = Barrel(Fedora("a generic-looking fedora", 15))
    var lootBarrel: Barrel<Loot> = Barrel(Coin(15))

    lootBarrel = fedoraBarrel
    lootBarrel.item = Coin(15)
    val myFedora: Fedora = fedoraBarrel.itemlootBarrel.item
}
```

All errors are resolved. What has changed?

There are two roles a generic parameter can be assigned: *producer* or *consumer*. The role of producer means that a generic parameter will be readable (but not writable), and consumer means the generic parameter will be writable (but not readable).

When you added the out keyword to Barrel<out T>, you specified that the generic would act as a producer – that it would be readable, but not writable. That meant that defining item with the var keyword was no longer permitted – otherwise, it would not simply be a producer of **Fedora**s, but would also be writable and support consuming one.

By making the generic a producer, you assure the compiler that the dilemma pointed out earlier is no longer a possibility: Since the generic parameter is a producer, not a consumer, the item variable will never change. Kotlin now permits the assignment of fedoraBarrel to lootBarrel, because it is safe to do so: lootBarrel's item now has type **Fedora**, not **Loot**, and cannot be changed.

Take a closer look at the assignment of the myFedora variable in IntelliJ. The green shading around lootBarrel indicates that a smart cast took place, and that is confirmed when you mouse over it (Figure 17.2):

Figure 17.2 Smart cast to **Barrel<Fedora>**

```kotlin
val myFedora: Fedora = lootBarrel.item
```
Smart cast to Barrel<Fedora>

The compiler can smart cast Barrel<Loot> to Barrel<Fedora> because item can never change – it is a producer only.

By the way, Lists are also producers. In Kotlin's definition for List, the generic type parameter is marked with the out keyword:

```kotlin
public interface List<out E> : Collection<E>
```

Marking the generic type parameter for **Barrel** with the in keyword would have the opposite effect on reassigning the **Barrel**s: Instead of being allowed to assign fedoraBarrel to lootBarrel, you would be allowed to assign lootBarrel to fedoraBarrel – but not vice versa.

Update **Barrel** to use the in keyword instead of out. You will notice that **Barrel** will now require dropping the val keyword for item, since it could otherwise produce an item (a violation of the consumer role).

Listing 17.22 Marking **Barrel** with in (Variance.kt)

```
class Barrel<~~inout~~ T>(~~val~~ item: T)
...
```

Now, lootBarrel = fedoraBarrel in **main** has an error warning you of a type mismatch. Reverse the assignment:

Listing 17.23 Reversing the assignment (Variance.kt)

```
...
fun main(args: Array<String>) {
    var fedoraBarrel: Barrel<Fedora> = Barrel(Fedora("a generic-looking fedora", 15))
    var lootBarrel: Barrel<Loot> = Barrel(Coin(15))

    ~~lootBarrel = fedoraBarrel~~
    fedoraBarrel = lootBarrel
    ~~val myFedora: Fedora = lootBarrel.item~~
}
```

The opposite assignment is possible because the compiler can be certain you would never be able to produce **Loot** from a **Barrel** containing **Fedora**s – leading to the possibility of class cast exceptions.

You removed the val keyword from **Barrel** because **Barrel** is now a consumer – it accepts a value, but it does not produce one. Therefore, you also drop the item lookup. This is how the compiler is able to reason that the assignment you have made is a safe one.

By the way, you may have heard the terms *covariance* and *contravariance* used to describe what out and in do. In our opinion, these terms lack the commonsense clarity of in and out, so we avoid them. We mention them here because you may encounter them elsewhere, so now you know: If you hear "covariance," think "out," and if you hear "contravariance," think "in."

In this chapter you have learned how to use generics to expand the capabilities of Kotlin's classes. You have also seen type constraints and how the in and out keywords can be used to define the producer or consumer role for the generic parameter.

In the next chapter, you will learn about extensions, which allow you to share functions and properties without using inheritance. You will use them to improve NyetHack's codebase.

For the More Curious: The reified Keyword

There are cases where it is useful to know the specific type that is used for a generic parameter. The reified keyword allows you to check a generic parameter's type.

Imagine that you wanted to fetch loot from a list of different kinds of loot (**Coin**s and **Fedora**s, for example), and – depending on the type of loot that was randomly selected – you either wanted to provide a backup loot item of a desired type or return the one that was selected. Here is a **randomOrBackupLoot** function that attempts to capture that logic:

```
fun <T> randomOrBackupLoot(backupLoot: () -> T): T {
    val items = listOf(Coin(14), Fedora("a fedora of the ages", 150))
    val randomLoot: Loot = items.shuffled().first()
    return if (randomLoot is T)
        randomLoot
    } else {
        backupLoot()
    }
}

fun main(args: Array<String>) {
    randomOrBackupLoot {
        Fedora("a backup fedora", 15)
    }.run {
        // Prints either the backup fedora or the fedora of the ages
        println(name)
    }
}
```

If you typed this in, you would find that it does not work. IntelliJ would flag the type parameter T with an error (Figure 17.3):

Figure 17.3 Cannot check for instance of erased type

```
return if (randomLoot is T) {
    randomL
} else {          Cannot check for instance of erased type: T
    backupLoot()
}
```

Kotlin normally disallows the type check you performed against T because generic types are subject to *type erasure* – meaning the type information for T is not available at runtime. Java has the same rule.

If you were to look at the bytecode for the **randomOrBackupLoot** function, you would see the effect of type erasure on the expression randomLoot is T:

```
return (randomLoot != null ? randomLoot instanceof Object : true)
? randomLoot : backupLoot.invoke();
```

Where you used T, Object is used instead, because the compiler no longer knows the type of T at runtime. This is why type checking a generic defined in the usual way is not possible.

However, unlike Java, Kotlin provides the `reified` keyword, which allows you to preserve the type information at runtime.

`reified` is used on an inlined function:

```
inline fun <reified T> randomOrBackupLoot(backupLoot: () -> T): T {
    val items = listOf(Coin(14), Fedora("a fedora of the ages", 150))
    val first: Loot = items.shuffled().first()
    return if (first is T) {
        first
    } else {
        backupLoot()
    }
}
```

Now the type check `first is T` is possible, because the type information is reified. The generic type information that is normally erased is instead preserved so that the compiler can check the type of the generic parameter.

The bytecode for the updated **randomOrBackupLoot** shows that the actual type information for T is maintained, instead of `Object`:

```
randomLoot$iv instanceof Fedora
? randomLoot$iv : new Fedora("a backup fedora", 15);
```

Using the `reified` keyword allows you to inspect the type of a generic parameter without requiring *reflection* (learning a name or a type of a property or function at runtime – generally a costly operation).

18
Extensions

Extensions allow you to add functionality to a type without directly modifying the type's definition. You can use extensions with your own types and also types you do not control, like List, String, and other types from the Kotlin standard library.

Extensions are an alternative to the sharing behavior of inheritance. They are a good fit for adding functionality to a type when you do not control the definition of the class or when a class is not marked with the open keyword, making it ineligible for subclassing.

The Kotlin standard library frequently uses extensions. For example, the standard functions that you learned about in Chapter 9 are defined as extensions, and you will look at several examples of their declarations in this chapter.

For this chapter, you will be working first in the Sandbox project and then applying what you learned to streamline NyetHack's codebase. Begin by opening the Sandbox project and creating a new file called Extensions.kt.

Defining Extension Functions

Your first extension allows you to add a specified amount of enthusiasm to any String. Define it in Extensions.kt:

Listing 18.1 Adding an extension to String (Extensions.kt)

```
fun String.addEnthusiasm(amount: Int = 1) = this + "!".repeat(amount)
```

Extension functions are defined in the same way as other functions, with one major difference: When you specify an extension function, you also specify the type the extension adds functionality to, known as the *receiver type*. (Recall from Chapter 9 that the subject of an extension is called a "receiver.") For the **addEnthusiasm** function, the receiver type you specified is String.

addEnthusiasm's function body is a single-expression function that returns a new string: the contents of this plus 1 or more exclamation points, based on the argument passed to amount (1, if the default vaue is used). The this keyword refers to the receiver instance the extension function was called on (a String instance, in this case).

Now, you can invoke the **addEnthusiasm** function on any instance of String. Try out the new extension function by defining a string in a new **main** function, calling the **addEnthusiasm** extension function on it, and printing the result:

Listing 18.2 Calling the new extension on a String receiver instance (Extensions.kt)

```
fun String.addEnthusiasm(amount: Int = 1) = this + "!".repeat(amount)

fun main(args: Array<String>) {
    println("Madrigal has left the building".addEnthusiasm())
}
```

Run Extensions.kt to see that your extension function adds an exclamation point to the string, as expected.

Could you have subclassed String to add this functionality to String instances? In IntelliJ, view String's source definition by pressing the Shift key twice to open the Search Everywhere dialog and then searching for the "String.kt" file. Its header looks like this:

```
public class String : Comparable<String>, CharSequence {
    ...
}
```

Since there is no open keyword on the String class definition, there is no way to subclass String to add functionality through inheritance. As we said earlier, extensions are a good option when you want to add functionality to a class you do not control or that is ineligible for subclassing.

Defining an extension on a superclass

Extensions do not rely on inheritance, but they can be combined with inheritance to expand their scope. Try it in Extensions.kt: Define an extension on the Any type called **easyPrint**. Because it is defined on Any, it will be directly callable on all types. In **main**, change the call to the **println** function to instead call your new **easyPrint** extension function directly on the String:

Listing 18.3 Extending Any (Extensions.kt)

```
fun String.addEnthusiasm(amount: Int = 1) = this + "!".repeat(amount)

fun Any.easyPrint() = println(this)

fun main(args: Array<String>) {
    println("Madrigal has left the building".addEnthusiasm()).easyPrint()
}
```

Run Extensions.kt and confirm that the output has not changed.

Since you added the extension for the Any type, it is also available for use with other subtypes. Call the extension on an Int after the String:

Listing 18.4 **easyPrint** is available on all subtypes (Extensions.kt)

```
fun String.addEnthusiasm(amount: Int = 1) = this + "!".repeat(amount)

fun Any.easyPrint() = println(this)

fun main(args: Array<String>) {
    "Madrigal has left the building".addEnthusiasm().easyPrint()
    42.easyPrint()
}
```

Generic Extension Functions

What if you wanted to print the string "Madrigal has left the building" both before and after calling **addEnthusiasm** on it?

First, you would need to make the **easyPrint** function chainable. You have seen chained function calls before; functions can be chained if they return their receiver or another object that subsequent functions can be called on.

Update **easyPrint** to make it chainable:

Listing 18.5 Making **easyPrint** chainable (Extensions.kt)

```
fun String.addEnthusiasm(amount: Int = 1) = this + "!".repeat(amount)

fun Any.easyPrint()= println(this): Any {
    println(this)
    return this
}
...
```

Now, try calling the **easyPrint** function two times: once before **addEnthusiasm** and once afterward:

Listing 18.6 Calling **easyPrint** twice (Extensions.kt)

```
fun String.addEnthusiasm(amount: Int = 1) = this + "!".repeat(amount)

fun Any.easyPrint(): Any {
    println(this)
    return this
}

fun main(args: Array<String>) {
    "Madrigal has left the building".easyPrint().addEnthusiasm().easyPrint()
    42.easyPrint()
}
```

The code does not compile. The first **easyPrint** call was allowed, but **addEnthusiasm** was not. Take a look at the type information to understand why: Click on the first **easyPrint** and press Control-Shift-P (Ctrl-P), then, from the list of expressions that pops up, select the first ("Madrigal has left the building".easyPrint()") (Figure 18.1):

Figure 18.1 Chainable, but wrong type for adding enthusiasm

The **easyPrint** function returns the String it was called on, but uses Any to represent it. **addEnthusiasm** is only available on String, so it cannot be called on the return from **easyPrint**.

To solve this, you can make the extension generic. Update the **easyPrint** extension function to use a generic type as its receiver instead of Any:

Listing 18.7 Making **easyPrint** generic (Extensions.kt)

```
fun String.addEnthusiasm(amount: Int = 1) = this + "!".repeat(amount)

fun <T> AnyT.easyPrint(): AnyT {
    println(this)
    return this
}
...
```

Now that the extension uses the generic type parameter T for the receiver and returns T instead of Any, the particular type information for the receiver is passed forward in the chain of calls (Figure 18.2):

Figure 18.2 Chained function returning a usable type

String

`"Madrigal has left the building".easyPrint().addEnthusiasm().easyPrint()`

Try running Extensions.kt again. This time you will see the string printed twice:

```
Madrigal has left the building
Madrigal has left the building!
42
```

Your new generic extension function works with any type, and it also maintains the type information. Extensions used with generic types allow you to write functions that have a wide reach across a number of different types in your program.

Extensions on generic types appear throughout the Kotlin standard library. For example, take a look at the definition for the **let** function:

```
public inline fun <T, R> T.let(block: (T) -> R): R {
    return block(this)
}
```

let is defined as a generic extension function, allowing it to work with all types. It accepts a lambda that takes the receiver as its argument (T) and returns R – some new type that is whatever the lambda returns.

Notice that the inline keyword you learned about in Chapter 5 is also used here. The same guidance from before applies: Inlining the extension function if it accepts a lambda reduces the memory overhead required.

Extension Properties

In addition to adding functionality to a type by specifying extension functions, you can also define extension properties. Add another extension to String in Extensions.kt, this time an extension property that counts a string's vowels:

Listing 18.8 Adding an extension property (Extensions.kt)

```
val String.numVowels
    get() = count { "aeiouy".contains(it) }

fun String.addEnthusiasm(amount: Int = 1) = this + "!".repeat(amount)
...
```

Try out your new extension property by printing the numVowels extension in **main**:

Listing 18.9 Using an extension property (Extensions.kt)

```
val String.numVowels
    get() = count { "aeiouy".contains(it) }

fun String.addEnthusiasm(amount: Int = 1) = this + "!".repeat(amount)

fun <T> T.easyPrint(): T {
    println(this)
    return this
}

fun main(args: Array<String>) {
    "Madrigal has left the building".easyPrint().addEnthusiasm().easyPrint()
    42.easyPrint()
    "How many vowels?".numVowels.easyPrint()
}
```

Run Extensions.kt. You will see the new numVowels property printed:

```
Madrigal has left the building
Madrigal has left the building!
42
5
```

Recall from Chapter 12 that class properties have a backing field where their data is stored (except for computed properties) and that they are automatically assigned getters and, if needed, setters. Like computed properties, extension properties do not have a backing field – they must define **get** and/or **set** operators that compute the value that should be returned by the property to be valid.

For example, the following would not be allowed:

```
var String.preferredCharacters = 10
error: extension property cannot be initialized because it has no backing field
```

Instead, you could define a valid preferredCharacters extension property by defining a getter for the preferredCharacters val.

Extensions on Nullable Types

An extension can also be defined for use with a nullable type. Defining an extension on a nullable type allows you to deal with the possibility of the value being null within the body of the extension function, rather than at the call site.

Add an extension for nullable Strings in Extensions.kt and test it out in the **main** function:

Listing 18.10 Adding an extension on a nullable type (Extensions.kt)

```
...
infix fun String?.printWithDefault(default: String) = print(this ?: default)

fun main(args: Array<String>) {
    "Madrigal has left the building".easyPrint().addEnthusiasm().easyPrint()
    42.easyPrint()
    "How many vowels?".numVowels.easyPrint()

    val nullableString: String? = null
    nullableString printWithDefault "Default string"
}
```

The infix keyword, available for both extension and class functions that have a single argument, allows for the cleaner syntax you see in the function call. If a function is defined with infix, you can omit the dot between the receiver and the function call as well as the parentheses around the argument.

Here are versions of the call to **printWithDefault** with and without infix:

```
null printWithDefault "Default string"    // With infix
null.printWithDefault("Default string")   // Without infix
```

Making a function an infix allows you to clean up usage of the function and can be a nice refinement when you have an extension or class function that expects a single argument.

Run Extensions.kt. You will see that Default string is printed. Since the value of nullableString was null, **printWithDefault** coalesced the value to use the default you provided.

Extensions, Under the Hood

An extension function or property is called in the same style as a normal function or property, but it is not directly defined on the class it extends, nor does it rely on inheritance for adding functionality. So how are extensions implemented on the JVM?

To inspect how an extension works on the JVM, you can look at the bytecode that the Kotlin compiler generates when you define one and translate it back to Java.

Open the Kotlin bytecode tool window, either by selecting Tools → Kotlin → Kotlin Bytecode or by searching for "show Kotlin bytecode" in the Search Everywhere dialog (accessed by pressing the Shift key twice).

In the Kotlin bytecode window, click the Decompile button at the top left to open a new tab with the Java representation of the bytecode that was generated from Extensions.kt. Find the equivalent bytecode for the **addEnthusiasm** extension that you defined for String:

```
public static final String addEnthusiasm(@NotNull String $receiver, int amount) {
    Intrinsics.checkParameterIsNotNull($receiver, "$receiver");
    return $receiver + StringsKt.repeat((CharSequence)"!", amount);
}
```

In the Java version of the bytecode, the Kotlin extension is a static method that accepts what it extends as an argument when you compile it for the JVM. The compiler substitutes a call of the **addEnthusiasm** function.

Extracting to Extensions

Next, you will apply what you have learned to refine NyetHack. Open the project and the `Tavern.kt` file.

`Tavern.kt` contains duplicate chains of logic called on several collections: `shuffled().first()`.

```
...
(0..9).forEach {
    val first = patronList.shuffled().first()
    val last = lastName.shuffled().first()
}

uniquePatrons.forEach {
    patronGold[it] = 6.0
}

var orderCount = 0
while (orderCount <= 9) {
    placeOrder(uniquePatrons.shuffled().first(),
            menuList.shuffled().first())
    orderCount++
...
```

This duplication indicates an opportunity to extract the duplicate logic to a reusable extension.

Define a new extension called **random** at the top of `Tavern.kt`:

Listing 18.11 Adding a private **random** extension (Tavern.kt)

```
...
val patronGold = mutableMapOf<String, Double>()

private fun <T> Iterable<T>.random(): T = this.shuffled().first()

fun main(args: Array<String>) {
    ...
}
...
```

The combination of **shuffled** and **first** is called on both lists (like `menuList`) and a set –
`uniquePatrons`. To make your extension available on both types, you define their supertype as the
receiver type: `Iterable`.

Now, replace the old calls to **shuffled().first()** with a call to the extension function **random**. (You can press Command-R [Ctrl-R] to open the search and replace bar to make this easier. However, be sure not to replace the call to **shuffled().first()** in your extension definition.)

Listing 18.12 Using the **random** extension (Tavern.kt)

```
...
private fun <T> Iterable<T>.random(): T = this.shuffled().first()

fun main(args: Array<String>) {
    ...
    (0..9).forEach {
        val first = patronList.shuffled().first()random()
        val last = lastName.shuffled().first()random()
    }

    uniquePatrons.forEach {
        patronGold[it] = 6.0
    }

    var orderCount = 0
    while (orderCount <= 9) {
        placeOrder(uniquePatrons.shuffled().first()random(),
                menuList.shuffled().first()random())
        orderCount++
    }

    displayPatronBalances()
}
...
```

Defining an Extensions File

Your **random** extension is marked with the private visibility modifier:

```
private fun <T> Iterable<T>.random(): T = this.shuffled().first()
```

Marking an extension as private prohibits use of the extension outside of the file it is defined in. Right now, the extension you defined is only used in Tavern.kt, so it makes sense to mark it private to restrict access. The rule of thumb is the same for extensions as it is for functions: If the extension will not be used elsewhere, mark it private.

Having said that, you also defined your random extension so that it would work with any Iterable. Are there other places in your code, outside of Tavern.kt, where you could put it to use? As it turns out, there is one.

Take a look in Player.kt – you will see the same randomization code used to select a **Player**'s hometown:

```
...
private fun selectHometown() = File("data/towns.txt")
                                    .readText()
                                    .split("\n")
                                    .shuffled()
                                    .first()
...
```

It would be nice to be able to use your **random** extension there, as well.

Since the **random** extension will be used across several files, making it private is no longer appropriate – and neither is leaving it in Tavern.kt. A good place for extensions to be used across multiple files is within their own file – and, in fact, their own package.

Control-click (right-click) the com.bignerdranch.nyethack package and choose New → Package. Name the package extensions and add a file to it called IterableExt.kt (Figure 18.3). The naming convention for files that contain only extensions is typically the type the extension applies to plus -Ext.

Figure 18.3 Adding an extensions package and file

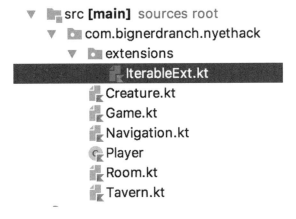

Move the **random** extension to IterableExt.kt, removing the old listing in Tavern.kt. Delete the private keyword from the extension when you move it to IterableExt.kt.

Listing 18.13 Removing the **random** extension from Tavern.kt (Tavern.kt)

```
...
private fun <T> Iterable<T>.random(): T = this.shuffled().first()

fun main(args: Array<String>) {
    ...
}
...
```

Listing 18.14 Adding the **random** extension to IterableExt.kt (IterableExt.kt)

```
package com.bignerdranch.nyethack.extensions

fun <T> Iterable<T>.random(): T = this.shuffled().first()
```

Now that you have moved the extension to its own file and made it public, you can use it in Tavern.kt and Player.kt. But you might notice that Tavern.kt is reporting errors. When an extension is defined in a separate package, you must import the extension in each file that uses it. Make sure that the import statement for the **random** extension is present at the top of both Tavern.kt and Player.kt:

```
import com.bignerdranch.nyethack.extensions.random
```

Now, within Player.kt, update the **selectHometown** function to use the **random** extension function in place of the old randomization code:

Listing 18.15 Using **random** in **selectHometown** (Player.kt)

```
...
private fun selectHometown() = File("data/towns.txt")
    .readText()
    .split("\n")
    .random()
    .shuffled()
    .first()
...
```

Renaming an Extension

Occasionally, you may want to use an extension or an imported class whose name is less than ideal in some way. Perhaps it is a difficult-to-remember acronym, or maybe you already have a class with the same name in your file. If you want the function of an imported function or class but not its name, you can use the **as** operator to assign a different name to be used within the file.

For example, in Tavern.kt you could change the name of the imported **random** function to **randomizer**:

Listing 18.16 The **as** operator (Tavern.kt)

```
import com.bignerdranch.nyethack.extensions.random as randomizer
...
private fun selectHometown() = File("data/towns.txt")
        .readText()
        .split("\n")
        .random()
        .randomizer()
...
```

And with that done, it is time to say farewell to NyetHack. Congratulations! You have accomplished quite a lot in your journey: You laid a foundation of conditionals and functions, defined your own classes so that you could represent objects in the world, built a game loop to take input from the player, and even built out a world to explore with monsters to defeat.

And all the while you leveraged Kotlin's language features to take advantage of the object-oriented programming paradigm.

Extensions in the Kotlin Standard Library

A large portion of the Kotlin standard library's functionality is defined via extension functions and extension properties.

For example, take a look at the source code file Strings.kt (note: Strings, not String), by pressing the Shift key twice to open the Search Everywhere dialog and entering "Strings.kt":

```
public inline fun CharSequence.trim(predicate: (Char) -> Boolean): CharSequence {
    var startIndex = 0
    var endIndex = length - 1
    var startFound = false
    while (startIndex <= endIndex) {
        val index = if (!startFound) startIndex else endIndex
        val match = predicate(this[index])
        if (!startFound) {
            if (!match)
                startFound = true
            else
                startIndex += 1
        }
        else {
            if (!match)
                break
            else
                endIndex -= 1
        }
    }
    return subSequence(startIndex, endIndex + 1)
}
```

Browse through this standard library file, and you will see that it consists of extensions to the String type. The excerpt above, for example, defines an extension function **trim** that is used to remove characters from a string.

Standard library files that contain extensions to a type are often named in this way, with an -s appended to the type name. If you look through the standard library files, you will notice other files matching this same naming convention: Sequences.kt, Ranges.kt, and Maps.kt are just some of the files that add functionality to the standard library through extensions to their corresponding type.

Heavy use of extension functions to define core API functionality is one of the ways that the Kotlin standard library keeps such a small footprint (~930k) but packs in so many features. Extensions use space efficiently because they can provide a feature for many types with one definition.

In this chapter, you have learned how extensions provide an alternative to sharing behavior with inheritance. In the next chapter you will delve into the fascinating world of functional programming.

For the More Curious: Function Literals with Receivers

It is possible to use function literals with the extension syntax to powerful effect. To understand what is meant by "function literals with receivers," take a look at the definition for **apply**, a function you met in Chapter 9:

```
public inline fun <T> T.apply(block: T.() -> Unit): T {
    block()
    return this
}
```

Remember what **apply** enables you to do: set up properties of a particular receiver instance within a lambda that you pass as an argument. For example:

```
val menuFile = File("menu-file.txt").apply {
    setReadable(true)
    setWritable(true)
    setExecutable(false)
}
```

This allows you to avoid explicitly calling each function on a menuFile variable. Instead, you can call them implicitly within a lambda. The bit of magic that **apply** provides is accomplished by defining a function literal with a receiver.

Looking again at the definition for **apply**, check out how the function parameter called block is specified:

```
public inline fun <T> T.apply(block: T.() -> Unit): T {
    block()
    return this
}
```

Not only is the block function parameter a lambda, it also is specified as an extension to generic type T: T.() -> Unit. This is what allows the lambda that you define to also have access to the receiver instance's properties and functions implicitly.

Specified as an extension, the lambda's receiver is also the instance that **apply** is called on – granting access to the receiver instance's functions and properties within the body lambda.

Using this style, it is possible to write what are known as "domain-specific languages" – an API style that exposes functions and features of a receiver context you configure using lambda expressions that you define to access them. For example, the Exposed framework from JetBrains (github.com/JetBrains/Exposed) makes extensive use of the DSL style for its API to allow you to define SQL queries.

You might add a function to NyetHack that uses this same style, allowing a room to be configured with a pit goblin. (Feel free to add this to your NyetHack project as an experiment.)

```
fun Room.configurePitGoblin(block: Room.(Goblin) -> Goblin): Room {
    val goblin = block(Goblin("Pit Goblin", description = "An Evil Pit Goblin"))
    monster = goblin
    return this
}
```

This extension to **Room** accepts a lambda that has **Room** as its receiver. The result is that the properties of **Room** are available within the lambda that you define, so the goblin can be configured using the **Room** receiver's properties:

```
currentRoom.configurePitGoblin { goblin ->
    goblin.healthPoints = dangerLevel * 3
    goblin
}
```

(Note that you would need to change the visibility of dangerLevel on **Room** to actually allow access to the dangerLevel property.)

Challenge: toDragonSpeak Extension

For this challenge, revisit Tavern.kt. Convert the **toDragonSpeak** function that you wrote to be a private extension function within Tavern.kt.

Challenge: Frame Extension

The following is a small program that allows a string of an arbitrary size to be displayed in a beautiful ASCII frame that is suitable for printing and hanging on any wall:

```
fun frame(name: String, padding: Int, formatChar: String = "*"): String {
    val greeting = "$name!"
    val middle = formatChar.padEnd(padding)
            .plus(greeting)
            .plus(formatChar.padStart(padding))
    val end = (0 until middle.length).joinToString("") { formatChar }
    return "$end\n$middle\n$end"
}
```

For this challenge, you will apply what you have learned about extensions. Try refactoring the **frame** function as an extension that is available for use with any String. An example of calling the new version would look like this:

```
print("Welcome, Madrigal".frame(5))

******************************
*     Welcome, Madrigal      *
******************************
```

19

Functional Programming Basics

For the last several chapters, you have been learning about and working with the object-oriented programming paradigm. Another prominent programming paradigm is *functional programming*, developed in the 1950s based on the mathematical abstraction lambda calculus. While functional programming languages have generally been more common in academia than in commercial software, the principles of the approach are useful in any language.

The functional programming style relies on data that is returned from a small number of higher-order functions (functions that accept or return another function) designed specifically to work on collections, and it favors composing chains of operations with those functions to create more complex behavior. You have worked with higher-order functions (which accept functions as parameters and return functions as their result) and function types (which enable you to define functions as values) already.

Kotlin supports multiple programming styles, so you can mix object-oriented and functional programming styles to suit the problem at hand. In this chapter, you will use the REPL to explore some of the functional programming features Kotlin offers and learn about the ideas behind the functional programming paradigm.

Function Categories

There are three broad categories of functions that compose a functional program: *transforms*, *filters*, and *combines*. Each category is designed to work on collection data structures to yield a final result. Functions in functional programming are also designed to be *composable*, meaning that simple functions can be combined to build complex behavior.

Transforms

The first category of function in functional programming is transforms. A *transform function* works on the contents of a collection by walking through the collection and transforming each item with a *transformer function* provided as an argument. The transform function then returns a copy of the modified collection, and execution proceeds to the next function in the chain.

Two commonly used transforms are `map` and `flatMap`.

The `map` transform function iterates through the collection it is called on and applies its transformer function to each element. The result is a collection with the same number of elements as the input collection. Enter the following into the Kotlin REPL to see an example:

Listing 19.1 Converting a list of animals to babies – with tails (REPL)

```
val animals = listOf("zebra", "giraffe", "elephant", "rat")
val babies = animals
    .map{ animal -> "A baby $animal" }
    .map{ baby -> "$baby, with the cutest little tail ever!"}
println(babies)
```

Functional programming emphasizes composable functions that can be combined with one another to act on data in series. Here, the first **map** applies its transformer function, { animal -> "A baby $animal" }, to transform each animal into a baby animal (or, at least, to stick "baby" in front of its name) and passes the resulting modified copy of the list forward to the next function in the chain.

The next function here is also a **map**, which runs through the same series of steps to add a cute tail to each baby animal. Reaching the end of the chain of functions, a final collection with the result of applying both **map** operations to each element is yielded:

```
A baby zebra, with the cutest little tail ever!
A baby giraffe, with the cutest little tail ever!
A baby elephant, with the cutest little tail ever!
A baby rat, with the cutest little tail ever!
```

We said earlier that transform functions return a modified copy of the collection they are called on. They do not directly modify the original collection. In the REPL, print the value of animals, the original list, to see that it has not changed:

Listing 19.2 Original collection not modified (REPL)

```
print(animals)
"zebra", "giraffe", "elephant", "rat"
```

The original animals collection was not modified in any way. **map** does its work by returning a new copy of the collection with the transformer you defined applied to each element.

In this way, variables that change over time are avoided. In fact, the functional programming style favors immutable copies of data that are passed to the next function in the chain. The idea behind this is that mutable variables lead to programs that are harder to debug and reason about. They also increase the amount of state programs rely on to do their work.

We said earlier that **map** returns a collection with the same number of elements as the input collection. (This is not the case for all transform functions, as you will see in the next section.) However, the elements do not need to be of the same type. Try entering the following in the REPL:

Listing 19.3 Before and after mapping: same number of items, different types (REPL)

```
val tenDollarWords = listOf("auspicious", "avuncular", "obviate")
val tenDollarWordLengths = tenDollarWords.map { it.length }
print(tenDollarWordLengths)
[10, 9, 7]
tenDollarWords.size
3
tenDollarWordLengths.size
3
```

`size` is a property available on collections that holds the number of elements in a list or set or the number of key-value pairs in a map.

In this example, three items were received on the lefthand side of **map**, and three items were returned on its righthand side. What changes is the type of data: The tenDollarWords collection is a List<String>, and the list generated by the **map** function is a List<Int>.

Take a look at the signature of the **map** function:

```
<T, R> Iterable<T>.map(transform: (T) -> R): List<R>
```

The functional programming style is enabled largely because of Kotlin's support for higher-order functions. **map**, as you can see in its signature, accepts a function type. It would not be possible to pass a transformer function to **map** without the ability to define a higher-order type. And **map** would not be nearly as useful if not for its generic type parameters.

Another commonly used transform function is **flatMap**. The **flatMap** function works with a collection of collections and returns a single, "flattened" collection containing all of the elements of the input collections.

Enter the following into the Kotlin REPL to see an example:

Listing 19.4 Flattening two lists (REPL)

```
listOf(listOf(1, 2, 3), listOf(4, 5, 6)).flatMap { it }
[1, 2, 3, 4, 5, 6]
```

The result is a new list with all the elements from the two original sublists. Note that the number of elements in the original collection (two – the two sublists) and the number of elements in the output collection (six) are not the same.

In the next section, you will combine **flatMap** with another category of function.

Filters

The second category of functions in functional programming is filters. A *filter function* accepts a predicate function that checks each element in a collection against a condition and returns either true or false. If the predicate returns true, the element is added to the new collection that the filter returns. If the predicate returns false, the element is excluded from the new collection.

One filter function is the aptly named **filter**. Let's start with an example of **filter** combined with **flatMap**. Enter the following into the REPL:

Listing 19.5 Filtering and flattening (REPL)

```
val itemsOfManyColors = listOf(listOf("red apple", "green apple", "blue apple"),
listOf("red fish", "blue fish"), listOf("yellow banana", "teal banana"))

val redItems = itemsOfManyColors.flatMap { it.filter { it.contains("red") } }
print(redItems)
[red apple, red fish]
```

Here, **flatMap** accepts the transform function **filter**, allowing you to do work on each of the sublists before they are flattened.

filter, in turn, accepts a predicate function with a condition to check: { it.contains("red") }. As **flatMap** iterates through all of the elements in its input lists, **filter** checks each against the condition in its predicate and includes only those elements for which the predicate is true in the new collections it returns.

Finally, **flatMap** combines the items from the resulting transformed sublists into one new list.

This series of functions is typical of functional programming. Enter the following into the Kotlin REPL to see another example:

Listing 19.6 Filtering non-prime numbers (REPL)

```
val numbers = listOf(7, 4, 8, 4, 3, 22, 18, 11)
val primes = numbers.filter { number ->
    (2 until number).map { number % it }
        .none { it == 0 }
}
print(primes)
```

You have implemented a solution to a fairly complex problem with only a handful of simple functions. This is the signature style of functional programming: bite-sized operations that do one thing and work together to produce a more complex result.

The **filter** function's predicate condition here is the result of another function: **map**. For each element in numbers, **map** divides the number by each value in the range from 2 until the number in question and returns the remainders. Next, **none** returns true if none of the returned remainders equal 0. If so, the predicate condition is true and the number checked is prime (because it is not evenly divisible by any number except 1 and itself).

Combines

The third category of functions used in functional programming is *combines*. Combining functions take different collections and merge them into a new one. (This is different than **flatMap**, which is called on one collection that contains other collections.) Enter the following into the Kotlin REPL:

Listing 19.7 Combining two collections, functional style (REPL)

```
val employees = listOf("Denny", "Claudette", "Peter")
val shirtSize = listOf("large", "x-large", "medium")
val employeeShirtSizes = employees.zip(shirtSize).toMap()
println(employeeShirtSizes["Denny"])
```

Here, you used the **zip** combining function to combine two lists: employees and their respective shirt sizes. **zip** then returns a new list, a collection of Pairs. You call **toMap** on the resulting list, as you can whenever you have a list of Pairs, to return a map that can be indexed into using a key – here, an employee name.

Another function that is useful for combining values is the **fold** function. **fold** accepts an initial accumulator value, which is updated with the result of an anonymous function that is called for each item. The accumulator value is then carried forward to the next anonymous function. Consider this example, where the **fold** function is used to accumulate a list of numbers, multiplied by 3:

```
val foldedValue = listOf(1, 2, 3, 4).fold(0) { accumulator, number ->
    println("Accumulated value: $accumulator")
    accumulator + (number * 3)
}

println("Final value: $foldedValue")
```

If you were to run this code, you would see the following result:

```
Accumulated value: 0
Accumulated value: 3
Accumulated value: 9
Accumulated value: 18
Final value: 30
```

The initial value for the accumulator, 0, is passed to the anonymous function, with the result that `Accumulated value: 0` is printed. That value, 0, is then carried forward into the calculation for the first element in the list, 1, with the result `Accumulated value: 3` (that is, 0 + (1 * 3)). In the next calculation, the accumulated value of 3 is added to (2 * 3), with the result `Accumulated value: 9` – and so forth. Once all the elements have been visited, the final accumulator value holds the result.

Why Functional Programming?

Look back at the example using **zip** in Listing 19.7. Imagine implementing the same task in the object-oriented paradigm or its broader class, called *imperative programming*. In Java, for example, this task might look something like this:

```
List<String> employees = Arrays.asList("Denny", "Claudette", "Peter");
List<String> shirtSizes = Arrays.asList("large", "x-large", "medium");
Map<String, String> employeeShirtSizes = new HashMap<>();
for (int i = 0; i < employees.size; i++) {
    employeeShirtSizes.put(employees.get(i), shirtSizes.get(i));
}
```

At first glance, the imperative version here may look like it accomplishes the task in roughly the same number of lines as the functional version in Listing 19.7. But a closer look shows that the functional approach offers a number of key benefits:

1. "Accumulator" variables (employeeShirtSizes, for example) are defined implicitly, reducing the number of stateful variables to keep track of.

2. The results from functional operations are added to accumulator variables automatically, reducing the risk of bugs.

3. New operations are trivially easy to add to the functional chain, since all functional operators work with the iterable you are performing work on.

Considering the first two of these benefits, new operations in the imperative style usually also involve the creation of more variables to hold more state. For example, an employeeShirtSizes collection is needed outside of the for loop to hold the loop's results.

This pattern requires manually adding the results to employeeShirtSizes with each loop. If you neglect to add the values to the employeeShirtSizes collection (a step that can be easy to overlook), the rest of the program will not work correctly. Each additional step increases the chances that this type of mistake will occur.

On the other hand, a functional implementation implicitly accumulates a new collection after each operation in the chain without requiring new accumulator variable definitions:

```
val formattedSwagOrders = employees.zip(shirtSize).toMap()
```

There are fewer mistakes to make in the functional style because the accumulation of the values in a new collection is performed implicitly, as part of the functional chain's work.

As for the third benefit listed above, since all of the functional operations are designed to work with iterables, it is trivial to add another step to the functional chain. For example, suppose the employeeShirtSizes map needed to be formatted to represent swag orders after building the hash map. In the imperative style, that would require an addition like this:

```
List<String> formattedSwagOrders = new ArrayList<>();
for (Map.Entry<String, String> shirtSize : employeeShirtSizes.entrySet()) {
    formattedSwagOrders.add(String.format("%s, shirt size: %s",
            it.getKey(), it.getValue());
}
```

A new accumulator value and a new for loop that works to populate the accumulator with results: more entities, more state, more to keep track of.

With the functional style, subsequent operations are easily added to the chain without the need for additional state. The same program could be implemented functionally with the simple addition of:

```
.map { "${it.key}, shirt size: ${it.value}" }
```

Sequences

In Chapter 10 and Chapter 11, you were introduced to the collection types List, Set, and Map. These collection types are all known as *eager collections*. When an instance of any of these types is created, all the values it contains are added to the collection and can be accessed.

There is another flavor of collection: *lazy collections*. You learned about lazy initialization, in which a variable is not initialized until it is first accessed, in Chapter 13. Lazy collection types, similar to lazy initialization of other types, provide better performance – specifically when working with very large collections – because their values are produced only as needed.

Kotlin offers a built-in lazy collection type called Sequence. Sequences do not index their contents, and they do not keep track of their size. In fact, when working with a sequence, the possibility of an infinite sequence of values exists, because there is no limit to the number of items that can be produced.

With a sequence, you define a function that is referred to each time a new value is requested, called an *iterator function*. One way to define a sequence and its iterator is by using a sequence builder function provided by Kotlin, **generateSequence**. **generateSequence** accepts an initial seed value, the starting place for the sequence. When the sequence is acted on by a function, **generateSequence** calls an iterator you specify that determines the next value to produce. For example:

```
generateSequence(0) { it + 1 }
        .onEach { println("The Count says: $it, ah ah ah!") }
```

If you were to run this snippet, the **onEach** function would execute forever.

So, what is a lazy collection good for, and why choose it over a list? Let's go back to the example of finding primes in Listing 19.6. Suppose you wanted to adapt this to generate the first N number of primes – say, 1,000. A first shot at an implementation might look like this:

```
// Extension to Int that determines whether a number is prime
fun Int.isPrime(): Boolean {
    (2 until this).map {
        if (this % it == 0) {
            return false // Not a prime!
        }
    }
    return true
}

val toList = (1..5000).toList().filter { it.isPrime() }.take(1000)
```

The problem with this implementation is that you do not know how many numbers you have to check to get 1,000 primes. This implementation takes a guess – 5,000 – but in fact this is not enough. (It will only get you 669 primes, if you want to know.)

This is a perfect case for using a lazy collection, instead of an eager one, to back the chain of functions. A lazy collection is ideal, because you do not need to define an upper bound for the number of items to check for the sequence:

```
val oneThousandPrimes = generateSequence(3) { value ->
    value + 1
}.filter { it.isPrime() }.take(1000)
```

In this solution, **generateSequence** produces a new value, one at a time, starting from 3 (the seed value) and incrementing by one each time. Then it filters the values with the extension **isPrime**. It continues doing this until 1,000 items have been produced. Because there is no way to know how many candidate numbers will have to be checked, lazily producing new values until the **take** function is satisfied is ideal.

In most cases, the collections you work with will be small, containing fewer than 1,000 elements. In these cases, worrying about using a sequence or a list for a constrained number of items will be of little concern, because the performance difference between the two collection types will be negligible – on the order of a few nanoseconds. But with more sizable collections, with hundreds of thousands of elements, the performance improvement to be realized by switching the collection type can be significant. In these cases, you can convert a list to a sequence quite simply:

```
val listOfNumbers = (0 until 10000000).toList()
val sequenceOfNumbers = listOfNumbers.asSequence()
```

The functional programming paradigm can require frequent creation of new collections, and sequences provide a scalable mechanism for working with large collections.

In this chapter, you saw how to use basic functional programming tools like **map**, **flatMap**, and **filter** to streamline how you work with data. You also saw how to use sequences to work efficiently as your data set grows larger.

In the next chapter, you will learn how your Kotlin code *interoperates* with Java code as you write Kotlin code that calls Java code and vice versa.

For the More Curious: Profiling

When the speed of code is an important consideration, Kotlin provides utility functions for profiling code performance: `measureNanoTime` and `measureTimeInMillis`. Both functions accept a lambda as their argument and measure the execution speed of the code contained within the lambda. `measureNanoTime` returns a time in nanoseconds, and `measureTimeInMillis` returns a time in milliseconds.

Wrap the function to measure in one of the utility functions like so:

```
val listInNanos = measureNanoTime {
    // List functional chain here
}

val sequenceInNanos = measureNanoTime {
    // Sequence functional chain here
}

println("List completed in $listInNanos ns")
println("Sequence completed in $sequenceInNanos ns")
```

As an experiment, try profiling the performance of the list and sequence versions of the prime number examples. (Change the list example to check numbers through 7,919 so that it can find 1,000 primes.) How much does the change from a list to a sequence affect the performance time?

For the More Curious: Arrow.kt

In this chapter you saw some of the functional programming-style tools that are included in Kotlin's standard library, like `map`, `flatMap`, and `filter`.

Kotlin is a "multiparadigm" language, meaning it mixes the styles of object-oriented, imperative, and functional programming. If you have worked with a strictly functional programming language like Haskell, you know that Haskell offers useful functional programming ideas that go further than the basics included in Kotlin.

For example, Haskell includes the `Maybe` type – a type that includes support for either something or an error – and allows operations that might result in an error to be represented using a type instead. Using a `Maybe` type allows you to represent an exception, like incorrectly parsing a number, without throwing an exception – which allows you to not need try/catch logic in your code.

Representing an exception without dealing with try/catch logic is a good thing. Some view try/catch as a form of GOTO statement: More often than not, it leads to code that is difficult to read and maintain.

Many of the functional programming features found in Haskell can be brought to Kotlin through libraries like Arrow.kt (`http://arrow-kt.io/`).

For example, the Arrow.kt library includes a flavor of the `Maybe` type found in Haskell called `Either`. Using `Either`, it is possible to represent an operation that could result in failure without resorting to throwing exceptions and try/catch logic.

Consider, for example, a function that parses some user input from a string to an `Int`. If the value is a number, it should be parsed as an `Int`, but if it is invalid, it should instead be represented as an error.

Using `Either`, the logic would read as follows:

```
fun parse(s: String): Either<NumberFormatException, Int> =
    if (s.matches(Regex("-?[0-9]+"))) {
        Either.Right(s.toInt())
    } else {
        Either.Left(NumberFormatException("$s is not a valid integer."))
    }

val x = parse("123")

val value = when(x) {
    is Either.Left -> when (x.a) {
        is NumberFormatException -> "Not a number!"
        else -> "Unknown error"
    }
    is Either.Right -> "Number that was parsed: ${x.b}"
}
```

No exceptions, no `try`/`catch` blocks – just easy-to-follow logic.

Challenge: Reversing the Values in a Map

Using the functional techniques you learned in this chapter, write a function called **flipValues** that allows you to flip-flop the keys and values in a map. For example:

```
val gradesByStudent = mapOf("Josh" to 4.0, "Alex" to 2.0, "Jane" to 3.0)
{Josh=4.0, Alex=2.0, Jane=3.0}

flipValues(gradesByStudent)
{4.0=Josh, 2.0=Alex, 3.0=Jane}
```

Challenge: Applying Functional Programming to Tavern.kt

`Tavern.kt` could be improved by using some of the functional programming features you learned about in this chapter.

Consider the **forEach** loop that you use to generate the unique patron names:

```
val uniquePatrons = mutableSetOf<String>()

fun main(args: Array<String>) {
    ...
    (0..9).forEach {
        val first = patronList.random()
        val last = lastName.random()
        val name = "$first $last"
        uniquePatrons += name
    }
    ...
}
```

The loop mutates the state of the `uniquePatrons` set every iteration. This works – but it is possible to do better using a functional programming approach. You might express the `uniquePatrons` set like this instead:

```
val uniquePatrons: Set<String> = generateSequence {
    val first = patronList.random()
    val last = lastName.random()
    "$first $last"
}.take(10).toSet()
```

This is an improvement over the old version, because the mutable set is no longer required and you can make the collection read-only.

Notice that the number of uniquePatrons currently varies, depending on chance. For your first challenge, use the **generateSequence** function to generate exactly nine unique patron names. (Look back at the example in this chapter that generated exactly 1,000 prime numbers for a hint.)

For a second challenge, using what you learned in this section, upgrade the code in Tavern.kt that populates the patron gold map with initial values:

```
fun main(args: Array<String>) {
    ...
    uniquePatrons.forEach {
        patronGold[it] = 6.0
    }
    ...
}
```

The new version should perform the setup for the patronGold set where the variable is defined, rather than within the **main** function.

Challenge: Sliding Window

For this advanced challenge, begin with this list of values:

```
val valuesToAdd = listOf(1, 18, 73, 3, 44, 6, 1, 33, 2, 22, 5, 7)
```

Using a functional programming approach, perform the following operations on the valuesToAdd list:

1. Exclude any number less than 5.
2. Group the numbers in pairs.
3. Multiply the two numbers in each pair.
4. Sum the resulting products to produce a final number.

The correct result is 2,339. Walking through each step, here is what the data should look like along the way:

```
Step 1: 1, 18, 73, 3, 44, 6, 1, 33, 2, 22, 5, 7
Step 2: 18, 73, 44, 6, 33, 22, 5, 7
Step 3: [18*73], [44*6], [33*22], [5*7]
Step 4: 1314 + 264 + 726 + 35 = 2339
```

Notice that step 3 groups the list into sublists of two elements each – this is commonly known as a "sliding window" algorithm (and is where the challenge gets its name). Solving this tricky challenge will require consulting the Kotlin reference documentation – particularly the collections functions at kotlinlang.org/api/latest/jvm/stdlib/kotlin.collections/index.html. Good luck!

20

Java Interoperability

Throughout this book, you have learned the fundamentals of the Kotlin programming language, and we hope you are inspired to use Kotlin to improve existing Java projects you may have. Where do you start?

You have seen before that Kotlin compiles down to Java bytecode. This means that Kotlin is *interoperable* with Java – that is, it functions alongside and works with Java code.

This is likely the most important feature of the Kotlin programming language. Full interoperability with Java means that Kotlin files and Java files can exist in the same project, side by side. You can invoke Java methods from Kotlin and Kotlin functions from Java. This means you can use existing Java libraries from Kotlin, including the Android framework.

Full interoperability with Java also means that you can slowly transition your codebase from Java to Kotlin. Maybe you do not have the opportunity to rebuild your project entirely in Kotlin – consider moving new feature development to Kotlin. Perhaps you would like to convert the Java files in your application that will see the most benefit from a move to Kotlin – consider converting your model objects or your unit tests.

This chapter will show you how Java and Kotlin files interoperate and discuss the things you should consider when writing code that will interoperate.

Interoperating with a Java Class

For this chapter, create a new project in IntelliJ called Interop. Interop will contain two files: Hero.kt, a Kotlin file that represents the hero from NyetHack, and Jhava.java, a Java class that represents a monster from another realm. Create these two files as well.

In this chapter, you will write both Kotlin code and Java code. If you do not have experience writing Java code, fear not, as the Java code in these examples should be intuitive given your Kotlin experience.

Start by declaring the **Jhava** class and giving it a method called **utterGreeting** that returns a String:

Listing 20.1 Declaring a class and method in Java (Jhava.java)

```java
public class Jhava {
    public String utterGreeting() {
        return "BLARGH";
    }
}
```

Now, in Hero.kt, create a **main** function. In it, declare an adversary val, an instance of **Jhava**:

Listing 20.2 Declaring a **main** function and **Jhava** adversary in Kotlin (Hero.kt)

```
fun main(args: Array<String>) {
    val adversary = Jhava()
}
```

That is it! With that, you have written a line of Kotlin code that instantiates a Java object and bridged the gap between the two languages. Java interoperability in Kotlin really is that easy.

But we do have more to show you, so let's press on. As a test, print out the greeting that the **Jhava** adversary utters.

Listing 20.3 Invoking a Java method in Kotlin (Hero.kt)

```
fun main(args: Array<String>) {
    val adversary = Jhava()
    println(adversary.utterGreeting())
}
```

You have now instantiated a Java object and invoked a Java method on it, all from Kotlin. Run Hero.kt. You should see the monster's greeting (BLARGH) printed out to the console.

Kotlin was created to interoperate seamlessly with Java. It was also created with a number of improvements over Java. Do you have to give up the improvements when you want to interoperate? Not at all. With some awareness of the differences in the two languages and the help of annotations available on each side, you can enjoy the best of what Kotlin has to offer.

Interoperability and Nullity

Add another method to **Jhava** called **determineFriendshipLevel**. **determineFriendshipLevel** should return a value of type String and, because the monster does not understand friendship, a value of null.

Listing 20.4 Returning null from a Java method (Jhava.java)

```
public class Jhava {
    public String utterGreeting() {
        return "BLARGH";
    }

    public String determineFriendshipLevel() {
        return null;
    }
}
```

Call this new method from Hero.kt, storing the monster's friendship level in a val. You are going to print this value out to the console, but, remembering that the monster yelled its greeting at you in all caps, go ahead and lowercase the friendship level before printing it out.

Listing 20.5 Printing the friendship level (`Hero.kt`)

```
fun main(args: Array<String>) {
    val adversary = Jhava()
    println(adversary.utterGreeting())

    val friendshipLevel = adversary.determineFriendshipLevel()
    println(friendshipLevel.toLowerCase())
}
```

Run `Hero.kt`. Although the compiler did not alert you to any problems, the program crashes at runtime:

```
Exception in thread "main"
java.lang.IllegalStateException: friendshipLevel must not be null
```

In Chapter 6, we told you that in Java all objects can be null. When you call a Java method like **determineFriendshipLevel**, the API seems to advertise that the method will return a `String`, but that does not mean that you can assume that the return value will play by Kotlin's rules about nullity.

Because all objects in Java can be null, it is safer to assume that values are nullable unless otherwise specified. However, while this assumption is safer, it can lead to considerably more verbose code, as you will have to handle the nullability of each and every Java variable you reference.

In `Hero.kt`, hold down the Command (Ctrl) key and mouse over **determineFriendshipLevel**. IntelliJ reports that the method returns a value of type `String!`. The exclamation mark means that the return value could either be `String` or `String?`. The Kotlin compiler does not know whether the value of the string being returned from Java is null.

These ambiguous return value types are called *platform types*. Platform types are not syntactically meaningful; they are only displayed in the IDE and in other documentation.

Fortunately, authors of Java code can write Kotlin-friendly code that advertises nullity more explicitly using nullability annotations. Explicitly declare that **determineFriendshipLevel** can return a value of null by adding a @Nullable annotation to its method header.

Listing 20.6 Specifying that a return value will possibly be null (`Jhava.java`)

```
public class Jhava {
    public String utterGreeting() {
        return "BLARGH";
    }

    @Nullable
    public String determineFriendshipLevel() {
        return null;
    }
}
```

(You will need to import `org.jetbrains.annotations.Nullable`, which IntelliJ will offer to do for you.)

@Nullable warns the consumer of this API that the method can return null (not that it *must* return null). The Kotlin compiler recognizes this annotation. Return to `Hero.kt` and note that IntelliJ is now warning you about invoking **toLowerCase** directly on a `String?`.

297

Replace this direct invocation with a safe call.

Listing 20.7 Handling nullability with the safe call operator (Hero.kt)

```
fun main(args: Array<String>) {
    val adversary = Jhava()
    println(adversary.utterGreeting())

    val friendshipLevel = adversary.determineFriendshipLevel()
    println(friendshipLevel?.toLowerCase())
}
```

Run Hero.kt. Now, null should be printed to the console.

Because friendshipLevel is null, you may want to provide a default friendship level. Use the null coalescing operator to provide a default to be used when friendshipLevel is null.

Listing 20.8 Providing a default value with the Elvis operator (Hero.kt)

```
fun main(args: Array<String>) {
    val adversary = Jhava()
    println(adversary.utterGreeting())

    val friendshipLevel = adversary.determineFriendshipLevel()
    println(friendshipLevel?.toLowerCase() ?: "It's complicated.")
}
```

Run Hero.kt, and you should see It's complicated.

You used @Nullable to signify that a method could return null. You can specify that a value will definitely not be null using the @NotNull annotation. This annotation is nice, because it means that the consumer of this API does not need to worry that the value returned could be null. The **Jhava** monster's greeting should not be null, so add a @NotNull annotation to the **utterGreeting** method header.

Listing 20.9 Specifying that a return value will not be null (Jhava.java)

```
public class Jhava {

    @NotNull
    public String utterGreeting() {
        return "BLARGH";
    }

    @Nullable
    public String determineFriendshipLevel() {
        return null;
    }
}
```

(Again, you will need to import the annotation.)

Nullability annotations can be used to add context to return values, parameters, and even fields.

Kotlin provides a variety of tools for dealing with nullability, including prohibiting normal types from being null. If you write Kotlin code, then the most common source of issues with null is interoperation, so take care when calling Java code from Kotlin.

Type Mapping

Kotlin's types often correspond one to one with Java types. A `String` in Kotlin is a `String` when compiled down to Java. This means that a `String` returned from Java methods can be used in the same way in Kotlin as a `String` explicitly declared in Kotlin.

There are, however, some type mappings that are not one to one between Kotlin and Java. For an example, consider basic data types. As we discussed in the section called *For the More Curious: Java Primitive Types in Kotlin* in Chapter 2, Java represents basic data types using what it calls primitive types. Primitive types are not objects in Java, but all types are objects in Kotlin – including basic data types. However, the Kotlin compiler maps Java primitives onto the most similar Kotlin type.

To see type mapping in action, add an integer called `hitPoints` to **Jhava**. An integer is represented by the object type `Int` in Kotlin and by the primitive type `int` in Java.

Listing 20.10 Declaring an `int` in Java (`Jhava.java`)

```java
public class Jhava {

    public int hitPoints = 52489112;

    @NotNull
    public String utterGreeting() {
        return "BLARGH";
    }

    @Nullable
    public String determineFriendshipLevel() {
        return null;
    }
}
```

Now, obtain a reference to `hitPoints` in `Hero.kt`.

Listing 20.11 Referencing a Java field from Kotlin (`Hero.kt`)

```kotlin
fun main(args: Array<String>) {
    val adversary = Jhava()
    println(adversary.utterGreeting())

    val friendshipLevel = adversary.determineFriendshipLevel()\
    println(friendshipLevel?.toLowerCase() ?: "It's complicated.")

    val adversaryHitPoints: Int = adversary.hitPoints
}
```

Although `hitPoints` is defined in the **Jhava** class as an `int`, you refer to it here as an `Int` with no problem. (You are not using type inference here only to illustrate the type mapping. Explicit type declarations are not required for interoperability: `val adversaryHitPoints = adversary.hitPoints` would work just as well.)

Now that you have a reference to this integer, you can invoke functions on it. Call a function on adversaryHitPoints and print out the result.

Listing 20.12 Referencing a Java field from Kotlin (Hero.kt)

```
fun main(args: Array<String>) {
    ...
    val adversaryHitPoints: Int = adversary.hitPoints
    println(adversaryHitPoints.dec())
}
```

Run Hero.kt to print out the adversary's hit points, decremented by 1.

In Java, methods cannot be invoked on primitive types. In Kotlin, the integer adversaryHitPoints is an object of type Int, and functions can be called on that Int.

As another illustration of type mapping, print the name of the Java class backing adversaryHitPoints.

Listing 20.13 Java backing class name (Hero.kt)

```
fun main(args: Array<String>) {
    ...
    val adversaryHitPoints: Int = adversary.hitPoints
    println(adversaryHitPoints.dec())
    println(adversaryHitPoints.javaClass)
}
```

When you run Hero.kt, you will see int printed to the console. Although you can invoke Int functions on adversaryHitPoints, the variable is a primitive int at runtime. As you may recall from the bytecode you looked at in Chapter 2, all mapped types are mapped back to their Java counterparts at runtime. Kotlin gives you the power of objects when you want them, but the performance of primitive types when you need them.

Getters, Setters, and Interoperability

Kotlin and Java handle class-level variables quite differently. Java uses fields and typically gates access via accessor and mutator methods. Kotlin, as you have seen, features properties, which restrict access to backing fields and may automatically expose accessors and mutators.

In the last section, you added a public hitPoints field to **Jhava**. This worked to illustrate type mapping, but it violates the principle of encapsulation – so is not a good solution. In Java, fields should be accessed or mutated using methods called getters and setters. Getters can be used to access data, and setters can be used to mutate data.

Make `hitPoints` private and create a getter method so that `hitPoints` can be accessed but not mutated.

Listing 20.14 Declaring a field in Java (`Jhava.java`)

```java
public class Jhava {

    ~~public~~private int hitPoints = 52489112;

    @NotNull
    public String utterGreeting() {
        return "BLARGH";
    }

    @Nullable
    public String determineFriendshipLevel() {
        return null;
    }

    public int getHitPoints() {
        return hitPoints;
    }
}
```

Now, return to `Hero.kt`. Note that your code still compiles. Recall from Chapter 12 that Kotlin can bypass the need for using getter/setter syntax, meaning that you can use syntax that looks like you are accessing fields or properties directly while still maintaining encapsulation. Because **getHitPoints** is prefixed with `get`, you can drop the prefix in Kotlin and refer to it simply as `hitPoints`. This Kotlin feature transcends the barrier between Kotlin and Java.

The same goes for setters. By now your hero and the **Jhava** monster are well acquainted and wish to communicate further. The hero would like to expand the monster's vocabulary beyond a single utterance. Pull the monster's greeting out into a field and add a getter and a setter so that the hero can modify the greeting in an attempt to teach the monster language.

Listing 20.15 Exposing a greeting in Java (`Jhava.java`)

```java
public class Jhava {

    private int hitPoints = 52489112;
    private String greeting = "BLARGH";
    ...
    @NotNull
    public String utterGreeting() {
        return ~~"BLARGH"~~greeting;
    }
    ...
    public String getGreeting() {
        return greeting;
    }

    public void setGreeting(String greeting) {
        this.greeting = greeting;
    }
}
```

In Hero.kt, modify adversary.greeting.

Listing 20.16 Setting a Java field from Kotlin (Hero.kt)

```
fun main(args: Array<String>) {
    ...
    val adversaryHitPoints: Int = adversary.hitPoints
    println(adversaryHitPoints.dec())
    println(adversaryHitPoints.javaClass)

    adversary.greeting = "Hello, Hero."
    println(adversary.utterGreeting())
}
```

You can use assignment syntax to mutate a Java field, rather than calling its associated setter. You have the syntax benefits provided in Kotlin, even while working with Java APIs. Run Hero.kt to see that the hero has taught the **Jhava** monster some language.

Beyond Classes

Kotlin affords developers greater flexibility with respect to the format of the code that they write. A Kotlin file can include classes, functions, and variables – all at the top level of the file. In Java, a file represents exactly one class. How, then, are top-level functions declared in Kotlin represented in Java?

Expand the interspecies communication with a proclamation from the hero. Declare a function called **makeProclamation** in Hero.kt, outside of the **main** function that you worked in before.

Listing 20.17 Declaring a top-level function in Kotlin (Hero.kt)

```
fun main(args: Array<String>) {
    ...
}

fun makeProclamation() = "Greetings, beast!"
```

You will need a way to invoke this function from Java, so add a **main** method to **Jhava**.

Listing 20.18 Defining a main method in Java (Jhava.java)

```
public class Jhava {

    private int hitPoints = 52489112;
    private String greeting = "BLARGH";

    public static void main(String[] args) {

    }
    ...
}
```

In that **main** method, print out the value returned by **makeProclamation**, referencing the function as a static method in the class **HeroKt**:

Listing 20.19 Referencing a top-level Kotlin function from Java (Jhava.java)

```
public class Jhava {
    ...
    public static void main(String[] args) {
        System.out.println(HeroKt.makeProclamation());
    }
    ...
}
```

Top-level functions defined in Kotlin are represented as static methods in Java and are called as such. **makeProclamation** is defined in Hero.kt, so the Kotlin compiler creates a class called **HeroKt** for the static method to be associated with.

If you would like Hero.kt and Jhava.java to interoperate a bit more fluidly, you can change the name of the generated class with the @JvmName annotation. Do this at the top of Hero.kt:

Listing 20.20 Specifying compiled class name using JvmName (Hero.kt)

```
@file:JvmName("Hero")

fun main(args: Array<String>) {
    ...
}

fun makeProclamation() = "Greetings, beast!"
```

Now, in **Jhava**, you can reference the **makeProclamation** function more cleanly.

Listing 20.21 Referencing a renamed top-level Kotlin function from Java (Jhava.java)

```
public class Jhava {
    ...
    public static void main(String[] args) {
        System.out.println(HeroKt.makeProclamation());
    }
    ...
}
```

Run Jhava.java to read your hero's proclamation. JVM annotations like @JvmName give you direct control over what Java code is generated when you write Kotlin code.

Another important JVM annotation is @JvmOverloads. Kotlin's default parameters empower you to replace verbose, repetitive method overloading with a streamlined approach to providing options in your API. What does this mean in practice? The following example should clarify things.

Add a new function called **handOverFood** to Hero.kt.

Listing 20.22 Adding a function with default parameters (Hero.kt)

```
...
fun makeProclamation() = "Greetings, beast!"

fun handOverFood(leftHand: String = "berries", rightHand: String = "beef") {
    println("Mmmm... you hand over some delicious $leftHand and $rightHand.")
}
```

The hero offers some food in the **handOverFood** function, and the function's caller has options for invoking it due to its default parameters. The caller can specify what is in the hero's left hand and/or right hand – or accept the default options of berries and beef. Kotlin gives the caller options without adding much complexity to the code.

Java, on the other hand, which lacks default parameters, would accomplish this with method overloading:

```
    public static void handOverFood(String leftHand, String rightHand) {
        System.out.println("Mmmm... you hand over some delicious " +
                leftHand + " and " + rightHand + ".");
    }

    public static void handOverFood(String leftHand) {
        handOverFood(leftHand, "beef");
    }

    public static void handOverFood() {
        handOverFood("berries", "beef");
    }
```

Method overloading in Java requires much more code than default parameters in Kotlin. Also, one option for calling the Kotlin function cannot be replicated in Java – the option of using the default value for the first parameter, leftHand, while passing a value for the second parameter, rightHand. Kotlin's named function arguments make this option possible: handOverFood(rightHand = "cookies") will result in Mmmm... you hand over some delicious berries and cookies. But Java does not support named method parameters, so it has no way to distinguish between methods called with the same number of parameters (unless the parameters are of different types).

As you will see in a moment, the @JvmOverloads annotation triggers the generation of the three corresponding Java methods so that Java consumers are, for the most part, not left out.

The **Jhava** monster abhors fruit. It would like to be offered pizza or beef instead of berries. Add a method called **offerFood** to Jhava.java that exposes a way for a **Hero** to offer food to a **Jhava** monster.

Listing 20.23 Only one method signature (Jhava.java)

```
public class Jhava {
    ...
    public void setGreeting(String greeting) {
        this.greeting = greeting;
    }

    public void offerFood() {
        Hero.handOverFood("pizza");
    }
}
```

This call to **handOverFood** causes a compiler error, because Java has no concept of default method parameters. As such, a version of **handOverFood** with only one parameter does not exist in Java. To verify, take a look at the decompiled Java bytecode for **handOverFood**:

```
public static final void handOverFood(@NotNull String leftHand,
                                      @NotNull String rightHand) {
    Intrinsics.checkParameterIsNotNull(leftHand, "leftHand");
    Intrinsics.checkParameterIsNotNull(rightHand, "rightHand");
    String var2 = "Mmmm... you hand over some delicious " +
            leftHand + " and " + rightHand + '.';
    System.out.println(var2);
}
```

While you have the option to avoid method overloading in Kotlin, your Java counterparts are not afforded the same luxury. The @JvmOverloads annotation will help your API consumers in Java by providing overloaded versions of your Kotlin function. Add the annotation to **handOverFood** in Hero.kt.

Listing 20.24 Adding @JvmOverloads (Hero.kt)

```
...
fun makeProclamation() = "Greetings, beast!"

@JvmOverloads
fun handOverFood(leftHand: String = "berries", rightHand: String = "beef") {
    println("Mmmm... you hand over some delicious $leftHand and $rightHand.")
}
```

Your invocation of **handOverFood** in **Jhava.offerFood** no longer causes an error, because it is now calling a version of **handOverFood** that exists in Java. You can again confirm this by looking at the new decompiled Java bytecode:

```
@JvmOverloads
public static final void handOverFood(@NotNull String leftHand,
                                      @NotNull String rightHand) {
    Intrinsics.checkParameterIsNotNull(leftHand, "leftHand");
    Intrinsics.checkParameterIsNotNull(rightHand, "rightHand");
    String var2 = "Mmmm... you hand over some delicious " +
            leftHand + " and " + rightHand + '.';
    System.out.println(var2);
}

@JvmOverloads
public static final void handOverFood(@NotNull String leftHand) {
    handOverFood$default(leftHand, (String)null, 2, (Object)null);
}

@JvmOverloads
public static final void handOverFood() {
    handOverFood$default((String)null, (String)null, 3, (Object)null);
}
```

Note that the single-parameter method specifies the first parameter from the Kotlin function: leftHand. When this method is called, the default value for the second parameter will be used.

To test offering food to the monster, call **offerFood** in Hero.kt:

Listing 20.25 Testing out **offerFood** (Hero.kt)

```
@file:JvmName("Hero")

fun main(args: Array<String>) {
    ...
    adversary.greeting = "Hello, Hero."
    println(adversary.utterGreeting())

    adversary.offerFood()
}

fun makeProclamation() = "Greetings, beast!"
...
```

Run Hero.kt to confirm that the hero hands over pizza and beef.

If you are designing an API that may be exposed to Java consumers, consider using @JvmOverloads for an API that is nearly as robust for Java developers as it is for Kotlin developers.

There are two more JVM annotations that you should consider when writing Kotlin code that will interoperate with Java code, and they both have to do with classes. Hero.kt does not yet have a class implementation, so add a new class called **Spellbook**. Give **Spellbook** one property, spells – a list of string spell names.

Listing 20.26 Declaring the **Spellbook** class (Hero.kt)

```
...
@JvmOverloads
fun handOverFood(leftHand: String = "berries", rightHand: String = "beef") {
    println("Mmmm... you hand over some delicious $leftHand and $rightHand.")
}

class Spellbook {
    val spells = listOf("Magic Ms. L", "Lay on Hans")
}
```

Recall that Kotlin and Java handle class-level variables quite differently: Java uses fields with getter and setter methods, while Kotlin has properties with backing fields. As a result, while in Java you can access a field directly, in Kotlin you will be routed through an accessor – even though the access syntax may be identical.

So, referencing spells, a property of **Spellbook**, in Kotlin would look like this:

```
val spellbook = Spellbook()
val spells = spellbook.spells
```

And in Java, accessing spells would look like this:

```
Spellbook spellbook = new Spellbook();
List<String> spells = spellbook.getSpells();
```

In Java, calling **getSpells** would be necessary because you cannot directly access the spells field. However, you can apply the @JvmField annotation to a Kotlin property to expose its backing field to Java consumers and avoid the need for a getter method. Apply JvmField to spells to expose it directly to **Jhava**:

Listing 20.27 Applying the @JvmField annotation (Hero.kt)

```
...
@JvmOverloads
fun handOverFood(leftHand: String = "berries", rightHand: String = "beef") {
    println("Mmmm... you hand over some delicious $leftHand and $rightHand.")
}

class Spellbook {
    @JvmField
    val spells = listOf("Magic Ms. L", "Lay on Hans")
}
```

Now, in Jhava.java's **main** method, you can access spells directly to print out each spell:

Listing 20.28 Accessing a Kotlin field directly in Java (Jhava.java)

```
...
public static void main(String[] args) {
    System.out.println(Hero.makeProclamation());

    System.out.println("Spells:");
    Spellbook spellbook = new Spellbook();
    for (String spell : spellbook.spells) {
        System.out.println(spell);
    }
}

@NotNull
public String utterGreeting() {
    return greeting;
}
...
```

Run Jhava.java to confirm that the spells in the spellbook are printed out to the console.

You can also use @JvmField to statically represent values in a companion object. Recall from Chapter 15 that companion objects are declared within another class declaration and initialized either when their enclosing class is initialized or when any of their properties or functions are accessed. Add a companion object containing one value, MAX_SPELL_COUNT, to **Spellbook**.

Listing 20.29 Adding a companion object to **Spellbook** (Hero.kt)

```
...
class Spellbook {
    @JvmField
    val spells = listOf("Magic Ms. L", "Lay on Hans")

    companion object {
        val MAX_SPELL_COUNT = 10
    }
}
```

Now attempt to access MAX_SPELL_COUNT from **Jhava**'s **main** method using Java's static access syntax.

Listing 20.30 Accessing a static value in Java (Jhava.java)

```
public static void main(String[] args) {
    System.out.println(Hero.makeProclamation());

    System.out.println("Spells:");
    Spellbook spellbook = new Spellbook();
    for (String spell : spellbook.spells) {
        System.out.println(spell);
    }

    System.out.println("Max spell count: " + Spellbook.MAX_SPELL_COUNT);
}
...
```

The code does not compile. Why not? When referencing members of a companion object from Java, you must access them first by referencing the companion object and using its accessor:

```
System.out.println("Max spell count: " +
        Spellbook.Companion.getMAX_SPELL_COUNT());
```

@JvmField takes care of all this for you. Add a @JvmField annotation to MAX_SPELL_COUNT in **Spellbook**'s companion object.

Listing 20.31 Adding the @JvmField annotation to the member of a companion object (Hero.kt)

```
...
class Spellbook {
    @JvmField
    val spells = listOf("Magic Ms. L", "Lay on Hans")

    companion object {
        @JvmField
        val MAX_SPELL_COUNT = 10
    }
}
```

Once that annotation is in place, your code in Jhava.java will compile, because you can access MAX_SPELL_COUNT just like any other Java static. Run Jhava.kt to confirm that the maximum spell count is printed to the console.

Although Kotlin and Java handle field access in different ways by default, @JvmField is a useful way to expose fields and ensure equivalent access to your Java counterparts.

Functions defined on companion objects run into similar issues when accessed from Java – they have to be accessed via a reference to the companion object. The @JvmStatic annotation works like @JvmField to allow direct access to functions defined on companion objects. Define a function on **Spellbook**'s companion object called **getSpellbookGreeting**. **getSpellbookGreeting** returns a function to be invoked when **getSpellbookGreeting** is called.

Listing 20.32 Using @JvmStatic on a function (Hero.kt)

```
...
class Spellbook {
    @JvmField
    val spells = listOf("Magic Ms. L", "Lay on Hans")

    companion object {
        @JvmField
        val MAX_SPELL_COUNT = 10

        @JvmStatic
        fun getSpellbookGreeting() = println("I am the Great Grimoire!")
    }
}
```

Now, invoke **getSpellbookGreeting** in Jhava.java.

Listing 20.33 Invoking a static method in Java (Jhava.java)

```
...
public static void main(String[] args) {
    System.out.println(Hero.makeProclamation());

    System.out.println("Spells:");
    Spellbook spellbook = new Spellbook();
    for (String spell : spellbook.spells) {
        System.out.println(spell);
    }

    System.out.println("Max spell count: " + Spellbook.MAX_SPELL_COUNT);

    Spellbook.getSpellbookGreeting();
}
...
```

Run Jhava.java to confirm that the spellbook's greeting is printed to the console.

Although statics do not exist in Kotlin, many commonly used patterns compile down to static variables and methods. Employing the @JvmStatic annotation gives you greater control over how Java developers interface with your code.

Exceptions and Interoperability

The hero has taught the **Jhava** monster language, and the monster will now extend its hand in friendship … or maybe not. Add a method, **extendHandInFriendship**, to Jhava.java.

Listing 20.34 Throwing an exception in Java (Jhava.java)

```java
public class Jhava {
    ...
    public void offerFood() {
        Hero.handOverFood("pizza");
    }

    public void extendHandInFriendship() throws Exception {
        throw new Exception();
    }
}
```

Invoke this method in Hero.kt:

Listing 20.35 Invoking a method that throws an exception (Hero.kt)

```kotlin
@file:JvmName("Hero")

fun main(args: Array<String>) {
    ...
    adversary.offerFood()

    adversary.extendHandInFriendship()
}

fun makeProclamation() = "Greetings, beast!"
...
```

Run this code, and you will see that a runtime exception is thrown. It is not wise to trust a monster.

Recall that exceptions are unchecked in Kotlin. In calling **extendHandInFriendship**, you called a method that throws an exception. In this instance, you knew that when you called the method. Another time, you may not be so lucky. You should take extra care to understand the Java APIs that you are interfacing with from Kotlin.

Wrap your invocation of the **extendHandInFriendship** method in a try/catch block to thwart the monster's treachery.

Listing 20.36 Handling exceptions using try/catch (Hero.kt)

```kotlin
@file:JvmName("Hero")

fun main(args: Array<String>) {
    ...
    adversary.offerFood()

    try {
        adversary.extendHandInFriendship()
    } catch (e: Exception) {
        println("Begone, foul beast!")
    }
}

fun makeProclamation() = "Greetings, beast!"
...
```

Run Hero.kt to see that the hero deftly avoids the monster's duplicitous attack.

Calling Kotlin functions from Java requires some additional understanding when it comes to handling exceptions. All exceptions in Kotlin, as we have said, are unchecked. But this is not the case in Java – exceptions can be checked, and they must be handled at the risk of a crash. How does this affect calling a Kotlin function from Java?

To see, add a function to Hero.kt called **acceptApology**. It is time to exact revenge on the monster.

Listing 20.37 Throwing an unchecked exception (Hero.kt)

```kotlin
...
@JvmOverloads
fun handOverFood(leftHand: String = "berries", rightHand: String = "beef") {
    println("Mmmm... you hand over some delicious $leftHand and $rightHand.")
}

fun acceptApology() {
    throw IOException()
}

class Spellbook {
    ...
}
```

(You will need to import java.io.IOException.)

Now, call **acceptApology** from Jhava.java.

Listing 20.38 Throwing an exception in Java (Jhava.java)

```
public class Jhava {
    ...
    public void apologize() {
        try {
            Hero.acceptApology();
        } catch (IOException e) {
            System.out.println("Caught!");
        }
    }
}
```

The **Jhava** monster is clever enough to suspect the hero of trickery and wraps its invocation of **acceptApology** in a try/catch block. But the Java compiler warns you that an IOException is never thrown in the contents of the try block – that is, in **acceptApology**. How can this be? **acceptApology** clearly throws an IOException.

Understanding this scenario requires a peek into the decompiled Java bytecode:

```
public static final void acceptApology() {
    throw (Throwable)(new IOException());
}
```

You can see that an IOException is thrown in this function, but nothing about the function's signature notifies the caller that an IOException should be checked for. When the Java compiler complains that **acceptApology** does not throw an IOException when invoked from Java, this is why. It has no idea.

Fortunately, there is an annotation to solve this problem, too: @Throws. When you use @Throws, you include information about the exception that the function throws. Add a @Throws annotation to **acceptApology** to augment its Java bytecode.

Listing 20.39 Using the @Throws annotation (Hero.kt)

```
...
@Throws(IOException::class)
fun acceptApology() {
    throw IOException()
}

class Spellbook {
    ...
}
```

Now, look at the resulting decompiled Java bytecode:

```
public static final void acceptApology() throws IOException {
    throw (Throwable)(new IOException());
}
```

The @Throws annotation adds a throws keyword to the Java version of **acceptApology**. Looking back at Jhava.java, you should see that you have now satisfied the Java compiler, as it can now recognize that **acceptApology** throws an IOException that requires checking.

The @Throws annotation smooths over some of the ideological differences between Java and Kotlin with respect to exception checking. If you are writing a Kotlin API that may be exposed to a Java consumer, consider using this annotation so that your consumer can properly handle any exception thrown.

Function Types in Java

Function types and anonymous functions are novel inclusions in the Kotlin programming language that provide a streamlined syntax for communicating between components. Their concise syntax is made possible via the -> operator, but lambdas are not supported in versions of Java prior to Java 8.

So what do these function types look like when called from Java? The answer may seem deceptively simple: In Java, your function type is represented by an interface with a name like **FunctionN**, where N is the number of arguments taken as parameters.

To see this in practice, add a function type called translator to Hero.kt. translator should take a String, lowercase it, capitalize the first letter, and print out the result.

Listing 20.40 Defining the translator function type (Hero.kt)

```
fun main(args: Array<String>) {
    ...
}

val translator = { utterance: String ->
    println(utterance.toLowerCase().capitalize())
}

fun makeProclamation() = "Greetings, beast!"
```

translator is defined like many of the function types that you saw in Chapter 5. It is of type (String) -> Unit. What will this function type look like in Java? Store the translator instance in a variable in **Jhava**.

Listing 20.41 Storing a function type in a variable in Java (Jhava.java)

```
public class Jhava {
    ...
    public static void main(String[] args) {
        ...
        Spellbook.getSpellbookGreeting();

        Function1<String, Unit> translator = Hero.getTranslator();
    }
}
```

(You will need to import kotlin.Unit; be sure to choose the option from the Kotlin standard library. You will also need to import kotlin.jvm.functions.Function1.)

This function type is of type Function1<String, Unit>. Function1 is the base type because translator has exactly one parameter. String and Unit are used as type parameters because the type of translator's parameter is String and it returns the Kotlin type Unit.

There are 23 of these `Function` interfaces, ranging from `Function0` to `Function22`. Each of them includes one function, **invoke**. **invoke** is used to call a function type, so any time that you need to call a function type, you call **invoke** on it. Call `translator` in **Jhava**:

Listing 20.42 Calling a function type in Java (Jhava.java)

```java
public class Jhava {
    ...
    public static void main(String[] args) {
        ...
        Function1<String, Unit> translator = Hero.getTranslator();
        translator.invoke("TRUCE");
    }
}
```

Run `Jhava.kt` to confirm that `Truce` is printed to the console.

While function types are useful in Kotlin, be mindful of how they are represented in Java. The concise, fluid syntax that you have grown fond of in Kotlin is quite different when called from Java. If your code is visible to Java classes (e.g., as a part of an API), then the more considerate route may be to avoid function types. But if you are comfortable with the more verbose syntax, then Kotlin's function types are indeed available to you in Java.

Interoperability between Kotlin and Java is the foundation of Kotlin's growth trajectory. It provides Kotlin with the ability to leverage existing frameworks, such as Android, and to interface with legacy codebases, giving you a path to gradually introduce Kotlin in your projects. Fortunately, interoperation between Kotlin and Java is straightforward, with a few small exceptions. Writing Java-friendly Kotlin code and Kotlin-friendly Java code is useful skill that will pay dividends as you continue your Kotlin journey.

In the next chapter, you will build your first Android app with Kotlin, which will generate the starting attributes for new players in NyetHack.

Building Your First Android Application with Kotlin

Kotlin is a first-class language for developing Android applications, with official support from Google. In this chapter, you will write your first Android application using Kotlin. The app, which rolls a new NyetHack player character's starting attributes, is called Samodelkin, honoring a Russian cartoon android from the 1950s who created himself.

Android Studio

To create an Android project, you will use the Android Studio IDE instead of IntelliJ. Android Studio is built on IntelliJ, and while they share many similarities, Android Studio includes extra features required for developing Android applications.

Download Android Studio from `developer.android.com/studio/index.html`. Once the download has completed, follow the installation instructions for your platform at `developer.android.com/studio/install.html`.

Note that this chapter is based on Android Studio 3.1 and Android 8.1 (API 27). If you have a more recent version, some of the details may have changed.

Before creating a new project, confirm that the Android SDK package you will need has been downloaded for your system by selecting Configure → SDK Manager from the Welcome to Android Studio dialog (Figure 21.1):

Figure 21.1 Bringing up the SDK Manager

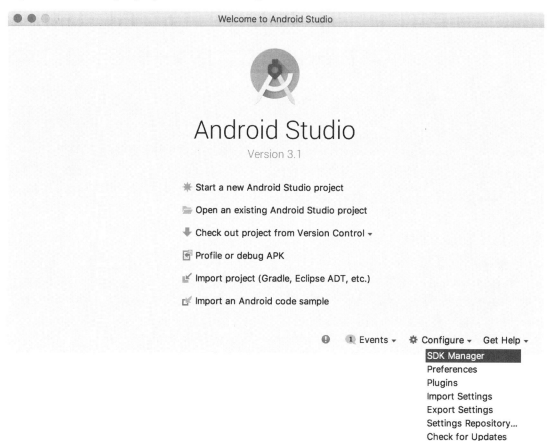

In the Android SDK window, ensure that Android 8.1 (Oreo) (API 27) is checked and marked Installed in the status column (Figure 21.2). If it is not, check the box next to it and click OK, which will download the required API. If it is installed, click Cancel to return to the Welcome to Android Studio dialog.

Figure 21.2 Confirming API 27 is installed

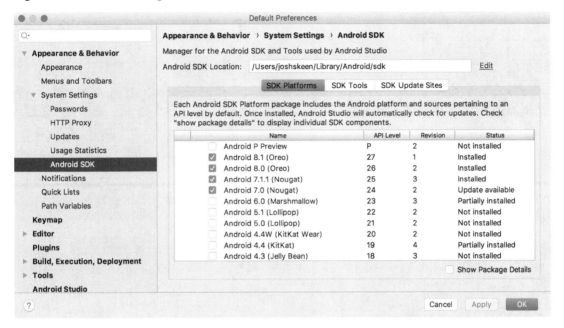

Back at the Welcome to Android Studio dialog, click Start a new Android Studio project.

In the Create Android Project dialog, enter "Samodelkin" for Application name and "android.bignerdranch.com" for Company domain. Make sure that Include Kotlin support is checked (Figure 21.3).

Figure 21.3 The Create Android Project dialog

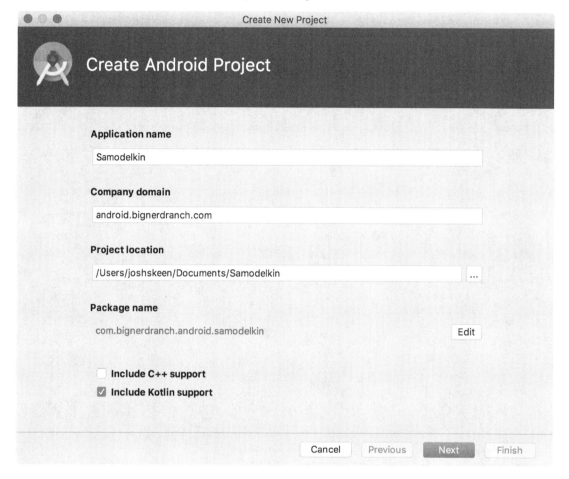

Click Next and, in the Target Android Devices dialog, make sure Phone and Tablet is checked. Leave the default in the API dropdown below as is (even if it looks different from ours) (Figure 21.4). Click Next.

Figure 21.4 The Target Android Devices dialog

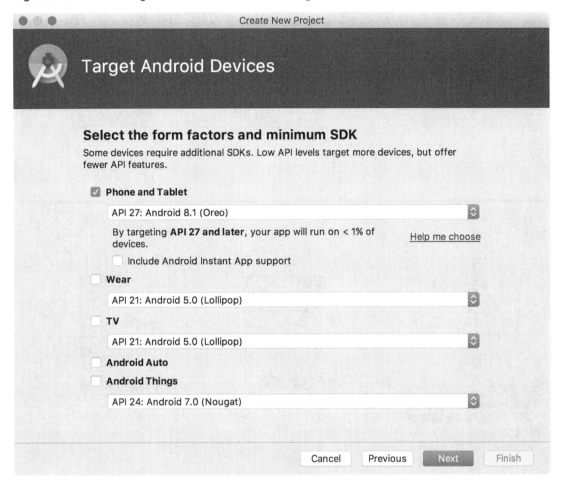

319

In the Add an Activity to Mobile dialog, select Empty Activity and click Next (Figure 21.5).

Figure 21.5 Adding an empty activity

Last, you will be presented with the Configure Activity dialog. Enter "NewCharacterActivity" for the Activity Name and leave the other defaults as they are.

In this step, you specified an *activity* that will be created, `NewCharacterActivity`. You can think of an activity using your common-sense definition of the word – it is something a user of your application will be able to do when using your app. For example, composing an email, searching for a contact, or, in the case of Samodelkin, creating a new character – these are all activities.

In Android, activities consist of two parts – a user interface and an `Activity` class. The user interface, or UI, defines the elements a user will see and interact with in the app, and the `Activity` class defines the logic required to bring that UI to life. You will work with both of these when building the app.

Click Finish. A small dialog appears, showing that the project is being configured (Figure 21.6):

Figure 21.6 Configuring project

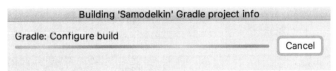

After a minute or two, your new project will open.

A new project configuration, directory structure, and default definitions for the activity's class definition and UI have been generated and added to your project. Let's take a quick tour.

Gradle configuration

First, take a look at the directory structure for your project, visible in the project tool window on the left. Make sure that Android is selected in the dropdown for the project tool window (Figure 21.7):

Figure 21.7 Android project tool window perspective

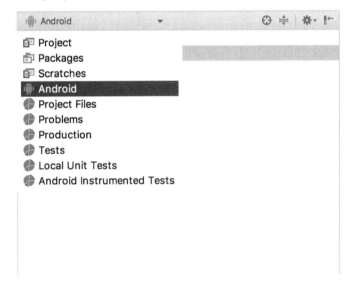

Now, find the Gradle Scripts section at the bottom of the project tool window and expand it (Figure 21.8):

Figure 21.8 Gradle Scripts

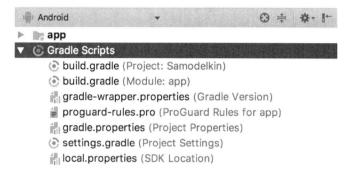

Android uses a popular build automation tool called Gradle to manage your application dependencies and compilation. Gradle configuration is defined using a lightweight DSL. An Android project's Gradle settings are configured using two `build.gradle` files, automatically added when the Android project is created.

Certain Gradle configuration steps Android Studio took care of for you enable your Android project to be developed using Kotlin. Let's take a look.

The (`Project: Samodelkin`) Gradle configuration file defines global settings for the project. Double-click on `build.gradle` (`Project: Samodelkin`) to open it in the editor, the main Android Studio window area. You will see contents similar to the following:

```
buildscript {
    ext.kotlin_version = '1.2.30'
    repositories {
        google()
        jcenter()
    }
    dependencies {
        classpath 'com.android.tools.build:gradle:3.1.0'
        classpath "org.jetbrains.kotlin:kotlin-gradle-plugin:$kotlin_version"
    }
}

allprojects {
    repositories {
        google()
        jcenter()
    }
}

task clean(type: Delete) {
    delete rootProject.buildDir
}
```

The shaded lines add the classpath configuration for the Kotlin Gradle plug-in, enabling Gradle to compile Kotlin files.

Next, open and look at the build.gradle (Module: app) file:

```
apply plugin: 'com.android.application'
apply plugin: 'kotlin-android'
apply plugin: 'kotlin-android-extensions'

android {
    compileSdkVersion 27
    defaultConfig {
        applicationId "com.bignerdranch.android.samodelkin"
        minSdkVersion 19
        targetSdkVersion 27
        versionCode 1
        versionName "1.0"
        testInstrumentationRunner "android.support.test.runner.AndroidJUnitRunner"
    }
    buildTypes {
        release {
            minifyEnabled false
            proguardFiles getDefaultProguardFile('proguard-android.txt'),
                    'proguard-rules.pro'
        }
    }
}

dependencies {
    implementation fileTree(dir: 'libs', include: ['*.jar'])
    implementation"org.jetbrains.kotlin:kotlin-stdlib-jre7:$kotlin_version"
    implementation 'com.android.support:appcompat-v7:27.1.0'
    implementation 'com.android.support.constraint:constraint-layout:1.0.2'
    testImplementation 'junit:junit:4.12'
    androidTestImplementation 'com.android.support.test:runner:1.0.1'
    androidTestImplementation
            'com.android.support.test.espresso:espresso-core:3.0.1'
}
```

The shaded lines here add two plug-ins to your project. The kotlin-android plug-in enables Kotlin code to be correctly compiled when used in conjunction with the Android framework. It is required for any Android project that will be written using Kotlin.

The kotlin-android-extensions plug-in adds a number of conveniences for improving your Android application when working with Kotlin. You will be using a feature that kotlin-android-extensions provides soon.

Gradle also manages the library dependencies that are required for your Android project. Toward the end of the app/build.gradle file, you will see the listing of the required libraries that are downloaded and included automatically by the Gradle build management tool.

Dependencies for a Gradle Android project are defined in the dependencies block of app/build.gradle. Note that the Kotlin standard library is included in the list of dependencies: implementation"org.jetbrains.kotlin:kotlin-stdlib-jre7:$kotlin_version".

Project organization

Next, expand the `app/src/main/java` directory in the project tool window. You will see a package called `com.bignerdranch.android.samodelkin` and a file called `NewCharacterActivity.kt` (which may have opened in the editor when your project was created).

All source code for your project will live within the `com.bignerdranch.android.samodelkin` package. Do not be fooled by the directory name – your project will be written in Kotlin, not Java. The default naming convention for the `src` directory is a holdover from the days of Java.

Finally, expand the `app/src/main/res` directory in the project tool window. This is the home of your app's resources. UI XML files, images, localized string definitions, and color values are all examples of Android resources.

Defining a UI

Your first work in developing Samodelkin will be in the `res` directory. In Android, a UI layout resource is an XML file that describes the elements the user will see and interact with.

Open the `res/layout` folder. You will see an XML file called `activity_new_character.xml`, which was created for you using the name you specified for your first activity in the project setup process.

Double-click on `activity_new_character.xml`. The file opens in the UI graphical layout tool (Figure 21.9):

Figure 21.9 The UI graphical layout tool

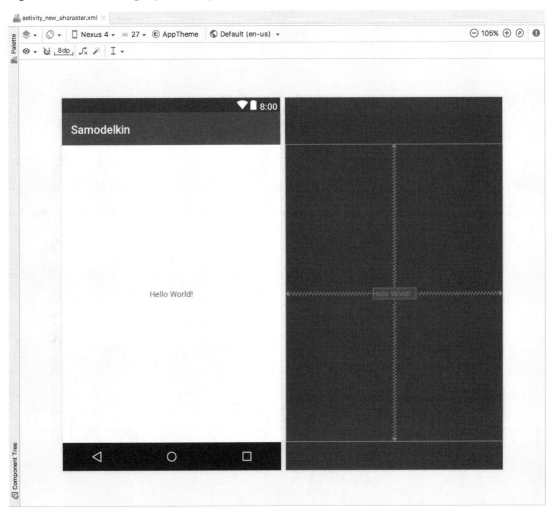

The UI for Samodelkin will display five attributes for the new character: name, race, wisdom, strength, and dexterity. The character creation screen also requires a button to randomly generate the character's stats, allowing the user to "re-roll" the stats to get a different character build.

Click on the Text tab at the lower left of the editor. UIs for Android applications are written in XML. The details of the XML are outside the scope of this book, so – to allow you to focus on the Kotlin aspects of project development – we have provided the XML for the new character UI for you at `bignerdranch.com/solutions/activity_new_character.xml`.

Overwrite the XML content in the file with the XML content in the link. Save the file with Command-S (Ctrl-S) and click on the Design tab at the lower left. Your UI will now look like Figure 21.10.

Figure 21.10 The new character UI

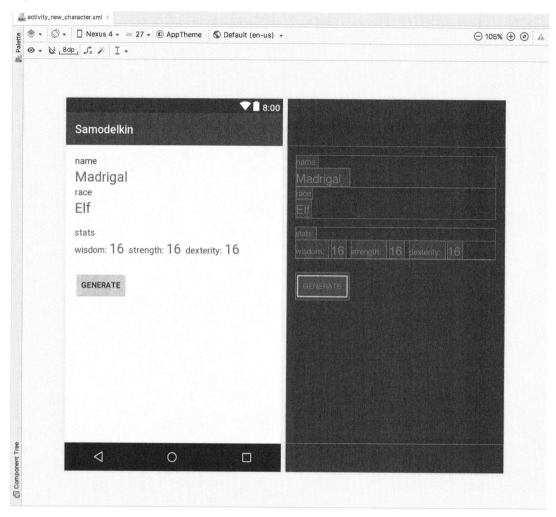

Switch back to the Text tab to look more closely at the XML. Press Command-F (Ctrl-F) to search for the text "android:id" in the file. You will find that there are five android:ids in the XML – one for each attribute (name, race, wis, str, and dex), like this one:

```
<TextView
    android:id="@+id/nameTextView"
    android:layout_width="wrap_content"
    android:layout_height="match_parent"
    android:textSize="24sp"
    tools:text="Madrigal" />
```

For each view element that displays data or allows the user to interact with the app, you specify an id attribute. An id attribute allows you to programmatically access the view element it is defined on (often called a *widget*) in your Kotlin code. You will be using these id attributes shortly to associate your app's logic with its UI.

Running the App on an Emulator

Next, you are going to deploy and run the application on an Android emulator to test it.

The first step is to configure an emulator. From the Android Studio menus, select Tools → AVD Manager (Figure 21.11).

Figure 21.11 Showing the AVD Manager

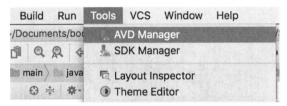

At the lower left of the window, click + Create Virtual Device... (Figure 21.12).

Figure 21.12 Android Virtual Device Manager

Your Virtual Devices
Android Studio

Type	Name	Play Store	Resolution	API	Target	CPU/ABI	Size on Disk	Actions
	Nexus 5X API 19		1080 × 1920: 420dpi	19	Android 4.4 (Google APIs)	x86	1.6 GB	▶ / ▾
	Pixel C API 25		2560 × 1800: xhdpi	25	Android 7.1.1 (Google APIs)	x86	2.6 GB	▶ / ▾
	Pixel C API 19		2560 × 1800: xhdpi	19	Android 4.4 (Google APIs)	x86	4.5 GB	▶ / ▾
	Pixel XL API 26		1440 × 2560: 560dpi	26	Android 8.0 (Google APIs)	x86	2.3 GB	▶ / ▾
	Pixel XL API 25		1440 × 2560: 560dpi	25	Android 7.1.1 (Google APIs)	x86	1.7 GB	▶ / ▾
	Nexus 9 API 25		2048 × 1536: xhdpi	25	Android 7.1.1 (Google APIs)	x86	2.2 GB	▶ / ▾
	Nexus 4 API 19		768 × 1280: xhdpi	19	Android 4.4 (Google APIs)	x86	1.7 GB	▶ / ▾
	Nexus 5X API 25 x86		1080 × 1920: 420dpi	25	Android 7.1.1 (Google APIs)	x86	3.1 GB	▶ / ▾
	Pixel API 25		1080 × 1920: xxhdpi	25	Android 7.1.1 (Google APIs)	x86	2.7 GB	▶ / ▾

? + Create Virtual Device...

In the Select Hardware dialog, select a phone model (the default choice should be fine) and click Next. In the System Image dialog, select the Oreo API Level 27 release (and download it, if necessary). Click Next. When the system image has finished downloading, click Next again. Finally, on the Android Virtual Device (AVD) dialog, click Finish. Close the Android Virtual Device Manager window.

Back at the main Android Studio window, look at the row of buttons in the top right. To the left of the run button is a dropdown box. Make sure that it says app, then click the run button (Figure 21.13). This opens the Select Deployment Target dialog.

Figure 21.13 Running Samodelkin

Select the virtual device you configured and click OK. The emulator will launch and display the new character activity UI, in all of its current (unpopulated) glory (Figure 21.14):

Figure 21.14 Samodelkin, running in the emulator

The UI shows no values for the character's stats yet. In the next section, you will fix that.

Generating a Character

Now that you have defined the UI, it is time to generate and display a new character sheet. Since the focus of this chapter is Android and Kotlin, and the details of the implementation have been the focus of the previous chapters, we will move quickly with the implementation for **CharacterGenerator**. Add a new file to the project by right-clicking on the com.bignerdranch.android.samodelkin package and selecting New → Kotlin File/Class.

Name the new file CharacterGenerator.kt and fill it in like so:

Listing 21.1 The **CharacterGenerator** object (CharacterGenerator.kt)

```kotlin
private fun <T> List<T>.rand() = shuffled().first()

private fun Int.roll() = (0 until this)
        .map { (1..6).toList().rand() }
        .sum()
        .toString()

private val firstName = listOf("Eli", "Alex", "Sophie")
private val lastName = listOf("Lightweaver", "Greatfoot", "Oakenfeld")

object CharacterGenerator {
    data class CharacterData(val name: String,
                            val race: String,
                            val dex: String,
                            val wis: String,
                            val str: String)

    private fun name() = "${firstName.rand()} ${lastName.rand()}"

    private fun race() = listOf("dwarf", "elf", "human", "halfling").rand()

    private fun dex() = 4.roll()

    private fun wis() = 3.roll()

    private fun str() = 5.roll()

    fun generate() = CharacterData(name = name(),
                                   race = race(),
                                   dex = dex(),
                                   wis = wis(),
                                   str = str())
}
```

The **CharacterGenerator** object you define exposes one public function, **generate**, which returns the data representing a randomly generated character wrapped in a **CharacterData** class. You also define two extensions, **List<T>.rand** and **Int.roll**, to shorten the code for selecting an element at random from a collection and for randomly rolling a six-sided die a set number of times.

The Activity Class

NewCharacterActivity.kt may already be open in an editor tab. If it is not, expand the
app/src/main/java/com.bignerdranch.android.samodelkin directory and double-click
NewCharacterActivity.kt.

The initial class definition appears in the editor:

```
class NewCharacterActivity : AppCompatActivity() {

    override fun onCreate(savedInstanceState: Bundle?) {
        super.onCreate(savedInstanceState)
        setContentView(R.layout.activity_new_character)
    }
}
```

This code was generated along with your project. Notice that **NewCharacterActivity**, the activity you
defined during the setup process, subclasses **AppCompatActivity**.

AppCompatActivity is part of the Android framework and serves as a base class for the
NewCharacterActivity you will define in your app.

Also, notice that the **onCreate** function has been overridden. **onCreate** is an *Android lifecycle function*:
a function that the Android operating system invokes for you when, in this case, your activity is
initially created.

The **onCreate** function is where you retrieve view elements from the UI XML and where you wire up
associated interactive logic for a particular activity. Take a look at its definition:

```
class NewCharacterActivity : AppCompatActivity() {

    override fun onCreate(savedInstanceState: Bundle?) {
        super.onCreate(savedInstanceState)
        setContentView(R.layout.activity_new_character)
    }
}
```

Within **onCreate,** the **setContentView** function is called with the name of the XML file you defined,
activity_new_character. **setContentView** takes a layout resource and *inflates* it – converting the
XML to a UI view that is displayed on the phone, tablet, or emulator for a particular activity.

Wiring Up Views

To display the character data in the UI, you will first retrieve each view element that will display
text using a function available on **NewCharacterActivity** (via inheritance) called **findViewById**.
findViewById accepts a view element id (the android:ids defined in the XML) and returns the view
element if a match is found.

In NewCharacterActivity.kt, update **onCreate** to look up each view element that will display data by
its id and assign it to a local variable:

Listing 21.2 Looking up view elements (NewCharacterActivity.kt)

```
class NewCharacterActivity : AppCompatActivity() {
    override fun onCreate(savedInstanceState: Bundle?) {
        super.onCreate(savedInstanceState)
        setContentView(R.layout.activity_new_character)
        val nameTextView = findViewById<TextView>(R.id.nameTextView)
        val raceTextView = findViewById<TextView>(R.id.raceTextView)
        val dexterityTextView = findViewById<TextView>(R.id.dexterityTextView)
        val wisdomTextView = findViewById<TextView>(R.id.wisdomTextView)
        val strengthTextView = findViewById<TextView>(R.id.strengthTextView)
        val generateButton = findViewById<Button>(R.id.generateButton)
    }
}
```

Android Studio will complain about all your references to TextView and Button. You need to import the classes that define these widgets in your file to access their properties. Click on the first red TextView and press Option-Return (Alt-Enter). The line import android.widget.TextView appears at the top of your file, and the red error underlines disappear. Repeat the process for Button.

Next, assign the character data to a property on the **NewCharacterActivity** class:

Listing 21.3 Defining the characterData property (NewCharacterActivity.kt)

```
class NewCharacterActivity : AppCompatActivity() {
    private var characterData = CharacterGenerator.generate()

    override fun onCreate(savedInstanceState: Bundle?) {
        ...
    }
}
```

And to the views that you looked up at the end of the **onCreate** function:

Listing 21.4 Displaying the character data (NewCharacterActivity.kt)

```
class NewCharacterActivity : AppCompatActivity() {
    private var characterData = CharacterGenerator.generate()

    override fun onCreate(savedInstanceState: Bundle?) {
        ...
        characterData.run {
            nameTextView.text = name
            raceTextView.text = race
            dexterityTextView.text = dex
            wisdomTextView.text = wis
            strengthTextView.text = str
        }
    }
}
```

There are several details to notice about the code that assigns the character data to the text views. First, you use the **run** standard function to shorten the amount of code required to configure the view elements from the character data – scoping each character data property access to be implicitly called on characterData.

Also, you assign the text using property assignment syntax, like this:

```
nameTextView.text = name
```

To do this with Java, instead of Kotlin, you would write:

```
nameTextView.setText(name);
```

Why is there a difference here? Android is a Java framework, and the standard Java convention for accessing a field is to use getters and setters. Remember that **AppCompatActivity**, the TextView elements, and all of the components of the Android platform are in fact written in the Java language, and you interface with them when using Kotlin to write an Android app.

If you were to interface with the nameTextView from a Java class, you would use the standard Java getter/setter syntax (**setText**, **getText**) to set the text for the TextView.

Because you interfaced with the **TextView** Java class using Kotlin, Kotlin translates Java's getter/setter convention to the equivalent Kotlin convention: property access syntax. This required no additional code or extra changes. Kotlin bridges Java style and Kotlin style automatically, since Kotlin was designed with seamless Java interoperability in mind.

Run Samodelkin on the emulator again. This time, you will see character data that was loaded from **CharacterGenerator** and populated in the UI (Figure 21.15):

Figure 21.15 Samodelkin, showing data

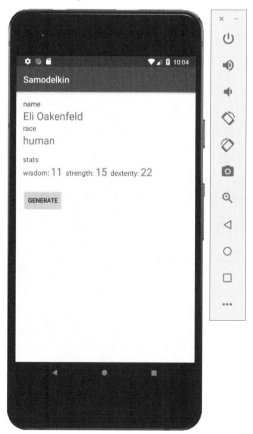

Kotlin Android Extensions Synthetic Properties

One problem – your **onCreate** function is getting somewhat lengthy and disorganized. (Also, the GENERATE button does nothing yet. You will fix that in a moment.)

As you pack more code into **onCreate**, it becomes harder to follow what is going on. In a more elaborate application, this lack of order could be problematic. Even in a relatively simple app like Samodelkin, it is good practice to keep things tidy.

You are going to move the assignment of the character data to the views to a separate function, instead of cramming it all into the **onCreate** function. Using functions to organize your activity can preserve your sanity as the interface and functionality of the activity grow more complex.

To do this, you need a way to use the views that you looked up in **onCreate**. One solution is to make the view elements you retrieved with **findViewById** properties of **NewCharacterActivity**, allowing them to be accessed in other functions beyond **onCreate**.

However, an even more convenient solution, available because your project includes the kotlin-android-extensions plug-in, is to use synthetic properties, which expose a view via its id attribute. These properties correspond to all the widget properties defined in the named layout file, activity_new_character.xml.

Update **NewCharacterActivity** with a **displayCharacterData** function to see what this means. (You can cut and paste **characterData.run** to save typing.)

Listing 21.5 Refactoring to **displayCharacterData** (NewCharacterActivity.kt)

```
import kotlinx.android.synthetic.main.activity_new_character.*

class NewCharacterActivity : AppCompatActivity() {
    private var characterData = CharacterGenerator.generate()

    override fun onCreate(savedInstanceState: Bundle?) {
        super.onCreate(savedInstanceState)
        setContentView(R.layout.activity_new_character)
        val nameTextView = findViewById<TextView>(R.id.nameTextView)
        val raceTextView = findViewById<TextView>(R.id.raceTextView)
        val dexterityTextView = findViewById<TextView>(R.id.dexterityTextView)
        val wisdomTextView = findViewById<TextView>(R.id.wisdomTextView)
        val strengthTextView = findViewById<TextView>(R.id.strengthTextView)
        val generateButton = findViewById<Button>(R.id.generateButton)

        characterData.run {
            nameTextView.text = name
            raceTextView.text = race
            dexterityTextView.text = dex
            wisdomTextView.text = wis
            strengthTextView.text = str
        }
        displayCharacterData()
    }

    private fun displayCharacterData() {
        characterData.run {
            nameTextView.text = name
            raceTextView.text = race
            dexterityTextView.text = dex
            wisdomTextView.text = wis
            strengthTextView.text = str
        }
    }
}
```

Kotlin Android extensions are a suite of extras included by default with your new project, via Gradle. The line import kotlinx.android.synthetic.main.activity_new_character.*, enabled by the kotlin-android-extensions plug-in, adds a series of extension properties to your **Activity**. As you can see, synthetic properties greatly simplify your view lookup code – no **findViewById** needed. Instead of each view being a local variable in the **onCreate** function, you now have properties that correspond to each view's id defined in the layout file.

Now the view assignment behavior also has its own function, **displayCharacterData**.

Setting a Click Listener

You have displayed a character's stats, but the user currently has no way to generate another character. The GENERATE button needs to be wired up with the details of what to do when it is pressed. It should update the character data property and display the results.

Update **onCreate** to implement this behavior by defining a click listener. (Even though you "press" things in Android, the listener is called "click.")

Listing 21.6 Setting a click listener (NewCharacterActivity.kt)

```
class NewCharacterActivity : AppCompatActivity() {
    private var characterData = CharacterGenerator.generate()

    override fun onCreate(savedInstanceState: Bundle?) {
        super.onCreate(savedInstanceState)
        setContentView(R.layout.activity_new_character)
        generateButton.setOnClickListener {
            characterData = CharacterGenerator.generate()
            displayCharacterData()
        }

        displayCharacterData()
    }
    ...
}
```

Here, you define a click listener implementation that determines what happens when the button is pressed. Run Samodelkin again and press the GENERATE button several times. You will see a new character sheet loaded each time the button is pressed.

The **setOnClickListener** method expects an argument that implements the **OnClickListener** interface. (You do not have to take our word for it; you can look it up yourself at developer.android.com/reference/android/view/View.html.) The **OnClickListener** interface has only one abstract method defined on it – **onClick**. Interface parameters like this are called *SAM types* – single abstract method types.

In older versions of Java, the implementation for the click listener interface would be provided using an anonymous inner class:

```
generateButton.setOnClickListener(new View.OnClickListener() {
    @Override
    public void onClick(View view) {
        // Do stuff
    }
});
```

Kotlin includes a feature called *SAM conversions*, allowing you to use a function literal as a valid argument in place of an anonymous inner class. Any time you interface with Java code that requires an argument implementing an SAM interface, traditionally accomplished with an anonymous inner class, Kotlin supports using a function literal instead.

Note that if you were to look at the bytecode for the click listener code that you have written, you would see that a full anonymous inner class was used to provide the implementation, just like in the traditional Java code above.

Saved Instance State

Your character attribute app is really shaping up. You can press GENERATE and create character stats to your heart's content. But there is still a problem. To see it, run the emulator, then simulate rotating the phone by clicking on one of the rotation icons in the emulator options window (Figure 21.16):

Figure 21.16 Rotating the emulator

The UI shows different character data (Figure 21.17):

Figure 21.17 Different character data after rotating

The data shown in the UI changed because of how Android's activity lifecycle works. When a device is rotated (Android calls this a *device configuration change*), Android destroys and re-creates the activity – and, in the process, re-creates the UI by calling the **onCreate** function on a new instance of the **NewCharacterActivity** class.

One way to fix this issue is to carry the displayed character data forward to the next instance of the activity by storing it in the activity's *saved instance state*. The saved instance state can be used to store data that you would like to reuse when the activity is re-created after a device configuration change.

First, update the **NewCharacterActivity** class to *serialize* the character data:

Listing 21.7 Serializing the characterData (NewCharacterActivity.kt)

```kotlin
private const val CHARACTER_DATA_KEY = "CHARACTER_DATA_KEY"

class NewCharacterActivity : AppCompatActivity() {
    private var characterData = CharacterGenerator.generate()

    override fun onSaveInstanceState(outState: Bundle) {
        super.onSaveInstanceState(outState)
        outState.putSerializable(CHARACTER_DATA_KEY, characterData)
    }
    ...
}
```

Serialization is a process by which objects are stored. When you serialize an object, you break it down into basic data types, like String or Int. Only serializable objects can be stored in a Bundle.

You will have an error on characterData because you tried to pass non-serializable data to the **putSerializable** function. To fix it, you need to add the **Serializable** interface to the **CharacterData** class so that **CharacterData** is serializable:

Listing 21.8 Making the **CharacterData** class **Serializable** (CharacterGenerator.kt)

```
object CharacterGenerator {
    data class CharacterData(val name: String,
                             val race: String,
                             val dex: String,
                             val wis: String,
                             val str: String) : Serializable
    ...
}
```

The **onSaveInstanceState** function is called once before the activity is destroyed. It exposes the **savedInstanceState** bundle, which allows an activity's instance state to be persisted.

You add the current characterData to the saved instance state bundle using the **putSerializable** method, which expects a serializable class and a key. The key is a constant and will be used later to retrieve the serializable data, and the value is the **CharacterData** class, which you updated to implement **Serializable**.

Reading from the saved instance state

You have taken care of the problem of serializing **CharacterData** to the saved instance state, and now you need to deserialize it and set the UI back up using the old data. You do so in the **onCreate** function:

Listing 21.9 Fetching the serialized character data
(NewCharacterActivity.kt)

```kotlin
private const val CHARACTER_DATA_KEY = "CHARACTER_DATA_KEY"

class NewCharacterActivity : AppCompatActivity() {
    ...
    override fun onCreate(savedInstanceState: Bundle?) {
        super.onCreate(savedInstanceState)
        setContentView(R.layout.activity_new_character)

        characterData = savedInstanceState?.let {
            it.getSerializable(CHARACTER_DATA_KEY) as CharacterGenerator.CharacterData
        } ?: CharacterGenerator.generate()

        generateButton.setOnClickListener {
            characterData = CharacterGenerator.generate()
            displayCharacterData()
        }

        displayCharacterData()
    }
    ...
}
```

Here you read the serialized character data from the saved instance state bundle, casting it back to **CharacterData** if the saved instance state is non-null. On the other hand, if the saved instance state is null, you use the null coalescing operator (?:) to generate new character data.

Either way, you assign the result of this expression (either the deserialized character data or new character data) to the characterData property.

Try running Samodelkin again and rotating the emulator. This time, you will see that the data is retrieved from the bundle and displayed again after rotating, because you set character data from the saved instance state.

Refactoring to an Extension

The saved instance state serialization and deserialization work correctly, but the code can be improved. Notice that, currently, you are required to manage the key and type of data (you must manually cast it to **CharacterData**) when you get and put the **CharacterData** on the savedInstanceState bundle:

```
private const val CHARACTER_DATA_KEY = "CHARACTER_DATA_KEY"

class NewCharacterActivity : AppCompatActivity() {
    private var characterData = CharacterGenerator.generate()

    override fun onSaveInstanceState(outState: Bundle) {
        super.onSaveInstanceState(outState)
        outState.putSerializable(CHARACTER_DATA_KEY, characterData)
    }

    override fun onCreate(savedInstanceState: Bundle?) {
        super.onCreate(savedInstanceState)
        setContentView(R.layout.activity_new_character)

        characterData = savedInstanceState?.let {
            it.getSerializable(CHARACTER_DATA_KEY)
                    as CharacterGenerator.CharacterData
        } ?: CharacterGenerator.generate()
        ...
    }
    ...
}
```

To improve on this, add an extension property definition to NewCharacterActivity.kt:

Listing 21.10 Defining a characterData extension property (NewCharacterActivity.kt)

```
private const val CHARACTER_DATA_KEY = "CHARACTER_DATA_KEY"

private var Bundle.characterData
    get() = getSerializable(CHARACTER_DATA_KEY) as CharacterGenerator.CharacterData
    set(value) = putSerializable(CHARACTER_DATA_KEY, value)

class NewCharacterActivity : AppCompatActivity() {
    ...
}
```

Now you can access the characterData from the saved instance state bundle as a property. You no longer need the key to retrieve the data, and you no longer require casting the **Serializable** to **CharacterData** when you retrieve it.

The extension property provides a clean abstraction over the bundle's API, removing the need for tracking the details of how the character data was stored and which key was used each time you wish to read or write the characterData.

Now, update the **onSaveInstanceState** and **onCreate** functions to use the new extension property:

Listing 21.11 Using the new extension property (NewCharacterActivity.kt)

```
private const val CHARACTER_DATA_KEY = "CHARACTER_DATA_KEY"

class NewCharacterActivity : AppCompatActivity() {
    private var characterData = CharacterGenerator.generate()

    override fun onSaveInstanceState(outState: Bundle) {
        super.onSaveInstanceState(outState)
        outState.putSerializable(CHARACTER_DATA, characterData)
        outState.characterData = characterData
    }

    override fun onCreate(savedInstanceState: Bundle?) {
        super.onCreate(savedInstanceState)
        setContentView(R.layout.activity_new_character)

        characterData = savedInstanceState?.let {
            it.getSerializable(CHARACTER_DATA_KEY) as CharacterGenerator.CharacterData
        } ?: CharacterGenerator.generate()
        characterData = savedInstanceState?.characterData ?:
            CharacterGenerator.generate()

        generateButton.setOnClickListener {
            characterData = CharacterGenerator.generatw()
            displayCharacterData()
        }

        displayCharacterData()
    }
    ...
}
```

Run Samodelkin again, putting the application through its paces by rotating the emulator and pressing the GENERATE button several times. You will see that the character data is persisted correctly as before.

Congratulations! You have created your first Android application using Kotlin. You have learned about some of the ways Kotlin supports working with the Java code that the Android framework is written in, and you have also seen an example of how kotlin-android-extensions makes your coding life easier. Finally, you have seen how features in Kotlin, like extensions and standard functions, can make your Android code more clean.

In the next chapter, you will learn about Kotlin coroutines, an experimental feature that provides a lightweight and elegant alternative to other models for specifying work in the background.

For the More Curious: Android KTX and Anko Libraries

There are many open-source libraries designed to enhance the developer experience when working with Kotlin and Android. We will highlight two here to give an idea of what is possible.

The Android KTX project (github.com/android/android-ktx) provides a number of useful Kotlin extensions for Android app development, often also granting a more Kotlinesque interface to the

Android Java APIs than would otherwise be possible. For example, consider the following code, which uses Android's shared preferences to persist a small amount of data for later use:

```
sharedPrefs.edit()
        .putBoolean(true, USER_SIGNED_IN)
        .putString("Josh", USER_CALLSIGN)
        .apply()
```

With Android KTX, you can shorten the expression and write it in a more idiomatic Kotlin style:

```
sharedPrefs.edit {
    putBoolean(true, USER_SIGNED_IN)
    putString("Josh", USER_CALLSIGN)
}
```

Android KTX enables many nice, if small, improvements to your Kotlin Android code, and it allows you to work with the Android framework in a style that is a closer match to Kotlin, rather than Java.

Another popular Kotlin project for use with Android, Anko (github.com/Kotlin/anko), provides a variety of enhancements for Kotlin Android development, including a DSL for defining Android UIs and a number of helpers for working with Android intents and dialogs, SQLite, and many other aspects of an Android project. For example, the following Anko layout code programmatically defines a vertically oriented linear layout containing a button that displays a toast (a pop-up message) when clicked:

```
verticalLayout {
    val username = editText()
    button("Greetings") {
        onClick { toast("Hello, ${username.text}!") }
    }
}
```

Compare this with the large amount of code to do the same programmatically in classic Java:

```
LayoutParams params = new LinearLayout.LayoutParams(
                    LayoutParams.FILL_PARENT,
                    LayoutParams.WRAP_CONTENT);
LinearLayout layout = new LinearLayout(this);
layout.setOrientation(LinearLayout.VERTICAL);
EditText name = new EditText(this);
name.setLayoutParams(params);
layout.addView(name);
Button greetings = new Button(this);
greetings.setText("Greetings");
greetings.setLayoutParams(params);
layout.addView(greetings);
LinearLayout.LayoutParams layoutParam = new LinearLayout.LayoutParams(
        LayoutParams.FILL_PARENT,
        LayoutParams.WRAP_CONTENT);
this.addContentView(layout, layoutParam);
greetings.setOnClickListener(new OnClickListener() {
    public void onClick(View v) {
        Toast.makeText(this, "Hello, " + name.getText(),
                Toast.LENGTH_SHORT).show();
    }
}
```

Kotlin is still a relatively young language, and useful libraries are being developed every day. Keep your eye on kotlinlang.org for up-to-date news on developments in the language.

22

Introduction to Coroutines

Android apps perform all kinds of functions. You may want your app to download data, query a database, or make a request to a web API. These are all useful operations – but they can all require a considerable amount of time to complete. You do not want your user to be stuck waiting for them to complete before they can continue using your app.

Coroutines allow you to specify work that happens in the background of your application, or *asynchronously*. Instead of requiring the user to wait while that work completes, coroutines allow the user to continue interacting with your app while the work completes in the background.

Coroutines are considerably more resource efficient and easier to work with than the solutions offered by some other programming languages, such as the threads used by Java and other languages (which you will learn more about in this chapter). Complex code can be required to handle the delivery of results between threads, and they are faced with performance issues because it is all too easy to "block" a thread.

In this chapter, you will add coroutines to your Samodelkin Android app to fetch new character data from a web API.

Parsing Character Data

The new character data web API is located at `chargen-api.herokuapp.com`. (By the way, the new character web API is written in Kotlin, using the Ktor web framework (`github.com/ktorio/ktor`). If you are interested, you can check out the source code for the web API at `github.com/bignerdranch/character-data-api`.)

When the web API data is requested, a comma-separated list of new player attributes is returned with values for the `race`, `name`, `dex`, `wis`, and `str` attributes. Try visiting `chargen-api.herokuapp.com` to see a set of attribute values like:

```
halfling,Lars Kizzy,14,13,8
```

Reload your web browser several times to see different responses from the service.

Your first task is to convert the comma-separated string of player character data returned from the web API to a **CharacterData** instance that can be displayed in the UI.

Let's get started. Open `CharacterGenerator.kt` in Android Studio and define a **fromApiData** conversion function:

Listing 22.1 Adding the **fromApiData** function (`CharacterGenerator.kt`)

```
...
object CharacterGenerator {
    data class CharacterData(val name: String,
                             val race: String,
                             val dex: String,
                             val wis: String,
                             val str: String) : Serializable
    ...
    fun fromApiData(apiData: String): CharacterData {
        val (race, name, dex, wis, str) =
                apiData.split(",")
        return CharacterData(name, race, dex, wis, str)
    }
}
...
```

The **fromApiData** function takes a comma-separated string from the character data service, splits it at the commas, and destructures the results into a new `CharacterData` instance.

Test **fromApiData** by calling it when the GENERATE button is pressed. For now, pass some fake data:

Listing 22.2 Testing the **fromApiData** function (`NewCharacterActivity.kt`)

```
...
class NewCharacterActivity : AppCompatActivity() {
    ...
    override fun onCreate(savedInstanceState: Bundle?) {
        super.onCreate(savedInstanceState)
        setContentView(R.layout.activity_new_character)

        characterData = savedInstanceState?.let {
            it.getSerializable(CHARACTER_DATA_KEY) as CharacterGenerator.CharacterData
        } ?: CharacterGenerator.generate()

        generateButton.setOnClickListener {
            characterData = CharacterGenerator.generate()
                            fromApiData("halfling,Lars Kizzy,14,13,8")
            displayCharacterData()
        }
        ...
    }
    ...
}
```

Run Samodelkin on the emulator to confirm that the application builds. Press the GENERATE button. You will see the test data that you passed to the conversion function displayed in the UI (Figure 22.1):

Figure 22.1 Displaying test data

Fetching Live Data

Now that you have tested the conversion function, it is time to fetch some live data from the character data web API.

Before starting with the implementation, you will need to add several permissions to your Android manifest to enable network requests. Find and open the manifest at src/main/AndroidManifest.xml. Add the permissions as shown:

Listing 22.3 Adding required permissions (AndroidManifest.xml)

```
<?xml version="1.0" encoding="utf-8"?>
<manifest xmlns:android="http://schemas.android.com/apk/res/android"
    package="com.bignerdranch.android.samodelkin">

    <uses-permission android:name="android.permission.INTERNET" />
    <uses-permission android:name="android.permission.ACCESS_NETWORK_STATE" />

    <application
        android:allowBackup="true"
        android:icon="@mipmap/ic_launcher"
        android:label="@string/app_name"
        ...
    </application>
</manifest>
```

Now to request the data from the web API. A simple way to fetch the web API data is to use a java.net.URL instance. Kotlin includes an extension function to URL, **readText**, that provides simple support for connecting to a basic web API endpoint, buffering the data, and converting that data into a string – everything you need here.

Define a new constant in **CharacterGenerator** for the web API endpoint as well as a new function called **fetchCharacterData** that reads data from the web API using **URL**'s **readText** function. Make sure to import the **URL** class at the top of the file, as shown:

Listing 22.4 Adding the **fetchCharacterData** function (CharacterGenerator.kt)

```
import java.io.Serializable
import java.net.URL

private const val CHARACTER_DATA_API = "https://chargen-api.herokuapp.com/"

private fun <T> List<T>.rand() = shuffled().first()

object CharacterGenerator {
    ...
}

fun fetchCharacterData(): CharacterGenerator.CharacterData {
    val apiData = URL(CHARACTER_DATA_API).readText()
    return CharacterGenerator.fromApiData(apiData)
}
```

Now, put the new function to use. Update the GENERATE button's click listener to call
fetchCharacterData:

Listing 22.5 Calling **fetchCharacterData** (CharacterGenerator.kt)

```
...
class NewCharacterActivity : AppCompatActivity() {
    ...
    override fun onCreate(savedInstanceState: Bundle?) {
        ...
        generateButton.setOnClickListener {
            characterData = CharacterGenerator.
                            fromApiData("halfling,Lars Kizzy,14,13,8")
                            fetchCharacterData()
            displayCharacterData()
        }

        displayCharacterData()
    }
    ...
}
```

Run Samodelkin again and click the GENERATE button. Instead of new character attributes, you will
see the dialog in Figure 22.2.

Figure 22.2 Samodelkin has stopped

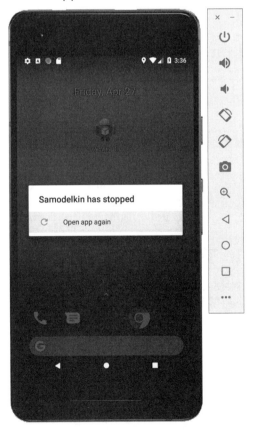

Samodelkin crashed. Why? To find out, take a look in the Logcat output, where the Android application logs are displayed. Click on the Logcat tab at the bottom of Android Studio and scroll up until you reach the red text that starts with FATAL EXCEPTION: main (Figure 22.3):

Figure 22.3 Logcat output

```
Logcat

Emulator Pixel_2_API_2    com.bignerdranch.androi    ...    Q·         ☑ Regex    Show only selected applic

04-27 15:35:52.147 18876-18876/com.bignerdranch.android.samodelkin D/NetworkSecurityConfig: No Network Security Config specifie
04-27 15:35:52.154 18876-18876/com.bignerdranch.android.samodelkin D/AndroidRuntime: Shutting down VM
04-27 15:35:52.158 18876-18876/com.bignerdranch.android.samodelkin E/AndroidRuntime: FATAL EXCEPTION: main
    Process: com.bignerdranch.android.samodelkin, PID: 18876
    android.os.NetworkOnMainThreadException
        at android.os.StrictMode$AndroidBlockGuardPolicy.onNetwork(StrictMode.java:1450)
        at java.net.Inet6AddressImpl.lookupHostByName(Inet6AddressImpl.java:102)
        at java.net.Inet6AddressImpl.lookupAllHostAddr(Inet6AddressImpl.java:90)
        at java.net.InetAddress.getAllByName(InetAddress.java:787)
        at com.android.okhttp.Dns$1.lookup(Dns.java:39)
        at com.android.okhttp.internal.http.RouteSelector.resetNextInetSocketAddress(RouteSelector.java:175)
        at com.android.okhttp.internal.http.RouteSelector.nextProxy(RouteSelector.java:141)
        at com.android.okhttp.internal.http.RouteSelector.next(RouteSelector.java:83)
        at com.android.okhttp.internal.http.StreamAllocation.findConnection(StreamAllocation.java:174)
        at com.android.okhttp.internal.http.StreamAllocation.findHealthyConnection(StreamAllocation.java:126)
        at com.android.okhttp.internal.http.StreamAllocation.newStream(StreamAllocation.java:95)
        at com.android.okhttp.internal.http.HttpEngine.connect(HttpEngine.java:281)
        at com.android.okhttp.internal.http.HttpEngine.sendRequest(HttpEngine.java:224)
        at com.android.okhttp.internal.huc.HttpURLConnectionImpl.execute(HttpURLConnectionImpl.java:461)
        at com.android.okhttp.internal.huc.HttpURLConnectionImpl.getResponse(HttpURLConnectionImpl.java:407)
        at com.android.okhttp.internal.huc.HttpURLConnectionImpl.getInputStream(HttpURLConnectionImpl.java:244)
        at com.android.okhttp.internal.huc.DelegatingHttpsURLConnection.getInputStream(DelegatingHttpsURLConnection.java:210)
        at com.android.okhttp.internal.huc.HttpsURLConnectionImpl.getInputStream(Unknown Source:0)
        at java.net.URL.openStream(URL.java:1058)
        at kotlin.io.TextStreamsKt.readBytes(ReadWrite.kt:145)
        at com.bignerdranch.android.samodelkin.CharacterGeneratorKt.fetchCharacterData(CharacterGenerator.kt:39)
        at com.bignerdranch.android.samodelkin.NewCharacterActivity$onCreate$2.onClick(NewCharacterActivity.kt:35)
        at android.view.View.performClick(View.java:6294)
        at android.view.View$PerformClick.run(View.java:24770)
        at android.os.Handler.handleCallback(Handler.java:790)
        at android.os.Handler.dispatchMessage(Handler.java:99)
        at android.os.Looper.loop(Looper.java:164)
        at android.app.ActivityThread.main(ActivityThread.java:6494) <1 internal call>
        at com.android.internal.os.RuntimeInit$MethodAndArgsCaller.run(RuntimeInit.java:438)
        at com.android.internal.os.ZygoteInit.main(ZygoteInit.java:807)
04-27 15:35:52.164 1664-1997/system_process W/ActivityManager:  Force finishing activity com.bignerdranch.android.samodelkin/.
04-27 15:35:52.169 1664-1680/system process E/memtrack: Couldn't load memtrack module

▶ 4: Run    ⚙ TODO    ☰ 6: Logcat    🔀 Android Profiler    ✔ 9: Version Control    ⬛ Terminal    🔨 Build        3 Event Log
```

Two lines below FATAL EXCEPTION, the log shows the cause of the error: an android.os.NetworkOnMainThreadException. The exception occurred because you attempted to make a network request on the *main thread* of the application, an operation that is not allowed.

The Android Main Thread

A *thread* is a pipeline that handles a sequence of work to be performed. The main thread of an Android application is reserved for processing the work required for keeping the UI responsive: handling button presses, rendering updates when the user scrolls, and updating the text box as characters are generated, for example. For this reason, it is sometimes called the "UI thread."

When you requested data from the web API, the UI would have been unresponsive while that request completed. This is called "blocking a thread", because the thread cannot move forward to the next work to process until the current – possibly long-running – work completes. Android explicitly forbids networking on the main thread because it blocks the main thread for an unknown amount of time, leading to an unresponsive UI.

Enabling Coroutines

To solve the crash, you need a way to move the network request to a background thread instead of the main thread. Kotlin 1.1 and all versions since include a coroutines API that gives you a way to do so concisely.

As of this writing, coroutines are considered experimental (though they are expected to become a permanent feature of Kotlin), so to use them you must opt in by enabling them. You also need a coroutine library extension to use coroutines with Android. Click the Logcat tab again to hide it, and open your app/build.gradle file. Enable coroutines and add the new dependency there:

Listing 22.6 Enabling coroutines (app/build.gradle)

```
...
kotlin {
    experimental {
        coroutines 'enable'
    }
}

dependencies {
    implementation fileTree(dir: 'libs', include: ['*.jar'])
    implementation "org.jetbrains.kotlin:kotlin-stdlib-jre7:$kotlin_version"
    implementation "org.jetbrains.kotlinx:kotlinx-coroutines-android:0.22.5"
    ...
}
```

Once you add the entry to your app/build.gradle file, click the Sync Now button that appears at the top right of the screen to sync the Gradle files.

Specifying a Coroutine with async

One way to create a coroutine is to use the **async** function provided with the coroutine library. The **async** function requires one argument: a lambda that specifies the work you want to happen in the background.

In **fetchCharacterData**, move the blocking **readText** function call into a lambda and pass it to the **async** function. Also, update the return type to be a Deferred<CharacterGenerator.CharacterData>, the result of the **async** function:

Listing 22.7 Making **fetchCharacterData** async (CharacterGenerator.kt)

```
    ...
    fun fetchCharacterData(): Deferred<CharacterGenerator.CharacterData> {
        return async {
            val apiData = URL(CHARACTER_DATA_API).readText()
            return CharacterGenerator.fromAPIData(apiData)
        }
    }
```

Now, instead of returning **CharacterData**, the **fetchCharacterData** function returns a Deferred<CharacterGenerator.CharacterData>. A Deferred is like a promise for future results: No data is returned until you request it.

Return to NewCharacterActivity.kt and add the following, which converts the deferred web API results into **CharacterData** and displays the results. (We will walk through this code after you enter it.)

Listing 22.8 Awaiting the API results (NewCharacterActivity.kt)

```
...
class NewCharacterActivity : AppCompatActivity() {
    ...
    override fun onCreate(savedInstanceState: Bundle?) {
        ...
        generateButton.setOnClickListener {
            launch(UI) {
                characterData = fetchCharacterData().await()
                displayCharacterData()
            }
        }

        displayCharacterData()
    }
    ...
}
```

Android Studio will prompt you to import **launch** and UI. Make sure to import the kotlinx.coroutines.experimental versions.

Run your new and improved app and click the GENERATE button. This time, the data you see has been fetched from the web service and displayed in the UI. Let's take a closer look at how this happens.

First, you created a new coroutine by calling the **launch** function. **launch** starts the work that you specify in a new coroutine immediately.

You included UI as the first argument to launch. UI specifies the coroutine context – where the work specified within the lambda will be performed – as Android's UI thread.

Why the UI thread? The call to **displayCharacterData** must be performed on the UI thread because it contains code that updates the UI. That call will happen only after the character data is downloaded, so it does not block the main thread.

As we said above, networking is forbidden on the main thread. The default argument for the coroutine context is CommonPool, a pool of background threads available for executing coroutines. This is the argument that was used, by default, for the **async** function in **fetchCharacterData**, so the request to the web API is executed using the thread pool when you call **await**, instead of the Android main thread.

launch vs async/await

The **async** and **launch** functions that you used to perform the request and update the UI are called *coroutine builder functions*, functions that set up a coroutine to perform work in a certain way. **launch** builds a coroutine that performs the work you specify right away – in this case, calling **fetchCharacterData** and updating the UI.

The **async** coroutine builder works differently than **launch** in that it builds a coroutine that returns a Deferred, a type that represents work that has not been completed yet. Instead of starting the work immediately, a Deferred is a promise of work to be completed some time in the future.

The Deferred type provides a function called **await** that you call when you would like the work to be performed. **await** also suspends execution of the next work to do (the UI update) until the deferred work has completed. This means that you call **displayCharacterData** after the response from the web service has been returned. If you are familiar with the concept of a Java Future, a Deferred works in a very similar manner.

Even though the web request was performed in the background, you were able to structure the code imperatively because of Deferred's **await** function: You await the result and then call the UI update function. Compared to a traditional approach (like a callbacks interface), you were able to structure the code as if the request to the web service was synchronous. This is because of a coroutine's ability to suspend execution and resume at a later time – all without blocking the thread.

Suspending Functions

Notice the ⚡ icon in Android Studio next to where you called the **await** function. The IDE indicates that you made a *suspend function call* on that line. What does this mean?

Coroutines are said to "suspend," whereas a traditional thread is said to "block." This difference in terminology hints at why coroutines offer better performance than threads: When a thread is blocked, it can no longer be used to do any work until it is unblocked. A coroutine is executed by a thread – for example, the Android UI thread, or a thread in the common pool – but does not block the thread that executes it. Instead, a thread executing a function that suspends can be used to execute other coroutines. This is why a coroutine offers significantly better performance than a standard thread.

Under the hood, suspend functions are marked with the suspend keyword. Here is **await**'s function signature:

```
public suspend fun await(): T
```

In this chapter, you completed the Samodelkin app (*Do svidaniya, Samodelkin!*) and saw that Android's main thread is reserved for processing UI events. You also learned the basics of using coroutines to perform work in the background without blocking Android's main thread.

Challenge: Live Data

Currently, the data that is initially shown in the app is static data from the **CharacterGenerator** object, which is replaced with live data when the GENERATE button is pressed. For this challenge, you will fix that. Make the initial data that is shown in the application live data from the web service instead.

Challenge: Minimum Strength

A character with a strength value lower than 10 will not last more than a few rounds of play in NyetHack. For this challenge, discard any response with a strength value less than 10. Perform new requests until you receive a response with a value of 10 or greater.

23

Afterword

That is it. You have learned the fundamentals of the Kotlin programming language. Pat yourself on the back!

This is where the real work begins.

Where to Go from Here

Kotlin is a language that can be used in many contexts, be it as a replacement for your backend server code or as the language driving your hot new Android app. At this point, you likely have an idea of where you will use your new knowledge, so *use it*. That is the key to making the most of this book and writing good Kotlin code.

If you are looking for Kotlin documentation to dig into, we recommend `kotlinlang.org`. For reference material, we hold *Kotlin in Action* (`manning.com/books/kotlin-in-action`) in high regard.

You do not have to write code alone: Kotlin's community is vibrant and excited about the future of the language. Kotlin is open source, so if you would like to see it developed in real time (or even contribute), you can find it on GitHub: `github.com/jetbrains/kotlin`. We encourage you to reach out to local Kotlin user groups or, if your community does not have one, start one.

Shameless Plugs

If you would like to follow up with the authors, you can find us on Twitter. Josh is @mutexkid, and David is @drgreenhalgh.

If you would like to know more about Big Nerd Ranch, take a look at `bignerdranch.com`. We offer a bevy of other great guides, which you can find at `bignerdranch.com/books`. Might we suggest *Android Programming: The Big Nerd Ranch Guide*? Android development is a great way to put your newfound Kotlin knowledge to use.

We also offer intensive training courses and develop apps for clients. If you can dream up a way to use some great code, Big Nerd Ranch can help.

Thank You

Lastly, we just have to say thank you. Without you – yes, *you* – this book would not be possible.

We hope that you have enjoyed reading it as much as we have enjoyed writing it. Now go out there and write the next great application in Kotlin.

Of the top 25 apps in the U.S., 19 are built by companies that brought in Big Nerd Ranch to train their developers.

APP & PRODUCT DEVELOPMENT

Big Nerd Ranch designs, develops and deploys applications for clients of all sizes—from small start-ups to large corporations. Our in-house engineering and design teams possess expertise in iOS, Android and full-stack web application development.

TEAM TRAINING

For companies with capable engineering teams, Big Nerd Ranch can provide on-site corporate training in iOS, Android, Front-End Web, Back-End Web, macOS and Design.

CODING BOOTCAMPS

Our all-inclusive, immersive bootcamps are like none other. As soon as you arrive, we take care of everything, from the airport shuttle to hotels to meals. Our Georgia and California retreats are perfect for intermediate to advanced developers who can't spend months away from home.

FRONTIER SCREENCASTS

Take advantage of bite-sized tutorials on a variety of topics, including Converting Your Java Project to Kotlin. Our authors and developers have prepared a variety of topics to keep you leveled up. New screencasts released weekly. Ask about our free trial.

www.bignerdranch.com

Appendix
More Challenges

Now that you have completed the book, you may be wondering, "OK, what's next?" This section is for you.

Leveling Up with Exercism

The Exercism project (exercism.io) is a great way to level up with Kotlin (and over 30 other languages). Exercism provides a command-line interface (CLI) to a sizable suite of challenges and puzzles and also offers community-driven code reviews of your solutions.

To get started with Exercism, first follow the CLI setup instructions for your platform at exercism.io/clients/cli. Exercism also requires the Gradle build tool. If you have not installed Gradle already, follow the installation instructions for your platform at gradle.org/install. Finally, you will need a GitHub account to log in to Exercism; create one at github.com if you do not have one already.

Once you have installed and configured the CLI, you can begin fetching challenges to work on. You can fetch challenges from a particular language track sequentially or by name. To fetch the next available challenge in the Kotlin track, for example, you use the command-line command exercism fetch kotlin. If you know the name of the exercise you want to fetch, add it to the end of the command: exercism fetch kotlin name.

To walk you through the process, we will use the example of the "two-fer" challenge. Fetch the two-fer challenge by name:

```
exercism fetch kotlin two-fer
```

Once the challenge has been fetched, the path to the challenge will be returned. It will look something like:

```
Not Submitted:   1 problem
kotlin (Two Fer) /Users/joshskeen/exercism/kotlin/two-fer
```

Open IntelliJ and select File → Import. Enter the path to the challenge in the import dialog (/Users/joshskeen/exercism/kotlin/two-fer, in our example). (You can use the ... button to the right to select it rather than typing it in.) Make sure to select the Use gradle wrapper task configuration option in the import dialog (Figure A.1), and click OK.

Figure A.1 Importing the two-fer challenge

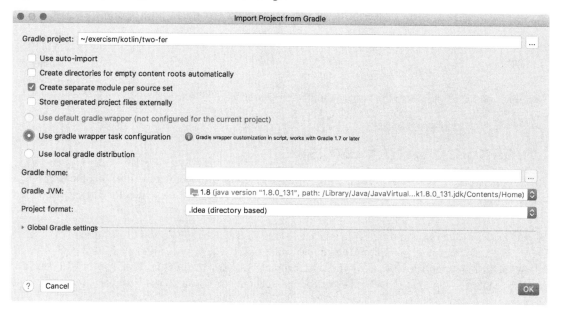

After a few moments, the configured challenge will open. From the root directory of the project, open the README.md file to read the problem description (Figure A.2):

Figure A.2 Reading the problem description

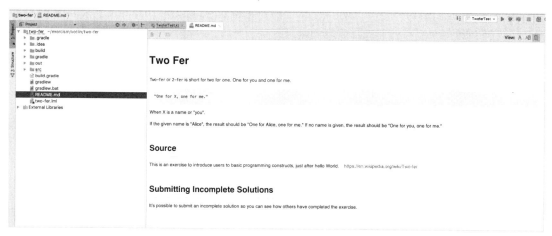

An Exercism challenge is provided as a test file. Initially, all of the tests defined in the file will fail. Your objective is to make them all pass. Open the test file by opening `src/test/kotlin/TwoferTest.kt`. You will notice the test currently has errors, since you have not yet defined a solution file (Figure A.3):

Figure A.3 Examining the test file

To define a solution file, open `src/main/kotlin` and create a new file called `Twofer.kt`. It is helpful to open this file alongside the test file in a split pane to keep track of which test you are solving, which you can do by right-clicking in either tab at the top of the editor and selecting Split Vertically (Figure A.4).

Figure A.4 Creating the solution file

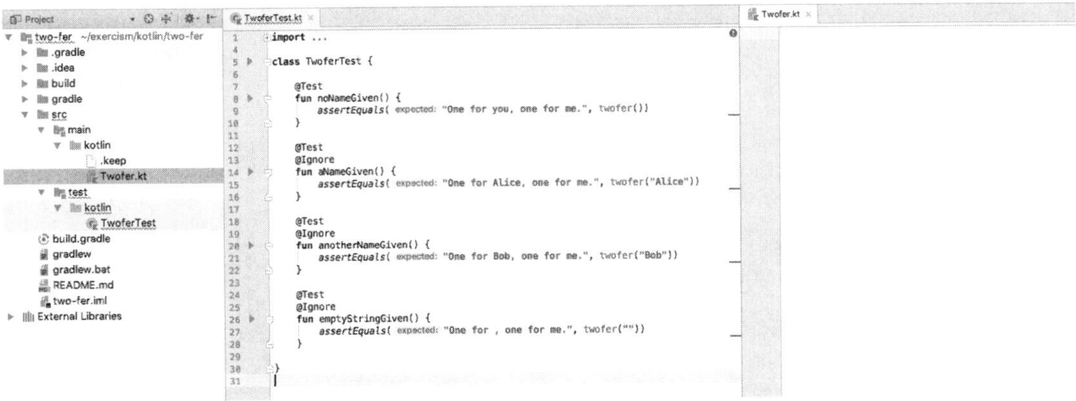

Looking at the test file, it appears that the solution should be a function called **twofer**. And it appears that two different version of the **twofer** function are required: one with no arguments and one that accepts a string. Define both versions, using **TODO** as a placeholder for the implementation:

Listing A.1 Defining two twofer functions (`Twofer.kt`)

```
fun twofer(): String {
    TODO()
}

fun twofer(name: String): String {
    TODO()
}
```

Now that the test file is runnable, try running the tests. Run `TwoferTest.kt` by clicking on the circle next to the class name and selecting Run 'TwoferTest' (Figure A.5):

Figure A.5 Running the tests

You will see the following output, since your solution currently uses the **TODO** function:

```
kotlin.NotImplementedError: An operation is not implemented.

    at TwoferKt.twofer(Twofer.kt:2)
    at TwoferTest.noNameGiven(TwoferTest.kt:9)
```

Time to make the first test pass. Go back and look at the first test. Notice what the assertion expects:

```
@Test
fun noNameGiven() {
    assertEquals("One for you, one for me.", twofer())
}
...
```

If **twofer** is called, the string "One for you, one for me." is expected. Update the **twofer** function in your solution file to return that string:

Listing A.2 Implementing a solution for the first test (Twofer.kt)

```
fun twofer(): String {
    TODO()
    return "One for you, one for me."
}
...
```

Run the test file again. This time, you will notice that the run pane in the lower left shows a green check next to the first test, **noNameGiven** (Figure A.6).

Figure A.6 **noNameGiven** passed

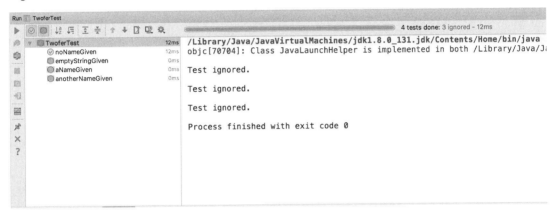

Proceed to the next test. First, remove the @Ignore annotation in the test file:

Listing A.3 Removing @Ignore (TwoferTest.kt)

```
...
@Test
@Ignore
fun aNameGiven() {
    assertEquals("One for Alice, one for me.", twofer("Alice"))
}
...
```

Run the test file again, and you will see a fail for the second test. Update your solution file to make the second test pass. Continue in this way through all the tests in the file, making each one pass.

Once you have completed a solution, you can submit it to be peer reviewed via the command line:

```
exercism submit path_to_solution/file.kt
```

Once the command completes, a URL will be displayed where you can review other solutions to the same exercise. You will find the community input for your solutions, as well as reviewing the solutions of others, to be a useful way to acquire new techniques with Kotlin.

As of this writing, there are 61 Kotlin exercises available. You can view them at `exercism.io/languages/kotlin/exercises`. We have listed our favorites in Table A.1, along with our rating of their difficulty:

Table A.1 Exercism challenges

Challenge	Rating: 1 = easy 5 = hardest
kotlin two-fer	1
bob	1.5
robot-name	1.5
sum-of-multiples	2
nucleotide-count	2
pig-latin	3
isogram	2.5
triangle	2.5
sieve	2.5
secret-handshake	2.5
binary	3
collatz-conjecture	3
diamond	3
bracket-push	3
roman-numerals	IV
saddle-points	5
spiral-matrix	5

By the way, you can find Josh's solutions at `exercism.io/mutexkid`.

Glossary

addition and assignment operator	Adds or appends the value on its righthand side to the element on its lefthand side: +=
algebraic data type	A type that allows the representation of a closed set of possible subtypes, such as an enumerated class. (See also class, enumerated; class, sealed)
application entry point	The starting place for a program. In Kotlin, this is the `main` function.
argument	An input to a function.
argument, default	A value assigned to a function argument to be used if no value is provided by the caller.
argument, named	A function argument assigned a name that can be used by the caller.
arrow operator	Operator used in lambda expressions to separate parameters from the function body, in when expressions to separate the condition from the result, and in function type definitions to separate parameter types from result types: ->
assignment operator	Assigns the value on its righthand side to the element on its lefthand side: =
branch	A set of code executed conditionally.
bytecode	The lower-level language used by the Java Virtual Machine.
called on, implicitly	Called on a receiver that is scoped but not specified. (See also scoping, relative)
class	A definition of a category of objects represented in code.
class, abstract	A class that is never instantiated but is used to create common features among its subclasses.
class, data	A class with special features for data management.
class, enumerated	A class defining a collection of constants called enumerated types; all instances of the class are of one of the defined types. Compared to a sealed class, an enumerated class prohibits inheritance, and its subclasses cannot contain different states or have multiple instances. (See also class, sealed; type, enumerated)
class, nested	A named class defined within another class.
class, sealed	A class with a defined set of subtypes, allowing the compiler to check whether a when expression contains an exhaustive set of branches. (cont.)

	Compared to an enumerated class, a sealed class permits inheritance, and its subclasses can contain different states and can have multiple instances. (See also algebraic data type; class, enumerated)
class body	The portion of a class definition, designated by curly braces, that holds its behavior and data definitions.
class function	A function defined within a class.
class property	An attribute required to represent the state or characteristics of an object.
closure	Another term for a Kotlin anonymous function. Anonymous functions in Kotlin may reference local variables defined in the scope outside of the anonymous function because they persist, or "close over," local variables they reference. (See also function, anonymous)
code comment	A note in code; comments are ignored by the compiler.
collection, eager	A collection whose values are accessible when it is instantiated. (See also collection, lazy)
collection, lazy	A collection whose values are produced only as needed. (See also collection, eager; function, iterator)
comparison operator	An operator that compares the elements on its lefthand and righthand sides.
compilation	The translation of source code into a lower-level language to create an executable program.
compiled language	A language that is translated into machine-language instructions prior to processing by a compiler. (See also compilation; compiler)
compiler	A program that performs compilation. (See also compilation)
compile time	See compilation.
compile-time error	An error that occurs during compilation. (See also compilation)
conditional expression	A conditional statement assigned to a value that can be used later.
console	A pane in the IntelliJ IDEA window that displays information about what happened when a program was executed, along with any outputs from the program. Also called the run tool window.
constant	An element that holds a value that cannot be changed.
constructor	A special function that prepares a class for use during instantiation.

constructor, primary	A class constructor defined in the class header.
consumer	A generic parameter that is writeable but not readable.
contravariance	Marking a generic parameter as a consumer.
control flow	Rules for when code should be executed.
coroutine	Experimental Kotlin feature that allows work to be performed in the background.
covariance	Marking a generic parameter as a producer.
delegate	A way of defining a template for property initialization.
destructuring	Declaring and assigning multiple variables in a single expression.
dot syntax	Syntax that connects two elements with a dot (.); used when calling a function defined on a type and when referring to a class property.
editor	The main area of the IntelliJ IDEA window, where code can be entered and edited.
encapsulation	The principle that an object's functions and properties should be visible to other objects only as needed. Also the process of hiding function and property implementations using visibility modifiers.
equality, referential	Of two variables: referring to the same type instance. (See also equality, structural)
equality, structural	Of two variables: having the same value. (See also equality, referential)
escape character	Distinguishes characters that have special meaning to the compiler: \
event log tool window	A pane in the IntelliJ IDEA window that displays information about what IntelliJ did to make a program ready to run.
exception	A disruption to the execution of a program; an error.
exception, unchecked	An exception generated by code that is not wrapped in a `try/catch` statement.
exception, unhandled	An exception that is not managed in the codebase.
expression	A combination of values, operators, and functions that produces another value.
extend	Gain functionality through inheritance or interface implementation.
extension	A property or function added to an object without inheritance.
field	Storage for the data associated with a property.

floating point	A number represented using a decimal that can be positioned at an arbitrary place based on its significant digits.
function	A reusable portion of code that accomplishes a specific task.
function, abstract	A function declared without an implementation in an abstract class. (See also class, abstract)
function, anonymous	A function defined without a name; often used as an argument to another function. (See also function, named)
function, combining	A function that takes multiple collections and combines them into a single new collection.
function, composable	A function that can be combined with other functions.
function, extension	A function that adds functionality to a particular type.
function, filter	A function that works on the contents of a collection by applying a predicate function to check a condition for each element; elements for which the predicate returns true are added to a new collection returned by the filter function.
function, iterator	A function referred to each time a value is requested from a lazy collection.
function, mutator	A function that changes the contents of a mutable collection.
function, named	A function defined with a name. (See also function, anonymous)
function, precondition	A Kotlin standard library function that defines conditions that must be met before some code is executed.
function, single-expression	A function with a single expression. (See also expression)
function, transform	In functional programming, a function that works on the contents of a collection by transforming each element using its transformer function; transform functions return a modified copy of the collection they are called on. (See also functional programming)
function, transformer	In functional programming, the anonymous function passed to a transform function that specifies the action to be taken on each element in the collection the transform is called on. (See also functional programming)
functional programming	A style of programming that relies on higher-order functions, designed to work on collections, that are chained to create complex behavior.

function body	The portion of a function definition, designated by curly braces, that holds its behavior definitions and return type.
function call	A line of code that triggers a function and passes it any necessary arguments.
function call, chainable	A function call that returns its receiver or another object that a subsequent function can be called on.
function header	The part of a function definition that includes the visibility modifier, function declaration keyword, name, parameters, and return type.
function inlining	A compiler optimization commonly used to reduce the memory overhead for functions that accept anonymous functions as arguments.
function overloading	Defining two or more function implementations with the same name and scope but different parameters.
function reference	A named function converted to a value that can be passed as an argument.
function type	The type of an anonymous function, defined by its input, output, and parameters.
generics	A type system feature that allows functions and types to work with unknown types.
generic type	A class that accepts a generic input - i.e., an input of any type.
generic type parameter	The parameter specified for a generic type, such as <T>.
getter	A function defining how a property is read.
higher-order function	A function that takes another function as an argument.
imperative programming	The programming paradigm that includes object-oriented programming.
increment operator	Adds 1 to the value of the element it is affixed to: ++
index	An integer corresponding to the position of an element in a series.
indexed access operator	Gets the element at a particular index from a collection: []
inheritance	An object-oriented programming principle in which the properties and behavior of classes are shared by their subclasses.
initialization	Preparation of a variable, property, or class instance for use.
initialization, late	Initialization of a variable that is delayed until its value is assigned.
initialization, lazy	Initialization of a variable that is delayed until it is first accessed.

initializer block	A block of code, prefixed with `init`, that will be executed during initialization of an object instance.
instance	A particular occurrence of an object.
instantiate	Create an instance of.
interface	A set of abstract functions and properties used to create common features among objects not related by inheritance.
interoperate	Interact with another programming language natively.
iteration	Repeating a process, as for each element in a range or collection.
Kotlin REPL	A tool in IntelliJ IDEA that allows code to be tested without creating a file or running a complete program.
Kotlin standard library functions	A set of extension functions available for use with any Kotlin type.
lambda	Another term for an anonymous function. (See also function, anonymous)
lambda expression	Another term for an anonymous function's definition. (See also function, anonymous)
lambda result	Another term for an anonymous function's return. (See also function, anonymous)
logical operator	A function or operator symbol that performs a logical operation on its input(s).
logical 'and' operator	Returns true if and only if the elements on its lefthand and righthand sides are both true: `&&`
logical 'or' operator	Returns true if either of the elements on its lefthand and righthand sides is true: `||`
method	Java terminology for a function. (See also function)
module	A discrete unit of functionality that can be run, tested, and debugged independently.
modulus operator	Returns the remainder when one number is divided by another; also called the remainder operator: `%`
mutable	Able to be changed. (See also read-only)
non-nullable	Unable to be assigned a null value.

non-null assertion operator	Calls a function on a nullable element, returning an exception if the element it is called on is null: `!!`
null	Nonexistent.
nullable	Able to be assigned a null value.
null coalescing operator	Returns the element on its lefthand side if it is non-null; otherwise returns the element on its righthand side: `?:`
object, companion	An object defined within a class and marked with the `companion` modifier; companion objects allow their members to be accessed by referencing the outer class name only. (See also object declaration; object expression; singleton)
object declaration	A named singleton created with the `object` keyword. (See also object, companion; object expression; singleton)
object expression	An unnamed singleton created with the `object` keyword. (See also object, companion; object declaration; singleton)
operator overloading	Defining an implementation for an operator function on a custom type.
override	Provide a custom implementation for an inherited function or property.
parameter	An input required by a function.
parameterized type	The type defined for the contents of a collection.
pass an argument	Provide an input to a function.
platform type	Ambiguous types returned to Kotlin from Java code; they may be nullable or non-nullable.
polymorphism	The ability to use the same named entity (such as a function) to produce different results.
predicate	A true/false condition provided to a function as a lambda to define how work should be performed.
producer	A generic parameter that is readable but not writeable.
project	All the source code for a program, along with information about dependencies and configurations.
project tool window	The pane on the left of the IntelliJ IDEA window that shows a project's structure and files.
property, computed	A property defined such that its value is computed each time it is accessed.
property, inline	A class property defined in the primary constructor.

race condition	A condition that occurs when some state is modified simultaneously by two or more elements in a program.
range	A sequential series of values or characters.
read-only	Able to be read but not changed. (See also mutable)
receiver	The subject of an extension function.
receiver type	The type an extension adds functionality to.
refactor	Change the presentation or location of code without changing its functionality.
referential equality operator	Evaluates whether the variable on its lefthand side points to the same type instance as the value on its righthand side: === (See also equality, referential)
reflection	Learning the name or type of a property at runtime. (See also type erasure)
regular expression, regex	A defined character search pattern.
remainder operator	See modulus operator.
reserved keyword	A word that cannot be used as a function name.
return, implicit	Data that is returned without an explicit return statement.
return type	The type of output data a function returns after completing its work.
runtime	When a program is executed.
runtime error	An error that occurs after compilation, during program execution.
run tool window	A pane in the IntelliJ IDEA window that displays information about what happened when a program was executed along with any outputs from the program. Also called the console.
safe call operator	Calls a function only if the element it is called on is non-null: ?.
scope	The portion of a program in which an entity, such as a variable, can be referred to by name.
scoping, relative	The scoping of standard function calls within a lambda to the receiver the lambda is called on. (See also called on, implicitly)
setter	A function defining how a property's value is assigned.
signed numeric type	A numeric type that includes both positive and negative values.

singleton	An object declared with the `object` keyword; singletons are limited to a single instance throughout program execution.
smart casting	The tracking by the compiler of information that has been checked for a branch of code, such as whether a variable has a null value.
statement	An instruction in code.
string	A sequence of characters.
string concatenation	Combining two or more strings in a single output.
string interpolation	Using a string template.
string template	Syntax that allows a variable name to stand in for its value in a string.
structural equality operator	Evaluates whether the value on its lefthand side is equal to the value on its righthand side: == (See also equality, structural)
subclass	A class defined as inheriting properties from another class.
superclass	The class that a subclass inherits from.
target (a platform)	Design a program to run on a platform.
throw (an exception)	Generate an exception.
type	A classification of data; a variable's type determines the nature of the values it can hold.
type, enumerated	A type defined as one of the elements of an enumerated class. (See also class, enumerated)
type casting	Treating an object as though it were an instance of a different type.
type checking	Confirmation by the compiler that the value assigned to a variable is of the correct type.
type checking, static	Type checking performed as code is entered or edited.
type erasure	The loss of type information for generics at runtime.
type inference	The ability of the compiler to recognize a variable's type based on the value assigned to it.
types, collection	Data types that represent groups of data elements, such as lists.
type system, static	A system in which the compiler labels source code with type information for checking.
Unicode character	A character defined in the Unicode system.

variable	An element that holds a value; variables may be read-only or mutable.
variable, file-level	A variable defined outside of any function or class.
variable, local	A variable defined within a function's scope.
visibility	The accessibility of an element from other code elements.
visibility modifier	A modifier added to function and property declarations to set their visibility.
zero-indexed	Using the value 0 for the first index (in a series or collection).

Index

Symbols

!
    for platform types, 297
    logical 'not' operator, 33
`!!.` (double-bang/non-null assertion operator), 89
`!=` (non-equality operator), 29
`!==` (referential non-equality operator), 29
`$` (for string interpolation/templating), 40
`%` (modulus/remainder operator), 120
`&&` (logical 'and' operator), 33
`+` (addition operator), 28, 234
`++` (increment operator), 147
`+=` (addition and assignment operator), 15, 234
`+=` (plus assign operator), 135, 146, 154, 156
`–` (minus operator), 156
`–=` (minus assign operator), 135, 146, 156
`–>` (arrow operator)
    in anonymous function definitions, 71
    in function type definitions, 69
    in when expressions, 38
`.` (dot)
    for class property references, 168
    for function calls, 67
`..` (range operator), 37, 234
`:` operator
    for interface implementation, 244
    for subclassing, 207
`::` operator, for function references, 79
`<` (less-than operator), 29
`<=` (less-than-or-equal-to operator), 29
`<>` (for parameterized type definitions), 130
`=` (assignment operator)
    for maps, 156
    for variable values, 14
    in single-expression function syntax, 57
`==` (structural equality operator), 28, 234
`===` (referential equality operator), 29
`>` (greater-than operator), 29, 234
`>=` (greater-than-or-equal-to operator), 29
`?.` (safe call operator), 88
`?:` (null coalescing operator), 91
`@JvmField` annotation, 307
`@JvmName` annotation, 303
`@JvmOverloads` annotation, 303
`@JvmStatic` annotation, 309
`@NotNull` annotation (Java), 101, 298
`@Nullable` annotation (Java), 297
`@Throws` annotation, 312
`[]` (get/index operator), 106, 130, 155, 234
`[]=` (set operator), 134
`\` (escape character), 104
`_`, for temporary variables, 188
`||` (logical 'or' operator), 33

A

abstract classes
    about, 243, 248-250
    abstract functions, 248
    interface implementation, 250
    subclassing, 249
    vs interfaces, 250
abstract functions, 248
`abstract` keyword, 248
add function, 133, 135, 146
addAll function, 135, 146
addition and assignment operator (+=), 15, 234
addition operator (+), 28, 234
algebraic data types, 240
also function, 126, 128, 185
and(number) function, 121
Android
    accessing view elements, 330, 333
    activities, 320
    Android KTX Kotlin extensions library, 341
    Anko Kotlin enhancements library, 342
    click listeners, 335
    creating a project, 318
    Gradle build automation tool, 322
    importing classes, 331
    Kotlin library dependencies, 323
    Kotlin plug-ins, 322
    Kotlin single abstract method conversions, 335
    Kotlin synthetic properties, 333
    lifecycle functions, 330
    manifest, 346
    project organization, 324
    saved instance state, 337-339
    SDK packages, 316
    threads, 348
    user interfaces, 324-327
    using coroutines, 349-351